'So much expertise collected together fills me with hope. This book usefully combines essentials of understanding, recognising, and working with traumatic dissociation with practical specialist chapters. It has something for everyone whatever your profession, level of knowledge or stage of career. I wish it had been available during the decades of my own re-traumatising journey through mental health services and eventually into recovery. I believe that many of the dissociative trauma survivors I met and worked alongside during the 26 years of First Person Plural's existence would echo this sentiment.'

Kathryn Livingston, *BEM, Expert-by-experience,*
Co-founder of First Person Plural

'This response to the growth in recognition and awareness of trauma and dissociation is an impressive and significant breakthrough. A practical, comprehensive and inclusive guide to dissociation-informed care and services, it fulfils its aims to inform, empower and provide guidance for good practice. A highly accessible resource, it presents a powerful case for change supported by the clinical and research literature and illuminated by the voices of those with lived experience. It will boost knowledge, skills and confidence for practitioners, supervisors and managers in all settings and for anyone involved with survivors of trauma, including survivors themselves.'

Sue Richardson, *Psychotherapist, co-founder of European*
Society for Trauma and Dissociation – UK

'This evidence-informed treatment guide provides outstanding support to multidisciplinary professionals in assessing and responding to dissociation. Written by those with clinical expertise and lived experience, it outlines culturally competent and person-centred care across mental health services. The book addresses the diverse needs of clients including those with neurodivergence. It includes a competency and training framework aligned with national and international trauma-informed care guidelines. With a wealth of practical suggestions, clinical vignettes, and stakeholder-reviewed recommendations, it offers strategies for improving assessment and treatment outcomes, reducing harm, and supporting training among service providers.'

Professor Bethany Brand, *co-author of the Finding Solid*
Ground program / books, and Author of The Concise Guide
to the Assessment and Treatment of Trauma-related Dissociation

'Trauma-based dissociation, as a means of psychological and relational defence, is present in the lives of many people struggling with a wide variety mental health difficulties. It has a history of not being recognised or understood by services, from the individual practitioner through to the commissioning level. Dissociation, as so well described in this marvellously comprehensive book, can be a fundamental means of maintaining the best possible attachment relationships and well-being when growing up in truly dire circumstances. In adult life it can cause great difficulties with functioning, managing feelings, and the ability to form secure supportive relationships.

This book is an essential and accessible addition to the understanding of this often complex issue, including how to see the ways in which it can present across a broad range of mental health issues and with clear and thorough guidelines on thinking and practicing from a dissociation informed foundation. I highly recommend this book for all those professionals working in the field of mental health.'

Mark Linington, *CEO CDS UK (Clinic for Dissociative Studies) and member of The Bowlby Centre, London*

'Multi-disciplinary psychiatric services may regard themselves as trauma-informed yet display a pervasive blindness to the clinical, personal, societal, economic and generational consequences of the most severe trauma-related conditions, namely the dissociative disorders, despite these being clearly described in major international classifications. This valuable book provides information from diverse sources that will make such neglect by health services harder to justify. The arguments for appropriate treatment provisions that are not re-traumatising are lucid, caring, and based in a wealth of published data as well as descriptions of personal experiences, essential reading for all providers of psychiatric services.'

Frank Corrigan, *MD, FRCPsych, Developer of Deep Brain Reorienting*

'Dissociation, often a response to the unbearable, is frequently misunderstood. As a survivor of child sexual abuse, deeply uncomfortable with the medicalisation of dissociative experience, I recognise the urgent need for practitioners working within clinical frameworks to understand dissociation in all its complexity. This book bridges the gap between the language of 'disorder' and the reality of survival. As someone who dissociates in medical settings - often misread as crisis or instability - it gives me hope for a shift in practitioner awareness, empathy, and support.'

Sophie Olson, *Author and Founder of The Flying Child*

'While there is increasing recognition of dissociation in psychological therapies, there is less written about how best to work with it. In this book, the authors argue thoughtfully for a change in approach to mental health problems, and a recognition of the complex and multifaceted nature of dissociation as a route into working with difficulties that have often been with the sufferer for years. This book, very much a team effort, examines the urgent problem of how to be helpful in complex trauma.'

Dr Alasdair Forrest, *Consultant Forensic Psychiatrist, Medical Psychotherapist, and Group Analyst, Aberdeen, Chair, Royal College of Psychiatrists in Scotland Psychotherapy Faculty, Chair, Training Committee of Institute of Group Analysis in Scotland*

Working with Dissociation in Clinical Practice

Working with Dissociation in Clinical Practice brings together current literature and the contributing authors' professional and lived experiences to provide practical recommendations for supporting the mental health and wellbeing of individuals with dissociative difficulties.

Readers will benefit from learning how to apply this advice for best practice to a range of settings and client groups, ensuring more positive service user outcomes. Written in dialogue between Experts-by-Training and Experts-by-Experience, this essential edited volume covers practical strategies for practitioners working with dissociative clients. Authors address areas such as common misconceptions, assessment, comorbidity, risk management and providing care and therapy within a trauma-informed and multidisciplinary context. The book further explores support for dissociation within more specialist clinical areas, tailoring guidance to a range of client groups including children, older people, those with learning disabilities, and those in forensic settings. It provides guidance for health systems and organisations to become more dissociation aware, within exisiting frameworks for trauma-informed care.

This book is a compelling read for clinical psychologists, other psychological and mental health practitioners, people with lived experience of dissociative difficulties and those who support them.

Helena Crockford, past chair of the ACP-UK Complex Mental Health Network, is a Consultant Clinical Psychologist, Attachment-Based Psychoanalytic Psychotherapist and MBT Supervisor with 30+ years working in NHS complex mental health settings.

Melanie Goodwin is an Expert-by-Experience, co-founder of First Person Plural (1997–2023) and past-Trustee of European Society for Trauma and Dissociation-UK. She raises awareness of complex dissociation and DID through writing, speaking at conferences, developing resources, and co-delivering training alongside clinicians across public, private and voluntary service sectors.

Paul Langthorne is a Clinical Psychologist working in NHS community mental health services with many years experience of supporting people who experience trauma-related dissociation. He is currently in receipt of an NIHR pre-application support fund award and hopes to develop a programme of clinical research that helps to advocate for change in the NHS for people experiencing trauma-related dissociation.

Working with Dissociation in Clinical Practice

Guidance for Mental Health Professionals and Multidisciplinary Teams

Edited by Helena Crockford,
Melanie Goodwin and
Paul Langthorne

Routledge
Taylor & Francis Group

LONDON AND NEW YORK

Designed cover image: Getty Images

First published 2026
by Routledge
4 Park Square, Milton Park, Abingdon, Oxon OX14 4RN

and by Routledge
605 Third Avenue, New York, NY 10158

Routledge is an imprint of the Taylor & Francis Group, an informa business

British Library Cataloguing-in-Publication Data
A catalogue record for this book is available from the British Library

ISBN: 9781041038450 (hbk)
ISBN: 9781041038443 (pbk)
ISBN: 9781003625650 (ebk)

DOI: 10.4324/9781003625650

Typeset in Times New Roman
by Newgen Publishing UK

Access the Support Material: www.routledge.com/9781041038450

Editors' Dedications

Helena

For the first client who 'taught' me, both about living with dissociation and how mental health care needed to improve; and for the many others since who have added to that.

For Melanie Goodwin and Remy Aquarone who have supported my learning in this complex field every step of the way.

For Dr. Pete Cairns, Dr. Roger Kingerlee and Paul Junge, my colleagues-in-arms in Norfolk and Suffolk Foundation Trust, with whom all the magic came alive.

Melanie

Remy Aquarone and Sue Richardson worked closely with the International Society for the Study of Dissociation (ISSD), as it was then known, and used their training resources to do a lot of the early training in the UK. They then committed many years to developing and supporting the European Society for Trauma and Dissociation (ESTD) and the ESTD-UK.

Mike Fisher was founder of Trauma and Abuse Group (TAG) that ran for 25 years. He remained the chair and trainer of the organisation and worked closely with Remy, Sue and FPP. TAG became a well- respected forum in the UK.

Kathryn Livingston co-founded First Person Plural (FPP) and was involved with the ESTD-UK, helping to write their various training programmes, alongside her dedicated and extensive roles within FPP.

Dr. Ruth Cureton worked alongside Mike Fisher for many years ensuring that lived experience stayed central to their work.

Valerie Sinason started the Clinic for Dissociative Studies, London, while training worldwide. Her steadfast voice remains integral to the work today.

Sandra Buck took over the Ritual Abuse Information Network and Support (RAINS) and is very involved after 20+ years. She spoke out about DID in the very early days from her role as a paediatrician and would not be silenced.

These descriptions do not do justice to the roles they have fulfilled.

Paul

This book is dedicated to that most precious of things – hope – and the community of survivors, family members, advocates, clinicians and academics that keep it alive.

Thank you to the survivors I have worked with over the years in Derbyshire. I hope this book honours your teachings.

Thank you to my fellow travellers and mentors, many of whom have contributed to this book in various ways.

Thank you to my manager Dr. Helen Cadman, and before that Dr. Petrina Brown for supporting and empowering me to advocate for change in this area, initially in Derbyshire and now on a wider platform.

Finally, my beautiful family – thank you for always being there to keep my feet on *terra firma*. x

Contents

Acknowledgements

This book represents the collaborative efforts of over 100 people who have contributed their time, thoughts, writing, experiences, interest and commitment to this topic. We are indebted to you all. One way or another, you are people who understand the importance and value of recognising and working with trauma-based dissociation. You are all champions of hope, champions for what is possible, even within stretched and pressured mental health services. There is much work to do to ensure everyone who needs it receives a healing experience of care and treatment, but with your collective efforts behind the wheel, this goal is getting closer.

We would like to thank our colleagues on the Steering Group which initiated and cheered on this project: Dr. Rebecca Andrew, Consultant Clinical Psychologist, Surrey & Borders Partnership NHS Trust and Dr. Stuart Mitchell, Consultant Clinical Psychologist, Sport and Exercise Psychologist in Training, Northumbria University, Newcastle. We thank also colleagues in the ACP-UK Complex Mental Health Network who supported the original proposal, and the ACP-UK Board of Directors for understanding why this was so important.

We would like to thank all those who engaged in initial discussions about particular chapters, or offered their invaluable and thoughtful feedback as stakeholder reviewers of final chapter drafts: Remy Aquarone, Psychoanalyst; Dr. Ellie Atkins, Consultant Clinical Psychologist, ACP-UK Children, Young People and Families Network Lead; Dr. Jessica Austin, Principal Clinical Psychologist; Richard Barber, Director, Visible Project; Dr. Peter Cairns, Principal Clinical Psychologist; Dr. Rosemary Carter, Consultant Clinical Psychologist; Dr. Neil Clapton, Clinical Psychologist; Andrew Coburn, Assistant Director of Legal, Governance and Mental Health Legislation, Derbyshire Healthcare NHS Foundation Trust; Dr. Heather Cogger-Ward, Clinical Psychologist, Research Tutor/Assistant Professor; Dr. Christine Collinson, Clinical Psychologist; Dr. Ruth Cureton, Trustee, Clinic for Dissociative Studies; Dr. Elinor Currey, Highly Specialist Clinical Psychologist; Dr. Gillian Dyker, Principal Clinical Psychologist; Dr. Selma Ebrahim, Consultant Clinical Psychologist, Past Chair, Complex Mental Health Network ACP-UK; Dr. Laura Edwards, Consultant Clinical Psychologist; Dr. Brad English, Highly Specialist Clinical Psychologist; Kate Elliott, Assistant Psychologist; Elizabeth Gallant, Senior Therapeutic Radiographer; Dr. Zainab Hameed, Psychiatrist;

Dr. Elly Hanson, Clinical Psychologist; Rashida Harries, Psychotherapist; Dr. Laura Hayward, Clinical Psychologist; Dr. Roisin Jack, Neuropsychologist; Lawrence Jones, Consultant Clinical and Forensic Psychologist; Peter Jones, Chair, Growing Compassionate Communities and Counselling in Prisons Network; Dr. Laura Leanour, Clinical Psychologist; Dr. Megan Kendall, Clinical Psychologist; Dr. Carolien Lamers, Clinical Psychologist/Clinical Lecturer; Mark Linington, Consultant Psychotherapist; Kathryn Livingston, BEM, Co-Founder, First Person Plural; Dr. Renée P Marks, Therapist/Clinical Lead, Integrate Families; Dr. Roxanna Mohtashemi, Clinical Psychologist; Dr. Lina Papista, Principal Clinical Psychologist; Dr. Helen Philpott, Consultant Clinical Psychologist/ Clinical Neuropsychologist; Nikki Roome, Adult Safeguarding Lead; Dr. Eva Rogers, Specialist Clinical Psychologist; Dr. Rachel Sabin-Farrell, Consultant Clinical Psychologist; Kinga Simko, Trainee Clinical Psychologist; Dr. Stephanie Sneider, Consultant Clinical Psychologist; Valerie Sinason, Psychoanalyst; Dr. Allan Skelly, Consultant Clinical Psychologist; Dr. Sarah Swan, Clinical Psychologist; Dr. Michelle Trollope, Clinical Psychologist; Dr. Eirini Vasilaki, Clinical Psychologist; Dr. Danielle Watson, Lecturer in Law; Lizzie Watt, Trauma Informed Care Lead, Public Health Derbyshire; Dr. Jamie Wright, Consultant Psychiatrist.

We benefitted from some additional administrative help from Lucie Carwardine-Saunders, Trainee Clinical Psychologist; Lauren Currell, Senior Assistant Psychologist; Charlie Gardiner-Banks, Trainee Clinical Psychologist. Thank you all.

We have a particular vote of thanks for the Stakeholder Reviewer Panel with a remit to consider diversity issues: David Gibbs, Expert-by-Experience and Dr. Kiki Hassan, Clinical Psychologist. You never flagged and the guidance is richer, more inclusive and more widely applicable for your input.

Our special appreciation goes to the many who have generously shared their lived experience. Your contributions have brought the guidance to life and enabled all of us to understand the issues better from the inside. We thank you, whether you have chosen to share your full name, your first name, a pseudonym, your name as a part, or have preferred to remain anonymous: Sally Adams; Iris Benson, MBE; Ruth Cureton; Kathryn Livingston, BEM; Kelly Simpson; Alex; Angela; Becci; Ben; Gita; Hannah; Hayley; JC; Jill; Laura; Little Beth; Liv *et al*; Lizzie; Lizzie; Lizzie; Lucy; Maz; Simon; Sonia; Stephen; Tamarisk; Zoe; Child's Voice; and others who have contributed anonymously.

Finally, we would like to thank Dr. Penelope Cream, Director of Operations, ACP-UK, who has calmly supported and guided us to get this project to publication; and Lauren Redhead, our Editor at Routledge who has translated the publication process into language we could understand, and made the end-goal seem achievable, even when we doubted it.

Contributors

Remy Aquarone, Psychoanalyst, Director, Pottergate Centre, Norwich

Richard Barber, Director, Visible Project

Gordon Barclay, retired NHS consultant psychiatrist, now in private practice, Glasgow, Scotland

Melanie Bash, Consultant Clinical Psychologist, Tees, Esk and Wear Valleys NHS Foundation Trust

Paula Biles, Senior Consultant Trauma and DID Psychotherapist, Paula Biles Psychotherapy Ltd

Jo Burrell, Consultant Clinical Psychologist, Norfolk and Norwich University Hospitals NHS Foundation Trust

Reed Cappleman, Consultant Clinical Psychologist, Royal Edinburgh Hospital

Emma Černis, Clinical Psychologist, University of Birmingham and Midlands Dissociation and Depersonalisation Centre

Angela Dhanda, Mental Health Nurse, Surrey and Borders Partnership NHS Foundation Trust

Pat Frankish, Consultant Clinical Psychologist, Frankish Psychological Services

Elizabeth Gallant, Senior Therapeutic Radiographer, Norfolk and Norwich University Hospitals NHS Foundation Trust

Amanda Green, Peer Support Lead, Norfolk and Suffolk NHS Foundation Trust

Louise Harriss, Consultant Clinical Psychologist, Berkshire Healthcare NHS Foundation Trust

Kiki Hassen, Clinical Psychologist

Andrew Holding, Consultant Clinical Psychologist, Mersey Care NHS Foundation Trust

Darren James, Consultant Clinical Psychologist, Cwm Taf Morgannwg University Health Board, Wales

Angela Kennedy, Consultant Clinical Psychologist, Innovating for Wellbeing

Ruth Leaper, Principal Clinical Psychologist, Clinic for Dissociative Studies, London

Claire Lee, Highly Specialist Clinical Psychologist, Derbyshire Healthcare NHS Foundation Trust

Mike Lloyd, Consultant Clinical Psychologist, Director, Cheshire Psychology Ltd and The CTAD Clinic

Stuart Mitchell, Consultant Clinical Psychologist, Sport and Exercise Psychologist in Training, Northumbria University, Newcastle

Roxanna Mohtashemi, Clinical Psychologist, Dorset HealthCare University NHS Foundation Trust

Vivian Okoye, Neurodiversity and Inclusion Lead at Afrikindness

Andrew Rayner, Chartered Clinical Psychologist, Complex Trauma and Dissociation Clinic (CTAD) & The Compassionate Mind Foundation (CMF)

Anthony Redhead, Clinical Psychologist, Tees, Esk and Wear Valley NHS Foundation Trust

Janice Rigby, Consultant Clinical Psychologist, South London and Maudsley NHS Foundation Trust

Beth Ryan, Peer Support Worker, Norfolk and Suffolk NHS Foundation Trust

Lynne Ryan, BACP Registered Counsellor, South Yorkshire

Rachel Sabin-Farrell, Consultant Clinical Psychologist, Derbyshire Healthcare NHS Foundation Trust

Kelly Simpson, Expert-by-Experience

Fiona Summers, Consultant Clinical Neuropsychologist, Aberdeen Royal Infirmary, NHS Grampian

Vicky Sutton, Clinical Psychologist in Independent Practice

Jon Taylor, Consultant Forensic Psychologist, Derbyshire Healthcare NHS Foundation Trust

Hannah Wilson, Consultant Clinical Psychologist, MediaCity Psychology

Caroline Wyatt, Consultant Clinical Psychologist, South West Yorkshire NHS Foundation Trust

Foreword

The world is in pain from unknown generational trauma – wounds that are centuries old. But there is another kind of transmission too and we feel proud parents and grandparents to read these confident, clear, courageous and inclusive guidelines where the voices of Experts-by-Experience shine through. It is a privilege for us both to write this.

The Clinic for Dissociative Studies, London and The Pottergate Centre, Norwich, both still providers to NHS services, were our precious babies, born from the deep impact on our hearts and minds of survivors, victims and Experts-by-Experience. We named the subject because it mattered so much and was so discredited, attacked and misunderstood. And we spoke to each other because nearly 40 years ago there was so little understanding of organised abuse, relational trauma, extreme abuse, ritual abuse and disorganised attachment.

After nearly four decades we can see the positive changes that have happened: the way science, neurobiology, memory studies, research, the courage of survivors and Experts-by-Experience in writing papers, chapters, books, creating trainings, have transformed the national and international picture – all powerfully and thoughtfully represented by the pioneer authors of this book.

This book is a crucial step into the future. All the key organisations supporting this work understand that thoughtful reflective guidelines provide help. Guidelines are a guide. They are not commands written in concrete (although fear and defensiveness can attempt to do that). Whilst internationally we have the European Society for the Study of Trauma and Dissociation (ESTD) and the International Society for the Study of Trauma and Dissociation (ISSTD), we also have a need for national professional thinking; and whilst psychotherapists in this field have a range of theories and organisations they can link to, mental health professionals are in a far harder position.

One issue that stands out for us, is the courage of the co-authors and their contributors, many of whom have worked under the radar of inevitably dissociative organisations where isolation, secrecy, fear of attack (and job security) and ridicule, has parallels with people living with dissociation.

We hope that survivors will feel strengthened by this fine, detailed work, realising that their own courage to hope and connect has helped inspire it.

Thank you Helena Crockford, Melanie Goodwin and Paul Langthorne.

Rémy Aquarone, Adult Psychoanalyst, past President of ESTD,
past International Director of ISSTD
Valerie Sinason, Child Psychotherapist (retired),
Adult Psychoanalyst, President of Institute for Psychotherapy and
Disability, Fellow of ISSTD

Introduction

Helena Crockford, Melanie Goodwin and Paul Langthorne

Dissociation first entered my awareness as a clinical psychologist a decade into practice in secondary care mental health services. 'Jason', diagnosed with paranoid schizophrenia, revealed to me how he had survived a horrific history of childhood abuse and neglect by having different personalities he 'could go into', which now helped him cope with different life situations. He began 'teaching' me about complex dissociation, and with more training and supervision, I recognised how common this was. I also learned about widespread myths regarding dissociation, well represented within the multidisciplinary team (MDT) I worked with. This formed a complex, sometimes painful, context for 'Jason's' care. Through national leadership roles, including chairing the Personality and Complex Trauma Network, Division of Clinical Psychology, British Psychological Society, and the Complex Mental Health Network of the ACP-UK, I have met colleagues from all four nations of the UK encountering similar dilemmas. Coproducing a training strategy to raise dissociation awareness and skills (Crockford et al., 2019) we saw how keen MDT staff were to learn more, and how many held cases they felt baffled and deskilled by. Witnessing their 'lightbulb' moments – dissociation named and demystified, relief at the possibility of doing something more helpful – reinforced for me how small changes can go a long way. The value of coproduction – Melanie always working with us – was immense. **Helena**

Despite the growing recognition for health and social care services to be trauma-informed, people experiencing trauma-based dissociation continue to face inaccurate diagnosis, inadequate treatment and services that can inadvertently cause further harm. Trauma-related dissociation is as common as other serious mental health difficulties, yet remains one of the most misunderstood and under-recognised experiences in mental health care. This book has grown from our own journeys learning about or living with dissociation.

DOI: 10.4324/9781003625650-1

Alongside the national policy emphasis on trauma-informed care, many voices have worked with us, supported by the ACP-UK, to develop the range of chapters within this book. These include a combination of professional and lived experience.

My personal introduction to DID was after several years of therapeutic help it became obvious that we were many and a slow painful journey began. My innate drive to educate others saved us. I began to understand what an amazing way my brain had developed allowing us to lead a relatively normal life. Co-founding First Person Plural (FPP), an organisation for survivors and their allies, provided a forum for this work. Naively, I assumed that something as logical as DID would quickly be taken on board and become embedded within the NHS. If only! But through people like Paul and Helena willing to stay steadfast to their beliefs, often putting their heads above the parapet, things have changed and these guidelines are only now possible because of this. I would like to pay tribute to an occupational therapist working within my Trust. He spent nearly an hour very early on in my journey talking and listening kindly and respectfully. He did not try and rescue me but that phone call began the foundation on which the rest of my journey was built, thank you. **Melanie**

Contributors have come from a range of training backgrounds, service settings and geography across the UK. Psychological practitioners are the largest author group, representing the primarily psychologically informed nature of care and treatment for people experiencing trauma-based dissociation, but the importance of the multidisciplinary context of care is underlined. Each chapter has undergone a process of stakeholder comment and review, holding intersectional diversity in mind. Experts-by-Experience ensured the material was grounded, respectful and resonated with the lived experience. It also provided a quality assurance layer, giving Experts-by-Experience a role in shaping not only what was said, but also how it was expressed.

The chapters cover the main speciality areas of mental health practice. Each aims to summarise the, sometimes limited, evidence base, and to suggest questions for further research. They also address common myths and misconceptions, and provide practical clinical guidance illustrated with quotes from contributors with lived experience, and with clinical vignettes. These latter have been blended or anonymised to protect confidentiality, except where consent has been received.

Beginning work as a clinical psychologist in an MDT I saw how the ripples of trauma impacted the lives of people I worked with and was very committed to working to help address this. One person painfully highlighted the limits of my understanding of trauma-related dissociation. Unprepared by my clinical training I neither saw nor heard what was being communicated. I sadly became part of their 'silencing' and as a result my input was largely harmful rather than helpful. Thankfully, when I recognised this, my service listened and supported my development and I was fortunate to find some very patient guides along the way. It became apparent that trauma-related dissociation was being missed across many of our services, from inpatient wards to memory clinics. We shared training, some of it coproduced, and supervision within our department and with our multidisciplinary colleagues. More people now gain access to dissociation-informed care. It felt an important start. **Paul**

The chapters address the spectrum of dissociative difficulties. They emphasise trauma-informed principles, meaning authors talk more about 'people', their 'experiences' and 'what happened to them', than they do about 'patients', their 'symptoms' and 'what is wrong with them'. Medicalised and diagnostic language is used where specifically relevant. Trauma happens within cultural contexts of power and disadvantage, and the role of intersecting minoritised experiences are considered throughout, including culturally relevant perceptions, explanations and resources for dissociation.

While aimed initially at multidisciplinary mental health professionals, this book is also for people with lived experience and those supporting them – recognising that many people experiencing dissociation face multiple barriers to accessing safe, culturally responsive and inclusive care. The language aims to be accessible rather than technical where possible. Most authors have been front-line clinicians, and know how stretched mental health care is. Yet chapters convey therapeutic optimism, offering pragmatic advice achievable within current contexts. They also argue for socially just and cost-effective best practice service developments.

The chapters are in three sections. Section 1 provides seven core chapters, including general information about dissociation and models of understanding (Chapter 1), screening and assessment (Chapter 2), treating dissociative experiences in multidisciplinary teams (Chapter 3) and in psychological therapy (Chapter 4), issues relevant to children and families (Chapter 5), managing safety (Chapter 6), and addressing complexity and comorbidity with other mental health difficulties (Chapter 7). Section 2 offers seven chapters applying this guidance to specialist clinical areas: physical health (Chapter 8), perinatal mental health (Chapter 9), people with a learning disability (Chapter 10), older people (Chapter 11), eating disorders (Chapter 12), forensic settings (Chapter 13), and the independent practice context (Chapter 14). Section 3 provides three chapters summarising the guidance from previous chapters, on cultural considerations (Chapter 15), on dilemmas for organisations and commissioners (Chapter 16), and on a competency and training framework (Chapter 17). Finally, Melanie's Epilogue summarises what good practice looks like from her own rich lived experience (Chapter 18). Some authors have included additional free-to-access online resources listed by chapter, at www.routledge.com/9781041038450.

We hope this book will help, to inform and empower clinicians, but also people seeking help and their supporters, to realise the prevalence and pervasive impact of trauma-related dissociation; and towards shaping services and pathways of care to listen, respond, adapt, and importantly, avoid further harm.

Core Knowledge and Skills in Working with Trauma-Related Dissociation

Chapter 1

Understanding Trauma-Related Dissociation

Louise Harriss, Paul Langthorne, Mike Lloyd and Helena Crockford

1. Note on Terminology

Dissociation involves a disconnection within conscious awareness between aspects of a person's experience. The International Society for the Study of Trauma and Dissociation (ISSTD) define dissociation as:

> The disconnection or lack of connection between things usually associated with each other. Dissociation is a process in which a person disconnects from their thoughts, feelings, memories, behaviours, physical sensations, or sense of identity.
>
> (ISSTD, 2011)

There is a broad and growing consensus that this is a psychobiosocial process that occurs beyond conscious awareness and control; that varies in intensity and impedes the person being able to integrate aspects of their experience. Dissociation can potentially disrupt any and every area of a person's functioning at any stage of the life-course: including memory, sense of self, perception, consciousness, and bodily/somatic experiences. It can therefore encompass a broad range of different experiences and symptoms.

2. Background

2.1 The Context of Trauma-Informed Health Care

There are well-documented links between the experience of early childhood trauma and later physical and mental health problems in adulthood (Felitti et al., 1998). This understanding contributes to the drive for more trauma-informed approaches across public health services, especially mental health care in the UK and internationally (NHS Education for Scotland, 2017). All who work in health and care services have a role to play in adopting a trauma-informed approach.

Trauma-informed services will (see Substance Abuse and Mental Health Services Administration, 2014):

DOI: 10.4324/9781003625650-3

1. **Realise** the widespread impact of trauma and understand potential paths for recovery.
2. **Recognise** the signs and symptoms of trauma in clients, families, staff and others involved with the system.
3. **Respond** by fully integrating knowledge about trauma into policies, procedures and practices.
4. Seek to actively **Resist Retraumatisation.**

In addition, trauma-informed approaches emphasise the central importance of the relational context in which care is provided (NHS Education for Scotland, 2017).

Much mental distress has its origins within adverse experiences and trauma of some kind, and this understanding is a paradigm shift from the more traditional medicalisation of mental health problems. Formulation-led approaches, such as the *Power Threat Meaning Framework* (Johnstone & Boyle, 2020) provide an alternative way of making sense of people's difficulties, asking not *'what's wrong with you?'* but instead *'what has happened to you and how has it shaped you?'*.

Within the UK, the government set out a vision for transformation in health services including trauma-informed psychobiosocial formulation-based approaches to people's mental health difficulties (NHS England, 2019). This has led to a national drive to ensure health services embed trauma-informed approaches in their service delivery.

2.2 Dissociation-Informed Healthcare

Dissociation has been described as 'the hallmark of trauma' (Van der Kolk, 2014). People who have experienced chronic severe childhood trauma and abuse are more likely to develop a range of significant mental health problems, including trauma-related dissociative experiences (Dutra et al., 2009; Kate et al., 2020; Kate et al., 2021; Ogawa et al., 1997; Putnam & Trickett, 1997).

Despite this, in the UK specifically, but also internationally, services

- Often do not *realise* the significance of trauma-related dissociation for mental health
- Often do not *recognise* trauma-related dissociation when it is present
- Often do not *respond* with dissociation-informed or specific care.

which results in:

- Further *retraumatisation* for people when services do not see, accept or appropriately respond to their needs (Lloyd, 2019; Mitchell & Crockford, 2019; Salter, 2023)

Professionals who find themselves working with people who experience trauma-related dissociation, frequently report that their training and supervision has not prepared them to meet the challenges posed. This is often exacerbated by the professional isolation that occurs in the context of services that 'do not believe' in trauma-related dissociation (Herman, 1992). As a result, such clinical presentations often remain unrecognised (Foote et al., 2006).

The concept of dissociation dates to the seminal work of Pierre Janet in the 1900s (Loewenstein, 2018; Van der Hart et al., 2006) and the diagnostic classifications of what are now known as Dissociative Disorders (DDs) have been in international diagnostic systems for the past 40 years, with international best practice professional consensus guidelines in existence since 1994 (ISSTD, 2011). Despite this, there remains a relative lack of training or guidance for mental health professionals, including psychologists, in understanding and working with complex dissociative difficulties.

Within the UK NHS mental health services and other sectors of healthcare lack clearly defined assessment and treatment pathways specifically for people with dissociative experiences and for trauma-based conditions in general.

> 'The NHS do not have services for people with complex dissociation and therefore [people] end up on unhelpful pathways.' **Sally Adams, Expert-by-Experience**

As depicted in Figure 1.1, dissociation can therefore present as a 'disorder of hiddenness' (Howell, 2005, 2011) and go unrecognised. This, combined with the lack of training amongst health professionals, means that often it is only co-occurring difficulties that are recognised, or dissociative clinical presentations are misunderstood as other conditions.

The costs of failing to understand and respond appropriately to trauma-related dissociation are high, to the individual, their networks and the health-care system. Given the inter-generational transmission of trauma these costs may go on to impact subsequent generations (Yehuda & Lehrner, 2018). Increasing understanding and recognition should generate more appropriate dissociation-informed and dissociation-specific care pathways, better outcomes, more cost-effective care and reduce iatrogenic harm (see Chapter 16, Commissioning).

> 'Not everyone needs to be an expert but within the health service it would be beneficial if everyone has an awareness of complex dissociation including DID and knows the right service pathway.' **Melanie Goodwin, Expert-by-Experience**

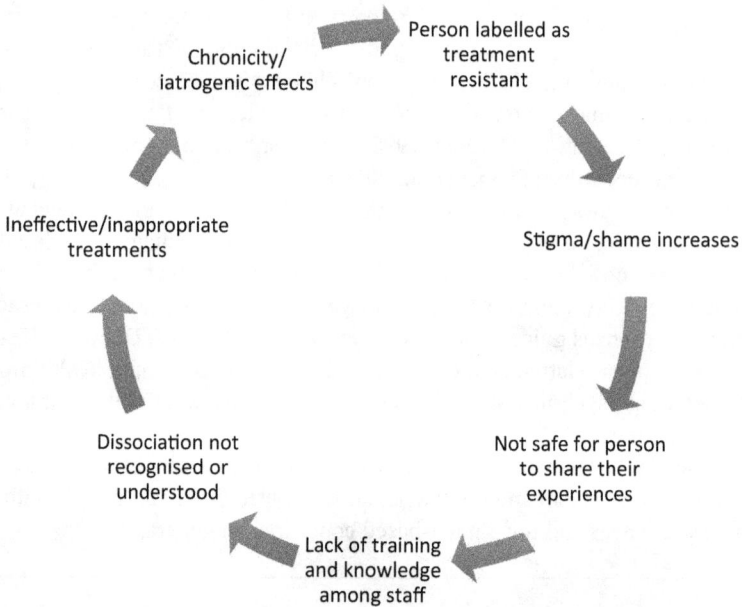

Figure 1.1 Cycle of Costs Associated with Dissociation-Uninformed Care.

As depicted in Figure 1.2, to address this, services should incorporate the following functions:

- Earlier identification and formulation/diagnosis of the person's difficulties
- Staff who are trained and supported to work with people who experience trauma-related dissociation
- Improved understanding and engagement (for both the person with dissociation and those around them)
- More appropriate treatment pathways, and the risk of inappropriate/ ineffective treatments reduced
- Improved outcomes for the person with dissociation
- Foster hope for people within a trauma-informed framework of understanding
- Improved cost-effectiveness through reductions in inappropriate longer term service utilisation and costs.

The current guidelines argue that people with trauma-related dissociation represent a marginalised group. This marginalisation both creates and compounds harm. The current guidelines are part of a wider movement that aims to reduce inequalities in health and promote a fair and just society (Herman, 2023). The inter-sectionality with other forms of marginalisation requires acknowledgement and further study (Ford, 2024).

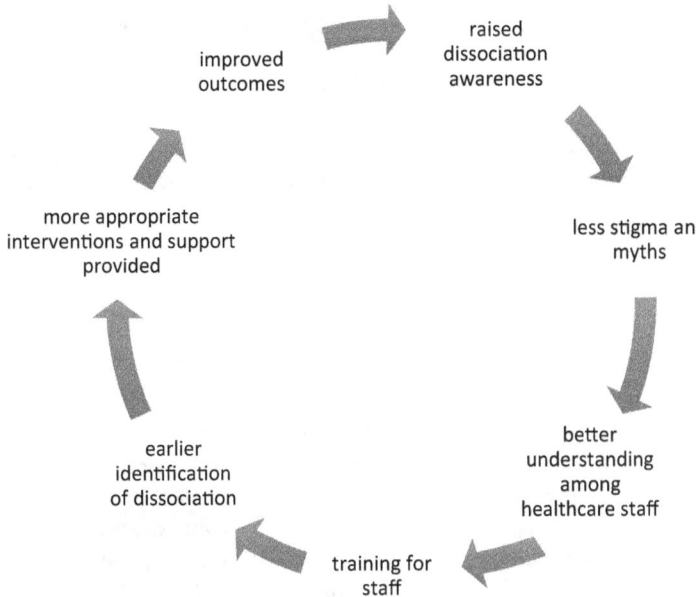

Figure 1.2 Cycle of Benefits of Dissociation-Informed Care.

3. Understanding Dissociation

3.1 Types of Dissociative Experiences

Dissociation can manifest in different ways in the form of different types of experiences. These experiences may occur in isolation or in combination. Steinberg (2023) has described five main dissociative experiences. These can be considered problematic when they are the source of distress or negatively impact the person's social and occupational functioning:

- **Amnesia** – the inability to recall important personal information
- **Depersonalisation** – feeling detached from one's body
- **Derealisation** – feeling the world surrounding you is unreal
- **Identity confusion** – a subjective feeling of uncertainty, puzzlement, or conflict about one's identity
- **Identity alteration** – recurring changes in behaviour or switches in role/identity.

Dissociative experiences can be psychological ('psychoform') or physical ('somatoform') in nature and can result in the person feeling either too much (which are termed 'positive symptoms') or too little (termed 'negative symptoms').

3.2 Psychoform Dissociative Experiences

Some people report only mild experiences in some areas (e.g., depersonalisation/derealisation) whereas others experience more severe experiences in all areas and are likely to meet criteria for a DD diagnosis. It is important to recognise that dissociative experiences may be a 'transdiagnostic' feature of a range of diverse mental health presentations (Spiegel, 2018; Şar, 2014).

3.2.1 Amnesia

Case Example: *Alison has difficulty remembering her daily activities and can lose time for 3 to 4 hours each day. Sometimes she finds herself in places and doesn't recall how she gets there. Her work colleagues have told her she has been argumentative and rude towards them but she has no recollection of this. She finds evidence of things she has done (e-mails she has sent and items she has bought) but doesn't remember doing this. On one occasion she woke up next to a man she didn't recall going to bed with.*

'It's scary ... it feels like you have lost a massive chunk of time ... a time warp ... like you are transported forwards in time and don't know how you arrived there.'

Amnesia refers to the inability to recall important personal information that is so extensive that it is not due to ordinary forgetfulness. People with dissociative amnesia will report time loss in the here and now (e.g., blocks of time missing), indirect evidence of time-loss (e.g., evidence of actions not remembered) as well as amnesia for past events. Sometimes people report having travelled somewhere and cannot recall how they got there (dissociative fugue). Time loss can range from minutes to years. Typically, there will be the experience of micro-amnesias, where discussions engaged in are not remembered or the content of a conversation is forgotten from one moment to the next. People with dissociative amnesia often try to hide this, covering up for it in conversation with others, or minimising the experiences if asked directly about this due to embarrassment or shame.

Many people may have non-dissociative difficulties with memory (poor memory, concentration, absorption problems) for a variety of reasons, exacerbated at times of stress.

3.2.2 Depersonalisation and Derealisation

Depersonalisation is the sense of being detached from one's body. Often referred to as an 'out-of-body' experience and is not related to taking alcohol or other substances.

> **Case Examples**: *'Suddenly all the colours go funny, my eyes go weird and then I'm not there anymore like I've taken a strange drug.'*
> *'An odd sinking feeling ... you feel yourself being sucked away ... almost like I'm melting away, a bit like a shrinking melting feeling.'*
> *'I can see my hand on the table, but it is not my hand ... it doesn't belong to me.'*
> *'I'm starting to go hazy.'*

Some people report persistent and recurrent feelings of depersonalisation, as if an outside observer of one's mental processes or body (e.g., feeling as though one were in a dream, feeling a sense of unreality of self, or of their body or of time moving slowly). Some report more severe symptoms of depersonalisation in the form of profound alienation from their bodies, such as not recognising themselves in the mirror or not recognising, feeling or connecting with parts of their bodies, in ways that they find difficult to articulate.

> **Case Examples**: *'Its like I'm looking through soup.'*
> *'I can't see or hear clearly, the speed is out of sync and things around me slow down...'*
> *'It's like Deja Vue ... I don't know where I am, but there is something very familiar about it ... it's very confusing.'*
> *'People I know start to look different, like I don't recognise them.'*

Derealisation is the sense of the world and one's surroundings not being real. Some people report that the world looks foggy, distant, dreamlike or distorted in some way. Some describe seeing the world as if detached from it, or as if watching a movie (Steinberg, 1995). Some report more severe symptoms of derealisation, such as feeling like a visitor to their own home or not recognising familiar places or people.

Depersonalisation and derealisation are common experiences, which may be present in many mental health problems, however, people who meet criteria for a DD are likely to report more severe difficulties in these areas that may indicate structural dissociation or 'division of self'. For example, a mild or common experience of depersonalisation might be feeling unreal and discon-nected, whereas a more severe symptom (suggesting 'division of self') might be feeling that parts of one's body is completely numb or not belonging to one-self. A mild or common experience of derealisation might be feeling the world far away or foggy, whereas a more severe 'symptom' (suggesting 'division of self') might be not recognising someone you are close to or not recognising a familiar place.

> **Case Examples**: *'I feel like a stranger to myself, I don't really know who I am … it doesn't make sense.'*
>
> *'I can feel one way one day, and very different the next, very fragile and then very competent, either not sure or highly opinionated.'*
>
> *'I felt fragmented and lost, frightened of looking at myself … like lost bits that got stranded.'*

3.2.3 Identity Confusion and Identity Alteration

Identity confusion refers to a subjective feeling of uncertainty, puzzlement or conflict about one's identity, often accompanied by a struggle as to who one is, or an inner battle regarding identity and decisions. The person may feel confused when their thoughts and feelings fluctuate, or when their sense of who they are is muddled and not always coherent or consistent. These difficulties are more persistent and marked than normal identity confusion that may occur in adolescence or midlife crises

Identity alteration represents recurring changes in behaviour or marked shifts in how the person experiences their role or identity, and a sense of acting like a different person some of the time. Often (but not always) this occurs outside of conscious awareness. This may be a subjective change which can only be self-reported, or it can result in either subtle or more notable changes in how the person presents (e.g., different voice, posture, behaviours, thinking pattern, preferences) that are observable to others.

> **Case Examples**: *David's wife has noticed that he has been getting up and wandering around the house at night. When she calls to him, he doesn't recognise his name, and says he is not David. In the morning, he sometimes finds things he has done on his computer or woodwork items he has made with remarkable skill and doesn't know how he did it or have any recollection of it.*
>
> *Sally, aged 33 is talking to her therapist, when she suddenly seems distracted by something, then her posture and voice change and she looks confused. She looks around the room and asks where she is. She doesn't recognise the handbag or car keys next to her as belonging to her, and when told it is hers, she says in a puzzled voice that it can't be because she is 15 and cannot drive.*

Recognisable signs of identity alteration might include referring to the self by different names and/or the self as plural 'we', possessing a skill one cannot recall learning, discovering items in one's possession that one is unaware of acquiring.

People who experience identity alteration commonly report a sense of involuntariness to the phenomena. They are aware of the presence of thoughts, feelings, behaviours, memories and events but that these do not belong to them and have a quality of 'not me' or 'not mine'.

Most people who meet criteria for a DD do not come with specific complaints about their identity or sense of self, indeed sometimes such difficulties may be outside of the person's awareness. It can be difficult for people to find the words to express their experiences, and the information may not be volunteered, unless asked.

3.2.4 'Schneiderian' Symptoms

> **Case Examples**: *'Its like my legs are walking and someone else is making them move, my words come out but it is not me doing the talking.'*
>
> *'There is something pulling it back down. I don't know what it is but it is controlling me, there are different perspectives, voices directing me, it feels like I am just an observer of a movie that I have no part in.'*

Many 'symptoms' typically thought to be experienced by people with schizophrenia and other psychoses, are also commonly experienced by people who experience trauma-related dissociation. Schneider's first-rank symptoms of schizophrenia (auditory hallucinations, somatic passivity, thought withdrawal, insertion and broadcasting, delusional perception, and delusions of control such as 'made' actions, drives or feelings) can be highly prevalent in people who meet criteria for a DD. For example, when people report experiences of hearing voices, feeling passively controlled, or of their actions not belonging to them, this can indicate a dissociative identity alteration.

3.3 Somatoform Symptoms

Somatic symptoms of dissociation are common among people with trauma-related dissociation, and often overlooked as a part of the bigger picture of the person's dissociative experiences (see Chapter 8, Physical Health). These can include the presence or absence of physical experiences, indicating a lack of integration of experiences that are usually connected (Scaer, 2014).

Examples of 'positive' (feeling too much) somatoform dissociation include:

- Non epileptic seizures
- Unexplained pain
- Tics
- Involuntary movements
- Sensory perceptions, such as touch, hearing, vision, taste, smell

- Sensory intrusions, such as feeling as if your legs are moving but it is not you moving them.

Examples of 'negative' (feeling too little) somatoform dissociation include:

- Partial or total paralysis
- Loss of strength/tension in muscles
- Loss of hearing vision, speech, smell or taste
- Loss of sensation, such as not feeling hunger, temperature, pain, touch, arousal, anaesthesia.

Case Examples: *'Suddenly there is this strange smell ... and a vision of blackness ... I don't know where it comes from...'*
'I feel a weight on top of me and the sensations of being raped.'
'I can see shadows, moving, and feel very afraid.'
'Its like a brain zap ... I feel electrical sensations all around me.'

Unusual visual or somatic experiences can sometimes be an intrusion experience (e.g., flashback) from a past trauma, disconnected from and unaware of their origins due to dissociative amnesia.

3.4 Accompanying Trauma-Related Symptoms

Most people who present with the above experiences of trauma-related dissociation will also present with wider difficulties associated with traumatisation (e.g., re-experiencing, hyper-arousal, avoidance of triggers).

Other secondary experiences may include emotional dysregulation, negative self-concept and relational disturbances (Cloitre et al., 2021).

In situations where a trauma-history is not disclosed it is important to consider that this may be due to lack of recollection of a trauma history, due to amnesia or very early pre-verbal developmental experiences.

In these cases, people will often present with disturbing trauma-related symptoms and the re-experiencing symptoms may present more bodily, as unexplained somatic flashbacks that are harder to locate in time or convey in a verbal narrative.

Diagnostically, most meeting criteria for a DD will also meet criteria for diagnoses of PTSD (79–100%), depression (83–96%) and have a history of past or current substance misuse (83–96%) (Lanius et al., 2010; Spiegel et al., 2011). There are also high levels of dissociative presentations among people who have a diagnosis of eating disorders, (see Chapter 12) particularly bulimia nervosa (Brewerton et al., 2020) and also in people with diagnoses of somatoform disorders and medically unexplained symptoms (Nijenhuis et al., 1998).

Some people who meet criteria for a DD may also be given a diagnosis of Emotionally Unstable Personality Disorder (EUPD) (Al-Shamali et al., 2022). Evidence suggests that there are discrete differences between these two presentations both clinically and neurobiologically (Brand & Lanius, 2014; Brand, Şar, et al., 2016)

Likewise, the presence of auditory hallucinations which are reported in 47-90% of people who meet criteria for a DD (Renard et al., 2017) may result in a diagnosis of schizophrenia despite such experiences being more prevalent in people experiencing trauma-related dissociation (see Chapter 7).

There appears to be an association between dissociation and poor physical health outcomes (Kendall-Tackett & Klest, 2009). Evidence suggests that traumatic experience impacts on the physiological systems involved in the human stress response, including the endocrine and immune system, with these impacts seen at the level of gene expression (Maté, 2022). Untreated dissociation can also impact on adherence to physical health treatment or willingness to present to services (Kendall-Tackett & Klest, 2009; Keuroghlian et al., 2011) (see Chapter 8).

3.5 Dissociative Experiences as a Protective Response to Threat

Dissociation is currently best understood as an adaptive defence to overwhelming trauma. It represents an automatic, reflexive evolutionary response to threat, serving to protect the person by reducing their awareness of intolerable (traumatic) experience.

We all have the natural ability to dissociate at times and this can allow us to get on with life and function effectively at times of heightened emotional stress or trauma. For example, dealing with an emergency calmly in the moment but feeling the shock and emotion later or having amnesia for aspects of a traumatic event such as childbirth or a road traffic collision.

As a coping response dissociation can help to maintain attachment in the face of overwhelming threat, betrayal or neglect, with aspects of experience held by distinct aspects of the self.

Dissociation can involve a wide array of experiences, from mild to severe, from temporary to chronic. However, for people who have experienced overwhelming trauma, often early in life and without a secure attachment to create safeness, more chronic patterns of severe dissociation may develop over time that become entrenched and problematic. It is often this delayed impact of dissociation or a breakdown in protective avoidance that drives people towards seeking help later in life (see Chapter 11).

Recognising and understanding the adaptive survival function of dissociation is very important.

Dissociation as a survival strategy can:

- Help prevent feeling overwhelmed in the moment
- Anesthetise physical and psychological pain
- Allow a degree of functioning for the person to be able to continue in their daily life.

However, when dissociative experiences persist and become the default for managing stress:

- The ability to be fully present is diminished
- Attention and new learning can be impaired
- Managing and regulating emotions can be more problematic
- Relationships and functioning are affected
- Risk/safety issues can increase
- A fragmented sense of self is experienced including a lack of continuity across time.

3.6 Dissociative Disorder Diagnoses

In some UK mental health services care pathways are diagnostically informed. In addition, for some people seeking a diagnosis is an important part of accepting and validating the impact of past trauma (see Chapter 2).

Both DSM-V and ICD-11 provide specific sections for the diagnostic classification of DDs which have been listed in diagnostic classifications since DSM-III was published in 1980. There is much overlap between classifications in DSM-V and ICD-11. See Table 1.1 for a list of current DD Classifications.

Both diagnostic frameworks include main diagnoses of Dissociative Identity Disorder (DID), Dissociative Amnesia (DA) and Depersonalisation Derealisation Disorder (DP/DR D), as well as an 'other-specified' or 'un-specified' category.

Table 1.1 DSM-V and ICD 11 Dissociative Disorders

DSM-V	ICD-11
Dissociative Identity Disorder (DID)	Dissociative identity disorder
Other Specified Dissociative Disorder (OSDD)	Partial dissociative identity disorder
Depersonalisation/Derealisation Disorder (DPDRP)	Depersonalisation-derealisation disorder
Dissociative Amnesia (with or without dissociative fugue) (DA)	Dissociative amnesia
Unspecified Dissociative Disorder (USDD)	Dissociative disorder, unspecified
	Dissociative neurological symptom disorder
	Trance disorder
	Possession trance disorder
	Other specified dissociative disorder

The new ICD-11 classification has replaced the previous diagnosis of Multiple Personality Disorder (ICD-10) with DID, and included a new category of Partial DID. Whilst there is more overlap than previously between the systems, there continues to be some differences and 'somatoform dissociation' is categorised and termed differently. DSM-V lists this separately under 'Conversion Disorder', whereas ICD-11 includes it as Dissociative neurological symptom disorder.

The DSM-V diagnostic criteria for PTSD now includes a Dissociative Subtype (PTSD-DS) in which persistent symptoms of depersonalisation/derealisation are present, and the DDs section follows the Trauma and Stressor Related Disorders highlighting their inter-relationship. ICD 11 also includes the diagnosis of Complex PTSD.

From a diagnostic perspective, dissociative experiences can present as symptoms of other primary mental health difficulties and still require careful consideration in assessment. ICD-11 includes considerable attention to the issue of boundaries with other diagnoses to aid with differential diagnosis. In all cases the presence of dissociation is important to address in treatment as a transdiagnostic psychological factor.

In sum, from a diagnostic perspective, dissociative experiences can:

1. Be mild and/or transient,
2. Be part of a primary dissociative problem
3. Accompany other mental health difficulties

4. Epidemiology

4.1 How Common Is Dissociation?

> **Myth:** *Dissociative presentations are rare*
> **Response:** *Far from being rare, dissociative presentations are as prevalent as other kinds of severe mental health problems*

Studies have adopted a range of standardised assessment tools to research the prevalence of trauma-related dissociation, across different settings, populations, countries and continents. Studies show a high degree of variance in results, perhaps in part due to the different sensitivity and specificity of differing assessment methods (Loewenstein, 2018; Şar 2011).

Studies show that 10% of people seen in clinical settings appear to meet the criteria for a DD, with half of these (5%) representing DID (Şar, 2011). This rate is higher in more restrictive clinical settings, for example, two studies demonstrated that 13.0–20.7% of people in psychiatric inpatient settings in USA would meet criteria for a DD (Ross, 1991; Saxe et al., 1993). Lipsanen et al. (2004) reported psychiatric inpatients (21.0%) were more likely than outpatients (14%) to meet criteria for a DD. Şar et al. (2007) found 35.7% of emergency admissions into a university psychiatric clinic in Istanbul met criteria for a DD. Mueller et al. (2007) found 25.0% of chronic and severely impaired psychiatric outpatients met criteria for a DD.

In clinical settings therefore trauma-related dissociation is relatively common, with higher rates seen in more intensive and crisis settings and in people with more chronic and severely impaired mental health presentations. Populations known to be at particularly high risk for experiencing trauma-related dissociation include substance users, forensic populations, sex-workers, eating disorder populations, as well as people who were looked after children. Many people who have been given the diagnostic label of EUPD may meet the diagnostic criteria for a DD (Brand & Lanius, 2014).

In the general population the prevalence of dissociative presentations is similar to other common mental health problems. A recent study by Simeon and Purnam (2022) reported on the prevalence of 'pathological dissociation' in a representative US national sample of some 6,644 participants. The one month prevalence of a likely DD was reported to be 4.1%. Regarding DID specifically, Simeon and Putnam (2022) reported 1.5% of the sample as likely meeting criteria for DID. This is consistent with other general population studies estimating the prevalence of DID within New York State and Turkey respectively (Johnson et al., 2006; Şar et al., 2007).

4.2 Functioning and Risk

There are often high levels of risk and impairment of functioning for many people with trauma-related dissociation. Leonard et al. (2005) found 60% of a sample of people who met criteria for a DD reported being 'disabled' with difficulties in functioning across multiple domains of life. A total of 76% reported significant delays in their dissociative difficulties being recognised and that this delay had had negative consequences for their functioning. They had significant health service utilisation, with 48% having been hospitalised and 68% of these more than five times. Outside of health costs, people who meet criteria for a DD have higher rates of social service utilisation due to additional impairments and needs associated with medical illness, disability, and other consequences of dissociation (Langeland et al., 2020). In their national prevalence study, Simeon and Putnam (2022) reported people with 'pathological dissociation' had poorer mental and physical health, marked comorbidity with major psychiatric disorders and greater likelihood of inpatient psychiatric admission.

> 'The cost to the person is so often ignored, it is impossible to measure the human cost.' **Melanie Goodwin, Expert-by-Experience**

For people meeting diagnostic criteria of a DD there is a completed suicide rate of 1–2% (Şar 2011), 60–80% report a history of suicide attempts and over 68%

report non-suicidal self-harm (Foote et al., 2008; Spiegel et al., 2011). The presence of a DD diagnosis is an independent risk factor for multiple suicide attempts (Foote et al., 2008) and represent a greater predictor of suicide risk than self-injury, depression, or PTSD (Xu et al., 2023). The majority of DD patients (92.31%) report only partial awareness of precipitants to their self-injury (Nester et al., 2022). Dissociation has also been found to be a predictor related to both suicide attempt and self-harm independent of other concurrent diagnoses (Calati et al., 2017). (See Chapter 6).

Additional coping behaviours such as substance misuse (Şar, 2011), eating disturbance, impulsivity or risk-taking behaviours (Ross et al., 1989) are more common among people who experience trauma-related dissociation (Boyer et al., 2022). Dissociative experiences are also strongly linked to higher rates of revictimisation, including sexual assault and intimate partner violence (Zamir et al., 2018).

> 'Many people with dissociative disorders do much to keep themselves away from services. Often it's my parts that hurt me, yet explaining that to professionals who have limited to no knowledge of dissociative disorders, often left me feeling like I was some kind of freak. Our coping behaviours centre on self-harm, eating difficulties and risk taking behaviours, yet I manage the consequences of those personally, so for example I self-sutre the cuts inflicted on the body to avoid interaction with health services that are often demeaning and unhelpful for someone with a dissociative disorder.' **Sally Adams, Expert-by-Experience**

4.3 Treatment Pathway and Outcome

Across studies, the evidence suggests people may spend on average between 5–12 years in the mental health system before having complex dissociation accurately recognised, with 3–4 incorrect prior conceptualisations or diagnoses (Loewenstein, 2018). This inability to recognise the presence of trauma-related dissociation means many people 'may suffer iatrogenic worsening of their difficulties due to years of misdiagnosis and mistreatment' (Spiegel et al., 2011) (see Chapter 7).

> 'Many of these experiences retraumatise the person so by the time they get a correct diagnosis there may be several extra layers of trauma that will need addressing, often within the setting that inflicted more recent traumatic experiences (i.e., hospital or mental health settings). **Melanie Goodwin, Expert-by-Experience**

> **Practice Point**: *Regardless of diagnosis, it has been found that elevated dissociation predicts poorer clinical outcomes unless the dissociation is directly addressed and treated.*
>
> (Brand, Sar, et al., 2016; Lyssenko et al., 2018)

Prognostic studies have looked at the long-term likely outcomes for people with complex dissociative difficulties (Baars et al., 2011) with a range of factors impacting on treatment course (e.g., on-going abuse, lack of supportive relationships or daily structure). These highlight there is much heterogeneity and 'no one size fits all' with some people responding very well to treatment and others less so due to a range of factors (Kluft, 1994).

For people who do not receive help to address trauma-related dissociation then their difficulties are unlikely to resolve (Al-Shamali et al., 2022; Brand, Vissia, et al., 2016). A generic trauma treatment delivered in a Norwegian inpatient setting did not address dissociative symptoms and failed to reduce amnesia or dissociative identity alteration (Jepsen et al., 2014). High levels of dissociation have been shown to reduce the effectiveness of NICE-recommended treatments for other clinical presentations. For example, standard protocol Eye Movement Desensitisation and Reprocessing (EMDR) therapy for PTSD and Dialectical Behaviour Therapy (DBT) for EUPD have both been found to have reduced effectiveness in populations experiencing high levels of dissociation (Bae et al., 2016; Kleindienst et al., 2011). This suggests that treatment approaches need to be able to be adapted around the specific needs associated with trauma-related dissociation (NICE, 2018).

The evidence base suggests effective recognition and treatment of dissociation can lead to positive outcomes and cost effectiveness. Langeland et al. (2020) report a systematic review finding that appropriate diagnosis and access to specialist treatment significantly reduces costs (by 25%-64%) by decreasing treatment length, emergency care utilisation, and hospitalisations. Marked improvement in functioning and reductions in cost through the delivery of dissociation informed- and specific-care have also been reported as part of the international TOP DD studies (Brand et al., 2025; Brand et al., 2022; Myrick, Webermann, Langeland, et al., 2017; Myrick, Webermann, Loewenstein, et al., 2017) and by Lloyd (2016) within the context of an NHS mental health service (see Chapter 4).

5. Models of Understanding Dissociation

There are several ways in which the experience of dissociation is described in the literature.

5.1 Dissociation as a State of Being

Some authors argue that dissociation reflects different states of being (SoB), each associated with a particular cognitive, emotional, motor, behavioural, sensory and memory profile (Loewenstein & Putnam, 2023). Safeness and secure attachment facilitate the integration of differing SoB, leading to smooth transitions from one state to the other relevant to the context the person is in. Early experiences characterised by neglect or abuse however impairs this integrative capacity, resulting in highly differentiated SoB characterised by ongoing shifts and sudden switches between *discrete behavioural states* (Loewenstein & Putnam, 2023). These differing levels of integration can account for the proposed continuum between 'normal dissociation' (such as daydreaming or absorption) at one end and 'pathological dissociation' characterised by discrete behavioural states at the other (e.g., Bernstein & Putnam, 1986).

5.2 Dissociation Categorised by Behavioural Function or Form

Some authors have attempted to provide a clearer taxonomy of dissociation. For example, Holmes et al. (2005) consider dissociation to incorporate two categories of trauma-related responses; '*detachment*' (which incorporates lowering of consciousness, emotional numbing, derealisation, and depersonalisation) and '*compartmentalisation*' into different 'parts' of the personality (which incorporates experiences such as identity confusion and alteration).

Along similar lines, Lanius (2015) deconstructs the continuum of 'dissociation' across the four dimensions of *time, thought, body* and *emotion*. This 'four-dimensional' model of dissociation contrasts trauma-related and normal waking states of consciousness across each domain. For example, trauma-related states of consciousness may entail reliving/flashbacks in the domain of time; voice hearing or the intrusion of 'parts' in the domain of thought; depersonalisation in the domain of body and emotional numbing and affective shut down or intense emotionality in the domain of emotion.

Nijenhuis (2015) critiques the above conceptualisations of dissociation as being overly inclusive and including experiences (such as depersonalisation) that are commonplace across other presentations (such as panic disorder).

5.3 Dissociation as Structural Dissociation of the Personality

Other conceptualisations, such as the Theory of the Structural Dissociation of the Personality (Van der Hart et al., 2006) advocate for greater specificity. Proponents of this view adopt the following definition of 'dissociation':

> *A division of the personality as a whole organism-environment system into two or more conscious and self-conscious subsystems or dissociative parts during or following traumatic/traumatising events.*
>
> (Nijenhuis, 2015, p.273)

This 'structural dissociation' varies in intensity across individuals and clinical presentations. At its simplest this presents as primary structural dissociation (as in PTSD). At its most complex, in tertiary structural dissociation there is a more marked *'division of self'* resulting in marked difficulties with amnesia, identity confusion and alteration. The model distinguishes between parts of the personality fixated in action systems of 'daily life' (Apparently Normal Parts of the Personality; ANP) and parts of the personality fixated in action systems of defense (Emotional Parts of the Personality; EP). See Table 1.2.

6. The Development of Dissociation

Complex dissociative difficulties often have childhood origins, having developed over time as a survival response to experiences of trauma and abuse, within a background of disorganised attachment.

6.1 The Importance of Attachment

Infants need connection and attachment to survive. Healthy attachment relationships for infants also provide a 'secure base' for promoting exploration, development and learning and 'safe haven' for the regulation of threat. Children learn the capacity for self-regulation of emotions through the early process of co-regulation with a caregiver. This learning through healthy attachment promotes integration through the development of 'internal working models' of relationships (both self-other relationships and self-self relating). The benefits of secure attachment are reflected at a neurobiological level (Gerhardt, 2004).

Table 1.2 Structural Dissociation of the Personality

Type	Description	Diagnostic link
Primary Structural Dissociation	A single split between ANP and EP	PTSD
Secondary Structural Dissociation	More than one EP emerges	C-PTSD, EUPD, DDNOS
Tertiary Structural Dissociation	Multiple ANPs and EPs develop	DID

Attachment models provide a useful framework to understand how early attachment disruption (Dutra et al., 2009) in addition to severe trauma/abuse may underpin the development of dissociation.

People who present with severe levels of dissociation have usually experienced early attachment disruption within the context of severe childhood trauma, neglect and abuse (Loewenstein, 2018). From a diagnostic perspective people who meet criteria for a DD report the highest frequencies of childhood psychological trauma among all psychiatric disorders, including childhood sexual, emotional, physical abuse and neglect (Şar, 2011) with childhood sexual abuse found in 70% to 100% of people with DID (Spiegel et al., 2011). Studies of children who met criteria for DID have found 95% of maltreatment reports substantiated by social services (Hornstein & Putnam, 1992).

When attachment figures are chronically 'frightening or frightened' (Hesse & Main, 2000) the child has an unsolvable dilemma of needing attachment from the figure who engenders fear. Dissociation and splitting off awareness provides a means of escape when there is no other escape (Liotti, 2006).

An example of this is where 'the night-time child' endures sexual abuse and then dissociates entirely from the 'day-time child' to be able to function as a 'good girl' for an abusive parent. As powerfully described by Marilyn Van Derbur (2003);

> *'Without realising it, I fought to keep my two worlds separated. Without ever knowing why, I made sure, whenever possible that nothing passed between the compartmentalisation, I had created between the day child and the night child'*

Dissociation enables the child to adapt and engage in more normal maturation and development in other areas, whilst developing discrete dissociative self-states to encapsulate intolerable trauma.

6.2 The Neurobiological Impact of Trauma

The neurobiological systems that process emotions can be significantly compromised in individuals with chronic trauma. Growing neurobiological evidence supports the trauma model conceptualisation of dissociation (Brand et al., 2022; Kearney & Lanius, 2022; Reinders et al., 2023). Neuroimaging studies show that patterns of brain activation differ significantly in patients with dissociative subtype PTSD (increased frontal system activation and decreased amygdala activation) compared with those with non-dissociative PTSD (increased amygdala activation) (Lanius et al., 2012). PET and fMRI studies of people meeting criteria for DID found simulating controls had markedly different brain activation and psychophysiological patterns from those who met criteria for DID (Reinders et al., 2016). One study showed people who met criteria for DID have

Table 1.3 Composite Neurobiological Model of Dissociation

Type	Description	Neurobiological underpinning
Supracortical dissociation	Involuntary turning away from pain 'not me, not mine'	Superior colliculi, brainstem
Intracortical dissociation	Depersonalisation and derealisation	Higher cortical areas in response to shock
Neurochemical dissociation	Stress-induced analgesia involving endogenous-cannabinoids (numbing, fuzziness, light headiness) and -opioids (loss of muscle tone, feelings of sleepiness, submission)	Descending inhibitory pain pathway to neurochemically 'cap' severe affective responses from the mid-brain limbic region/periaqueductal gray matter
Structural dissociation	See Table 1.2	Functionally segregated cortical loops

significantly reduced hippocampal and amygdala volumes compared to healthy controls (Vermetten et al., 2006).

Corrigan et al. (2025) have postulated four primary neurobiological pathways accounting for different forms of dissociation, each with their own distinct neurobiological signature and phenotype as outlined in Table 1.3.

These central nervous system dissociative mechanisms and responses are also associated with different mobilising and immobilising responses in the autonomic nervous system, as outlined by Porges (2011) for example in poly-vagal theory.

6.3 Alternative Theories

Some authors view experiences associated with DDs as fictitious, and tend to ascribe to one of the following models:

- The Iatrogenic Model views complex dissociative presentations as a condition produced in highly suggestible patients by clinicians
- The Socio-cognitive Model sees complex dissociative presentations as developing in North American culture caused by the media focus on childhood sexual abuse, repressed memories
- The Fantasy Model sees dissociation as a cognitive trait leading to fantasies and confabulations of traumatic experiences.

However, there are no studies in clinical populations to support the above models, and substantial research confounds these theories and supports the trauma model of dissociation (Brand, Şar, et al., 2016; Brewin & Andrews, 2017; Reinders & Veltman, 2021).

> *'I have DID and I work in a mental health service in the NHS. My manager believes DID to be fictitious as have some other professionals we have worked with. That in itself feels like a further retraumatisation in that the essence of "me and us" do not exist and are invalid and contributes to a deeper sense of shame and further hiddenness.'* **Sally Adams, Expert-by-Experience**

Herman (1992) outlines the long-standing societal denial of childhood sexual abuse as a key barrier to the acceptance of trauma-related dissociation. Powerful groups such as the USA-based False Memory Syndrome Foundation were very influential in the discreditation of the experiences of trauma-survivors (Salter & Blizard, 2022). Such groups perpetuated the myth that 'recovered' memories of childhood sexual abuse were not to be believed or were an artefact of over-zealous clinicians. Such claims have not been supported by the empirical literature (Brewin & Andrews, 2017).

Myths and misconceptions have also been perpetuated by media portrayals and dramatisations which have increased scepticism and stigma (Snyder et al., 2024).

7. Conclusion

In sum, dissociative responses, including DID, are more common than is often assumed. Untreated dissociation is associated with multiple poor outcomes for the person across multiple dimensions of health. Efforts to improve the ability of services to realise, recognise and respond to trauma-related dissociation will help to benefit not just people who experience trauma-related dissociation but also their families, social networks and society.

Chapter 2

Screening and Assessment of Dissociation

Paul Langthorne, Louise Harriss, Mike Lloyd and Helena Crockford

As summarised in Figure 2.1, the current guidelines propose a stepped model to aid the screening and assessment of trauma-related dissociation. These steps are intended to be offered flexibly, and in collaboration with the person. Attunement to the needs and wishes of the person in the moment and building consensus is important across each step. Each step will require adjustment, so they are applied in a culturally sensitive way. Placing the person at the centre of their care and empowering them to make choices is at the heart of this approach. Readers are directed to Brand (2024) for a full overview of issues related to the assessment of trauma-related dissociation.

1. Raising Awareness of Trauma-Related Dissociation

Helping clinicians to understand that trauma-related dissociation underlies a diverse range of clinical presentations and is often undetected is a key starting point for service improvement (Kezelman & Stavropoulos, 2020).

Such awareness-raising needs to engage with and address a range of barriers which are still significant across service areas currently. The voice of lived experience is key in helping to address such barriers.

See Chapter 17 for a proposed training and support framework to help raise awareness of trauma-related dissociation for staff working in various health and social care settings.

2. Barriers to Seeking Help

When working to raise the awareness of trauma-related dissociation, professionals need to be aware of the barriers that exist to the acknowledgement and disclosure of these experiences. Such barriers may inter-sect with other sources of marginalisation. To make services more accessible for people with dissociative difficulties it is important that providers use this awareness to address such obstacles.

DOI: 10.4324/9781003625650-4

Step 1. Awareness raising

Dissociation-informed. For all. Undertaken by any health professsional in any context.

Step 2. General screening

Dissociation-informed. For all. Undertaken by any health professsional in any context.

Enquire about dissociative experiences using specific questions

Step 3. Specific screening.

Dissociation-specific. Undertaken by any health professsional where role requires assessment of dissociative experiences. Requires access to training, supervision, consultation.

Use of dissociation screening tools (e.g., DES-II, SDQ 20) either stand-alone or as part of wider assessment.

Step 4. Structured assessment

Dissociation-specific. Undertaken by mental health professional with expertise in assessment of trauma and dissociation and access to appropriate supervision/consultation (e.g., psychiatry, psychologist).

Use of structured clinical assessment tools (e.g., SCID-D; DDIS) either stand-alone or as part of wider assessment.

Step 5. Formulation/Diagnosis

Dissociation-specific. Undertaken by mental health professional with expertise in trauma and dissociation and access to appropriate supervision/consultation (e.g., psychiatry, psychologist).

Helping to incorporate an understanding of dissociation into psychological formulations and where appropriate considerations regarding diagnosis.

Step 6. Psychoeducation

Dissociation-specific. Undertaken by mental health professionals with awareness of trauma-related dissociation.

Psychoeducation to increase understanding and normalisation of dissociative experiences. Education of person and network.

Step 7. Collaborative care planning

Dissociation-informed (for all) and specific. Building understanding of dissociation into care planning and delivery. Including delivery of 'routine aspects of care' and dissociation-specific needs (e.g., psychological treatment)

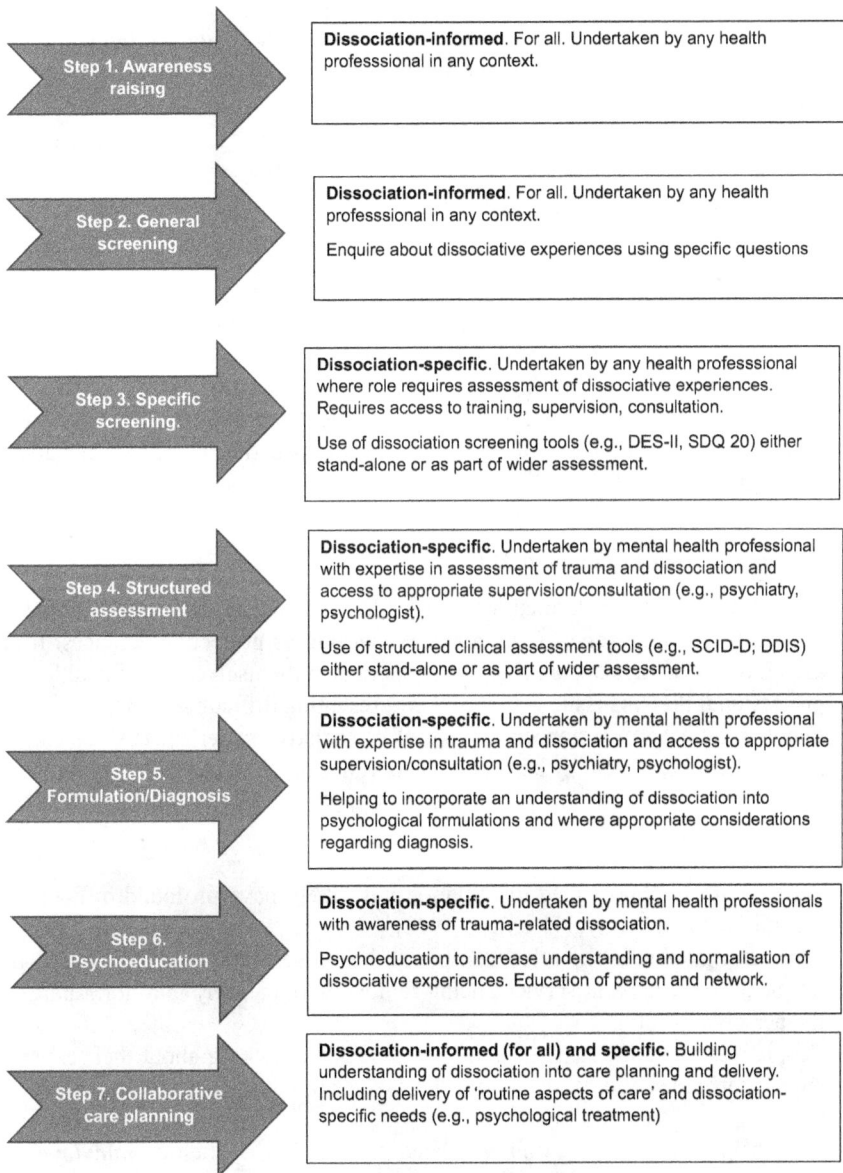

Figure 2.1 Stepped Approach to Facilitate the Realisation and Recognition of Trauma-Related Dissociation.

> *'When services do not operate in a trauma-informed way the impact of this can be devastating to the service user.'* **Sally Adams, Expert-by-Experience**

2.1 Internal Barriers

2.1.1 Shame and Stigma

- Fear or shame about their experiences, and coping strategies including denial, may have developed to push the symptoms into the background
- Societal stigma of mental health often adds to difficulties in help-seeking, particularly for people with trauma histories which have involved not being believed and fears of speaking out in case this results in negative consequences.

2.1.2 Dissociation of Dissociation

- Dissociation has been termed a 'disorder of hiddenness' (Howell, 2011) with the symptoms themselves (e.g., amnesia) serving as protective defences. It is therefore not always apparent to either the person themselves or the healthcare professional that this issue is part of their presenting difficulties
- People may have experienced a range of dissociative experiences since childhood which therefore may be experienced as normal and natural for them.

2.1.3 Fear of Others

- People with trauma-related dissociation will likely have profound difficulties around trust and betrayal (Herman, 1992)
- This can manifest in the relationship with health services, where invalidation, not being believed and services being removed prematurely may form part of the person's history
- People may have internalised strong messages that talking about their experience is forbidden and dangerous for themselves or others.

Seeking help for underlying trauma-related dissociation is often *a many-layered process* with which the person may have struggled for years. Professionals should be prepared for mixed reactions to dissociative experiences being recognised. Indeed, for some people the recognition of trauma-related dissociation may be accompanied by both relief and an adverse reaction and as such should be navigated with care (Armstrong, 1996, 2002; Brand, 2024).

> *'This is not an indication the person is 'getting worse' rather that they are able to engage, and more parts contribute allowing a bigger picture of the whole.'* **Melanie Goodwin, Expert-by-Experience**

2.2 External Barriers

- There can be professional and societal resistance to recognising and understanding trauma-related dissociation, which further complicates access to appropriate care and treatment (Nester et al., 2022)
- Services may not be prepared to work with the 'approach-avoidance' conflicts that can be a key part of relational trauma and dissociation. For example, services may only offer input to people who can demonstrate that they are 'ready, willing and able' for goal-focused work
- High thresholds to access services, may be especially difficult for people who experience trauma-related dissociation, where issues such as shame or amnesia make it difficult for the person to specify the difficulties, they are requiring support with
- Such service-barriers may intersect with other barriers that exist for marginalised groups (see Chapter 15, Cultural Considerations).

> *'I have faced more shame and stigma working with a psychologist who does not believe in dissociation and Dissociative Identity Disorder (DID) specifically.'* **Sally Adams, Expert-by-Experience**

3. Factors which Facilitate Help-Seeking and Receiving

When someone has reached out for help, it is important they feel listened to respectfully, without prejudice, without invalidation of their experiences and without overhasty diagnosis.

> *'Our solution is two-fold. First, to create a society within which such trauma can be spoken of without shame or repercussion - this is a huge task and the responsibility of us all. Second, we can believe the person when they come forward. We can approach their story with respect and understanding, patience and expertise, we can reassure and offer them the help they need, not just whatever happens to be available. We can engage with them,*

share the journey with them and walk them through it.' **Mike Lloyd, Clinical Psychologist**

3.1 General Guiding Principles for the Clinician to Facilitate Help-Seeking

An awareness and understanding of dissociation embedded within the relational principles of a *trauma-informed approach* are key (Armstrong, 2002; Brand, 2024). For people with fragmented experiences, a disorganised attachment style and profound interpersonal mistrust, these principles become even more important (Brand et al., 2022; Steele et al., 2001). These guiding principles are relevant across each interaction.

- **Build trust/safety**. Expect mistrust and validate this as understandable in the context of the person's experience. The person may not feel safe about revealing their experiences and there may be parts of them which do not wish this. Provide time and space and pay attention to whether the person feels uncomfortable with questions asked
- **Be collaborative**. Provide choice, transparency, and ensure the person has a clear understanding of what to expect. Putting the person at the heart of their care and allowing choice to shape decision making is important. Such collaboration allows for a consensus to be built over time and models a relationship where power can be shared
- **Provide clear and consistent boundaries**. Boundary violation is a key component of most interpersonal trauma, and it is therefore essential to model safe and consistent boundary setting (e.g., clear appointment times and duration, clarity around any contact between appointments)
- **Be aware that any relationships can be triggering.** Clinicians can inadvertently trigger re-activation of traumatic reliving, including a somatic or felt sense of being unsafe. A collaborative relational approach is essential in navigating this
- **Be aware of the potential for multiple experiences and responses**. Bear in mind the person may be functioning on different levels and from different dissociative parts or self-states during any interaction. The person's account may appear fragmented, or contradictory at times. This is a feature of unprocessed trauma and disorganised or dissociated states of mind (Hesse & Main, 2000). Differing views need to be welcomed, recognised, and acknowledged explicitly. *'You seem keen to have the assessment; are there any other views around?'.* Time should be spent negotiating a working consensus between parts/views before proceeding with any task. These different views should be checked in on regularly

- **Provide containment.** This includes clear structure to the interaction. If the person experiences dissociation during the appointment, acknowledge this, and consider strategies to enable grounding if needed (note standard grounding may need modifying for clients with complex dissociation)

Case Example: *John complained to his therapist that he could not remember any of the content of their sessions together. In exploring the issue, John was able to share that he was being shouted at by dissociative parts of the personality for suppressing their views and that this struggle consumed most of his attention, rather than the content of the session.*

The therapist and John agreed an agenda would be set and mutually agreed between all parts of John in advance of the session. This led to an increased sense of collaboration, a reduced need to suppress and an increased ability to attend and remember the session.

When episodes of 'not remembering' did take place, John and his therapist were able to relate this to the above pattern, think about who was being suppressed and why, and with this understanding consider how to proceed.

- **Pacing.** Session pace should be carefully managed, checking the person's current emotional state. If the person requires help with regulation, then support the person to utilise and develop their own strategies or offer grounding and other psychoeducational tools. This includes looking out for both heightened affect and the absence of affect. Attention should be paid to amnesia, within or between sessions, and its potential impact on the retention of information. Strategies to scaffold this can be collaboratively and creatively discussed. In some scenarios there may be a case to increase (or decrease) the length of a session. The pros and cons of this should be considered on an individual basis and in the boundaries of what is possible for the professional to deliver.

3.2 Micro-skills of Therapeutic Relationship

- Micro-skills can help to attunement and consensus building (Gilbert & Leahy, 2007) within the therapeutic relationship
- **Build engagement and rapport.** Use respectful listening, pay attention to the person's anxieties about attending appointments, and to any relational ruptures which may occur
- **Listen to and use the person's own language.** Professionals need to be guided and led by the language that makes most sense to the individual in describing their experiences

- **Be both direct and sensitive.** For example, when enquiring about examples of dissociative experiences, which may not be volunteered unless asked about directly.

3.3 Help to Balance 'Approach-Avoidance' Conflicts

- **Offer balanced therapeutic warmth.** Over-activating the attachment system by being overly warm or empathic can trigger emotional destabilisation. Aim for a balance between being warm, and information-gathering, being collaborative, transparent, curious, non-judgemental, and respectful (i.e., 'not too hot or too cold')
- **Gather history carefully.** Obtaining background history, including on trauma and early attachments, is important but should be done with care. Premature eliciting of trauma memories can be destabilising

> *'In highly dissociative clients they may not be able to offer much if any background, insight into relationships or general history that has any sense of depth. Please do not dismiss this person as not co-operating it should make you wonder what is happening?'* **Melanie Goodwin, Expert-by-Experience**

- **Highlight and validate existing strengths and resources.** Again, this requires attunement to the person; and as with all steps in this guide need to be offered at a pace that matches the needs of the person.

> *'In highly traumatised and dissociative clients our core beliefs can often be denigrated (i.e., I am useless, pathetic, a waste of space) and therefore having a professional telling us we are good at this and brilliant at that can be overwhelming and effect the trust we are building with a practitioner. Therefore, we need our strengths and resources shared slowly and gently.'* **Sally Adams, Expert-by-Experience**

4. General Screening for Dissociation: The What and the How

All healthcare professionals should be able to enquire about a person's current dissociative experiences (ISSTD, 2011; Kezelman & Stavropoulos, 2020). Brief straight-forward screening questions can be asked, within the context of a wider conversation. For an example see Table 2.1.

Table 2.1 Example Questions to Help Screen for Trauma-Related Dissociation

Have you ever experienced…?

Large gaps in your memory? Losing chunks of time? *(Amnesia)*

Felt you were watching yourself from a point outside of your body, as if you were seeing yourself from a distance? *(Depersonalisation)*

Felt as if familiar surroundings or people you knew seemed unfamiliar or unreal? *(Derealisation)*

Travelled away from home unexpectedly and been unable to remember your past or who you were? *(Fugue)*

Felt as if there were a struggle going on inside you, or felt confused as to who you are? *(Identity confusion)*

Felt as if there were different distinct people inside of you? Acted as if you were a completely different person or still a child? Been told by others they see you this way? *(Identity alteration)*

If yes, were you under the influence of drink or drugs at the time?

Do these experiences only occur when you are under stress?

Has this experience caused you distress and/or had a significant impact on your life?

4.1 How to Manage the Emergence of Dissociation During an Appointment

> **Case Example: Managing Dissociation During a Session.** *'Ah, I can see that the question I asked has caused something to happen. It looks like you have gone somewhere far away, but I think you can still hear me. It's ok, nothing is going on apart from us talking, and you are safe. Nothing has changed in the room. I will keep talking to you, so try and hold onto my voice and follow it back into the room, where we are sitting. Try and look around the room and focus on something you notice. If you can, point or tell me what you have seen. That's great, I like that object, too. It looks like you're back with me. It's ok, nothing has happened, but you went away for a few minutes, and I kept talking to you. You spotted that object and we talked about it. Maybe you can keep that object in mind in case you go away again? That's great. You did fine, shall we continue?'*

During the initial stages of an assessment, even basic questions can trigger dissociative responses, requiring careful observation and sensitive management. An example of managing this is offered in the box below.

Note the person's responses, acknowledge them (they may not be aware it is happening), and then encourage them to return to their usual adult functioning self-state, by supporting grounding back into the present moment as far as possible.

- Remain aware of boundaries (how long you have for the meeting, what you both need to be safe, limits of role)
- Reassure about safety and orientate to the present
- Ask them to notice what is in the room
- Reflect on dissociative episodes gently
- Agree together what to do it if happens again
- If there are adverse reactions to the environment then work out any immediate triggers and seek solutions collaboratively (e.g. a word, or smell)
- Ask the person if there is anything they need or want to do to help them feel safer (sitting in a different chair or place in the room)
- If needed, slow the assessment down, to support the person to ground and self-regulate

---

Case Examples: Checking in with Parts. *'Can you check in with all of you to see if you are ok with what we are doing here today?'*

'Is there any part of you that does not wish to/feels uncomfortable to answer that question?'

- Check consent from all parts of the person to continue with the assessment. Afford respect to the whole system of the person and assume that there may be inner conflict or uncertainty about the process

---

Case Example: Help from Parts. *During assessment Sally appeared to have dissociated into a child self-state. The therapist asked, 'Is there a part of you that can help you to get home safely?'*

- Be aware dissociative parts of the person may be listening or having an internal dialogue in the background and may have been triggered by something in the assessment process. They may also be willing to help if asked
- Such signs provide useful information towards the assessment (see below).

'If direct questions seem impossible to answer maybe using statements like those used in the DES-II. It may be that examples are needed to allow the person's brain to engage in a more enquiring way for the first time. I would have been totally unable to answer or even think about these questions, but the DES got me wondering and prevented shame taking over. It became a safe space to start thinking.' **Melanie Goodwin, Expert-by-Experience**

5. Dissociation Screening Tools

Specific screening tools can be useful to elicit further information (see Brand, 2024).

- There are many brief self-report screening tools available for dissociation. See Table 2.2 for a non-exhaustive summary
- The most widely used and validated measures are the Dissociative Experiences Scale II (DES-II), and the Somatoform Dissociation Questionnaire (SDQ-20). These can be administered by any health care professional
- Scoring and interpretation however require knowledge and skill, as does providing informed feedback. Clinicians unfamiliar with scoring and interpretation should consult with a psychologist or other professional with suitable expertise
- Particular items of the DES-II may be particularly indicative of the presence of a complex dissociative disorder (DD) and should prompt further exploration with the person (Simeon & Putnam, 2022)

Table 2.2 Common Screening Measures for Trauma-Related Dissociative Experiences

Screening Measure	Description
The Dissociative Experiences Scale (DES-II; (Carlson & Putnam, 1993).	28-item self-report screening measuring range of dissociative experiences. Scores >30 indicate 'pathological dissociation'. DES-Taxon score derived from subset of 8 items, most predictive of a DD diagnosis.
The Somatoform Dissociation Questionnaire (SDQ-20; Nijenhuis et al., 1996).	20-item measure focused on somatoform dissociative symptoms. Scores above 40 may be indicative of possible DD diagnosis, above 50 possible DID diagnosis. A shortened scale (SDQ-5) is also available.
Multiscale Dissociation Inventory (Briere et al., 2005).	30-item-scale measuring range of dissociative experiences.
Dissociation-Integration of Self-States Scale (Lord et al., 2025)	To assess relationship with different self-states.
The Dissociation Questionnaire (Vanderlinden et al., 1993).	63-item measure includes the DES, and additional items to include identity confusion and alteration, loss of control, amnesia and absorption.
Shutdown Dissociation Scale (Schalinski et al., 2015)	13-item structured interview for assessing dissociative sub-type of PTSD.

- The DES-II has been translated into many languages (e.g., Turkish, Japanese, Spanish, Chinese, Arabic, Farsi). Some studies have examined its validity across cultures such as Turkey, though results suggest variability in how items are interpreted (Sar, 2011). When using the DES-II it is essential to interpret results within a culturally informed lens. High scores on these tools might reflect culturally normative or spiritually sanctioned experiences, rather than pathology
- The SDQ-20 has been used in Turkey, India, Iran, and Sri Lanka, and it was deemed particularly useful in non-Western settings where dissociation often presents somatically (Chaturvedi & Sinha, 2011; Lewis-Fernández et al., 2007; Şar, 2022)
- Screening tools are not diagnostic instruments. Results should be interpreted with clinical care, including consideration of clinical reasons for under or over reporting (for example significant amnesia for the dissociation)
- With repeated measurement as part of outcome reporting, note that it is not unusual for highly dissociative individuals to have scores which initially increase on the DES-II as internal awareness of the dissociation increases
- Clinically, these tools can also be useful to develop a wider conversation about the experience of trauma-related dissociation
- If initial screening suggests the presence of significant dissociative experiences, consider with the person whether a more detailed assessment would be a helpful next step. This should be considered collaboratively with the person, clarifying their aims and the rationale for further assessment.

6. Structured Assessment of Dissociative Experiences

If dissociation is suspected, then it may be helpful to consider with the person whether more detailed assessment would be beneficial as part of their care. More detailed assessment of dissociation should be undertaken by a qualified professional with appropriate expertise and training in trauma and dissociation alongside a sound knowledge of general mental health and risk. This includes Practitioner Psychologists, other Psychological Therapists, and Psychiatrists, and may draw upon the contributions of other multidisciplinary colleagues.

If the screening and assessing clinicians are different, information sharing processes should be discussed to remain sensitive, collaborative, trauma-informed and avoid unnecessary repetition.

6.1 General Considerations for Dissociation-Specific Assessment

Clarify the purpose and intended outcome of assessment:
Discuss and agree the aims and process transparently and collaboratively, e.g., to develop a formulation, reach a diagnosis, access appropriate treatment pathways or guide care planning.

The format of the assessment:
Assessments may be undertaken face to face or on-line with people with complex mental health problems and dissociation (Parry et al., 2022).

The assessment should include:

- A thorough general mental health assessment
- Detailed exploration of the five main areas of dissociative experience
- Other trauma-related and somatic symptoms
- Impact on day-to-day functioning and relationships
- Coping mechanisms/behaviours
- Strengths/resources/support networks
- Risk and safety assessment including any current sources of threat or abuse
- Previous therapeutic interventions, including what helped or hindered these, the likes, dislikes and preferences of the person.

Other sources of information can be helpful:

- Case-note review
- A third person perspective can be helpful with the person's consent
- The use of further structured or semi-structured assessment tools (see below).

6.2 Structured Clinical Tools for Assessing Dissociative Disorders

Several structured and semi-structured diagnostic interviews for dissociative disorders have demonstrated good validity and reliability (Brand, 2024), see Table 2.3. for an overview. Appropriate training and supervision should be accessed for using these tools.

6.3 Observed Signs and Symptoms During Assessment

Many people with complex dissociation may hide or mask their experiences due to fear or shame. Some people may appear high functioning in work, education or social activity, whereas others may present with significantly impaired functioning and extensive mental health histories. Observations of dissociative cues during the assessment can provide valuable information. The SCID-D documents a list of 'intra-interview dissociative cues' which can be helpful to consider.

Some people who dissociate do so visibly, as their manner, voice and general behaviour fluctuate within and between appointments. Others may show this in more subtle ways (for example their voice becomes a little higher or language a little simpler). Some people may refer to themselves in the first person plural ('we') or third person ('he/she/they') or may present inconsistently between appointments.

People who meet criteria for DID may have strong avoidant reactions to some of their internal experiences and appear uncomfortable when asked about them.

Table 2.3 Diagnostic Assessments for Dissociative Disorders

Diagnostic Assessment	Description
The Structured Clinical Interview for Dissociative Disorders (SCID-D; Steinberg, 1995, 2023).	'Gold standard' assessment for diagnosis of DD. Allows for differential diagnosis with other overlapping presentations A semi-structured clinical interview, covering 5 domains, including clinician observations. Requires knowledge of dissociation and training on the instrument. Approximately 3 hours to administer. Limited cross-cultural validity studies of the SCID-D.
Dissociative Disorders Interview Schedule DSM-5 version (D-DIS; Ross et al., 1990).	Structured interview for trained clinicians to diagnose DDs (excluding depersonalisation/ derealisation disorder).
Trauma and Dissociation Symptoms Interview (TADS-I; Boon, 2023).	Semi-structured interview to assess dissociative symptoms and provide a DD diagnosis. Includes items to assess presence of imitative DID.
Multi-dimensional Inventory of Dissociation (MID; Dell, 2006).	218-item clinician administered client self-report measure. Assesses 14 major facets of dissociation and uses 23 scales to diagnose DDs. Briefer 60-item version (Kate et al., 2021) for screening.

7. Formulation and Diagnosis: Developing Shared Understanding

7.1 Formulation

> 'It [psychological formulation] also needs to be done *with* the dissociative person. My experience of this is that it's a powerful tool to understanding selves.' **Sally Adams, Expert-by-Experience**

A collaboratively and gradually developed individualised psychobiosocial formulation offers understanding of the development and protective functions served by trauma-related dissociation. Formulation draws on a broad based, integrated and multi-modal perspective which locates peoples' unique personal meaning within its wider social, religious and cultural contexts. This is particularly important for complex mental health difficulties where people have significant experiences of trauma and dissociation.

Formulation helps inform the individualised and person-centred direction of care and treatment. The formulation should reflect an appropriate therapeutic model including relevant adaptations for dissociation. It should be informed by a relational/attachment-oriented approach and include a means of understanding dissociation. Clinicians vary in preferred therapeutic modalities, and several models have provided adaptations for working with dissociation (see Chapter 4, Therapy). Whichever model is used the following are useful considerations:

- Psychological formulation needs to be developed gradually and at a pace and level to remain within tolerable levels for the person
- An initial formulation may not be longitudinal or involve detailed early history. A more detailed longitudinal formulation may be developed over time. This contributes to developing a more coherent narrative around sense of self and the function of dissociative experiences
- Maintaining factors can be considered, e.g., current threats, or protective avoidance/ defence against traumatic reliving. These may inform early treatment goals in the stabilisation phase of treatment.

A dissociation-focused formulation will likely include the following:

- Understanding of the triggers and processes around different dissociative states.
- An outline or map of different dissociative parts of the personality
- An understanding of the origins and functions of the development of dissociative processes, often for example as a survival function
- The broad personal history of attachment relationships, experiences of trauma, adversity, oppression and inequalities
- Factors which may be maintaining the continued need for the dissociation, for example continued lack of safety, adversity or oppression.

In addition the formulation may consider wider domains including:

- Trauma-related symptoms
- Somatic symptoms
- Risk to self and others
- Attachment difficulties
- Relational experiences
- Current life problems/family issues
- Work, financial and social issues
- Existing personal strengths
- Resources (internal or external)
- Previous therapy experiences
- The person's personal and cultural strengths and resources, past and present.

7.2 Diagnosis

There are arguments both for and against using a diagnostic framework for understanding complex dissociative difficulties. For some people, a diagnosis may represent a key step in the person beginning to accept their dissociation as a valid and understandable response to trauma. The relational context in which a diagnosis is offered will have a significant impact on whether it is experienced as helpful or harmful.

The advantages and disadvantages of a diagnosis should be considered on an individual basis (see Table 2.4). In a dissociative presentation, an added complexity is that different dissociative parts may hold different views, questions or concerns. These should be invited and considered, where possible being supported to reach a decision based on internal consensus.

When diagnosis is pursued it should be offered with an explicit recognition that the set of 'symptoms' someone presents with are *'expectable and adaptive reactions to traumatic childhood experiences'* (Kezelman & Stavropoulos, 2019, p.38).

Despite the prevalence data, at present only a small percentage of people with difficulties meeting the criteria for a DD are likely to receive an accurate diagnosis (Foote et al., 2006). This contributes to barriers to accessing appropriate treatment pathways and experiences of treatment failure and concomitant loss of hope.

Several factors have contributed to making formal diagnosis of dissociative disorders complex and problematic historically (Chien & Fung, 2022):

- Previous diagnostic classification systems provided differing perspectives (for example ICD-10 and DSM-IV). However, ICD-11 and DSM-5 are now, helpfully, more closely aligned
- Standard diagnostic tools and mental state examinations most clinicians have been taught have not routinely included questions about dissociation

Table 2.4 Common Pros and Cons of Diagnosis

Benefits of Diagnosis	Disadvantages of Diagnosis
Can help the person feel understood and less alone with their difficulties.	Not always wanted or necessary
Can help others to understand and be more aware of the person's difficulties.	May feel stigmatising or cause worry about impact upon future life opportunities.
Facilitates access to appropriate information and psychoeducation.	May overwhelm someone's dissociative barriers and prove destabilising.
May facilitate access to more appropriate treatment pathways.	May act as a barrier to receiving help in some services.
May support access to appropriate wider support.	Diagnosing without following up with timely information and/or treatment can be destabilising.

- The lack of treatment pathways and core professional trainings on dissociative conditions result in a reluctance to diagnose DDs (Corrigan & Hull, 2022)
- There have been historic myths and misconceptions surrounding dissociation and DID (Brand et al., 2016)
- As a 'disorder of hiddenness' (Howell, 2011) people with severe levels of dissociation may rarely volunteer information about dissociative experiences

---

Myth: DID is easy to spot.

Response: Contrary to popular belief, most people with complex dissociation such as DID, will not present floridly but often hide or minimise their dissociative experiences and symptoms, seeking help with a multitude of other complaints instead.

- There are potential 'red flags' in assessment for helping to identify and understand imitative presentations (Pietkiewicz et al., 2021), this requires a significant level of expertise (Boon, 2023).

8. Psychoeducation

Understanding and normalising experiences of dissociation forms an important part of early engagement and assessment. Troubling experiences, symptoms or behaviours can be re-framed as survival strategies with unintended consequences. Psychoeducation should address issues of shame and offer hope about the prospect of recovery and living a meaningful life with trauma-related dissociation. Sharing of the neurobiological underpinnings of trauma-related dissociation may be a helpful part of this work (Brand et al., 2022). Such psychoeducation may also be important for the person's support system. Signposting to a range of resources from both expert and lived-experience perspective can also be helpful for some (www.routledge.com/9781041038450).

Case Example: *When Carol's dissociative experiences were first noticed by her CPN she had a very mixed response.*

On the one hand, she felt great relief that finally her difficulties were being noticed and that someone appeared to want to understand.

On the other hand, she felt lots of shame and fear about what it meant about her to be experiencing such symptoms. Did this mean she was 'crazy'?

Carol and her CPN began to find stories of recovery and hope on-line with people who had lived experience of trauma-related dissociation. This helped to reduce her fear and shame and create a greater sense of empowerment and hope for the possibility of healing.

9. Collaborative Care Planning

9.1 Dissociation-Informed Care

For those with more significant functional impairment, mental or physical health comorbidities or complex social needs a multidisciplinary care plan focused on stabilisation will be the first step (see Chapter 3).

Such input will require many of the routine aspects of care. However, it is important that such care is adapted and led by the needs of the person experiencing trauma-related dissociation.

> **Practice Point**: *It can be helpful to keep in mind the metaphor of planning with a 'whole family' in relation to the individual with complex dissociation; consider and discuss the range of needs of the person's different parts or states and develop a plan which seeks to coordinate and address all of these.*
> **Helena Crockford, Consultant Clinical Psychologist**

Relevant care plans goals may include:

- Extended assessment towards a psychobiosocial formulation
- Psychoeducation
- Assessment and stabilisation of social care needs
- Practical support from a support worker
- Occupational or employment retention support
- Identification of any carer's support needs
- Developing risk management and safety plans
- Addressing ongoing threats or abuse
- Consideration of any dilemmas about mental capacity decision making
- Medication management or review
- Establishing consistent, boundaried engagement through regular, containing contact
- Psychological therapy which may be time-limited or longer-term depending on goals

9.2 Dissociation-Specific Care

For some people current needs may be more specific to the experience of trauma-related dissociation. Dissociation-specific care may include self-guided learning, establishment, and connection with peer support networks of people who have similar experiences or a focused piece of therapy with a psychological practitioner (see Chapter 4, Therapy).

Assessment is an ongoing process and the use of tools to monitor progress in treatment, such as the Progress in Treatment Questionnaire (Schielke et al., 2017) can help to track progress as well as barriers to change from both the therapist and patient perspective. The use of regular reviews in this way can be important for the development of formulation, therapeutic alliance, treatment planning and clinical decision-making over time.

10. Conclusion

Psychologists and other health care professionals have an important role to play in raising awareness, encouraging screening and accurate assessment of dissociation related difficulties, and in supporting trauma-informed and formulation-based care to enable people with dissociation – and those who support them – to understand their experiences, access more appropriate care pathways, and have the hope of improved outcomes.

Chapter 3

The Multidisciplinary Context of Care for People with Dissociative Difficulties

Helena Crockford, Paul Langthorne, Andrew Holding, Gordon Barclay, Angela Dhanda, Beth Ryan, Amanda Green and Kelly Simpson

1. Introduction

Many people experiencing complex and enduring mental health difficulties, including trauma-based dissociation, receive care and support from a range of agencies, teams and professionals. Most secondary care NHS mental health services in the UK take place in this multidisciplinary team (MDT) context. Community mental health, as well as acute, crisis and mental health liaison teams, often make up the core of secondary mental health services. A spectrum of other services also contribute, from social care, housing and addiction services, to the voluntary, community and social enterprise (VCSE) sector. These teams are comprised of practitioners representing diverse cultural, religious and social perspectives, and serve communities who embody these also.

Case Example: *Jason was a young man living in supported accommodation with on-site staff. Under the care of the CMHT, with symptoms including delusional beliefs and voice hearing, he received a diagnosis of paranoid schizophrenia. He saw a psychiatric nurse regularly, and every few months the psychiatrist reviewed his mental state and anti-psychotic medication. Seeming settled he became a valued member of the group home. Then staff became concerned because he seemed increasingly withdrawn. The psychologist was asked to see him. He engaged well with an assessment and began some therapy sessions. What soon emerged was a significant history of childhood neglect, sexual, physical and emotional trauma, not previously disclosed. He described different people he would 'escape into' to cope in different situations, and a belief system which provided comfort and escape, all better understood as trauma-related dissociative difficulties.*

DOI: 10.4324/9781003625650-5

1.1 The Scale of the Problem (see also Chapter 1)

With prevalence rates of 1–3% of people in the general population estimated as meeting the diagnostic criteria for DID, this is equivalent to approximately one million people in the UK suffering the most complex and pervasive dissociative difficulties (Reinders & Veltman, 2021). With the number of people for whom dissociative experiences more broadly are a significant issue estimated at 9–12%, this need expands further. Within clinical populations, across a range of in-patient and community mental health settings, studies have found significant prevalence rates for dissociation, ranging from 4.6% to 46%, and up to 14% for those meeting criteria for a DID diagnosis (see Loewenstein, 2018). These findings extend across countries and cultures (Kruger, 2020), with a range of expressions and interpretations of dissociation to be considered (see Chapter 15).

Epidemiological studies suggest that for a significant proportion of the secondary care caseload, considering dissociation is an important aspect of clinical care and treatment. Loewenstein (2018) describes a 'major public health issue' and 'a large, under-served population whose lack of recognition leads to substantial human and societal costs'. The positive news is that an accumulating combination of research evidence and practice-based expert consensus suggests working to help people with their dissociative difficulties can improve outcomes and is less likely to compound their suffering through ineffective or even iatrogenic experiences of services. Considering structural inequalities and diverse perspectives can be assumed to be an important part of that (Ford, 2024; Gómez et al., 2021).

1.2 Multidisciplinary Care

MDTs in the UK are constituted of staff from a range of professional backgrounds, including psychological professionals, psychiatrists, mental health nurses, occupational therapists and social workers. They may also include assistant practitioners, support workers and staff working from a lived experience background, such as peer support workers. As in the case example above, these staff work together to provide a range of functions within the often multi-faceted care pathway for someone presenting with complex dissociative difficulties. MDTs can however experience significant challenges in doing this effectively.

1.3 Lack of Knowledge, Skills and Confidence

Consultation Question: 'I didn't have any training about dissociation in my core mental health training. How can I support people on my caseload?'

Many mental health professional trainings have historically given little if any training specific to dissociation (e.g., Loewenstein, 2018; Reinders & Veltman, 2021). This means dissociative experiences may not be directly assessed or identified.

Research Question: Survey mental health professionals to identify levels of training, knowledge, skills and confidence for working with dissociative presentations. This might consider professional groups as well as number of years post-qualification.

Even when a person's experience of dissociation is recognised, staff can lack the skills or confidence to 'know what to do', resulting in feeling they are operating outside of their competency (Lloyd, 2019). This represents a widespread and significant skills gap in the existing workforce, particularly when compared to training and knowledge in other areas of severe, complex and enduring mental health, such as psychosis or personality difficulties.

'The ways in which someone with a dissociative disorder may present can lead to a team responding with high levels of threat, which if not effectively integrated, can lead to the team or service acting out of their threat system with either an angry and rejecting or anxious and overly restrictive response.' **Paul Langthorne, Clinical Psychologist**

This creates challenges in accurately assessing and identifying dissociation. People may receive several different diagnoses before dissociative difficulties are accurately identified (see Chapters 1 and 2); many have been offered multiple unsuccessful attempts at treatments without dissociation being taken into account (Reinders et al., 2019). Clients may have been labelled as 'resistant to change' or 'lacking motivation' (Fisher, 2017). These may all be 'red flags' for unidentified dissociation. Temple (2019) summarises: 'The key for clinicians is to have a low threshold of suspicion for the presence of dissociative disorders.'

1.4 Service Pressures

Mental health teams are often subject to significant service pressures, around issues of demand and capacity, staff vacancies, or a top-down emphasis on 'throughput'. Services can struggle to balance person-centred and formulation driven care with more service-driven priorities, limits and constraints. This context can work against a trauma and dissociation informed response, where care requires a strong relational focus, paying attention to beginnings, changes, ruptures and endings in therapeutic relationships, and taking time to work with complexity such as 'approach-avoidance' dilemmas in engagement and building trust.

1.5 Reasons for Hope

The treatment evidence-base is increasingly suggesting that positive outcomes are achievable and hopeful for people with significant dissociation; and that appropriate care may well be cost-effective. As Steinberg (2023) has suggested, 'When … [people] … hear their experiences reflected back to them for the first time without judgement or misattribution, I watch hope return as fear dissolves', (p.xvi).

'My journey was a very long one, with misdiagnosis and other obstacles along the way. But it was a positive outcome thanks to certain teams within the Trust; but this did not need to take as long. My hope is that someone starting their recovery journey now would not take as long and that they would have the right help to guide them along the way.' **Kelly Simpson, Expert-by-Experience**

Reactive, even chaotic, care and treatment delivery, may in fact escalate distress and care-seeking. A planned, structured, consistent formulation-driven, trauma-informed approach can serve to contain and focus care provided (Lloyd, 2016).

Key questions for MDT staff include what, within their current roles, they can realistically do to accurately identify, inform, support and offer interventions to people presenting to services with dissociative experiences as a significant part of their presentation? This is complex. Awareness of potential pitfalls and how to avoid these leading to iatrogenic experiences of care, is an important consideration.

Myth: Identifying dissociation will mean expensive long-term care, outside the MDT's existing resources or skill set.

Fact: Planned and structured, trauma and dissociation informed care can be more cost-effective, through reductions in crisis, acute or emergency contacts, as well as by promoting a person's wellbeing, recovery and social functioning.

This chapter sets out key principles relevant to all MDT staff. It offers suggestions for individual professional groups for how to adapt core elements of their role for people with dissociation as a significant part of their presentation. Consideration of intersecting cultural, religious and social perspectives, inequalities and experiences should be held in mind for their possible impact on the development of, symptom manifestation (Kruger, 2020) and recovery from trauma-based dissociation as well as the experience of care not itself reinforcing inequalities (Gomez et al., 2021; see Chapter 15).

2. Key Principles of MDT Working with Dissociation

> *'My aim in sharing my story was not to lay blame at any single depart-ment's feet but to highlight what a profound and positive effect a multidisci-plinary team can have on a single person's recovery. When a patient's whole experience is taken into consideration and you can look beyond a difficult behaviour or conversation then you can start to see the reasons behind this. And YOU can adjust how YOU interact with them.'* **Kelly Simpson, Expert-by-Experience**

2.1 Working Together

A key process in the effective support of people presenting with dissociative difficul-ties is for the care network around the client to 'integrate' themselves (Kluft, 1993). The response to someone with dissociative difficulties can be one of fragmentation and 'dis-integration', both between professionals within one team, and between differ-ent teams or services with which a person is engaged. This fragmentation might arise from the person presenting differently at different times, or differently to different pro-fessionals; from differences of opinion about diagnosis; and from more unconscious counter-transference responses and re-enactments, which echo the person's own internal psychological struggles (ISSTD, 2011, p.147). The person accessing services can experience this as a series of conflicting and confusing responses to their care.

A key aim of interventions for people with significant dissociation is support-ing them to develop more internal communication and cooperation between dis-sociative parts of themselves. Professionals and teams model something valuable when they develop a shared understanding or formulation, and work to coordinate their efforts, respective roles and intersectional experiences around this plan (for example, Bostock & Armstrong, 2019).

2.2 Trauma-informed Care

The NHS Long Term Plan and programme of Community Transformation, described a 'community-based offer [that] will include access to ... personalised and trauma-informed care' (NHS England, 2019). NHS Trusts are developing lead-ership and strategies to improve trauma-informed practice. Improving dissociation-informed care is an important element of this (see Chapters 1, 16).

2.3 A Dissociation Focus

Related to this, where significant dissociation is present, care and treatment plans should consider an active focus on the person's dissociative experiences and how these interact with the range of goals developed and agreed with them.

2.4 Personalised Care

Clarifying the person's current level of need, as well as their strengths and resources, is important, as even within a complex dissociative presentation, the person's current level of daily functioning and care needs can exist on a wide spectrum. This feeds through into a range of personalised MDT plans for care, rather than a 'one-size-fits-all' approach.

Consideration of the person's intersecting cultural, religious and social contexts is an important factor here, including resources they might draw upon (see Chapter 15).

2.5 Training and Skills

Dissociation-specific awareness and skills will be beneficial for everyone within the person's network of care. However, a clinician's role within an MDT and specific service setting, will guide the level of knowledge, skill and competency required (see Chapter 17).

2.6 Supervision and Reflective Practice

All practitioners should have access to trauma-informed supervision, to promote reflection and receive support in relation to the complex clinical questions, relational dynamics and vicarious trauma which may arise.

Key Principles: Summary

- Trauma and Dissociation Informed care
- Recognise the dissociation
- All care goals are dissociation informed
- Personalised care, including attention to the intersection of cultural, religious and social influences
- Working together as a care network
- Appropriate training and skill
- Access to supervision.

3. Multidisciplinary Roles in the Care of Someone with Complex Dissociation

3.1 The Role of the Psychological Practitioner

Psychological practitioners within MDTs have a range of training backgrounds, including doctoral level Clinical, Counselling, Health or Forensic Psychologists, Psychotherapists, Psychological Therapists, Clinical Associate and Assistant Psychologists. Psychological practitioners typically offer 'interventions' at a number of different 'levels', including:

- direct client work
- indirect clinical work consulting to and supervising other MDT staff
- service development
- teaching and training other staff
- conducting audit and research.

Each are relevant for the MDT care of those with complex dissociative difficulties.

3.1.1 Early Identification and Screening within the MDT Pathway

Contributing to the early stages of a client's contact with an MDT – the initial referral, triage and screening processes – can be valuable and cost-effective, aiding early identification of significant dissociation, and informing the MDT care pathway going forward.

In Improving Access to Psychological Therapies (IAPT), Children & Adolescent Mental Health Services (CAMHS), or Early Intervention in Psychosis (EIP) services this is particularly important, as first time points of contact for clients on their mental health treatment and recovery journey. As with all mental health presentations, early identification can promote hope, empowerment and recovery, whilst avoiding inaccurate diagnostic labels and inappropriate care and treatment pathways (Lloyd, 2016).

Psychologists can support MDT colleagues with:

- Triage and initial team assessment appointments, particularly where referrals indicate possible dissociation
- Consulting to staff undertaking assessments
- Helping services develop trauma and dissociation informed tools and processes
- Cascading awareness-level training about dissociation and trauma to MDT colleagues (see Chapter 17, Training).

Case Example: Carol moved to a new area and was referred to the CMHT. She had previous psychological therapy which had helped her live better with a traumatic and neglectful early history. She was however struggling as a single parent because of lapses in memory – 'losing time'. She met the psychologist for an extended assessment over ten sessions, including dissociation screening measures and the SCID-D. Her experiences met the criteria for a diagnosis of DID, and a formulation of her difficulties and situation was developed together. Using this understanding her social worker was better able to help her with challenges of daily life and to access social support in the voluntary sector. She did not wish to undertake any further psychological therapy at that time.

3.1.2 Extended Assessment

Psychologists play a key role in the comprehensive assessment of dissociative difficulties, diagnostic clarity and the development of a formulation. (See Chapter 2.)

- This may be **a longer or slower process** than with other presenting difficulties due to complexity, and **attention towards relational processes** enabling building of a working alliance. Taking time here can constitute a valuable, therapeutic piece of work in itself, which may in some cases address the client's current needs (see Case Example as above)
- While this requires some specialist knowledge and skills regarding dissociation, this also **draws on existing psychological knowledge and skills**
- Complexity arises further from the **presence of dissociative experiences** during the assessment process
  - For someone with significant **depersonalisation or derealisation**, these experiences can manifest during appointments. This may be so aversive, upsetting or shameful to the client that they wish to leave or avoid appointments
  - For someone with current **amnesia or 'losing time'**, they may forget to attend appointments, or have little recall for what happened in previous sessions. Without identifying this, treatment plans may not progress, and the person may be wrongly assumed to be 'not ready to engage' or 'lacking in motivation'. Developing strategies in a collaborative way can help to scaffold this issue, for example, offering a summary of the previous session, or providing written or recorded material as reminders
  - The **existence of dissociative parts** may mean the person has a range of diverging or conflicting points of view towards engaging with services. A fearful or hostile part may seek to prevent the person from attending appointments or sharing information. Intersectional factors may play a part. These all need directly exploring to facilitate engagement even at this early stage. For example, stating early on that all parts and perspectives will be important and welcome to contribute; or enquiring regularly if there are any other points of view about attending the appointment, or other aspects of care

---

Myth: Reports of dissociative symptoms can be the product of leading questions and suggestibility, rather than genuine accounts.

Fact: Empirical evidence does not support the assertion that accounts of dissociative experiences result from being overly vulnerable to suggestibility (Dalenberg et al., 2012; Dalenberg et al., 2014). Assessment tools like the SCID-D have a high degree of validity and reliability (Steinberg, 2023).

- Timely and accurate identification of dissociative experiences can be incredibly valuable for future care. The recognition and validation of client's experiences can itself be therapeutic (Steinberg, 2023), even transformational, in helping people to feel normalised, less overwhelmed, improving self-compassion and increasing agency (see Chapter 2).

3.1.3 Contributing to Diagnostic Clarity

Not all psychological practitioners will wish to engage with formal diagnosis (see Chapter 2). However, there can be pragmatic advantages in doing so.

Case Example: Mary, a former primary school teacher, had an assessment for psychological therapy prior to being added to a six-month waiting list for therapy. Significant dissociation suggestive of a DID diagnosis was identified for the first time, despite previous EMDR therapy in primary care and lengthy acute psychiatric crisis and in-patient care. When therapy began, she reported how the assessment had changed her life. She felt she had found words for her experiences for the first time, and no longer feared that the intrusive voices she heard were 'evil spirits'. During the wait for therapy, she had accessed self-help resources and on-line communities and, together with her wife, had developed a number of helpful strategies for managing her amnesia, as well as understanding and communicating with her dissociative parts in daily life.

Currently there is no agreed non-medical terminology alternative to psychiatric diagnosis, so it remains embedded in aspects of health culture including NICE recommendations, NHS commissioning and clinical pathways, outcome measures, research and clinical governance. It also provides a point of reference in other areas of public life such as the social security and criminal justice systems. Finally, some service users and supporters seek diagnostic clarity, requesting formal diagnosis, and find this helpful. Psychologists can assist clients and supporters to think through potential advantages and disadvantages of diagnosis, and embed diagnostic categories within a wider psychobiosocial formulation, including the role of intersectional experiences of disadvantage, to place them within a personalised, culturally and trauma-informed framework of understanding (Johnstone & Boyle, 2018).

3.1.4 Developing a Psychobiosocial Formulation

This is a core competency for psychologists in all specialties and a distinctive feature of the profession (BPS, 2011). It represents a working hypothesis or model, based on psychological theory and evidence bases, which aims to explain the development and maintenance of a person's difficulties. Importantly, it also guides further intervention. Chapter 2, section 7.1 elaborates this further in relation to dissociation.

The 'Mentalising Stance' provides a useful summary of a collaborative therapeutic stance (e.g., Bateman & Fonagy, 2006)

- Curious
- Non-judgemental
- Not-knowing
- Genuine
- Empathic.

The process of developing the formulation is as important to consider. Formulation should be offered tentatively rather than imposed (Christofides et al., 2012), particularly so with clients who may find it difficult to disagree (Johnstone & Dallos, 2006), or have dissociative parts with multiple opinions and perspectives. They should be created collaboratively, with power shared and autonomy fostered, rather than from an authoritative expert position where decisions or interventions are prescribed or imposed. This supports building a working relationship based on collaboration, transparency and mutual respect, offering an important and explicit therapeutic counterbalance to a history of relationships experienced as neglectful, traumatic, abusive, secretive, coercive or discriminatory. A 'mentalising stance' – in which both professional and client are encouraged to remain curious and non-judgemental, openly sharing their uncertainty and gaps in knowing, and learning together – can be helpful and model a key skill that is useful in later therapy (Bateman & Fonagy, 2006; Mitchell & Steele, 2021).

Formulation as an intervention. The formulation may thus provide a powerful intervention in itself, supporting the person and their MDT care to move forward. It can promote a consistent and culturally competent team approach to intervention, enabling the service user and their care network to work together in a non-retraumatising way. It gathers key information into one place, enhancing team understanding, empathy and reflectiveness, and conveying hope for positive change (Christofides et al., 2012; Clarke & Nicholls, 2018).

Formulations remain partial and dynamic, open to revision, change and re-formulation.

3.1.5 Psychoeducation about Dissociation and Trauma
(see Chapter 2, Section 8)

Although some clients may not choose to engage in an extended assessment or therapy, they may benefit from a general understanding of the difficulties associated with experiences of dissociation and trauma. Such explanations can help to understand the adaptive and survival function of dissociation (e.g., Fisher, 2021).

Working with **clients' families and supporters** can help to scaffold the system of support around the client, to better understand, empathise and respond more helpfully, as well as helping them manage their own stress and burden.

Providing links to information and resources can help people connect to others with similar difficulties and feel less isolated.

3.1.6 Consultation with MDT Colleagues and Partner Agencies

Psychologists may:

- Support MDT staff with ongoing **risk assessment and safety planning**, with for example crisis-specific formulations and strategies around managing dissociation where this has an impact on risk and safety (see Chapter 6).
- Explain the formulation-driven rationale and necessity for a **joined-up approach** to the multidisciplinary or multiagency network around the client. This can be hard to achieve in already fragmented and over-stretched systems. However helping to maintain continuity and consistency of care is a vital therapeutic component, including during transitions between mental health teams such as inpatient wards, crisis and community teams, or between CAMHS and adult services. Neglecting this can risk serious destabilisation and potential iatrogenesis for the client's mental state
- Consult to **MDT or multi-agency meetings** including social services, housing or advocacy services. This supports other professionals to understand the client's presentation and broader needs, and how interventions may be suitably adapted
- Consult to **client reviews and re-assessment** as the client's episode of care progresses. This may benefit someone who has long been in the mental health system, as dissociative difficulties emerge gradually over time, particularly where staff have previously lacked awareness and skill to identify this accurately
- **Consult within acute settings.** For psychologists working in acute crisis and in-patient settings the time-frame for intervention may be much shorter. Their role may be in supporting MDT staff to identify dissociative experiences evident

in real time, and to adapt care plans such as 'positive behaviour support plans' to be trauma and dissociation-informed. Additionally, a longer admission may provide opportunities to witness dissociative experiences, and engage the service user in a more thorough assessment to guide the care pathway following discharge (see Chapter 6)

- **Consult within physical health settings** (see Chapter 8). Psychologists may work with other professionals, including GPs or hospital medical specialists such as Neurology, to help differentiate somatic presentations with a dissociative basis, and clarify a trauma-informed understanding and treatment pathway

3.1.7 Psychological Therapy (See Chapter 4)

> **Case Example**: A young man who had previously suffered a homophobic assault, was so anxious leaving the house to come to the team base that he felt himself leave his body and look down on himself from above. He found this very distressing. However once this was identified and discussed, he found he was able to manage other situations better which he had previously been avoiding due to this experience of depersonalisation.

A key principle when considering psychological therapy, appropriate therapeutic models and time-frames, is **for any therapy intervention to be dissociation-informed, and adapted to the particular needs of the client at that time**.

Whatever therapy approach is planned, **the dissociation needs to be held in mind and actively engaged with** (ISSTD, 2011, p.140), including where this is not the only, or main, focus of treatment. For example, this might concern how day-to-day amnesia or 'loss of time' is managed so as to build continuity between sessions; or focus on building consensus between parts of the person around agreeing to the aims of a particular piece of work.

All standard therapy tasks, such as identifying therapeutic goals, socialising to the therapy frame, the boundaries that will be required, timekeeping, modes of communication, therapy transitions and endings, **need a dissociation-informed perspective**.

Transparency while building the working alliance is important for service users who may hold very different working models of relationships where words such as 'trust' or 'safety' have become loaded terms (Allen, 2013; Wallin & Ebscohost, 2007). Some authors go further, suggesting that 'trust' is not a requirement of therapy, only that client and therapist can agree to work together on a particular goal (Fisher, 2017, 2021).

Time-limited Therapy. In many MDT settings, therapy may be offered on a time-limited basis due to service constraints. However useful episodes of treatment can still be formulated within the available time-period. What is crucial is to have a shared and transparent understanding of the time-frame with the client, to plan together for realistic aims within this, and to maintain an active awareness and engagement with the dissociation.

Relational Process. Beginnings, breaks, ruptures and endings need attending to and carefully managing, and this relational process may be as significant as the explicit aims and content of the therapy (Wallin, 2007; Allen, 2013). [See Chapter 4 for fuller guidance on briefer and longer term therapy.]

Case Example: A client with a history of emotional neglect and complex trauma including racial abuse met criteria for a DID diagnosis. They were having difficulties engaging with physical health appointments, putting their physical health at risk. In time-limited therapy, in a CMHT setting, a formulation was slowly co-developed around the role different parts were playing in causing and maintaining this problem. Therapy helped their parts to work together. They then communicated their understanding to their GP. Their GP was then able to put in place simple trauma-informed adaptations to the medical procedures to enable them to go ahead.

3.1.8 Service Development and Strategy

Psychologists provide leadership at many levels in relation to psychologically and trauma-informed care. Partnering in this with experts-by-experience is highly effective and models coproduction and trauma-informed working.

Good Practice Example: Merseycare Trusts appointed a Consultant Clinical Psychologist as 'Psychological Lead for Trauma and Dissociation', with ringfenced time to offer consultation and supervision regarding complex dissociation cases within the trust.

Dissociation 'Champions' (see Chapter 17). Part of this can be championing the perspective that working with trauma-based dissociation is core business for mental health services, given both high prevalence rates, and good possibilities for hopeful outcomes. Psychological practitioners can encourage other professionals' interest and confidence in working with people who experience dissociation, challenge scepticism or outdated myths, and model hopeful, curious and compassionate attitudes.

Psychologists, particularly, are increasingly being encouraged to take up formal and statutory roles in clinical leadership, for example as Multi-Profession Approved Clinicians (Health Education England, 2020a). They are in a strong position to be effective in clinical leadership roles in relation to people with significant dissociation, along with other complex trauma presentations such as 'complex emotional needs' and 'personality disorder', all areas where aetiology and treatment are primarily psychologically informed.

Where resources are limited, it remains important for psychological practitioners to advocate for appropriate treatment. Psychologists can have a key role in recognising where specialist and out-of-area referrals may be required and are often well placed to support both the referral and review process of these placements.

> **Good Practice Example**: In Norfolk & Suffolk Foundation Trust, a group of consultant and principal clinical psychologists accessed specialist training and supervision to become local Dissociation Champions. With an Expert-by-Experience on the Strategy Group, they successfully cascaded their expertise to colleagues in their MDTs via consultation and supervision (Crockford et al., 2019). Their experience demonstrated how valuable such a role can be in initiating earlier identification, diagnosis and formulation, increasing the number of dissociation and trauma-informed therapy or care packages and reducing the risk of unhelpful, even iatrogenic, interventions. It seemed helpful in reducing the number of out of area specialist placements being requested.

Service and system development. In addition to clinical leadership, applied psychological professionals have been invited to adopt **strategic and executive leadership roles** as part of their contribution to service delivery (e.g., Psychological Professions Network, 2020). This encompasses working to influence wider system and organisational culture to improve services for those with dissociative experience (see Chapter 16).

Specific examples of this approach might include:

- Helping to enhance Trauma-informed Care strategies to include dissociation
- The development of dissociation champions to assist in developing clear local care pathways, improving access and reducing waiting times
- Liaising with commissioners to set out the arguments for investing resources, particularly in relation to gaps in access to longer term psychological therapies, the 'gold standard' for complex trauma presentations (including complex dissociation, people with a diagnosis of personality disorder etc) (NHS England, 2022).

3.1.9 Teaching and Training

Applied psychologists have also been asked to see themselves as providers of teaching, encouraging the workforce to be more psychologically minded (see Chapter 17).

They can be active in promoting greater awareness of dissociation and the developmental, social and cultural context of trauma and intersectional adversity, share skills and help others remain up to date with the latest developments and research. They can **offer practical staff training** on essential stabilisation and grounding skills and support staff to teach clients these skills. The evidence suggests that such techniques can prove helpful with even the most complex presentations (Brand et al., 2014; Dorahy et al., 2014; Fisher, 2017; ISSTD 2011).

Good Practice Example: Trauma-based Dissociation and Skills Training in Norfolk and Suffolk

A one-day training was coproduced and co-delivered with Experts-by-Experience for NHS MDT staff. Titled 'Working with Clients with Trauma-Related Dissociation', the training aimed to increase:

1. The level of knowledge and understanding of trauma-based dissociative difficulties, their causes and how to identify them.
2. Staff awareness around the lived experience of dissociation.
3. Skills in working safely and effectively with people who dissociate, reducing the risk of providing iatrogenic experiences of care.

This was well-subscribed. It covered the development of dissociation from an attachment and neurodevelopmental perspective and incorporated lived experience throughout. It included key 'Dos and Don'ts' as well as principles of engagement and promoting stabilisation, both within the person and in the wider system (e.g., care team and family). It also considered staff care and supervision staff fed back the following:

'I think the course was worthwhile in terms of time away from other commitments and I will get that time back in terms of my work being more effective and improving my confidence.'

'I particularly enjoyed how articulate the Expert-by-Experience was in describing difficult to capture phenomena'

'Inspiring reminder of the values necessary to underpin our work'

Colleagues can be kept aware of external training opportunities, articles, books, conferences etc. A **local library of resources** can be maintained for others to access.

Teaching on psychological practitioner and other mental health professional core trainings on the significance of trauma and dissociation, helps provide a foundation level understanding of dissociation from early career onwards.

Providing trainee placements can be vital in ensuring that students gain experience and some familiarity of working with people who experience dissociation early in their careers. In addition, supervising doctoral theses and other research into dissociation helps extend the current body of knowledge (see suggested Research Questions throughout the book).

3.2 The Role of the Psychiatrist

3.2.1 Professional Stance and Clinical Leadership

> '*A shared sense of intellectual inquiry and adventure… actively encouraged by the CMHT psychiatrist, will percolate down to the interactions also of different members of the CMHT with their service users.*' **Gordon Barclay, Consultant Psychiatrist**

Psychiatrists are usually senior clinicians within an MDT, often with formal or informal clinical leadership responsibilities. In this capacity they have an important role in shaping and modelling the clinical stance within the team. For this client group the recommended stance is to foster an atmosphere of professional curiosity – mutual support, enquiry and openness – within the team.

Service users with significant dissociation will usually have histories of abusive relationships and betrayal of trust by those in positions of power and authority (ISSTD, 2011). Reflection on how power is managed in the professional relationship is important for building working alliances between staff and service users which allow therapeutic and meaningful engagement to take place. This includes remaining thoughtful and reflective of the possibility that iatrogenic or harmful interactions and dynamic re-enactments can occur. Intersectional experiences of power, inequality or discrimination should be kept in mind here.

> '*It is fair to say that there is a very wide range of attitudes towards dissociation among UK psychiatrists relating to very different experience and understanding of dissociation in general.*' **Gordon Barclay, Consultant Psychiatrist**

3.2.2 Differential Diagnosis

Accurate identification of dissociative experiences is vital in guiding appropriate care.

> '*Misdiagnosis didn't need to happen. At first, I got a diagnosis of PTSD which I still have now but as time went on and more behaviours became*

apparent that is when different diagnoses were thrown around ... borderline personality disorder, bipolar disorder and a few others. This led to varying medications and varying psychological inputs. None of which were very helpful. As time went on and I still didn't have the right diagnosis, my crisis points became more frequent leading to more hospitalisations, more suicide attempts and much more frequent self harm. When I look back at that period of time, it makes me very sad because I feel like some of that didn't need to have happened. It took until I was in my thirties to get the right diagnosis. That's 15 years of not having the right help. Fifteen years of my life I can't get back.' **Kelly Simpson, Expert-by-Experience.**

- Temple (2019) summarises the **signs in routine practice** to be aware of for 'When to suspect the presence of a dissociative disorder' (p.22), including multiple previous diagnoses, lack of response to standard treatments and indications of amnesia. This accuracy can often be, by itself, a powerfully transformative process for the service user towards hope and recovery. (See Case Example 'Mary', above; also Chapter 2)
- Differential diagnosis can form a part of this (ISSTD, 2011). However, a diagnosis may **take time** to reach with accuracy, as dissociation can be a hidden phenomenon. Intersecting social and cultural factors can play a part here, for example Black individuals presenting with dissociative symptoms may be more likely to be misdiagnosed with psychosis (Metzl, 2009), despite significant trauma histories; and neurodiverse individuals may be at risk of 'diagnostic overshadowing', with dissociative symptoms seen as behaviours related to their neurodiversity rather than responses to feeling overwhelmed or traumatised (see Chapter 7)

Myth: Dissociative Identity Disorder is not a valid diagnosis.
Fact: A range of dissociative diagnostic categories have been in existence internationally for many years. These have been refined and consolidated in the current DSM-V and ICD-11 manuals.

- **Professional curiosity** may be more important than great expertise about dissociation or different dissociative presentations

'The experience of a supportive and non-judgemental receptive openness and curiosity is absolutely vital in facilitating the "unconcealing" of what may remain forever hidden within many layers of mistrust and "protection" unless met with such an "active receptivity".' **Gordon Barclay, Consultant Psychiatrist**

Establishing the information necessary for a diagnosis, it is important to hold an attitude of 'phenomenological openness', being receptive and listening well to the service user's descriptions of possible dissociative experiences. Invoking Bion (1964), this could be phrased as 'listening without thought, memory or desire'. With a **curious stance**, helpfully model for the team staying with anxiety associated with uncertainty, rather than rushing to action or an overhasty diagnosis. Crucially, if service users feel connected with, and heard, clinicians are more likely to learn about the symptoms and experiences associated with dissociation, which may remain deeply hidden by shame or fear if not met with an open and receptive attitude.

> *'Patients with dissociation will very often say – if we listen – what a powerful experience it can be to be really listened to, and to be heard. And patients will often say – if we can listen – what a powerful experience it has been **not** to have been listened to, and so not to have been heard. Positively, and negatively.'* **Gordon Barclay, Consultant Psychiatrist**

- Another challenge in accurately reaching a diagnosis for someone with a dissociative presentation is that **dissociation may be changeable in its presentation**, differing between different people with the same diagnosis, as well as showing variation in a person's presentation over time (see Crisis Management below, also Chapter 6)

> *'On my journey to recovery I have often come across to others as "acting like a completely different person" it has been told to me so often I just accepted that I was "different" or "strange". I started to judge myself "What's wrong with me?" "Who am I?" This has stuck with me until this day. It became nearly impossible to try to explain that the things I was doing wasn't me. I mean physically it was me but mentally it was not me. Imagine trying to explain that to someone when I didn't even understand it myself? The day I got my diagnosis it was strange but I felt reborn – finally I had an answer! Even though I feel much more myself than I have in years, I still experience judgment and I have heard this from other service users with DID.'* **Beth Ryan, Peer Support Worker**

- **Comorbidities,** as mentioned above, are also common (see also Chapter 1; Chapter 7; Chapter 8, Chapter 12) and can mask or obscure significant dissociation.

However, wherever dissociation is present it is important to identify this, and to engage actively with this during treatment planning. Without this, care and treatment can be impeded and less effective (for example by amnesia between appointments or by different dissociative parts having differing views on treatment plans)

- When a diagnosis is suggested, this should be clearly and openly discussed with the service user, including psychoeducation materials, and/or signposting to resources for further information and understanding (see Chapters 1 & 2)
- As important as a formal diagnosis, if not more so, are developing and sharing:
  - a full descriptive account of the person's difficulties,
  - and a collaborative individual psychobiosocial formulation (see above Psychologist's role).

Together these will help frame the MDT treatment plan.

- Sharing this information with anyone working with the client is important, facilitating discussion, and attending to team dynamics where the potential for fragmented responses and professional splits is a significant feature

3.2.3 Medication

> '*I have to start very slowly with as small a dose as possible and it may take up to six weeks to tolerate what is often not even considered a level that is therapeutic.*' **Lizzie, Expert-by-Experience**

> '*I would say that poly pharmacy is a big issue in this patient group. I have met patients who even at a young age have tried so many medications, without benefit, that their traumatic feelings of "being broken / damaged / worthless" are compounded further ("I really must be untreatable").*' **Jamie Wright, Consultant Psychiatrist.**

Making general recommendations about medication for people meeting criteria for a dissociative disorder diagnosis is challenging, due to widely varying presentations within each diagnostic category. Additionally, a person's mood, state and behaviour may fluctuate, almost by definition, over time, and dissociative parts can seem to have different responses to medication or different views on taking medication regularly (ISSTD, 2011, p. 150-6 provides a helpful summary of issues to be considered). Often, as with other mental health presentations where complex trauma is part of the aetiology (for example, for people meeting criteria for a personality disorder diagnosis), prescribing is more likely to address comorbid symptoms/diagnoses (Loewenstein, 2005). As with prescribing for borderline personality diagnosis, much prescribing for individuals with dissociative difficulties will be 'off-label' and done pragmatically to the end of reducing emotional dysregulation (Loewenstein, 2005); there is a corresponding lack of evidence base for prescribing for dissociative disorders (Sutar and Sahu, 2019).

> '*I hold onto a very fragile sense of mental well being...I would so welcome the possibility of being able to talk through my options with a DID informed prescriber and be able to get a little support at the times when I am seeking help.*' **Lizzie, Expert-by-Experience**

Anti-depressants, anxiolytics, mood stabilisers and antipsychotics have all been used in the context of dissociative presentations, often for named comorbid difficulties rather than the dissociative experiences per se. A crisis situation would be one example, (ISSTD, 2011, p.137) where dissociative experiences have decompensated to a point where the presentation appears psychotic. Anti-psychotic medication may contribute to short-term relief, while such symptoms persist. However, such prescribing must be followed up with timely review, as the antipsychotic medication will often not be needed once the acute distress and disorganisation has resolved. Over-prolonged use of antipsychotics in such a situation could indeed be considered to impede an individual's recovery.

Carefully considering the pros and cons of prescribing is also relevant to the context and stage of treatment and psychotherapy. Medications such as antidepressants and anti-psychotics may at times contribute to supporting the stabilisation of dissociative presentations, and so be helpful in treatment Phase 1: Stabilisation and Safety (see Chapters 4 & 18). However practice-based clinical experience can suggest that medication leaves individuals less able to access emotions, and so impede therapy once an adequately robust and well 'resourced' therapeutic container is available to support the therapeutic processing of emotions. Psychiatrist and psychological practitioner should here confer and communicate well, so prescribing decisions are made on the basis of nuanced discussion and a shared understanding of dissociation.

3.2.4 Crisis Management

Psychiatrists often have a significant role in assessing both **risk**, and issues relating to **mental capacity**. (See Chapter 6; and Chapter 13).

- **In relation to risk,** dissociation is increasingly being linked as a factor distinguishing suicidal acts (Calati et al., 2017; Rabasco & Andover, 2020) over suicidal ideation alone, and as such is critical to consider in effective risk assessment and safety planning

- However, risk can be more complex to assess where significant dissociation exists. The person may present as feeling fine, and yet shortly after present with significant risks, with sometimes little obvious warning. Risk assessment will be aided by gaining awareness and understanding of any dissociative parts or states; and involving the views or perspectives of these different parts when discussing with the person the risks and safety plan

- In relation to **mental capacity** decision making, there should be no blanket assumptions about lack of capacity. What will be important is to take the time to have a discussion in relation to the views of different parts of the person about the specific decision in question, and how the dissociation and parts of themselves can be supported to build consensus between them (see Chapter 6)

Case Example: A service user repeatedly tried to abscond from an acute psychiatric ward which the staff viewed as challenging behaviour. This behaviour began to be understood as a 'flight response' occurring when a post-traumatic dissociative state was triggered on the ward. In this state they believed they were back locked in their abuser's house and were once again trying to escape. When staff understood this, they were able to consider a more trauma-informed response.

- **In crisis**, people with complex dissociation can show decompensation in ways which overlap with other severe mental health states, such as psychosis or even a catatonic state. These may well however have a post-traumatic rather than organic basis. Keeping in mind the underlying dissociative presentation, and the individual case formulation, can help to understand and manage crises more appropriately; for example, the question might be asked whether this is a decompensation in response to stressful events, post-traumatic triggers, or perhaps an anniversary associated with past trauma

---

'Some of the things I heard as an inpatient was being called "difficult", "attention seeking", "and a hysterical woman" and "non-compliant". Not knowing any different and being in a vulnerable mental state, I believed what they were saying. I began to think I was wasting everyone's time and had no place asking for help. When I look back, I can now clearly see that these

behaviours were all manifestations of my DID. It was different parts driving at different times meaning there was huge contrast from one day to the next.'
Kelly Simpson, Expert-by-Experience

- **Acute use of psychotropic medication,** including antipsychotic medication, may be considered as above

Case Example: In crisis, a service user with a dissociative diagnosis, presented as apparently catatonic, as if their sense of agency was really impaired. However later, they were able to recall with crystal clarity each nuance of word and gesture of those involved in their assessment and management at that time.

- Remaining aware of the underlying dissociative presentation/ formulation will help to guide a **trauma-informed approach to care**, whether in A&E, under a mental health liaison team, or on an in-patient ward. As in the case example below and EbE testimony above, treating someone with appropriate dignity and sensitivity in a crisis situation contributes not only to being able to ground the immediate crisis, but also to the possibility that each interaction contributes to building a more long-lasting sense of trust, rather than mistrust, in helping relationships
- A **co-created care plan and safety plan** which are dissociation aware, trauma-informed, and culturally competent, can help the service user with significant dissociation to maintain a sense of agency about their care through a crisis. These plans could form the basis of a Health Passport (NHS England, 2024) which the person may carry with them to support their care in a range of situations

*'The phenomenon of splitting can happen in a potentially even more troubling manner with service users with significant dissociation. Awareness of and discussion around such dynamics is vital, for what we are not able to **engage with** proactively and consciously, we will often find ourselves being **engaged by**.'* **Gordon Barclay, Consultant Psychiatrist**

'One of the only ways to combat iatrogenic harm and overly defensive practice is to create a collaborative advanced statement with the patient about their wishes regarding admission, when to avoid, when to consider, if considering then what to keep in mind, etc. and to have this front and centre in their notes.' **Jamie Wright, Consultant Psychiatrist**

- **In-patient admissions and managing transfers of care.** When there is transfer of care across teams, for example between community mental health, crisis and in-patient teams, the psychiatrist has an important role in negotiating **a consistency of approach** and **joined up planning** across team interfaces. This is an important component of effective care where the person's internal state and experience is fragmented and disorganised. Systems and teams risk mirroring and reinforcing this where there are differences of opinion about diagnosis, care and treatment, arising perhaps in part due to the person's varying presentation. These differences must be brought together, with joined up conversations facilitated across the person's care network, building an over-arching framework of understanding of the person's struggles. Without this, divisions, splits and discontinuities develop, with unhelpful, even iatrogenic impacts on the person, their care, staff wellbeing and service effectiveness.

  The immediate focus of care may be on crisis stabilisation, but this can be trauma-informed and dissociation aware, based on the individual's formulation, and any previously co-created safety plan or health passport, perhaps in anticipation of being admitted.

'Recovery isn't linear. It doesn't go in a straightforward motion. You have times where you go forwards and times when you slip back. And times when you are just standing still. But none of that can happen if you don't have the right support around you. I was very fortunate that after many years of struggling, I found the right help. My work with Psychology was ... the hardest thing I have ever had to do. But throughout the process, I had the support of all of the different teams around me. This combined approach changed everything for me. It allowed me to move forward and allow myself to live my life in a positive way.' **Kelly Simpson, Expert-by-Experience**

3.3 The Role of the Mental Health Nurse (MHN)

Within UK mental health services MHNs are often frontline in the assessment, treatment and case management of service users, whether in community or acute settings. They may be the first MDT clinician engaging with a client and work to build therapeutic relationships with them and their supporters. MHNs may be the care co-ordinator or lead professional to the client over time, complete case management paperwork such as care and safety plans, and liaise with other agencies and services to work together, advocating for the client's needs and impact on their daily life.

The MHN may have a longer relationship with the client than other MDT members, and provide more continuity of care. They have a key role in coordinating components of treatment, bringing clients' often complex care network together to promote joined up working. In terms of the stages of trauma-informed care (Chapters 4 & 18), their role may often contribute to stabilisation and safety (Phase 1) of the client's psychological, physical and social needs.

3.3.1 Assessment Process

MHNs are often involved in initial client assessments. A knowledge of core symptoms of dissociation and basic screening questions, alongside knowledge of other mental health presentations and awareness of intersecting cultural, religious and social influences, will enable them to help someone begin to name their dissociative experiences, sometimes for the first time (see Chapter 2).

They must **develop a therapeutic relationship** with someone, building confidence to open up about experiences that are hard to speak about, or have been missed or dismissed previously. Not uncommonly clients have had several previous diagnoses – including psychosis, emotionally unstable personality disorder, depression, eating disorders etc. – and treatment and experience of services will have reflected this. It may be necessary to sensitively touch on histories of complex trauma and intersecting inequalities to support the person in developing an initial formulation of their needs. Discussion of preferred pronouns may be more complex where dissociative parts identify with different genders and sexualities.

3.3.2 MDT Discussion

The MHN may feedback their assessment to the MDT. Presenting clearly and confidently about a client's possible dissociative symptoms, will help in early planning of an appropriate trauma-informed and dissociation-aware care pathway. They will liaise with colleagues to formulate a MDT care plan, perhaps involving further dissociation screening or referral for diagnostic and formulation-based assessments of their difficulties, history, resources and strengths.

3.3.3 Key Working and Care Coordination

While UK national policies move away from the previous rigid Care Programme Approach, best principles of well-coordinated care remain (NHSE, 2022).

• **Extended assessment, care and safety planning.** For someone with complex mental health difficulties, a MHN key worker will continue to assess over time alongside building the therapeutic relationship. Where significant dissociation is present, this process will take longer, to build trust, to gain a full picture, and to complete core tasks such as care and safety planning. Symptoms of amnesia, depersonalisation and derealisation, identity alteration or intrusive voice hearing, may all impact on how much is covered in appointments or remembered between them. Identifying and making sense of what is happening with the person in the here-and-now, can help to distinguish dissociative features, which may otherwise be misinterpreted as lack of engagement or motivation

---

Case Example: Safety Planning Can Be Made 'Dissociation Friendly'. A MHN, and client who experienced high levels of dissociation, began developing **a safety plan for each part** of the personality. This helped the client gradually identify common triggers for each part; how each part typically responded; and things experienced as helpful and harmful. This helped the person develop their understanding of the parts and increased the range of options available to prevent and mitigate crisis situations. A clinical psychologist supported the MHN to understand how dissociation impacted the person's daily life. The MHN developed their understanding of person-centred working, and took this forward with other cases.

Additionally, different parts of the person may have different views on any aspect of care. These diverse views should be respectfully taken into account, a further reason processes may take more time to complete. The aim ultimately is to support the client to engage with the views of different dissociative parts and to reach an internal consensus within themselves as to each decision.

Dissociation can play a significant part in risk presentations, and make risk assessment and safety planning particularly complex (See Chapter 6; and; and Section 3.24 above). A client may appear settled and engaging well in an appointment, only to present with significant risks shortly after. Equally an immediate presentation of high risk can resolve more quickly than might be expected, if a sense of safety or grounding is regained, or a helpful part is able to come forward. This can result in less restrictive crisis management.

- **Liaison with family and supporters.** Working longer term as a keyworker with someone with significant dissociation, the MHN may form relationships with their family and supporters. This can aid further assessment, learning how dissociative experiences impact on family relationships, including loss of time, knowledge of important events, or changes to personality that may be distressing to loved ones. Supporters can bear a significant burden, particularly when the dissociation is not identified or well understood. They can be offered psychoeducation, helping them understand how dissociation manifests and common misunderstandings. They can help the MHN and client with awareness of the dissociation in daily life, contributing to knowledge of different dissociative experiences, or parts and their relationships with supporters. The MHN can help the client and supporters plan how to manage these experiences. This can be a priority in terms of scaffolding and maintaining relationships which are important to them

Complex issues of safeguarding may also arise and form part of this discussion (see Chapter 6). This includes considering any current risks or on-going threats to the client, including from within the family. Abuse is not always in the past, and past abusers may still present a risk to the next generation, or trigger a sense of threat and destabilisation for the client

- **Liaison with other agencies.** The historic lack of information about dissociative presentations extends to other agencies in a client's care network. The nurse can provide psychoeducation to other professionals involved in the client's care, but also support and empower the client to advocate for themselves and work out how to explain their difficulties and needs appropriately for each situation. Examples include communications with occupational health in relation to adaptations at work; with a medical team regarding a hospital procedure; or when state benefits are being reviewed. A health passport can be a useful and empowering tool (NHSE, 2024), as a document carried with someone to help them communicate what they might need or want in different settings and situations.
- Another core coordinating task is to **bring the client's wider network of care together on a regular basis.** This helps practically, because they may have complex mental, physical and social care needs, with many agencies involved. It enables all partners to work with shared understanding and aims alongside the client. However, crucially, it is also important for the client psychologically, because the fragmented nature of the person's internal experience, can be replicated and reinforced by splits, disagreements and omissions within the care system. Care providers who are able to work together around the client, model thinking together and collaboration, a potentially therapeutic experience in itself for someone whose history is of traumatic, conflictual or neglectful relationships.

3.3.4 Generalist Therapeutic Interventions

MHNs reinforce the interventions of psychological practitioners within the team and provide low-intensity psychological interventions such as grounding or trauma-stabilisation strategies. This might include consolidation of a piece of time-limited psychological therapy after this has ended.

A longer-term relationship between the client and MHN offers the opportunity and trust for dissociative experiences to be revealed for the first time even much further into the care and treatment journey. This might include the naming or recognition of different dissociative parts. The evolving picture requires clinicians to remain person-centred, curious and compassionate about someone's experiences.

In this context, MHNs may sometimes be the person to whom painful emotions and disclosures are first made. Sensitive, supportive responding will give the client space to work through what might seem a muddle to them. The MHN's role, listening and validating these experiences and emotions, can be significant for maintaining trust, whilst helping develop a more formal treatment plan towards addressing trauma, or moving forward in other ways with social recovery.

3.3.5 Physical Health Procedures

A MHN's role includes monitoring the effects of a prescribed psychotropic medication. With complex dissociation, a client can present what seem unusual or idiosyncratic responses to medication. (See Section 3.23 above.)

They may also carry out physical health checks and procedures. For someone with a history of trauma, these may be experienced as invasive, distressing and triggering of post-traumatic reactions, including dissociation. These interventions should be offered in a trauma-informed, sensitive and caring manner, sometimes with personalised adaptations. This may require liaison with other health care providers, including a GP, midwife, or hospital consultant (see Chapter 8). Examples include:

- A trusted other may be chosen by the client to be present, to help them to stay grounded
- Additional time may need to be planned for, to manage a heightened level of distress
- Support and education may be offered to the health care provider as carrying out the procedures can feel difficult if they feel responsible for triggering a post-traumatic reliving experience, or being mistaken for an abuser at the time of the intervention being carried out.

3.4 The Role of the Occupational Therapist (OT)

The OT's core role in mental health settings is to support people to 'enjoy everyday activities that lead to a sense of purpose and enhance their chances of recovery'. (www.rcot.co.uk/about-occupational-therapy/what-is-occupational-therapy). This might include improving self-care, such as building a morning routine, managing finances by developing a budget, building confidence to go out and join a local group, or developing professional skills to use in work.

OTs in MDTs may also have broader remits overlapping with other professionals, including care coordination or key worker functions, (see Section 3.33 above), or have additional training to deliver psychological therapies (see Section 3.1 above).

Making core OT interventions dissociation-aware and dissociation-adapted is important when engaging clients with complex dissociation with these tasks. This includes:

- Being aware of how someone's dissociation presents, and any existing formulation and care plan
- Assessing with the client how their range of dissociative states may appear or impact on the OT intervention being worked on
- With a client with dissociative parts of the personality, consider with them the different views these parts may have about the piece of work being done. The

engagement phase will involve working with the client and their internal system to build a shared view or consensus about the goals being attempted, and how these might be approached. This can be a mutually creative process. It might be that it is a particular part who will be the one who can 'front' to manage the task, for example driving or taking public transport, while other, perhaps younger parts, are 'being taken care of'. Equally, if a part is fearful or mistrustful about the plan, and this is not acknowledged and worked with, progress may be difficult to achieve

- This means a piece of work may need to be slower paced, taking more time at the planning stage, whilst addressing how dissociation may impact on the plan as it moves forward.

3.5 The Role of the Social Worker (SW)

Fung et al. (2019) summarised mental health SW as follows: *'Social work is a profession with a long tradition of helping people and solving social problems by intervening at the points where individuals interact with their environments... Social workers [may provide] individual counselling, but ... also focus on the system and community levels, such as tackling family problems and social problems and challenging unjust policies and practices ... In addition, social workers are the agents who aim at empowering people to develop their skills and use their own resources and those of their communities to solve their problems.'* With this in mind, they helpfully review the knowledge basis for core SW practice as applied to complex dissociation. They highlight significant gaps in the literature and evidence base, and the need for further research towards developing profession-specific guidelines. They helpfully propose **the potential areas** where SWs may intervene:

- Establishing safety – for example from current abusive or high-risk contexts (see Chapter 6)
- Addressing on-going relationship difficulties and promoting sources of positive social support
- Supporting clients with educational, financial, occupational and housing issues
- Supporting clients with legal issues, often as victims of crimes, but sometimes having committed crimes (see Chapter 13).

In addition, SWs are well placed to keep issues of intersecting social, religious and cultural inequalities and discrimination, but also cultural resources, in mind.

Key considerations for SWs will be:

- Working together with the rest of the care network (see Sections 3.24 and 3.33 above)
- Accessing and understanding existing assessments and formulations of the client's dissociative features, and how these may impact on any SW goals

- Assessing further dissociative features which come to light during SW interventions, and for this reason, understanding the main symptom areas of dissociation (see Chapter 1), and relevant screening questions (see Chapter 2)
- Paying attention to the therapeutic relationship with the client, throughout any goals and tasks, to consider any trauma dynamics which emerge. Through this, ensuring practice is trauma-informed and culturally competent
- This involves taking time to work with the dissociative features and to engage with the person's dissociative parts. This is relevant both when developing initial plans and goals with the person and when considering how these plans are progressing. In both cases the aim is to work with the client and their parts, to acknowledge the multiple internal points of view, and help to facilitate a consensus between these parts on the decision in hand.

Case Examples: One client would wander away from home at night in a dissociative state. This put them at physical risk, and their family, who lived elsewhere, were worried the client could no longer live independently. The SW helped them fund and install a movement alarm, which signalled if they left the house.

Another client was struggling to make progress addressing trauma and dissociation in psychotherapy, whilst living in an environment which felt unsafe. They felt trapped from moving independently due to financial pressures and managing dissociation and emotional instability. The SW helped them explore a range of accommodation options, addressed funding, and developed an individualised plan for their specific needs. With suitable accommodation and support in place, the client's use of psychotherapy, as well as their social recovery, improved rapidly.

- These issues are particularly crucial where issues of power, authority and control come into play, as when exercising SW's statutory powers and responsibilities involving the Mental Health or Mental Capacity Acts, or in relation to Child Protection Proceedings. (See Chapter 6).

As with the OT, the SW's role within an MDT may also be broad based with additional care coordination or psychotherapeutic skills (see Sections 3.33 and 3.1 above, respectively).

3.6 The Role of Support Workers (SuW)

SuWs may work in MDTs alongside qualified professionals, supporting clients with tasks of daily living, developing recovery goals to improve their quality of life, or putting into practice interventions recommended by other professionals. They may work within partner agencies in the person's care network – in drug and alcohol services, supported housing, or VCSE organisations. Sometimes they are the professional having most regular contact with the client, and seeing them more often in real-world settings – for example in their own home or during an activity. As such SuWs provide an important link between the client and other professionals or services. The charity First Person Plural (FPP) published a helpful guide for SuWs (https://www.firstpersonplural.org.uk/wp-content/uploads/2019/03/FPP-Support-Worker-leaflet-single-sheet-2019.pdf). This recommends:

- Having a basic understanding of the person's dissociation
- Establishing 'a relationship based on partnership working, openness and trust'
- Maintaining consistent boundaries
- Treating each dissociative part 'with genuine respect and interest, validating their reality; be[ing] non-judgemental'
- But at the same time being clear that the goal is helping the client with stabilisation – 'managing everyday life' – rather than any kind of trauma work, which is more appropriately addressed in a therapy setting
- That accessing supervision is vital.

Working alongside a person closely and in a range of settings, the SuW may be first to notice or hear about signs of dissociation. They should be aware of the kinds of dissociative experiences and also useful screening questions to ask (see Chapter 2), which can help guide early conversations with the client. This will help communication with MDT colleagues who may undertake formal assessment.

For someone with an existing dissociation-informed formulation or diagnosis, it will be important to be aware of this. It will be helpful to consult with MDT colleagues, for example psychological practitioners, on how the SuW role can be adjusted to be 'trauma-informed' for this person's care. It may help to discuss with the person their understanding of their formulation or diagnosis. It may help to support them with sourcing and working through psychoeducational resources and how to communicate with other people in their lives about their difficulties.

Holding a curious, compassionate and non-judgemental stance offers a helpful general approach.

One important adaptation is being aware how dissociation influences the person's choice of goals, and their progress towards these (see section 3.71 below). FPP's guide above, describes day-to-day challenges which someone with significant dissociation may benefit from support with – 'Making telephone calls, visiting the doctor, filling in forms, shopping, personal hygiene, eating and sleeping habits; these are just a few areas that are often problematic'.

'Learning to use public transport again was very challenging because there were so many triggers that would cause me to get scared or defensive. This would cause one of my more challenging alters to come out and they would then take it out of me physically or have open arguments with me which

in turn left other people staring and making a much more uncomfortable almost dangerous situation. Overcoming this was no easy task. I made a goal that I would attempt once a week to walk to the bus stop and look at the timetables. Next I would get on the bus and do a short trip and then I would do a dummy run of the place I needed to go so I could familiarise myself for the journey and I could feel more confident and this would mean my alters would also feel more comfortable as many times they would feed off my mood. I would use certain techniques to help me. I would listen to music through my earphones. I would concentrate on my breathing. I would also try to get a seat as close to the door as possible so if I became too overwhelmed I could make a quick exit. Thanks to these measures I can now freely travel for work and pass on what I have learnt to service users, especially if they have experiences like DID.' **Beth Ryan, Peer Support Worker**

3.7 The Role of Peer Support Workers (PSW)

MDTs may include practitioners employed on the basis of their lived experience of mental health difficulties. Health Education England (2020b) set out how 'the core of peer support is the value placed on the use of lived experience of mental health difficulties (including the experience of caring for someone with experience of mental health difficulties) and seeing this as a form of expertise'. PSWs draw on their experience of recovery as they support clients with their own recovery goals (Implementing Recovery through Organisational Change Programme, 2013) and aim to improve quality of life despite ongoing mental health challenges. The PSW may have their own experience of trauma and dissociation, or they may have experienced different mental health challenges.

Key adaptations for PSWs when working with someone with trauma-based dissociation are as follows:

3.7.1 Identifying Recovery Goals

Case Example: A person with a diagnosis of DID was avoiding using the bus because of the risk of being triggered and switching to an alter state. The PSW worked alongside them to practise a plan for how to manage this. As this became more achievable, it enabled attendance at an IT course, the next step on their pathway towards seeking employment.

Helping someone identify what matters to them may be a more involved discussion, with recognition that different parts may hold different views and needs. Allow space for these different views to be acknowledged, and support the person to negotiate internally how these different needs might be accommodated.

It is important to remain respectful and non-judgemental about the nature of these needs. For example, a dissociated younger part of the person may wish to have regular times to do age-appropriate activities, for example reading children's books or playing with toys. Planning regular, safe and appropriate times for these parts to 'have space', can help to settle the person's 'internal system' overall. Adult parts can then be freer to be present in a less interrupted way when needed, for example with a more 'adult' recovery-focused goal such as managing public transport.

The metaphor of a family can be a helpful image to hold in mind for the person's internal dissociative system. A family includes a range of people, with different ages, needs and preferences, who all need to be accommodated and time negotiated.

3.7.2 Overcoming Stigma and Self-Stigma

Dissociative experiences and states can be part of many mental health presentations but can be difficult to identify, and put into words. This can lead to misunderstandings ('The person is not engaging or not motivated'), and lead also to shame and self-blame ('I'm going mad' or 'I'm possessed by evil spirits'). Helping someone to name and describe what is going on for them day-to-day can be powerfully validating, normalising and empowering. Supporting someone to access psychoeducational materials (see Chapter 2), and offering guided self-help, can be helpful.

3.7.3 A Strengths Based Approach

The PSW is well placed to help someone identify and support their personal strengths and resources, which may well be significant. The impact of dissociative states can be episodic and fluctuating. Someone may be more destabilised at times of stress or specific post-traumatic triggers, and more settled and able to function well at other times. Dissociation itself can be understood as a strength, a creative survival response which enabled the person to come through traumatic or depriving experiences. This can be a helpful message to convey.

'Sometimes I advocate for service users, ensuring that our experiences and perspectives can be understood by others. Other times I share my experiences with service users because it can help that person feel more understood and they can be compassionate to themselves.' **Amanda Green, Peer Support Lead**

3.7.4 Stance of Compassionate Curiosity

> *'I can't change my past and what's happened to me, but I can positively affect my future. By identifying my values – what matters to me - and finding ways to live in line with these, I'm able to live a fulfilling, meaningful life. For example, I really value being independent, so I wanted to seek employment. This meant I needed to learn and practice ways to self-manage my mental health and wellbeing so I can stay safe and well at work.'* **Amanda Green, Peer Support Lead**

The PSW's role may be more aligned to being 'a companion on the recovery journey', walking with the person as they learn and grow rather than an expert providing answers. When someone shows mixed feelings or ambivalence about next steps, notice this, pause, stay curious and compassionate, and take time to understand this.

3.7.5 Making Use of Supervision

This can be highly complex work, and opportunities for supervision and reflection are important. This may be particularly so, where trauma and dissociation are closer to the PSWs own experience; or where there are disagreements within the MDT, including lack of recognition, understanding or overt stigma about dissociative presentations.

> *'Now, I've learnt to use my dissociation as an opportunity to learn about how my mental health is doing. For example, I know if I start to become more destabilised, that I need to do something to look after my wellbeing.'* **Amanda Green, Peer Support Lead**

3.7.6 Supporting Social Engagement, Hope and the Recovery Journey

> *'As a PSW who lives alongside a diagnosis of DID I find having goals beneficial. When working with service users I set myself goals. For example, if I have an appointment with a service user my goal is to have what I call "focus time". This means that I will have an agreement with my alters that this is*

my time. And explain I need to be present, as this is my time to help someone else and I need complete concentration and if they respect and help me I will respect them and try my best to give them the time they need.

As a rule, I try to focus on the younger alters as they can't always under-stand why I need the time that I ask of them. I will often try to make deals with them. For example, I will say if you let me work today when we get home after work you can have an hour of playtime and spend time with my partner who they see as "Mumma". Their favourite thing to do is cuddle with Mumma on the couch and watch funny animal videos or they love to play with cuddly toys. We also do joint activities like go to a local coffee shop for our favourite drinks. Sometime the system isn't perfect and sometimes the younger ones like to sneak out but often we will have discussions and remind-ers of boundaries and my mind is reset.' **Beth Ryan, Peer support worker**

Formal therapeutic interventions are one part of the story for recovery, but the PSW has a particular role in supporting someone to put strategies into practice in real life situations. These are vital albeit challenging steps. Without this, the person may reach a point of less immediate distress, but still significant impairment in their day-to-day functioning and quality of life.

4. Summary and Key Learning Points

KEY LEARNING POINTS for MDTs:

- Maintain **a collaborative stance**
- **Be accurate** in assessment, description, formulation and diagnosis of the five domains of dissociative experiences plus somatic symptoms
- Exercise **joined up working** of the care network around the client
- Be **trauma and dissociation-informed** in relation to all components of MDT care
- Clients can present **with a spectrum of need,** regardless of diagnostic category
- Consider intersecting cultural, religious and social influences, and **work with cultural competence**
- **A range of interventions** may have therapeutic benefits. These may include:
  - extended assessment
  - psychobiosocial formulation

- accurate diagnosis
- psychoeducation for the client, their supporters and other professionals;
- Phase 1 Stabilisation including addressing:
  - safety planning
  - physical health needs
  - medication
  - housing
  - relationships
  - daily structure
  - comorbid symptoms
  - intersectional discrimination
- social recovery, including utilising cultural resources
- time-limited psychological therapy
- longer term psychological therapy to address Phase 2 Trauma Processing.
- Pay **careful attention to relational dynamics** through every inter-action – beginnings, changes, ruptures, endings - including dynamics around power, authority and minority experience
- **Manage boundaries** clearly, collaboratively and consistently
- Access an **appropriate level of training** in dissociation awareness and skills (see Chapter 17)
- Seek and make use of trauma and dissociation informed **supervision**.

This chapter has described the multidisciplinary and multiagency context of care for many people who seek help with complex trauma-based dissociation. Key principles have been set out, including accurate identification of dissociation; personalised, trauma-informed, formulation-driven and culturally competent care packages; joined up working across a person's care network; and the need for all professionals to have an appropriate level of training, skill and supervision specifically for recognising and working with dissociation. The chapter has set out how each professional within the MDT can apply and adapt their specific role and remit for working to help and support someone with complex dissociation. Such adaptations should contribute towards better outcomes for people with complex dissociation as part of their presentation and reduce the risks of unhelpful experiences of care.

Acknowledgements

With thanks to Dr. Stuart Mitchell for his comments on an earlier version of this chapter.

Chapter 4

Psychological Therapy for Complex Dissociation

Stuart Mitchell, Andrew Holding, Paula Biles and Roxanna Mohtashemi

1. Introduction

Psychological therapy for people who experience dissociation from depersonalisation and derealisation to amnesia and dissociative identities, including dissociative identity disorder (DID), is much needed but often difficult to access. Clients with such difficulties often have these issues overlooked (e.g., 'it doesn't exist'; 'I don't know what to do with it') or (mis)understood through some other label, such as psychosis or personality difficulty. They may experience many assessments and attempts at therapy but feel it does not really address their needs. Staff providing care are often highly skilled and well intentioned but not trained in the recognition or treatment of dissociation. They may continue to provide psychological therapy for another problem in the hope it will work but find that effectiveness is limited as the level of dissociation experienced is not being worked with (Temple, 2019). This ends up in a frustrating and poor experience for both client and clinician.

Therapy can indeed be provided for people who experience dissociation, from mild to severe levels, to good effect. What is classed as 'normal' and 'clinically significant' may be culturally determined and linked to specific sociocultural contexts (Krüger, 2020). The growing evidence base and best practice expert consensus guidance supports this. Clinical psychologists, and other psychological practitioners, have many of the core therapeutic skills and competencies (e.g., assessment, formulation, safety planning, pacing and agenda setting) required to work with dissociation at the level presented with only modest further training and ongoing supervision (e.g., recognising dissociative experiences, understanding the neurobiology of trauma, using stabilisation strategies, addressing therapeutic relationship dilemmas, working with dissociative identities) to adapt what they already do in clinical practice.

In this chapter, we review the theoretical, clinical, practical, cultural and professional issues of providing psychological therapy for people experiencing dissociation. We start with a brief review of the current research evidence on treatments for the most complex and pervasive dissociative difficulties. We identify where research is lacking and point to best practice existing guidelines and further resources. We describe the widely and internationally accepted phased model of

DOI: 10.4324/9781003625650-6

trauma recovery, upon which existing therapeutic guidelines are broadly based. We do not repeat here the content of all existing guidelines, but do give key summary headlines, signposting to where to go for further detail. We then provide a practice overview for working with mild and more complex dissociation, including DID. We also discuss key myths and clinical dilemmas that appear in the literature and clinical practice, and address these through expert (professional and lived experience) opinion and research evidence where that exists. In the final section we provide pragmatic summaries of the clinical dilemmas and myths as discussed in the previous section and take-home messages for the best practice treatment of dissociation and people meeting criteria for a dissociative disorder diagnosis.

2. Psychological Therapy: Research Evidence Overview

There are several published clinical guidelines on the treatment of complex trauma, dissociative difficulties and DID based on expert consensus originating from the United States, Australia, Europe, and the UK (ISSTD, 2011; International Society for Traumatic Stress Studies, 2019; Kezelman & Stavropoulos, 2019, 2020; McFetridge et al., 2017). This has been aided by the recent introduction of complex post-traumatic stress disorder (CPTSD) as a diagnosis within the ICD-11 classification scheme where dissociation is a key feature (e.g., flashbacks, amnesia, numbing; ICD, 2019). However, this has not yet been included within the DSM-5-TR classification scheme, although a PTSD dissociative subtype and DID does exist. Other clinical practice guidance exists from leading world experts in the field of trauma and dissociation (Boon et al., 2011; Brand et al., 2022; Dana, 2018; Fisher, 2017, 2021; Frewen & Lanius, 2015; Ogden & Fisher, 2015; Rothschild, 2017; Steele et al., 2017).

Considerable research evidence exists showing the effectiveness of treatments for post-traumatic stress disorder (PTSD), but this has not until recently been extended to people experiencing complex trauma, dissociation, DID and other complex coexisting problems (Bradley et al., 2005). Whilst dissociation is found within many cultures and countries worldwide (Brand, Şar, et al., 2016), there are few studies which explore the complex intersection of culture, dissociation, multiple identities and social contexts (Krüger, 2020; Pierorazio et al., 2023). One notable exception is the study by Pierorazio et al. (2023). Using reflexive thematic analysis, these authors generated four themes regarding the meaning of culture to 197 participants experiences of dissociation and mental health treatment: (a) culture as multidimensional and complex, (b) culture as a dissociation-catalyst, (c) culture as dissociation-resistance, and (d) decontextualisation from culture. These themes were noted to intersect across multiple contexts within oppressive social systems, with the authors highlighting the need for therapists to develop empowering methodologies (e.g., qualitative research) and cultural competence in their therapeutic practice (Brown, 2008; Krüger, 2020) (see Chapter 15, Cultural Considerations).

A meta-analysis of 21 studies of treatment for PTSD where dissociation was also measured, concluded that dissociation did not moderate the effectiveness of psychotherapy for PTSD (Hoeboer et al., 2020). The quality of some of the studies reviewed was low, indicating a need for further high-quality trials in clients with PTSD. These authors only reviewed studies where dissociation was assessed using the Dissociative Experiences Scale (Carlson & Putnam, 1993), however it is not clear whether any further assessment of dissociation was undertaken or whether this was a focus for the treatment. This leaves the question of how more research can be developed for clients who experience various levels of dissociation, as they are often excluded from standard psychotherapy research trials for PTSD (Corrigan & Hull, 2022).

There have been many single case studies and case control studies on the treatment of severe dissociation, including DID, and several uncontrolled and few controlled outcome studies (Brand et al., 2009). These studies provide preliminary evidence of effectiveness of psychological interventions for dissociation, but suffer from severe methodological limitations, such as poor description of actual interventions, non-randomised research designs, statistical regression towards the mean and limited sample sizes (Brand et al., 2009). These studies highlight that working with dissociative identities is a complex and long-term undertaking requiring working with the inner system of dissociative identities, working towards greater cooperation and communication over time.

The prospective, longitudinal Treatment of Patients with Dissociative Disorders (TOP DD) study is the largest treatment outcome study conducted with clients with prominent levels of dissociation or diagnosable dissociative conditions (Brand et al., 2013). In an international naturalistic sample of dissociative clients treated by outpatient community therapists, these authors found significant decreases in clients' dissociative, depressive, and posttraumatic symptoms, incidence of self-harm, suicide attempts, drug use and hospitalisation and increases in productive and social activities (Brand et al., 2013). In a follow-up study 6 years later, these authors found that clients continued to demonstrate improved functioning, had less need for hospitalisation with no outcome assessed in this study worsening over time (Myrick et al., 2017). In a further prospective TOP DD longitudinal study, Brand et al. (2019) investigated the outcome of a web-based psychoeducational programme for an international sample of 111 participants diagnosed with dissociative conditions. The study used written, video, and behavioural practice exercises that provided education and skills training to both clinicians and clients on dissociation, emotion regulation, managing safety and reducing problem areas. All client groups showed improvements in functioning, reduced dissociation and self harm, and higher functional adaptation, with clients with the highest levels of dissociation (DID) or self-harm showing the most significant improvements (Brand et al., 2019). This was maintained at 2-year follow-up. These researchers have recently extended their TOP DD study into the *Finding Solid Ground* (FSG) program (Brand et al., 2022; Schielke et al., 2022). In a randomised controlled trial of 291 outpatients with severe dissociative and comorbid conditions, they found at 6 months (and 12 months) people showed significant improvements in emotion regulation, PTSD symptoms, self-compassion and adaptive functioning compared to a waiting list control group (Brand et al., 2025) and in qualitative research clients perceived it as helpful (Pierorazio et al., 2024).

In a randomised controlled trial in the Netherlands, Bækkelund et al. (2022) evaluated a structured protocol-driven group treatment delivered in a naturalistic clinical setting with clients with complex dissociative difficulties, as an add-on to individual treatment. Fifty-nine participants were randomised to 20 sessions of stabilising group–treatment, conjoint with individual therapy, or individual therapy alone, in a delayed-treatment design. The treatment was based on Boon et al. (2011) skills-based manual for therapists and clients. Results showed no significant differences between the groups from pre to post treatment, but significant improvements in psychosocial function, PTSD symptoms, and general psychopathology did occur at the 6-months follow-up period. This study highlights the finding that short-term stabilisation treatment requires further time for effects to be deepened and applied by clients in their daily lives.

A case series study is currently examining the effectiveness of schema therapy for people diagnosed with DID (Huntjens et al., 2019). This study considers dissociative identities as schema 'modes' or parts of modes which are common to us all with varying degrees of intensity. Amnesic barriers are not assumed to be present. Dissociative identities are also seen as extreme expressions of dysfunctional modes with greater disconnection from other modes. This was based on clinical observation of inpatients experiencing DID (Huntjens et al., 2019). However, it is important to realise that these authors' schema therapy model is also a phased approach to therapy for complex dissociation as recommended by ISSTD (Brand, Loewenstein, et al., 2019).

In summary, there are many case-control and case studies investigating the treatment of dissociation and dissociative conditions, with findings from studies with good external validity, which are therefore clinically encouraging, despite current methodological limitations. Some rigorous high quality-controlled studies do now exist and are underway based on the phase model of trauma (Brand et al., 2013, 2019, 2025; Huntjens et al., 2019). Multicultural experiences (see Chapter 15, Cultural Considerations) and neurodiversity (see Chapter 7 Comorbid Complexity), and their relationships with dissociation, have not been sufficiently investigated to date, although this is improving (Krüger, 2020).

3. The Phase Model of Recovery in Relation to Therapy

Expert consensus (Herman, 1992; ISSTD, 2011; Steele et al., 2017) recommends a **three-phase approach to recovery** which may be applied to any therapy model when therapy for complex trauma and dissociation is being considered. These are loosely defined as focusing on safety and stabilisation (phase one), acknowledging, and accepting past memories (phase two) and integrating parts of the self and further rehabilitation (phase three) (Herman, 1992). We therefore recommend when in therapy that a period of psychoeducation and stabilisation are carried out prior to any trauma processing. This may in fact be the entire work of therapy for more severely dissociated clients, although clients with DID may still benefit from carefully paced and negotiated work at all stages (Steele et al., 2017). In addition, for clients with DID, there may need to be a stage before phase two (memory work) where the memories are available within the shared consciousness between different identities through collaborative negotiation (Mosquera, 2019; Steele et al., 2017). This phase model may need to be adapted for clients who have developed multiple identities as a result of insidious trauma from oppressive systems or culturally induced stigma surrounding dissociation or seeking mental health treatment (Brand, Şar, et al., 2016; Pierorazio et al., 2023).

In the main, most professionals consider that attempting trauma processing before adequate stabilisation has occurred increases the risk of re-traumatisation and iatrogenic harm. Some authors have offered a different view, though this may be more relevant for less complex trauma presentations, such as simple PTSD (De Jongh et al., 2016). With more severe experiences of complex trauma and dissociation or DID however, it is important to acknowledge the trauma history but not invite detailed exploration before the client has the necessary resources to process their responses, as this may excessively trigger flashbacks or memories. If the client has a history of highly complex and sustained abuse, such as that arising within the context of organised or ritual abuse, it is wise to seek further professional advice on treatment as these are likely to be the most complex difficulties to work with and any professional will require significant supervision and support, if not further training (Miller, 2018).

All psychological practitioners in clinical practice may, with some brief additional training and appropriate supervision, support at least the first phase of dissociative work (stabilisation) delivered by themselves or through supporting interventions delivered by other mental health professionals, such as nurses and occupational therapists (see Chapter 3, Multidisciplinary Care). In this context, psychological practitioners may need to take a sensitive multidisciplinary approach to clients experiencing multiple somatic or physical health conditions or disabilities, so that diversity is respected, validated and its meaning considered fully in all assessment, formulation and any stabilisation-based interventions consistently across health care settings (Brown, 2008; Steele et al., 2017). However, transferring care and treatment to another professional for further work is a complex process, since developing a trusting therapeutic relationship takes considerable time and sensitive handling, if re-traumatisation is to be prevented (Steele et al., 2017).

Psychological therapy practitioners may also be able to deliver trauma processing (phase 2) work if they have further skills in trauma processing models, such as TF-CBT, EMDR or other relevant therapy models, including adaptations for cultural competence (Brown, 2008; Krüger, 2020).

They may also support intervention focused work indirectly through other professionals (see Chapter 17, Training).

4. Psychological Therapy: Practice Overview

Working with dissociation is complex and challenging for all practitioners. It requires patience, tolerance, compassion and flexibility of mind to help a person who has a fragmented sense of self. It also requires cultural competence in terms of openness and attunement to the multiple ways that identity and culture affect people, including the effects of insidious trauma due to different forms of systemic oppression (Brown, 2008).

Chapter 2 (Assessment) outlines the process of a dissociation-focused assessment and case formulation (see also Chapter 3, Multidisciplinary Care), noting the ways in which someone might have difficulties arising from trauma and dissociation, both internally and externally in their relationships and daily life. Following development of a shared formulation, careful **treatment planning** and **goal setting** will follow, linked to the person's current needs, and the resources available in the service and wider community, including cultural resources (see Chapter 15, Cultural Considerations).

Treatment based upon the phased model, as described above, has an initial focus on safety, stabilisation, skills building, enhancing internal communication and developing a collaborative therapeutic relationship. Treatment planning is helpful in supporting both client and therapist to stay grounded, on track, review and reset when things feel lost or confused. For example, it is common as a therapist to experience somewhat dissociative states of mind in response to a client who is dissociating, particularly when this is shifting and changing within or between sessions. The shared treatment plan should include an agreement about the treatment frame, such as frequency of sessions and availability of the therapist between appointments, the use of emails and other communications, short- and longer-term goals and what to do in the event of a crisis or emergency. In this part of the work, it may take longer to reach a shared consensus and agreement, particularly where dissociative identities hold different perspectives on for example goals and therapist availability.

Case Example: Multiple Gender Identities. *Stephen identified as male and gay, but felt he had to repress and decontextualise the feminine and cross-dressing aspect of his identity due to past experiences of bullying and homophobic attitudes in the culture where he lived. He really missed this part of his identity in his current life experiences. In therapy, with his therapist's help, he was able to reclaim this lost identity and enjoy its presence. Stephen felt heard and validated by his therapist in this regard, so did not have to conceal this aspect of his identity due to fear of its expression. Over time, Stephen reported being able to dance around his flat with his partner in full dress and attending events he had selected where men in drag were able to express themselves safely with enjoyment. Although not central to Stephen's* *traumatic experiences, this aspect of therapy made further improvements in his overall sense of being made up of multiple identities which all had a positive purpose and place in his life.*

Case Example: Managing Anger. *Jackie wanted help with her feelings of anger and the fact she felt deep down she was a dangerous person. There was no evidence in the assessment to support any dangerous behaviour ever being carried out. The therapist agreed with her to work on how she manages her anger in adaptive ways, but it became clear she would dissociate during these times and run after people in a rage when they had offended her in some way (e.g., stealing items from her shop). She could not remember all the details of this. Over time, Jackie agreed to explore the origins of her rage, where this was held inside her mind, perhaps in a dissociative separate younger part, and what scared her the most about it – that she might have killed her perpetrator when she was a child. Gradually, she became more accepting of her anger, less frightened of it and understood why a traumatised child part of her felt so afraid that she had harmed someone who had harmed her.*

Most clients who experience dissociation will require at least a brief period of stabilisation, and many a much longer time to develop safety and stability. Goals are linked to the phase and duration of therapy. For example, **Phase 1 goals** could include developing a safety plan, addressing initial fears about therapy, developing understanding and strategies to manage their range of dissociative states, developing internal communication between parts, and improving coping with aspects of daily life such as childcare or work. **Phase 2 goals** could include working through fears of traumatic memories, ensuring sufficient capacity is present to work with memories, reflecting on the implicit meaning of the trauma, and addressing attachment dilemmas. **Phase 3 goals** could include grieving past and future losses, adjusting to being more present in daily life and building capacity to develop meaning and purpose in life.

Case Example: Managing the Therapist's Window of Tolerance. A therapist became tearful and distressed in a session with a client who was describing her parents' reactions to her recent disclosure of abuse she suffered at age 6. The client noticed this and was alarmed, worried that her therapist was ok. He was able to acknowledge and validate (to himself) why he felt so distressed as he resonated with the terrible predicament his client was in and the lack of acknowledgment by her parents. He then was able to say to his client that he was ok and validate what a distressing story it was and how terrible it was to have no one acknowledge what had happened to her back then. This helped his client see that her therapist was able to be distressed but still carry on and hold the client's experience in mind at the same time.

Case Example: Moving on from Dissociation as a Way of Living. Susan had done considerable work in understanding her complex trauma history and learning to manage the effects of these in more adaptive ways by being present, mindful and regulating herself without excessive use of alcohol. This led her to identify that she was now feeling more in her daily life and that so many years had been wasted in 'just getting by' but 'not really living'. Her therapist spent some time on helping her grieve for these losses and explored how now she had the freedom to choose how she led her life without the need for dissociation

In general, it is important to **focus on process as well as content**, within the therapist's own model of therapy training. Learning skills and techniques can be helpful but so can learning to become more present and reflective about current experience, both internally and in relationships with other people, including the therapist. It is also key to provide treatment as much as possible within the window of tolerance (WoT) of both the therapist and the client. Further complexity arises for clients with DID, as different dissociated parts may experience different degrees of tolerance, rather than one global overall WoT for the whole person. For example, if a therapist tries to ground a client, the client may switch to another identity so that they are able to continue with the therapist's request. This may mean that certain issues never get the opportunity to be discussed, such as why some parts hold bits of information and others do not. It is helpful if this is considered early on in therapy but may require much further in-depth work with dissociative parts later in therapy as trust is developed.

Case Example: Session Structuring for Containment. *Jackie (already discussed), had great difficulty with feeling contained at the end of sessions. Her therapist worked with her on structuring her sessions into thirds, so that they could review her week, do some productive work on an agreed area (e.g., her anger), and then do a closure exercise (e.g., self-soothing, paced breathing or grounding) enabling her to leave feeling calmer and more regulated.*

Case Example: Managing a Phobia of Feeling. *Shania had great difficulty with tolerating any sort of feeling state in her mind or body. Her therapist explored this carefully and they came to understand that she felt it was*

not safe to have feelings and express them, as an angry teenage part of her believed this made her weak and liable to suffer more at the hands of her abusers. Further work was done on using the window of tolerance in collaboration with other parts as much as possible, so that different feeling states could be more acknowledged and allowed to be present, including sadness and everyday happiness and joy. This was done by using the WoT diagram, careful pacing and using titration strategies and structuring sessions so the client could leave sessions on time feeling relatively calm and stable (Steele et al., 2017).

5. Aspects of Therapy

Learning how to get grounded and stay present, separating the past from the present through mindful observation, learning to get and feel safer and diverse ways of improving emotional, physical and internal regulation are all key to effective therapy with clients who experience dissociation. Alongside standard ways of grounding, some clients may require techniques and strategies that are tailored to their intersectional identities, such as incorporating prayer or spiritual beliefs into grounding, or sensory grounding objects for neurodiverse clients (Kandeğer et al., 2022; Krüger, 2020) (see Chapter 15, Cultural Considerations; Chapter 7, Comorbid Complexities). Some further exploration of issues to address and keep in mind during therapy are shown below. These aspects will not be achieved in one go but can be integrated into the therapist's base therapy models, developing over time at a pace that feels manageable to client and therapist.

- **Building understanding of trauma-related dissociation. What is trauma and how did dissociative strategies enable them to survive? How is their nervous system affected now by past and present trauma? How did culture** (Krüger, 2020) **and race** (Zheng & Gray, 2015) **affect this and what language is best used to be more inclusive?** For example, Stephen recognised that he had a part of him that would go into freeze mode, whilst another part of him wanted to lash out and fight others, and yet another part felt weak and avoided taking any kind of responsibility. These were all his nervous system's ways of protecting him from further suffering. He also had multiple identities shaped by his culture, which he had learned to repress. These became a focus for therapy
- **How do they cope with the effects of past trauma now? What trauma-related dissociative difficulties do they experience and what tends to trigger them?** For example, Shania was often triggered by her angry teenage parts, who shouted at her angrily to not say anything to her therapist and to do what they demanded of her. She was also triggered by other people, when they became upset or angry with her. At these times, she felt the urge to run away
- **How to develop healthier ways of coping with trauma, lessen dissociative states and break unhelpful patterns.** This may include adapting learning

materials to client's learning styles and capacities, including neurodiversity. For example, Stephen often turned to cannabis as an escape to his difficulties, but also as a self-soothing strategy. His therapist helped him learn other ways to regulate and self soothe that did not lead to the longer-term problems of addiction

- **How to address trauma-related thinking that may support dissociation, and keep people stuck in old ways that are self-limiting.** This may include how someone perceives themselves, or how others perceive them within community values and cultural beliefs, such as hearing voices being a sign of possession (Krishnamurthy & Kumar, 2023). For example, Jack felt that he was a 'bad' and a 'nasty' person for what happened to him, and it was all his fault. His therapist helped him see how he had learned to blame himself for abuse that wasn't his fault as this gave him a sense of control and mastery over feeling helpless and scared. Over time, he learned to become more compassionate towards himself and less self-critical

- **How to contain and regulate emotions and unsafe behaviours connected to dissociation especially how to get grounded and feel safer.** For example, Irene learned to recognise when she was beginning to go outside her window of tolerance and feel too much, but also sometimes she would feel too little and become numb, depressed and lethargic. Different strategies were identified to help her with the early stages of either feeling too much or too little

- **How to identify and build up resources and resilience in daily life within different cultural contexts.** For example, Dennis was able to identify that he was a careful thinker and planner and did not rush headfirst into things. This was used to plan some exercises and activities he could practice helping him experience more emotion in his daily life

- **Managing traumatic attachment and fears and phobias linked to this.** For example, Jackie was fearful and avoidant of close attachment after years of childhood neglect and abuse. Through careful exploration of the felt sense experiences of safety in the therapeutic relationship, she was gradually able to appreciate how this made her feel lonely and isolated, and it then became something that she worked to change in her current life

- **Dealing with traumatic memories, fears and phobias.** For example, Stephen had several traumatic memories from his childhood, which kept him stuck in avoidance and cannabis use. With careful planning and adapted use of EMDR, he was able to process some core memories which then helped him feel better and able to cope with present experiences in more adaptive ways

- **Moving on and building progress and quality of daily life.** For example, Jackie had to take time to allow herself to recognise more feelings in herself, grow greater awareness of her life and experiences and become freer to choose how she wanted to lead her life, despite many years of childhood trauma

- **Working with dissociative self-sates or parts.** For example, Shania had several teenage parts that acted a little like some of her abusers, to whom the parts themselves remained attached to the extent of ensuring she returned to them on a frequent basis. She had no memory of this. This became a key focus of subsequent therapeutic work.

Whilst improving safety, stabilisation and regulation are key **phase one therapy tasks, collaborating with the client's inner system of self-states and parts is also important,** but also more complex, often benefitting from further training and supervision with an expert in complex trauma and dissociation. The inner system needs to be helped to stabilise, building up internal communication and cooperation over time. It is often a case of working towards something, and celebrating this with the dissociative parts, rather than having a blanket goal of achievement. Whilst many therapy models may be helpful for working with dissociation, the therapist must include ways of working directly with dissociative parts in a paced, systematic, and coordinated way (Steele et al., 2017). The number or appearance of parts, or switching between them, is less important than understanding their function, role and perspective. Therapy involves seeking ways to foster greater communication and cooperation between them. A key message to the client is that all parts of them are equally welcome. They also retain responsibility for each other, with the person as a whole remaining responsible for themselves, their wellbeing and behaviour. Many resources are available for further guidance on aspects of therapy (e.g., Fisher, 2017, 2021; ISSTD, 2011; Kezelman & Stavropoulos, 2020; Steele et al., 2017).

Case Example Continued: Working with Hostile Teenage Parts. Shania had two strong teenage parts who were mostly very angry and powerful, but who would place her in situations of significant risk. Her therapist worked carefully to understand this, and how the whole system was submitting to the teenage parts of behaviour and all of them were being put at risk. Over time, this strengthened the daily life adult self who then in turn took more responsibility for the overall safety and was able to resist returning to her abusers, but could communicate better with her teenage parts reframed as protector parts, rather than abuser-like parts.

Some **key texts** provide further detailed guidance when undertaking psychological therapy within different psychological models where dissociation in the main presenting problem. The International Society for the Study of Trauma and Dissociation (ISSTD, 2011) provide guidance for adults with DID and Dissociative Disorder Not Otherwise Specified (DDNOS) based on a synthesis of research evidence and clinical practice. The Blue Knot Foundation provide treatment guidelines, validated by ISSTD, for complex trauma and dissociation based on a thorough review and synthesis of the research literature (Kezelman & Stavropoulos, 2019, 2020).

From a CBT perspective, Kennedy and colleagues (Kennedy et al., 2013) provide a thorough overview of CBT and neurobiological models for working with dissociation, which is currently under review (Kennerley, personal communication).

From psychoanalytic and mentalising perspectives, Allen (2013), Mitchell and Steele (2021), Rüfenacht et al. (2023) and Howell and Itzkowitz (2016) all consider adaptations for complex dissociation.

Steele et al. (2017) outline a through overview of a practical integrative approach for working with trauma-related dissociation. They include a useful prognostic evaluation tool to assess progress and capacity for change during therapy, building on their earlier book on coping with trauma-related dissociation (Boon et al., 2011). These skills and areas of focus offer useful adjunctive tools to existing therapy models, all of which must have a relational and process perspective in addition to skills and strategies (Fisher, 2017).

Ogden and Fisher (2015) describe a sensorimotor psychotherapy approach outlining different practical strategies and exercises to help clients feel more grounded and safer in their bodies. Fisher (2021) has elaborated this further in a workbook on transforming the living legacy of trauma, including a range of exercises and suggestions for overcoming complex trauma and dissociation.

From an EMDR perspective, Mosquera (2019) described working with dissociation in a specialist service in Spain, recording sessions for supervision and training purposes. Her guidance covers how to work with the whole client, and also different parts of the client, each with their own function. She offers detailed therapy case examples, with case formulations and therapeutic strategies used. Other key papers and texts are recommended from Forgash and Copely (2008), Paulsen (2014), Gonzalez and Mosquera (2017) and Gonzalez-Vazquez (Gonzalez-Vazquez et al., 2018).

Finally, the Finding Solid Ground Workbook for therapists and clients by Brand and colleagues, based on their research programme is an evidence-based psychoeducational program structured for clients with severe difficulties, and can be delivered on an individual or group basis (Schielke, et al., 2022).

6. Addressing Myths and Dilemmas in Clinical Practice

Clinical practice when working with dissociation varies enormously but may hold ideas and beliefs which contain misunderstandings about dissociation and how it can be worked with therapeutically to good effect. Clinicians are often faced with complex clinical dilemmas which need understanding and carefully managing. These myths and dilemmas are explored below.

> *'I have 30 years plus experience of trying to get a diagnosis and find a treatment pathway within the NHS, but in reality, have had no choice but to choose the private therapy route to find any help at all.'* **Expert-by-Experience**

6.1 Services Have Nothing Specific to Offer for Trauma-Related Dissociation

This experience is unfortunately not uncommon in NHS mental health services, and may leave clients feeling frustrated, angry and misunderstood. Underpinning these experiences are often practitioner beliefs and attitudes about dissociation and psychological therapies which may compromise client care and treatment. Clinicians influenced by these beliefs and attitudes are less likely to carefully assess and identify dissociative experiences or plan targeted treatments, without which the difficulties are unlikely to resolve (Jepsen et al., 2014; Kluft, 2005). Such beliefs also influence decision makers and service planners to conclude that resources should not be allocated to training and therapy interventions in this area.

6.2 Therapy Is Unlikely to Work

One such myth is that **therapy for dissociation is unlikely to work or is so difficult it is not worth even attempting**. Clinicians are often concerned about several related issues. They may believe that clients will be unable to maintain focus or concentration due to amnesia, depersonalisation, derealisation, self-state shifts, etc; there may be discontinuity between sessions which prevents progress; clients may struggle to identify and maintain consistent therapeutic goals or even consent to treatment; therapists may struggle to develop a good therapeutic relationship with many of the dissociative parts; therapists may struggle to communicate with parts that appear to be unusual or non-human such as 'animal' or 'spiritual' parts and therapists may be unable to work with someone who is fragmented in relation to fundamental aspects of their character, such as their gender identity or sexual orientation constantly changing and in conflict.

These are understandable anxieties about working with dissociation, however they need updating with information and research evidence, as reviewed earlier in the chapter. The current evidence suggests that with appropriate adjustments to treatment, people with severe dissociative difficulties can be worked with effectively and positive treatment benefits can be gained. For example, a meta-analysis of eight treatment outcome studies for a range of dissociative disorders demonstrated moderate to strong within-patient effect sizes for dissociative focused treatment (Brand et al., 2009). Other studies have been reviewed above.

6.3 Working with Hostile or Angry Parts

Case Example: Working with an Angry and Hostile Part. Stephen had great difficulty with feeling and expressing his anger and, submitting to others, would often be taken advantage of by them. As this was explored in therapy, Stephen became much more aware of different angry parts of him that were highly protective, and even felt murderous. He was quite frightened of such a part. Initially, he labelled one such part 'rage', but this was felt to be too strong and did not give it a positive intention enabling it to feel included in the therapy. With careful dialogue and giving the part a positive name and labelling its function – to help Stephen stand up for himself – Stephen became less afraid of this part, and in fact he was able to stand up for himself by being present with this part and jointly being more assertive. The part was able then to enjoy the therapy sessions where he and the angry part were working together to solve their life problems.

Whilst some dissociative parts may initially appear to be hostile or overly protective of the client, others may manifest as having non-human or unconventional personas, sometimes referred to as 'Fictive' (based on a fictional character or person) or 'Factive' (based on a real person) internalisations. Working with such parts can be challenging for the clinician, but with a dissociation-informed framework, it is possible to work constructively with such parts. Models of trauma-based dissociation (e.g., Steele et al., 2017) suggest that all parts, however seemingly oppositional or novel, have developed in order to be functional, derived from adaptive necessity, to help the person survive. It is important to distinguish parts that carry rage and anger from traumatic experiences in childhood or re-traumatisation in adulthood, from parts who have taken on the role of protectors or internalised abusers (Mosquera, 2019; Steele et al., 2017). These latter may hold huge power over the whole dissociative system, leading to blocks in the therapeutic progress unless they are respectfully consulted, to understand the rules that have kept the person alive, for example 'not talking to anyone outside' the system. If consulted early on and throughout with respect, they can provide considerable help to the clinician (Steele et al., 2017; Mosquera, 2019). Clinical experience has suggested they can often be worked with constructively if they are accepted by the clinician, given equal respect as a part of the person, and their perspectives and roles understood.

Case Example: Pacing with the Whole System. Shania seemed eager to work on her trauma and dissociation and share information about the whole of her internal system with her therapist in one session. The therapist did not check the effects of doing this on the rest of her parts. The client subsequently self-harmed during the week as a teenage part did not like the client saying so much without their agreement. The therapist at the next session reviewed this and apologised for going too fast and agreed to work at a slower pace and invite views from all parts as much as possible before going into any new area of work so that more consensus could be built up.

6.4 Goals, Capacity and Consent

In terms of goals for and consent to treatment, the key is to work with the range of the client's parts to build a consensus about goals (Mitchell & Steele, 2021). Clinical experience indicates that sufficient agreement over goals can be reached within the collective system of the client with patience and creativity. This may require more negotiation and time from the clinician as they work with the dissociative system of the client, rather than working with the goals of only one part of the client (Steele et al., 2017).

In terms of capacity to consent, the Mental Capacity Act ('Mental Capacity Act', 2005) highlights the importance of assuming individuals have the capacity to make a decision unless there is a good reason to think otherwise. Many people who live with complex dissociative experiences, which may be hidden to others, are often highly functional, making important decisions and prioritising issues whilst holding down careers, providing childcare and so on. Issues relating to risk and safety are discussed more fully in Chapter 6.

6.5 Alliance Building

Case Example: Building a Safe Collaborative Relationship. Stephen had many years of support from a CMHT, with a diagnosis of 'mixed personality disorder' and psychotropic medication for his voice hearing. After a psychological assessment his difficulties were reformulated as resulting from attachment trauma with significant levels of dissociation identified and understood as a survival strategy. Using a phased therapy approach, he was able to assert himself in outside relationships, develop greater safety in his relationships with men, regulate his distress without use of cannabis and process some disturbing childhood trauma memories.

Following the phase model of recovery described above, clinicians can develop a positive working alliance and maintain the necessary therapeutic boundaries with dissociative clients, much as with any other presenting difficulty. However, it may take more time to actively attend to and work with the range of views within the client's internal system. Therapeutic skill, careful management of varying attachment dilemmas between parts and the help of good supervision (Steele et al., 2017), can support this work to be effective. These issues will need revisiting and elaborating at each of the phase-based stages of stabilisation, processing and integration.

6.6 Dissociating During Sessions

Case Example: Checking and Managing Dissociation as It Occurs. Shania would often appear glassy eyed at the beginning of therapy sessions, or say she felt very anxious but did not know why this was. Her psychologist developed a regular pattern with her of checking in at the start whether there was any activity inside from any parts, or body sensation she felt was making her feel too much or too little. He asked her to rate this on a 'How present do you feel right now?' scale from 1–5. Depending on the answer, they worked on a few simple grounding exercises over the first few minutes to help her either feel more or calm her nervous system, to regain her window of tolerance. He would then ask her to re-rate her degree of being present, which always improved. This also helped her internal parts feel safer and more trustworthy about the therapy process. He repeated this regularly during the session and towards the end if needed.

It is realistic to expect clients with complex dissociation will dissociate during the therapeutic process. These experiences can be identified, understood and managed within the therapeutic relationship, to enable direct work with all different parts of the client whilst building a solid and consistent therapeutic rapport.

6.7 Fabrication, Pretence, and Amnesia

Another myth encountered when working with dissociation, is that **such conditions are fabricated or iatrogenic in nature and that any treatment of them is likely to be harmful**. Some authors have suggested therapists can't intervene without leading or shaping and exacerbating a client's problems; even validating a client's narrative risks reinforcing dissociative difficulties (Paris, 2012). This implies clients are suggestive, open to a clinician's influence, and clinicians have therefore created the problem of dissociation. Recent authors (Brand, Vissia, et al., 2016; Loewenstein, 2018) describe these hypotheses as models to be tested, which currently lack empirical evidence with no treatment studies or studies in clinical populations.

Dissociative experiences are inherently about detachment from overwhelming experiences to make those experiences feel bearable and survivable. Clients may appear floaty, spacey, zoned out or absent and difficult to reach. The intention is not usually to lie or pretend, but to survive and protect the self. Fabrication has an entirely different intention to deceive and exaggerate some experiences over others, as in for example Munchausen syndrome by proxy. In dissociation, the intention is to protect and minimise mental and physical pain rather than deceive or exaggerate. Considerable evidence supports this view. A review of meta-analyses (Dalenberg et al., 2012; Dalenberg et al., 2014) concluded that there was little evidence to support the fantasy model of dissociation. Rather, there was a strong effect size of the trauma-dissociation relationship among those with dissociative conditions. Similarly, several studies have found evidence that a history of chronic childhood abuse and dissociative tendencies are present long before a severe dissociative condition is suspected and eventually diagnosed.

Other research has shown that dissociation predicts only 1–3% of the variance in suggestibility, not supporting the 'fantasy proneness' model assumption that dissociative individuals are highly suggestable. Supporting evidence also comes from prevalence research demonstrating the presence of people with complex dissociative conditions in cultures where conditions such as DID are not well known in local psychiatry practice or the culture more generally (Akyüz et al., 1999; Yu et al., 2010).

6.8 Is Therapy Harmful?

Concerns regarding the harmfulness of therapy for complex dissociative experiences are not supported by current evidence. A review by Brand et al. (2014) did not find any peer-reviewed studies demonstrating that treatment consistent with expert consensus guidelines harms patients. A single study that identified symptom deterioration among DID patients found that only a small minority (1.1%) worsened over more than one time-point in treatment and that deterioration was associated with revictimisation or stressors in the patients' lives rather than with the therapy they received.

Conducting a thorough semi-structured clinical assessment such as the SCID–D (Steinberg, 2023) can help ease concerns about being leading, especially where information is also gained from friends and family (see Chapter 2, Assessment). Experienced therapists, skilled in engaging clients in the exploration of their experiences without being overly suggestive, regardless of the type of clinical presentation, are typically very mindful of this issue with traumatised clients. In fact, appearing overly sceptical of client's experiences and narratives may be experienced as a repetition of childhood experiences, for example of not being believed when disclosing trauma, and is likely to reinforce mistrust and have a profoundly negative effect on recovery outcome (Briere, 1992). Furthermore, it is the very act of helping clients to articulate, mentalise and share information about current experiences, memories and self-states that eventually leads to greater internal cooperation and improved functioning.

6.9 Working with Amnesia

Clients with severe dissociative experiences may often experience **amnesia** of current daily life for periods from minutes up to hours, or even days, due to parts of themselves being triggered by threatening stimuli. This can be challenging to manage within the therapy frame and structure. Best practice recommends an explicit treatment structure with careful and detailed discussion and agreement regarding all aspects of the treatment frame, such as times of sessions, length of therapy, therapist availability, breaks, crisis contact, use of email and telephone contact, etc. (Steele et al., 2017).

6.10 Issues Around Working Online

Sessions normally take place in an agreed clinical place (e.g., a consulting room) but online working can be helpful for people who have difficulty with using public transport, live too far away or do not feel safe leaving their homes. Online working may require some adaptations, such as protecting the time and space, the client being in a confidential and safe setting, the use of cameras and ways the client can step away from the therapy at the session's end, for example doing something completely different, such as exercise or household chores. The clinician should be aware of the possible triggering effects of working online, for clients who dislike being seen on video due to body dysmorphia or who have experienced being filmed in the context of abuse. Clients may wish to turn off the 'self-view' feature or turn off the camera all together. This needs careful, collaborative discussion and agreement between the clinician and client, including the range of views and perspectives within dissociative parts. Other clients may not wish to work online at all, as this may feel less real and connected to the therapist.

If family members or friends are involved in the therapy in any way, with the consent of the client, it is important to consider the degree to which this is triggering or reinforcing dissociative defences. It cannot be assumed that family or friends who accompany them to sessions are acting in the client's best interests or are safe. The therapist should seek further senior or experienced consultation when working with those accessed by organised groups of perpetrators or where the client appears to be returning to perpetrators for continued ongoing present abuse, as discussed in Chapter 6.

> *'There are some parts of the country where the postcode lottery does not allow for the incredibly important work that those of you working successfully with dissociative disorders in the NHS to be offered to all who need it.'*
> **Expert-by-Experience**

6.11 Time Limited Therapy

A related myth and dilemma for clinicians when working with dissociation is a concern that **briefer therapeutic may not be effective or may even be harmful**.

Here, clinicians are sometimes of the mindset that only long-term therapy over years will be useful for clients where significant dissociative problems and attachment trauma are present. They worry that offering briefer treatment of several months will be of little use since the client takes so long to form a safe trusting relationship and begin the work of therapy.

> *'I do think that in places "rose tinted glasses" are being used – yes in an ideal world diagnosis and treatment would be available to all but this is still a long way from reality.'* **Expert-by-Experience**

Indeed, long-term specialist psychological therapies are typically the preferred and needed treatment of choice for many severe dissociative conditions. However, short term interventions, while not a replacement for long-term attachment informed dissociation and trauma treatment, can still have significant benefits (e.g., Brand et al., 2019). For example, developing emotional regulation, containment and grounding skills are likely to have practical value; whereas psychoeducation, brief family work and/or the development of a jointly produced psychological formulation may help bring reassurance, validation, insight, hope and access to a wider range of psychoeducational resources, which can be empowering. Equally, focused client goals (for example being able to access physical health appointments) may be achievable within a shorter time frame, though still requiring a dissociation-aware formulation and intervention to be effective.

Clients in fact present with **a range of needs**, regardless of the diagnostic category, or complexity of their presentation, and these are important to assess and consider. Some clients prefer not to engage in longer-term trauma or phase three integration work at a particular point in time, either due to personal preferences or their own current life circumstances. A shorter-term intervention over several months focused on phase one stabilisation or phase two processing may be more appropriate in this situation to match the client's stage of recovery journey.

Care needs to be taken to manage expectations, by having a realistic appraisal of what can be accomplished in a particular period without destabilising the client further, defining goals and having a clear treatment frame. Additionally, it remains important to acknowledge and validate complexity factors (e.g., autism). It is also important to recognise, and openly acknowledge any unmet needs, including where there is a service gap, or treatment appears too brief in time.

Where longer-term therapy is desirable and indicated but there is no resourced pathway designed to meet the client's needs, it may be possible to offer episodic periods of therapy, such as blocks of 20 sessions or a treatment period of say 6 months. Whilst not optimal, episodic therapy, which typically includes a break of a several months before another period of limited duration is offered, may still be useful. However, with this approach it may be harder to offer consistent support by the same therapist with the same felt sense of emotional containment and attachment security. We know of no research on the effects of episodic therapy delivery, and this approach may reflect an accommodation between clients' needs and what services have capacity to provide. Caution is recommended, with particular attention to attachment dynamics.

'I feel overwhelmed by how many crises my client has and the level of contact they seek with me and other services. They contact me frequently between sessions and most recently at 3am. They threaten self-harm or suicide one week and cry and cling to me in other sessions.' **Mental Health Professional**

6.12 Risk and Safety in Therapy

Clinicians often express **concerns regarding risk and safety issues** and how these may be understood and safely managed. Such concerns include the fear that clients may dissociate or unknown parts of them get triggered during therapy or daily life and place them in currently dangerous situations, or harm them in some way. The client then may not be able to recall details of such events for which they are partially or fully amnesic.

It is important to recognise that there may already be significant challenges, including risk behaviours, which are presenting within the client's daily life and in their use of and relationship with service providers. An example would be regularly phoning crisis services in a childlike state, which crisis staff feel ill-equipped to understand or respond to. In this situation, one suggestion for good practice would be to patiently ask for their name, how old they are and whether the person (name of the client) can come back so they are not left alone and have someone to take care of them (Mosquera, 2019). When dissociation is recognised, this can in fact offer a new and helpful framework for formulating and intervening with that client's difficulties.

These issues and concerns can be worked with in a more effective manner using dissociation-specific adaptations (Ogden & Fisher, 2015). Several studies suggest that people experiencing dissociation are at increased risk of self-injury, suicidality, detentions under mental health act legislation, and other unplanned hospital admissions, in several specific clinical populations (e.g., Foote et al., 2008; Langeland et al., 2020; Simeon & Putnam, 2022). However, no studies to date confirm that dissociative clients are at greater risk than similarly traumatised individuals in the general population.

There is significant variation in the level of vulnerability to risk amongst people experiencing complex trauma and dissociation, with many having motivational systems that have learnt to manage stressors relatively effectively (Steele et al., 2017). For other individuals, the threat of harm can be more complex and challenging, requiring careful and extensive handling by the clinician (Steele et al., 2017).

However, as noted previously, the treatment outcomes for clients experiencing complex dissociation who engage in appropriate evidence-based psychological therapy, are generally positive, suggesting that risk can be managed well enough. As earlier clinical guidance has suggested, effective assessment, risk management strategies and safety planning from both the 'grounded-connected', and 'dissociated' positions should be early components of any structured intervention prior to any processing type work that may be more destabilising (ISSTD, 2011). (See Chapter 6, Safety, for further discussion.)

'My client does not have one consistent and strong adult self (part of his personality) that functions in daily life. I do not know how to work with him. I keep meeting a different part each week as he seems to switch rapidly between parts within and during sessions. Child parts want me to befriend them and play with them. It is all very confusing.' **Mental Health Professional**

Case Example: Managing Amnesia and Unsafe Behaviour. Shania experienced episodes of dissociation where she could not remember hours or days of what she did or where she was. She would then see signs, such as dirty clothes, credit card spending and physical bruising of what she might have done. With gentle exploration, it became clear that other parts of her were engaging in some activity of which she was not aware. Her therapist showed interest in this and wanted to understand more about these other parts and how they were trying to help her in some way. At first, she did not think they were helpful, and she was afraid of them. With careful titration and listening in to what they had to say about issues discussed in therapy, they became more engaged in the therapy process. As this continued, Shania realised that she was being returned to the people who were currently abusing her, as they were in contact with her through a mobile phone. She knew these were dangerous people and became increasingly concerned that she was returning to them, especially when she had drunk alcohol. She therefore developed a plan with her therapist for how she could stay mindful and curious about the activity of these parts, keep alcohol in check and attempt to maintain her own present awareness as much as possible. This eventually resulted in her being able to say 'no' to invitations from these abusers and break the hold they seemed to have over her and the bond with some of her other parts.

6.13 Working with the Dissociative System: the Therapeutic Frame

When working with dissociation it is important to work with the whole dissociative system of the client and to give equal weight and value to all parts of the client's internal system. No part should be favoured over another and no part should be 'got rid of'. In fact, many clients may, perhaps surprisingly to practitioners, fear this latter as an outcome or intention of the clinician. Each intervention or comment should be monitored for its effect on other parts of the client's internal system. Some clients may appear to 'switch' between different parts or states before, during or following a therapy session.

This creates a significant dilemma for the clinician. How much do they work with the part(s) present and how much do they stimulate and strengthen the daily life adult self-part? In addition, who is the client who wants therapy? How do all parts feel about attending for therapy? Which parts are more in favour of it? How much cooperation is there over attending and doing the work of therapy? There is often significant internal conflict between a client's parts over these issues, inadvertently made worse by clinicians only 'listening to the part that is speaking', rather than checking the effects on the whole internal system, being clear about each having a value, and working together with them to reach some overall agreement. There needs to be careful attention to building a collaborative therapeutic relationship (Steele et al., 2017) with the client, and all parts of the client as far as possible.

This is likely to be an on-going process, and in fact, from an attachment perspective, may be a valuable part of the work overall, as it models a collaborative, non-abusive way of relating. It may be challenging to reach a consensus or full agreement with the whole system of the client. It will take careful negotiation to assess the presence and functioning of the daily life part and develop internal dialogue with dissociated parts to reach the best agreement possible, such as most of parts agreeing with a proposed plan of action. This may not be possible if a fight or flight part is present and has less mentalising capacity, and other functions or motivational systems are in operation (Mitchell & Steele, 2021). If so, it is best to work with the maximum consensus that can be achieved, whilst recognising that other parts may need something else you can return to at a later stage. Keep returning to the idea that some parts have their own separate functions, but form a key part of the client's whole, which needs to be worked with as much as possible to build connection and cooperation.

Besides sessions having a regular and agreed predictable time, with predetermined length, it is important to end sessions on time to ensure consistency and safety for the client. 'Attach' parts (i.e., a younger part that is focused on maintaining connection with the clinician) (Fisher, 2017) may seek to extend these boundaries and seek greater connection enjoying the attention and care of the therapist. This should be discussed with the client's daily life self, drawing attention to the needs of these 'attach' parts and how the client can meet them. The function, roles and expectations of different parts need discussing collaboratively at assessment and early in therapy, but also as they arise through being mentioned, activated by trauma triggers, or through a goal to work with that part. Over time a consistent therapeutic frame can be developed and a safe, collaborative working alliance, and growing trust established, within which the work will progress.

The physical building where sessions take place may also be of importance to the clinician and client in helping to build a sense of consistency, containment and coherence in relation to the treatment. Do clients feel safe in the building or is there anything that is inadvertently triggering a heightened trauma response? Is there a place they can go to if they become dysregulated and cannot immediately travel home? Does the clinician have a safety button or alarm system if help is needed? If they work alone, what lone-working practices are in place? These are general considerations for all clinical work, but with trauma-informed care principles in mind, may be even more important for working with clients who experience dissociation due to the complexity of presentation and possible risks. There is not necessarily one 'right way' of doing this, but careful formulation and collaborative discussion and consensus building is likely to be the way forward.

6.14 Extremely Unsafe Behaviour

Some parts of the client may be fixed in engaging in unsafe behaviour that threatens the well-being and life of the client as whole. This needs to be addressed either directly with the part(s) concerned or through the adult daily life part (Mosquera, 2019) to work to build whole system responsibility for safety and well-being. If this is being avoided by the client's adult self and other parts, then a robust approach to this may be required insisting on whole client responsibility for their own safety (Steele et al., 2017). Clients in such unregulated chronic crisis driven states are likely to require multidisciplinary support (see Chapter 3) alongside therapy. Steele et al. (2017) offer some alternatives to consider, for example agreeing a supportive session on one occasion and a therapy session on another, with a view to returning to the usual treatment contract once stabilisation is re-established. Mental capacity in dissociated states is considered further in Chapter 6.

6.15 Communication from Parts

Another dilemma concerns when parts communicate with the therapist (including by phone or email) without the knowledge of the adult self or other parts of the client. A general guide would be to aim to work with the client as a whole and to foster internal communication between parts. This may involve some careful discussion. The therapist may consider how to inform the client of these communications, the aim being **not** to hold secrets. One useful way may be to acknowledge the communication, with a simple 'thanks', and at the next therapy session to discuss these, what has happened for this communication to occur and how to understand and manage it going forward. Therapists may for a time function as a bridge or mediator between different parts to enable them to communicate and work with each other but is not usually aiming to have and hold onto an individual relationship with different parts. This is however subtle work and should be considered on a case-by-case basis with support from an experienced supervisor. On occasion, it may be helpful for the clinician to work out with the client how and when different parts of them are ready to know and hear the communicated information. Therapy does not necessarily benefit from telling the client what other parts have revealed in full, until the whole system is ready, but responsibility for holding this does ultimately lie with the client. Supervision and consultation will be important in working through these issues.

6.17 Practitioners' Emotional Responses when Working with Dissociation

> **Case Example: Managing Communication from Parts.** *For example, Sandra had a diagnosis of DID and was a therapist herself. Parts of her would often send in letters, pictures and emails to her therapist about what they liked and didn't like about therapy. Her therapist drew attention to these communications, left them on the table and asked the client about what they thought had happened that led to the picture, email, etc. Sometimes this was about their unexpressed feelings about the therapist or therapy situation. This helped to promote greater dialogue and cooperation between parts about how therapy could best be used to help them all. On one occasion, this led to the wish for some child parts to have a picnic outside the therapist's office on the grass. Whilst not actually agreeing to do this, a helpful conversation was had about how the client as a whole could attend to these child parts needs to help them feel cared for and they could have nice experiences again, such as picnics, brushing her hair and doing her make up.*

Working with dissociation may be stressful, but also rewarding and humbling. Clinicians may feel a range of emotions, including anxiety, dread, fear, shame, anger, compassion, pride or vulnerability. These responses may be normal and understandable given the complexity of clients' experiences, their traumagenic origins and how hard the client may be trying to hide their experiences from others due to shame, fear and self-protection. When clients are frequently self-harming or in crisis, it can be stressful and can take a heavy toll on the clinician over time. Formulating the crises in a trauma and dissociation-informed way can however prove helpful. Experienced supervision (see Chapter 17, Training) provides an important structure for reflection and support.

> 'I have a client who is very critical of me and gets angry and verbally abusive. They say I do not understand their condition. I feel scared and don't know what to do to help.' **Mental Health Professional**

As well as crisis situations, criticism and attack from protector or perpetrator-like parts of the client towards the therapist or therapy can present another source of stress, leaving practitioners feeling overwhelmed, helpless or afraid and unable to respond. Of course, the client or a part may be right in saying that the clinician does not understand them if this is true. The problem is more the way the client's system of parts is managing their distress and anger. Formulating the difficulty will be important. This may be understood for example as the fight part(s) of the client acting as a way of protecting the client from something that is happening in the therapy. The client may feel the therapy is going too fast or exposing the vulnerability of the client that the fight part is there to protect. If child parts are coming forward and the clinician is engaging with them without the consent of other fight parts, this may also be a reason for a verbal attack. Some clients may have critical or hostile parts, or parts that appear like the perpetrators of abuse (sometimes termed perpetrator introjects) (Mosquera, 2019). Each of these parts requires a different response, which includes working with the whole internal system of the client as much as possible to formulate and understand what is happening and to appreciate the function and value of every part. The clinician needs to feel safe enough to maintain their capacity to mentalise and function effectively as a therapist, and revisiting boundaries around safety in the treatment contract may be crucial. Accessing experienced supervision will be important, perhaps considering role-playing how to handle the situation sensitively with the client and providing some sense of personal protection and safety. The clinician could consider somatic or imaginal exercises, such as an imaginary protective suit, to use during the session in such a situation which could be rehearsed in supervision beforehand (Steele et al., 2017). This ensures the clinician is able to remain as far as possible mindfully present and within their own window of tolerance, so they are reflective and responsive to the client.

> 'I am fortunate to be working with a skilled private therapist who has experience of working with dissociation, but many people are not, and many others remain misdiagnosed. I am hopeful that this will change in the future.'
> **Expert-by-Experience**

7. Best Practice Summaries

This chapter has summarised the research and practice evidence base with regard to psychological therapy for people with complex dissociation. It has discussed myths and clinical dilemmas about dissociation and its treatment. Common myths have included: treatment is difficult and unlikely to be effective, dissociation is all fabricated or iatrogenic and risk and safety are often unmanageable. Common clinical dilemmas have included how to work with limited time or resources, how to work with amnesia or dissociative parts, how to manage severely unsafe behaviour, how to manage frequent dissociative switching in session and how to manage

- **Identify dissociation and work directly with it in therapy**
- **Treatment** should be based on a careful and **comprehensive assessment and formulation** over several sessions
- **Identify and adapt for cultural, neurodiverse and intersectional identity factors** using inclusive language
- **Many different models of therapy have been adapted for use with trauma-based dissociation** (e.g., CBT, EMDR, DBT, Psychodynamic, MBT, Internal Family Systems, Sensorimotor Psychotherapy) and evidence for differences is currently not well established
- **Goals for treatment** should be developed with the client's whole system as far as possible, **based on the phased model of recovery,** and negotiated collaboratively as therapy progresses
- There should be a **clearly agreed treatment frame covering roles, expectations, and responsibilities** (e.g., session times, location, breaks, clinician availability, safety planning)
- As part of this, a **safety plan** should be developed with the client over one or more sessions, and for this to consider the early warning signs and triggers for different parts, what to do to help or try not to do, and any service responses that are helpful or to avoid. This should be available and reviewed regularly, particularly in response to further crisis episodes
- **Treatment** should be **phased and focused on both skills' development plus a secure relational attachment to the therapist,** with phase 1 Stabilisation, phase 2 Acceptance and Processing of memories and phase 3 Integration and rehabilitation
- **The treatment path is not linear**, and clients may go back and forth between different phases as they move towards recovery, within a secure therapeutic alliance
- **A collaborative therapeutic relationship is a core component of treatment,** and is developed over time, with a focus of 'working together' on the problems
- Treatment should consider and appreciate **the whole internal and external systems** of the client, giving equal value to all parts whether overt or not. This includes a focus on relationships outside of therapy
- It is useful to take stock of and balance a **client's positive resources and strengths,** which may be considerable, to support and strengthen these, and promote more adaptive functioning
- **Liaison across the client's care network** is important, even vital, where multiple professionals, services or agencies are involved. This aims to model communication and 'working together', fostering communication, consistency and client safety (see Chapter 3, MDT Care).

Figure 4.1 Best Practice Guidance for the Treatment of Dissociation (adapted from Steele et al., 2017).

attachment complexity with the therapist. Some 'take home' best practice guidance for the treatment of dissociation is summarised in Figure 4.1. Together, this chapter has aimed to illustrate that with modest further knowledge and training, building on existing psychological therapy models, dissociation can be worked with. This enables the possibility of far greater numbers of clients receiving appropriate care and treatment within current service structures, to improve their recovery. While people with complex dissociation may well already be receiving care from mental health services, their particular needs may not be being adequately recognised, and their treatment therefore risks being less effective and their outcomes less hopeful than it could be otherwise. It is long overdue to incorporate these valuable changes into routine clinical practice.

Acknowledgements

With much gratitude and thanks to Helena Crockford, Melanie Goodwin, Nancy Borrett and Richard Colley for their contributions and comments on earlier versions of this chapter.

Chapter 5

Working with Children and Adolescents with Complex Dissociation

Lynne Ryan, Vicky Sutton and Melanie Goodwin

1. Introduction

This chapter provides information on how trauma-based dissociation specifically manifests in children and young people, reviews the existing evidence base, and outlines treatment implications. Due to the complexity and scope of this topic, it is not intended to be exhaustive, but to offer a starting point and summary, with signposts for further information.

The authors are aware that this chapter and the theories and experiences drawn upon, are predominantly from a Western, white, heterosexual centred perspective. There is an acknowledgment of the cultural bias, which reflects the absence of voices from other more diverse and often marginalised communities. Going forward, greater representation from professionals and people who experience dissociation is needed, in research and treatment. Henrich (2020) coined the term 'WEIRD' to describe Western Psychology (Western, Educated, Industrialised, Rich and Democratic) and yet less than 11% of the world's population come from this demographic (Thalmayer et al., 2021). Only when psychological research embraces inclusivity, can there be a broader understanding of potential differences in dissociative experiences, presentation and treatments, across different cultures (See Chapter 15, Cultural Considerations).

General definitions of dissociation, its history and evolution, have been covered in previous chapters, however, writings from the nineteenth century to the present, place childhood experiences as central to later adult trauma and dissociation pathology (Sinason & Potgieter-Marks, 2022). Despite growing acceptance of the links between early trauma and difficulties across the lifespan, a lack of recognition remains for the significance of childhood dissociation in clinical practice and research.

Where child dissociation has received attention, a child-focused perspective has often been lacking, with treatment defaulting to 'bolt on' adult information and methods, an 'adultomorphic' perspective which ascribes adult characteristics to children (Binet, 2023). However, as previous guidelines have stated, 'Without careful consideration of developmental issues, the simplistic application of treatment

DOI: 10.4324/9781003625650-7

approaches for adult dissociation to children, may be potentially dangerous to children' (ISSTD, 2004, p.1).

Children and young people, due to their developmental stages and attachment dependency, may be more likely to dissociate in response to trauma, since active defense mechanisms (e.g., fight or flight responses), may be less available to them. Paradoxically, their dissociative experiences may be less often recognised and treated, risking misdiagnosis, ineffective treatments and long-term impacts on mental health (Kezelman & Stavropoulos, 2020).

Adding a dissociation lens to the 4 R's of trauma informed care, (Realise, Recognise, Respond and Resist Re-traumatisation), (see also Chapter 1, Understanding; Chapter 2, Assessment; Chapter 17, Training), encourages clinicians working with children to become trauma- and dissociation-informed, increasing recognition, research and treatment effectiveness. This is also likely to be cost effective, financially but also in relation to the emotional and developmental costs borne by traumatised children, young people and their families, when dissociation remains hidden and untreated.

This chapter summarises definitions, epidemiology and models of understanding; it then outlines signs of dissociation in children and methods of screening and assessment. Treatment strategies and principles are discussed. Signposts to useful guidelines, literature and resources are offered. There is discussion of key misconceptions, issues of practitioner self-care, and suggestions for future research. This information is illustrated with clinical vignettes (either composite cases or used with permission and anonymised to ensure confidentiality) and Expert-By-Experience and 'child's voice' lived experience quotes. The interested reader is directed to Gómez and Hosey (2025) for a comprehensive overview of issues relating to the understanding, assessment and treatment of dissociation in children and young people.

2. Definitions of Child Dissociation

Defining childhood dissociation is the start of raising awareness and providing treatment. The following definitions normalise dissociation as a natural adaptive response and encourage recognition and treatment.

Wieland (2015) creatively describes dissociation as 'a secret trapdoor that allows a child who cannot physically escape from a terrifying experience, to mentally exit the situation … it is an instinctive biological survival mechanism … adaptive at the time of the trauma, later, it can interfere with the child's effectiveness in navigating the world' (p.14). Hasler (2022) additionally suggests, 'Dissociation is a spectrum… But it is only a disorder if it is not understood…' (p. 200).

DSM-5 takes a 'lifespan' perspective. It recognises the importance of developmental stages in presentation and treatment of trauma and that post-traumatic stress disorder (PTSD) manifests differently in children compared to adults. With their neurobiology still developing, trauma has a more pervasive and long-term influence on their understanding of the world, self-regulation and self-concept (DeAngelis, 2007).

Research Question: Explore further the links between ACES and child dissociation – the number of ACES, but also the types of ACES, where relational ACEs may be hypothesised to have a greater correlation with dissociation.

However, the significance of relational and attachment contexts for the development of dissociation, has been lacking in definitions focused on PTSD symptoms. Van der Kolk (2005) described 'Developmental Trauma', as trauma experienced by children at key developmental times, usually within caregiving relationships. The closeness of the child's relationship to the perpetrator, the child's age and the frequency of trauma perpetrated, are all significant factors. ACES research (Felitti et al., 1998) highlights the link between developmental trauma and later health problems and health risk behaviours.

Choi et al. (2017) found the dissociative subtype of PTSD (PTSD-D) differed between adolescents and adults, where adolescents tended to:

- Experience more dissociative symptoms such as daydreaming, forgetting things and blocking out thoughts
- Have more trauma experiences as well as more severe PTSD and problems with behaviour and
- Some teenagers with trauma and PTSD had dissociative amnesia.

For children and adolescents, problems associated with relationship difficulties and emotional dysregulation, often labelled as 'behavioural problems', may first bring them to the attention of mental health or other children's services, rather than underlying trauma and dissociation per se. Complicating this is the apparent similarity or overlap between childhood dissociative symptoms and other presentations including neurodiversity, conduct disorder and non-epileptic seizures. Dissociation can then be missed or mislabelled. The importance of this cannot be overstated, as trauma and dissociation interventions are very different compared to presentations which may respond to, for example, pharmacological interventions.

'Early recognition is vital. The cost is immeasurable in choosing to ignore a child's plight. As an adult managing DID, there is never a day that my abuse does not have an impact on me and my loved ones. Be it triggers, relationships, depression or seeking a continuous reassurance I have a right to live, it is exhausting.' **Expert-by-Experience**

---

3. Origins of Child Dissociation

The importance of the child's early experiences is a key factor in their subsequent use of dissociation as a defensive survival strategy. Dissociative symptoms in children have been associated with the following experiences:

- Traumatic experiences (Anda et al., 2006; Coons, 1996; Dell & Eisenhower, 1990; Hornstein & Putnam, 1992)
- Neglect (Brunner et al., 2000; Ogawa et al., 1997)
- Rejecting and inconsistent behaviour in caregivers (Liotti, 2006; Liotti, 2009; Mann & Sanders, 1994)
- Traumatic physical experiences such as medical treatment (Stolbach, 2005)
- Perpetrator introjects (defined as a dissociative part of the self that resembles and / or is a copy of the abuser, often a parent figure) (Potgieter-Marks, 2012; Vogt, 2012; Waters, 2016).

Loewenstein (2018) underscored the range of evidence which supports 'a powerful relationship between dissociation/Dissociative Disorders (DD) and psychological trauma, especially cumulative and/or early life trauma'. (p.20).

An attachment lens is key, with strong links between dissociation, early relational trauma, and the development of disorganised patterns of attachment. Explored further below, attachment theory provides a crucial framework when considering child dissociation. Sinason and Potgieter-Marks (2022) propose that a lack of secure attachment 'is a predisposing factor to the development of a dissociative disorder', while Mosquera et al. (2014) describe how, 'Disorganised early attachment generates vulnerability to extreme dissociation of the personality when combined with persistent childhood neglect and trauma. The caregiver is at the same time the source of protection and the source of danger.' For this, Epstein (2018) coined the term 'Scaregiver'.

The connection between disorganised attachment and dissociation supports the rationale for early intervention, beginning with perinatal mental health services (see Chapter 9) as does the suggestion that younger people may progress faster in treatment (Myrick et al., 2012).

4. Prevalence of Child Dissociation

While trauma specialists have a broad consensus that dissociation is common but often overlooked and underreported for people who have experienced trauma (Wilkinson & DeJongh, 2021), there is limited research evidence concerning the prevalence of dissociation in children (Hagan et al., 2015; Şar et al., 2012).

Martin et al. (2022) studied young children in foster care and found 45% scored on or above the clinical threshold on the Child Dissociative Checklist (CDC) (Putnam et al., 1993) suggestive of 'sustained pathological dissociation'. Martínez-Taboas et al (2006) studied a community sample of young people aged

11–17 years in Puerto Rico, using the Adolescent Dissociative Experience Scale (A-DES) (Armstrong et al., 1997). 4.9% reported dissociative symptoms in the pathological range. Hagan et al. (2015) studied a US sample of 140 high risk young children exposed to interpersonal trauma. Dissociative symptoms were assessed by interviewing biological mothers. A total of 24.3% presented with at least subclinical dissociation. Goffinet and Beine (2018) studied 93 adolescents hospitalised for mental health treatment in Belgium. A total of 33% self-reported pathological dissociative symptoms. They concluded that 'Dissociative symptoms were highly prevalent and typically had not been previously diagnosed clinically' with 'a link between accumulated exposure to various types of traumas and severity of dissociation.' Sun et al. (2019) found that of 66 young people with a first episode of psychosis, 36.4% also had clinical levels of dissociation.

Research Question: Explore the prevalence of dissociation in different child and adolescent populations.

This research, focusing mainly on Western samples, lacks a wider examination of how dissociative experiences may differ depending on cultural context.

5. Models of Understanding Dissociation in Childhood

Four core psychological theories are summarised below for their relevance in understanding and informing treatment models for childhood dissociation – Attachment Theory, Developmental Trauma, Polyvagal Theory and Interpersonal Neurobiology. (See also Chapter 1).

5.1 Attachment Theory

Infants come into the world with a biological imperative to attach to a caregiver (Bowlby, 1988). They are entirely dependent on their caregiver(s) to meet their every need – for comfort and emotional co-regulation, for sustenance to enable growth, for warmth and protection from harm. Attaching to caregivers who can respond to these needs ensures the infant's survival. How the caregiver responds, directly influences brain development (Gerhardt, 2004), and the development of internal working models for relationships going forward (Bowlby, 1988). For infants born into families where caregivers attune to the infant's internal states sensitively and consistently, the infant's brain becomes patterned for optimal healthy functioning (Schore, 2003).

Case Example: Harry was a bright, funny and charming 8-year-old. He attended therapy with his adoptive parents, who loved him dearly. Harry was creative, a talented musician who loved drama, arts and crafts. Often he was loving and affectionate towards his parents, telling them how much he loved them and how happy he was they were his 'forever mummy and daddy'. However, whenever they set boundaries or said 'no' to Harry's desires, Harry switched. He would verbally abuse his mother calling her dirty, lazy and stupid as well as physically attacking her. When he switched back to being 8-year-old Harry, he often had no memory of this and could not understand why his parents were so upset with him.

Where caregivers are neglectful or abusive, the same biological imperative to attach in order to survive continues, but the caregiver, by their actions or lack of action, is also a threat to that survival. The infant experiences an insurmountable biological paradox leading to disorganised patterns of attachment (Dutra et al., 2009; Hesse & Main, 2000). Dissociation serves as a survival response allowing the infant to maintain an attachment, in the face of abuse. Waters (2016) highlights the survival function of the dissociative response in allowing the child to segment intense, overwhelming feelings into different self-states, allowing the 'function in daily life' part of the child, to continue to attach and remain 'unaware' of the harm. She describes how 'to maintain the child's attachment to the parent, the child has to segment off the abusive experience along with feelings of abandonment, betrayal, rejection, loss of safety' (p.33). As a result, a child can behave in a loving and affectionate way towards the caregiver when in one particular state, then suddenly switch into an angry state, behaving with aggression and hostility. The child is observed vacillating between these rapidly switching self-states, with behaviour consistent with the seemingly chaotic responses of disorganised attachment patterns.

5.2 Developmental Trauma

Van de Kolk (2005) defined Developmental Trauma as capturing the enduring and pervasive problems resulting from relational trauma, in contrast to the single event trauma associated with PTSD. Children suffering relational trauma – repeated abuse and neglect by caregivers – experience significant difficulties across seven domains: attachment, biology, affect regulation, dissociation, behavioural control, cognition and self-concept.

5.3 Polyvagal Theory

Polyvagal theory (Porges, 2022) suggests that intrafamilial abuse results in the activation of both the infant's attachment behavioural system (social engagement system) as well as their defensive systems. The two systems function in opposition, approach and avoidance. If the threatening behaviour from the attachment figure is brief, the social engagement system is only temporarily shut down and then reactivated when the parent is in a more regulated state and able to repair. In the case of chronic traumatisation both systems remain activated simultaneously (Dana, 2018).

> '*When working with children who dissociate in therapy, we – the non-abusing, safe caregivers and I – often really celebrate the remarkable capacity the brain has to help babies to escape from unbearably painful experiences, so important when they are too little to run away and escape. It truly is a wonderful thing. This is the beginning of the therapeutic process which aims to help the child to understand themselves in a new way and take steps towards believing that all of their parts are loveable and can be integrated.*' **Vicky Sutton, Clinical Psychologist**

Whilst in a sympathetic state, cortisol prepares the body to *mobilise* into a 'flight or fight' survival responses, or if activating the parasympathetic dorsal vagal system, the infant's breathing and heart rate decreases, leading to an *immobilised* response (freeze, shut down). In infancy, the active 'fight / flight' response is unavailable to resolve the threat, leaving the infant in a sympathetic high activation freeze response or parasympathetic immobilised collapse response. As Fisher (2017, p.4) describes, 'When the source of danger *is* the attachment figure, the mind and body must find a way to maintain an attachment bond whilst simultaneously mobilising animal defense survival responses to protect the child. These two powerful innate drives (to attach and to defend) each remain highly activated, one drive dominating at times and then the other.' She described how, to enable continued functioning, there needs to be a strict separation between these innate survival responses. Dissociation provides the resolution to the conflict of both needing to seek and avoid attachment figures simultaneously. The process of 'splitting or fragmentation, allows for each instinct to be evoked independently of the other' (Fisher, 2017). Therefore, the part that is seeking attachment is split off from and functions separately from the part that wants to flee or freeze.

5.4 Interpersonal Neurobiology

Theories of interpersonal neurobiology, stress the importance of the quality of the relationship between child and caregiver in promoting the growth of neural pathways that regulate affect and create a stable sense of self. The infant's brain and consequently, their developing sense of self, is powerfully moulded, for better or worse, by parenting experiences (Sunderland, 2006; Waters, 2016). The caregiver who can attune to and respond empathically and sensitively to the needs of the infant, promotes adaptive connections within the brain. These attuned responses help promote an integrated mind. Conversely, caregivers who are unable to provide these attuned experiences and / or act in ways that traumatise the child, alter the trajectory of brain development in significant ways.

There is growing evidence of structural brain changes in adults with trauma histories who present with dissociation (Kearney & Lanius, 2022). The hippocampus, which plays a pivotal role in memory, learning and emotion, is smaller in volume. The hippocampus is involved in processing emotional experience into long-term memory and contextualising the experience in time and space. When impaired, the emotional experience remains unprocessed and reappears intrusively in flashbacks, nightmares, feelings of fear and threat, and somatic experiences (body memories). Fisher (2017) understands these unintegrated, unattached implicit memories as the split off, dissociated 'stuck in trauma' parts of the self that hold the traumatic experience.

Case Example: Simon was removed from his birth family home aged 10 months following severe physical abuse and suspected sexual abuse. He had no explicit memory for these experiences but the implicit memories, the fragments of disconnected sensory and bodily experiences, were clearly apparent through his psychophysiological responses to being parented by his non-abusing adoptive parents. The blueprint of these early relational experiences within his birth family were continually activated. Following triggering experiences such as the parents placing a limit or boundary around Simon's behaviour, he would scream at his adoptive father to stop hitting him (even though the father was standing some distance away) and scream at his mother to 'wake up' even though she sat beside him, holding his hand and speaking to him in reassuring tones. At age 13 years, Simon was still struggling to update his memory systems, despite living in safety in the present.

The theories highlighted, have been developed from a Western perspective and therefore are likely to contain some cultural bias. For example, several research papers have questioned the universality of Bowlby's Attachment Theory (Rothbaum et al., 2000). A biological imperative drives an infant to engage in attachment seeking behaviours towards their caregivers, however the particular patterns of behaviour may vary, depending on cultural context. In Western individualistic cultures, the infant is commonly raised within a nuclear family with greater emphasis placed on the relationship the infant has with one primary caregiver, a 'monotropic bond' (www.attachmentproject.com). However, in more collectivist cultures, there is greater emphasis on the quality of the infant's attachment with multiple caregivers. Sensitivity towards these cultural differences, mean erroneous judgements about the quality of the relationships based on expected norms from a Western perspective, are less likely.

6. Myths About Dissociation in Children and Adolescents

There are some common misconceptions regarding dissociation in children.

- **Dissociation is rare**: the prevalence of adult dissociation is better established (see Chapter 1), but epidemiological research is increasingly reporting significant rates of dissociation in children and young people, particularly in clinical samples (see Prevalence, above). Historically within children's services, a child has been unlikely to be screened for dissociation
- **Children do not experience significant or problematic dissociation**: complex dissociation in adults is understood to evolve in childhood, therefore it is important clinicians consider the early and developing signs for this differentially with other kinds of difficulty. Unless dissociation is recognised and addressed appropriately, sustainable change is unlikely
- **Dissociative children will all present in a similar way**: each child will be unique in the way their dissociation has developed and manifests. Children need age-appropriate assessments and will have their own ways of expressing their dissociative experiences
- **Dissociation always evolves because of abuse**: children may have experienced overt trauma but also important may be internal experiences of unbearable overwhelm, for example in the context of medical interventions, neurodiversity or emotional invalidation, lack of attunement or neglect within attachment relationships.

> **Child's voice**: *'Don't go in with assumptions. Don't assume every child's dissociation is the same – it's probably different for every child. Go in thinking dissociation will be different for every child, e.g., my sibling's dissociation was very different to mine, for example, his eyes would roll to the back of his head when he was dissociating, and he could physically move, whereas I felt stuck and frozen.'*

To summarise, dissociation arises as a survival response in children who have experienced enduring, complex developmental trauma, where animal defensive responses (engage, fight, flight, freeze) are either impossible or have put the child in further danger. The only resource left has been for the child to compartmentalise their experiences. Forner (2023), summarises this saying 'Dissociation is a normal response to abnormal events. It is the trauma that is abnormal, not dissociation or the person'.

7. Existing Practice Guidelines

A number of child-centred dissociation clinical guidelines and resources already exist:

The International Society for the Study of Trauma and Dissociation (2004) provides resources and training to promote understanding and treatment of child and adolescent dissociation. Their Frequently Asked Questions resources may prove particularly useful for practitioners new to the field (www.isst-d.org/resources/child-adolescent-treatment-guidelines/).

The European Society for Trauma and Dissociation (2017) offers guidelines for working with children and adolescents covering theoretical background, goals for treatment, and suggested training and qualifications for clinicians. Guidance is divided by age range – 0–4 years and 4-18 years – affirming that no child is too young or too old to receive treatment.

8. Identifying Dissociation in Children and Adolescents

> **Child's voice:** '*I don't think people noticed my dissociating – my parents realised when I was about 10 years old, when they could see I was not present, and I wouldn't be able to hear them when they spoke to me. My dissociation looked like I wasn't paying attention. I would also dissociate if I felt trapped, I would freeze. So if I wanted to leave the room because bad things were happening, I didn't feel able to physically leave, I would leave in my mind. No option felt right – to leave or to stay, so dissociation was an answer. I couldn't physically move but I found a way to remove myself.*'

Trauma-informed screening would ideally be standard for children presenting to health and social care services. Clinicians should be alert to signs and symptoms of dissociation, following up with specialist trauma and dissociation focused assessments where indicated (see Section 9 below).

8.1 Signs and Symptoms of Child Dissociation

Common signs of dissociation in children may include (ESTD, 2017):

- Have 'imaginary friends/persons', 'inside friends that nobody knows about', or talk about an 'invisible friend'
- Hear 'voices'
- Have a history of multiple unexplainable physical symptoms without organic basis
- Have amnesia (and may be perceived as lying)
- Have behaviour that rapidly changes from calm to aggressive, anxious, regressed or controlling
- Struggle to connect to reality while doing tasks at home or at school and prefer to move into fantasy

- Have reports from school regarding concentration problems, trance like states and learning difficulties
- Have inconsistent performance reported
- Have a history of self-harming, sexualised or aggressive and violent behaviour.

Cultural frameworks for dissociative phenomena should also be considered, for example the concept of 'possession'.

8.2 Categorisation of Signs and Symptoms

Wieland (2015) organises these signs into **four categories** – behavioural, emotional, cognitive and physical changes:

Case Example: B, aged 8, had a history of significant sexual abuse and domestic violence, perpetrated by her father. When introducing B to the therapy centre along with her mother, we entered a playroom furnished with a corner full of baby toys, dolls and equipment. B, suddenly dropped to the floor and crawled on her belly, uttering baby sounds. The mother looked at me in astonishment and stated, 'I don't know what she's doing?'. She called her name several times, and on the third occasion, B looked up, blinked, and rose to her feet, unaware of what had just happened. At the time, I did not know what to make of this 'aberrant' behaviour, which I assumed to be some kind of regression. However, through training and supervision, I understood that I had witnessed B's dissociative 'switch' into a younger dissociated baby state, triggered by the sight of the baby toys.

- **Behavioural changes:** often the most noticeable, should be carefully considered, particularly for children with a history of trauma, where 'regressed behaviour' may indicate the presence of a dissociated younger state
- **Emotional shifts:** emotions may be incongruous to the situation, or change rapidly, for example, a child suddenly beginning to laugh for no apparent reason or presenting as blank and shut down
- **Cognitive shifts:** a child may be competent in executing a task on one occasion but be unable to do so at another time. Internal voice-hearing, a relatively common dissociative experience in children, is included here

---

Practice Point: '*Voice-hearing is important to be aware of, since I have observed anxious and /or disbelieving responses to the child's disclosure of hearing voices. As children are supremely attuned to adults non-verbal, as* *well as verbal communication, particularly children who have experienced trauma, this risks shutting down the child's disclosure, and leaving them wary of revealing information about their internal world. As clinicians, we must manage our own reactions and responses and receive without judgement, shame or blame, whatever the child trusts to reveal.'* **Lynne Ryan, Counsellor**

Case Example: 12-year-old C was referred to a sexual abuse therapy service, after she suffered fainting fits in school without medical cause. Despite having functioned well for two years after disclosing sexual abuse, the fainting fits appeared suddenly. Her GP suspected a psychological cause. It took several months to understand C's behaviour, before a very logical explanation emerged. C had recently moved to high school, where her perpetrator, an older teenage male 'M', also attended. As there had been no criminal charges, there were no restrictions on M.

On first encountering M at school, C was confronted with a psychological threat to her life and promptly fainted – understandable as an adaptive, defensive, dissociative response. The school subsequently attempted to put in measures to prevent contact. However, C's knowledge that M was present in her school, meant her nervous system perceived a very real threat in the environment, resulting in C fainting *in anticipation* of encountering M, not only when she actually saw him. This triggered the frequent fainting episodes and medical referral. The school expressed powerlessness to place further restrictions on M in the absence of criminal charges – not an uncommon dilemma. The lack of psychological safety in C's environment, led to the decision for her to change school.

- **Physical difficulties:** these include physical symptoms with no medical explanations, for example an inability to feel pain, encopresis and enuresis without awareness, fainting spells or dissociative seizures. Differential diagnosis is important in clarifying medical disorders that may overlap in presentation.

8.3 Comorbid Mental Health Difficulties

Children experiencing dissociation often also have symptoms consistent with other mental health difficulties including obsessive-compulsive difficulties, disordered eating, post-traumatic symptoms, neurodivergence, depression or self-harm. These may be comorbid or may in fact be better explained by the dissociative presentation. Seeking a psychiatric diagnosis may be part of the multidisciplinary care of the child's mental health. A trauma-informed approach will, however, consider the child's current presentation within the context of their past experiences, where what may be categorised as 'disorders', are better understood as creative and adaptive strategies the child is using to survive. Accepting and being curious about the 'whole' child is therefore key.

8.4 Signals in Practitioner Counter-Transference

In addition to signs of dissociation present in the child, the therapist's own counter-transference responses and reactions, including thoughts, feelings and bodily responses, may be important clues to the presence of dissociation. These may include dissociative shut-down type experiences, such as feeling tired, sleepy or 'spacey'. Evidence of mirror neurons in the brain provide a mechanism for understanding how emotions and feeling states are thus shared (Rothschild, 2004).

Research Question: Explore therapists' internal experiences when working with childhood dissociation.

9. Screening and Assessment of Dissociation in Children and Adolescents

Directly assessing dissociation in children is essential to creating an accurate formulation to guide effective treatments. If the child has experienced early childhood developmental trauma, given the links to dissociation already outlined, it is better to ask, 'Why wouldn't dissociation be present?', rather than, 'Is dissociation present?'. Trauma and dissociation screening should therefore be standard in child health and psychological services including considering culturally-specific ways dissociation may present (see Chapter 15, Cultural Considerations).

9.1 Screening Tools

Child's voice: 'No one ever asked me or knew what was going on inside.'

Screening for dissociation will be a first step and may include standardised measures. Various child and adolescent tools specific to dissociation are available, and some trauma measures also include dissociation subscales. Some well-validated screening measures are listed in Figure 5.1:

Administering, scoring and interpretation of screening tools should be undertaken by suitably trained and qualified clinicians (ESTD, 2017).

Child Dissociative Checklist (CDC) (Putnam et al., 1993), designed to screen for dissociative symptoms in children 4–14 years old, is a 20-item observer-report measure completed by someone who knows the child well www.ce-credit.com/articles/102019/Session_2_Provided-Articles-1of2.pdf

The Child Dissociative Experience Scale and Post Trauma Inventory (CDES.PTSI) (Stolbach, 1997) is a 37 item self-report measure assessing trauma and dissociation symptoms in 7–12 years old. https://evemerrill.com/forms/DES_child.pdf

The Adolescent Dissociative Experience Scale (A-DES) (Armstrong et al., 1997) is a 30-item self-report measure assessing dissociative experiences in adolescents aged 11–18 years. www.emdrworks.org/Downloads/a-des.pdf

The Somatoform Dissociation Questionnaire (SDQ-20) (Nijenhuis et al., 1996) is a 20-item self-report measure for ages 16+, which focuses on somatic presentations of dissociation (see Chapter 2). www.enijenhuis.nl/sdq20

The Trauma Symptom Checklist for Children (TSCC) (Briere, 1996), a 54-item self-report measure for 8–16 year olds.

The Trauma Symptom Checklist for Young Children (TSCYC) (Briere et al., 2001), a 90-item carer report tool for children aged 3–12, both provide well-validated general trauma screening tools including a dissociation subscale.

Similarly, **the Achenbach forms** (Achenbach & Ruffle, 2000) include: **The Child Behaviour Checklist (CBCL)** for children aged 1–5 and 6–18; the **Teachers Report Form (TRF)** for children aged 6–18 and the **Youth Self Report (YSR)** for children aged 12–18.

Figure 5.1   Screening Tools for Child Dissociation

---

*'In my clinical experience, I am often amazed by how much children are willing to share, about their, often complex, inner worlds when I have been brave and curious enough to ask the 'right' questions. This does not come without risk for the child and their information must be handled with utmost sensitivity and care. Our responses, both verbal and, perhaps more importantly, non-verbal – their neuroception of us (Porges, 2022) – can have major implications for the child's future willingness to be vulnerable, engage in therapy and find a healing trajectory. It is crucial not to collude with the denial that can surround trauma and dissociation – **do not dissociate from the dissociation!**'* **Lynne Ryan, Counsellor**

9.2 Assessment and Formulation

Beyond initial screening, comprehensive assessment should include interviews, use of child-centred techniques such as drawings, play and projective activities, and direct observation. This latter includes intra-interview observation but also observing the child in other relationships, environments and systems, for example the school or family milieu, noting particularly that the nature of dissociation means children can present differently according to their environment.

Assessment should cover the child's current symptoms and triggers, current and past attachment relationships, their history including trauma, all within a systemic approach involving caregivers, school staff and other key adults / professionals. It should include asking dissociation-specific questions, even when dissociation may seem unlikely to be present. The assessment should be developmentally sensitive, and alert to the fact the child may not be functioning at their chronological age.

Case Example: 10-year-old Alice had experienced sexual abuse by her paternal grandfather. Dissociation seemed unlikely as Alice had lived in a loving birth family and the abuse had been understood to be infrequent across a short period of time. At assessment, Alice was asked 'Do you have friends inside that no one knows about?', and Alice described and drew several dissociative 'helper' parts. She had never disclosed these parts before and subsequent sessions revealed further parts. It also emerged her abuse had been extensive. These parts had enabled her survival of horrific abuse at the hands of a 'trusted' caregiver.

The possibility of experiences of pre-natal and perinatal trauma should also be considered (Potgieter-Marks, 2016) (see Chapter 9, Perinatal Mental Health). Sinason and Potgeiter-Marks (2021), propose that prenatal stress should be viewed in a similar way to other early life stressors. Music (2024) reiterates this, highlighting the impact of substances, intergenerational attachment issues and foetal programming.

An initial awareness of dissociative parts and working with the child's internal system (see Treatment Section below) is important throughout all stages of engagement.

Child's voice: 'If a child has been through trauma, they are more likely to dissociate because children want to survive. I would say if you look at a person who is dissociating, they look like they are physically in the room but mentally they are not. Their brain has taken them somewhere else that feels safer – each person will have a different place they go to. My place was a fantastical and fairy tale place inside – there were no people just me and a dog, I felt safer by myself, no humans. This started when I was in an unsafe family, my brain was trying to help me survive.' (N.B. this young person was reflecting on his earlier experiences after many years of therapy.)

'As a child no one asked me, "How are you?" I would not have had a language that could convey my sadness, distress, terror, isolation; even as an adult I struggle, no words feel big enough. My behaviour should have been a clue into my reality but no one was looking. I was regularly told I was sulking, miserable, selfish and what was deemed appropriate punishment handed out; a "whipped bottom" and then sexually abused. I cannot remember a time when I was not shaking inside with "hidden" anxiety.'
Expert-by-Experience

Comprehensive assessment leads to the development of a collaboratively developed psychobiosocial formulation, which can be shared, and guide interventions in each setting of the child's life.

An increase in social media awareness and discourse around dissociation and DID, particularly amongst younger people, may be experienced positively by some, but also present a complicating factor requiring careful consideration during assessment (Brand, 2024; Salter et al., 2025).

10. Treatment of Dissociation in Children and Adolescents

This section presents some key principles and then elaborates child-focused adaptations to the three-phased approach to treatment for trauma and dissociation.

10.1 Working Together

Treatment for dissociative children cannot occur in isolation. A key role for clinicians is to consult to and support the systems and networks around the child, bringing together the different experiences of the child in different settings, which may reflect dissociated parts of the child, all of which will need attending to. Importantly, the internal fragmentation of the dissociative child can be mirrored by the external system. Potgieter Marks (2017) summarised this 'professional fragmentation' as follows, 'The power of the structural dissociation in children should never be underestimated. Neither should the power of potential fragmentation in the adults around the child, family systems or organisations, be underestimated.' (p.10).

She argued for professionals to work to promote, 'cohesive systems around the child with an increased capacity to use cooperation and collaboration to assist the dissociative child on his/her way to integration.' (p.10). This includes families, carers, schools, health and social care professionals and so on.

10.2 General Therapeutic Stance

Treatment is primarily psychological. ESTD (2017) advises an eclectic and flexible therapeutic stance, which may draw on a number of therapeutic tools and approaches. Some examples include The Sleeping Dogs Method (Struik, 2019); Affect Avoidance Theory (Silberg, 2022); and The Star Theoretical Model (Waters, 2016). Whatever approach is used the relational style is important, being attuned to and interested in the child as captured by the PACE approach (Hughes, 2011) – being Playful, Accepting, Curious and Empathic.

10.3 Medication

There are no medications specifically for treating dissociative difficulties in children, although certain drugs may be helpful in managing associated symptoms such as anxiety, depression or ADHD symptoms. Stierum (2016) (quoted in Waters, 2016), concluded: 'Psychopharmacological interventions in the treatment of dissociative disorders in children and adolescents should be avoided when possible, but are sometimes necessary' (p.280), for example if symptoms of anxiety or depression become debilitating.

10.4 Costs of Treatment

Therapeutic work for trauma and dissociation is often costly in terms of time, finances, and the emotional reserves of all involved. However, these should be offset against the costs of not providing optimal treatment, including longer-term service utilisation via youth justice, mental and physical health services, and educational support (Oakwater, 2008).

10.5 Phased-based Approaches

The three-phased model of trauma treatment.is recommended as the overarching framework for treatment (see Chapters 2, 3, 4). The ESTD (2017) guidelines usefully summarise the child-specific goals for treatment in each phase:

- **Phase 1: Safety and stabilisation:** establishing safety for the child to the fullest extent possible, to recognise and prevent further trauma and traumatic re-enactments
- **Phase 2: Trauma processing:** providing ways for the child to process traumatic experiences, establishing integration of the dissociative states and enabling the child to develop an integrated sense of self
- **Phase 3: Recovery and integration:** re-integrating the child back into age-appropriate levels of functioning across all domains: cognitive, emotional, social and relational.

These phases are each discussed further below. It must be noted that the phases do not always progress sequentially, and safety and stabilisation are revisited throughout.

Additionally, progressing beyond Phase 1 to trauma processing may realistically not always be a possibility, either due to limited environmental or relational safety, or a lack of service-related resources. However, Phase 1 input may of itself still be of value by providing safe therapeutic relationships within which psychoeducation and regulation strategies are offered. These are not limited to the child-therapist relationship, but include therapeutic parenting and educational interventions. When therapy is available, even if limited, the experience of a positive therapeutic relationship can be crucially important in providing an often novel template of a healthy and secure relationship, something of value in itself which may lead to the child being more open to future therapy and help, when the situation allows.

10.6 Phase 1: Safety and Stabilisation

> *'I really wish more had been understood about the importance of Safety and Stabilisation when I first had therapy. I entered deep trauma work much too quickly without understanding the need for all of us to be resourced to cope with it. 'Trauma land' became our normal landscape for the next few years with no respite or an ability to contain it. It was a horrible time.'* **'Melanie and all', Expert-by-Experience**

Key components of Phase 1 work with children and adolescents, include the following:

a) Establishing safety (no apology is made for the repetition of this theme, which reflects its importance at the heart of trauma-focused therapy)
b) Psychoeducation
c) The importance of emotional regulation
d) Fostering the therapeutic relationship
e) Including the child's voice

> Often what the therapist thinks is important, I did not. As a 9-year-old, my priority was who would look after my rabbit Snowy if we had to go away from home, and would they be kind to her and not send her to the butchers to be eaten?' **Lizzie, 'I am 9'**

f) Including caregivers in the work

These six areas are each now elaborated further below:

a) **Safety** *is* the first phase of trauma therapy and the prerequisite to a child's engagement. As Van der Kolk (2014) emphasised, safe connections with other people may be the most important underpinning for mental health and meaningful lives. The groundwork for this is laid in Phase 1. It includes addressing:

- Physical safety within the child's current environments
- Relational safety with their primary carer/s and other adults
- Safety within the therapeutic relationship
- The internal 'felt' sense of safety within the child.

Struik's (2019) 'The Sleeping Dogs Method' outlined six 'tests' of safety, including measures and interventions which build or increase safety in readiness to engage in the trauma processing. Without safety, a child may need to keep their dissociative defenses intact. Levels of external and internal safety should be continuously assessed, and include the safety of the child's primary caregiver and their physical and emotional availability to the child.

A safety consideration specific to working with dissociation, arises when children are triggered into a dissociative state and lose their footing in the 'here and now' of day-to-day reality, reliving past experiences without awareness of the present. The child may become deeply confused as to whether experiences of abuse have been perpetrated by previous or current caregivers, sometimes leading to unsubstantiated allegations. Caregivers and therapist working together, can help ground the child and provide additional safety in bearing witness to the current reality. Clinicians must be mindful of the potential safeguarding implications of unsubstantiated allegations and disclosures, which may be helpfully reframed as 'a child's truth', which due to trauma and dissociation, has become a fragmented memory, with narrative, time, and place distorted. A thorough knowledge of the child's history helps to understand 'out of context' disclosures and trauma re-enactments. Practical tools such as risk assessments and safety plans should be incorporated into therapy agreements to strengthen safeguards.

Therapist safety is also a consideration here. Working with trauma and dissociation elicits strong positive and negative transference and countertransference reactions and bearing witness to serious trauma in the child's life risks secondary traumatisation. The need for self-awareness, self-care and adequate support is essential. Good, containing supervision, team working and up to date training and professional development, provide vital buffers to resource the clinician (Aquarone, 2020; Burton & Lane, 2001).

b) **Psychoeducation** is a key aspect of stabilisation. It can assist the child and their caregivers to understand:

- Trauma and its impact, contributing to 'normalising' trauma and dissociation responses and facilitating shifts in the child's core beliefs from 'It's all my fault', 'I'm bad,' 'I should have done something,' 'I'm crazy,' to 'My clever brain & body helped me survive', 'My behaviours are creative ways to cope with what happened to me'. Information should be tailored to the child's age and stage of development and functioning, and also cultural background, including creative tools and techniques, with concepts such as brain development, the window of tolerance and polyvagal theory, or more culturally meaningful explanations and resources, such as prayer and spiritual beliefs. Early introduction, can offer prompt relief through better understanding of present experiences, 'illogical' and involuntary trauma responses, and how survival takes precedence over logical thinking

- What to expect from the *process* of therapy, the different stages and what they may consist of
- The activities and aims of the interventions used

Child's voice: *'I could only remember negative things about my life and I thought it was my fault. This got reinforced in each placement – I thought it must be me that's the issue. Even now I sometimes get that feeling, even if it's very rarely. If a child is helped to understand themselves, they can understand the behaviour is not their fault.'*

- The field of child trauma and dissociation has developed a variety of toys, books, videos and other psychoeducational materials. For example, Russian dolls (also called nesting dolls or matryoshkas) provide a useful metaphor to illustrate different parts contained within one body. Other toys with a 'whole' made up of parts, such as jigsaws or puppets, may also be useful. A therapeutic toolbox containing a number of resources is useful, and should respect and reflect the child's uniqueness, cultural and racial heritage and any additional needs, such as disability and neurodivergence. Often children develop their own metaphors and tools to make sense of their experiences
- Creative methods such as drawing, sand tray, clay, paint, movement, sensory and body activities, and use of metaphor, may be used in playful, age-appropriate ways.

One adolescent used a blank jigsaw to draw his brain and the 'parts' inside. This inspired the 'Jigsaw Brain' story. Explaining the three-phased approach to treatment can be done using the 'Sailing Through Therapy' resource. This visual resource incorporates the metaphor of the therapy river to illustrate the three-phased approach with resources and tools to use in the therapeutic process. (See Chapter 5, Online Resources (www.routledge.com/9781041038450) for both these tools.)

Case Example: Resourcing the Child. In addition to co-regulation with her parent in the session, Sarah benefited from a range of other tools. These helped her stay within her 'window of tolerance' during therapy helping her make sense of her traumatic past and the protective roles her dissociative parts played in her young life. She regularly chewed strong flavoured gum, sipped water and wobbled on her cushion. However, her favourite regulating tool was her 'ventral vagal playlist'. Sarah loved music and developed a play list of songs matching her different nervous system states. Sarah practised moving 'up and down her poly vagal ladder' (Dana, 2018) by playing different songs reflecting how her body and mind felt during different emotional states. This increased recognition helped her spot more quickly when moving into a 'dorsal state', playing first a tune which helped her express this feeling, followed by one which helped her move into a more regulated state of safety and connection.

c) **Emotional regulation skills:** The Blue Knot Guidelines (Kezelman & Stavropoulos, 2019, 2020) emphasise the importance of building the skills and capacity to self-regulate before attempting to process complex trauma. There can be pressure, real or perceived, to shortcut this essential phase – from referrers, commissioners, caregivers, clients themselves – with urgency to 'get on with the therapy', or to 'fix the child'. This can be translated as undertaking trauma processing to complete therapy 'as quickly as possible'. Attempting trauma work too soon, however, risks precipitating overwhelming responses and re-traumatisation.

Strategies to build emotional regulation include enabling the child to become more aware of bodily sensations and manage hyper-arousal and hypo-arousal. Perry (2009, 2020) emphasises brain stem regulation in his Neurosequential Model of Therapeutics (NMT), and advocates that interventions begin at the lowest level of brain dysfunction, moving sequentially up to cognitive levels. Interventions aim to change neural networks via 'patterned, repetitive input,' using somatosensory activities the child finds rewarding, delivered within relationship. This may include the use of movement, dance and music.

'There is a knowing, whether it as a child, an adult or alter, when they are with someone who believes and validates their reality; they are respectfully interested and gently inquisitive about them; they are kind and show real caring in the moment. You may not be able to offer long term therapy but being believed can be a big cog in the turning wheel, never under-estimate the gift you are offering. Early recognition means the abuse STOPS. Be the one who "gets the child". The "unspoken magic in the room" – the attunement – is everything.' **Melanie Goodwin, Expert-by-Experience**

d) **Fostering the therapeutic relationship:** It is widely accepted that regardless of model, theoretical orientation, tools or interventions used in therapy, the therapeutic relationship is key to effective change. As Nuñez et al. (2022) stated, 'a positive therapeutic relationship facilitates early changes in the motivation of children and caregivers, and provides them with a healing, relational experience as it develops. A positive parent-therapist relationship is also key for changes to further progress'.

> **Child's voice:** 'The child needs to know the adult understands them. For me I felt no one really knew me. Social services didn't know what was best for me and my siblings, as they didn't know or understand us. If they don't know you, there isn't a feeling of care. It's important to feel someone cares, not letting children down – I had lots of people and placements and they start to feel 'no one cares' or that 'it's my fault, something is wrong with me'.'

Including the child's voice: Children and adolescents are often neither the instigators nor the drivers of their own therapy. Working on consent issues, power imbalances and the differing agendas of the child and their systems, is often challenging. For example, when seeking the child's wishes and feelings, these may need balancing between their 'needs' vs their 'wants'. Good practice guidelines facilitate this process, particularly for those involved in health and social care systems. The protective or defensive nature of dissociation may additionally contribute to children 'not wanting' therapy, no matter how pressing their need. Psychoeducation can help to raise a child's awareness of trauma and its impact now and in the future, and increase their motivation to engage with help (Struik, 2019).

e) **Including caregivers in the work:** The child usually has multiple relationships within multiple systems: the caregiver/child relationship, the family system, community, school, medical and social care teams, their cultural contexts etc. The work with children needs to reflect this holistic reality and it is not recommended to work with the child in isolation, but rather have a trauma-informed, collaborative, empowering and strengths-based approach, recognising that the **safe** caregiver is the child's most valuable resource and a powerful agent of healing. A therapist may spend one hour per week with the child compared with caregivers, family members, teachers etc. who have extensive contact and influence, in effecting change. This may mean directly involving caregivers in the child's therapy, a significant difference of working with children compared to adults.

If safety is sufficient, the therapist can work to build a trusting relationship with caregivers and provide them with psychoeducation to support the therapeutic process. The caregivers themselves may then act as sources of safety and as 'co-therapists' (Hughes, 1997), co-regulating the child within and outside of therapy sessions.

This further serves to strengthen the attachment relationship (Golding & Hughes, 2012). The 'Star Theoretical Model' for working with child dissociation (Waters, 2016), includes family systems theory and highlights the importance of 'building a secure attachment with the parents as an anchor for traumatised children to be able to release dissociative defenses and face the horrors of the past traumatic life'.

Case Example: Creating Safety with a Parent: Kerry adopted Emily at 5 years old. From the first day, Emily rejected any attempt Kerry made to love and care for her. She felt Emily knew exactly how to 'push her buttons', to say the things that would cause her maximum pain and keep her at 'a safe distance'. For example, Emily once told her mother, 'God knew you would make a crap mother, that's why he made sure you could never have children of your own!!'. Kerry held a deep Christian faith and Emily's words went deep inside her body to her most vulnerable parts. Understandably, Kerry had moved into a place of 'blocked care' (Hughes & Baylin, 2012), a psychological state of self-protection. Working with Kerry in therapy, she addressed her own pain and became open once again to empathise with Emily's pain. She could then provide the safety Emily needed within and outside therapeutic sessions.

Unfortunately, before accessing therapy, caregivers have often lived for years with the child's intense, distressed behaviour, leaving them feeling helpless and hopeless. The therapist is uniquely placed to scaffold caregivers to understand the child's behaviours with a trauma and dissociation informed lens, fostering empathy for the child, and facilitating commitment to an often difficult therapeutic journey.

When engaging caregivers, it is also necessary to ensure their psychological safety and consider if they have unresolved primary trauma (Hesse & Main, 1999). They may need personal therapy to avoid risking re-traumatisation by witnessing and supporting their child's therapy. Many caregivers carry secondary trauma as a result of living with their child's trauma and this should also be addressed.

10.7 Phase 2: Trauma Processing

Key aspects of Phase 2 include:

a) Facilitating the processing of trauma memories
b) Working with the child's dissociative parts
c) Integration and/or internal cooperation between dissociative parts

These are elaborated further below.

a) **Processing trauma memories.** Trauma processing is a collaborative process where the therapist assists the client to find ways to externalise their internal world, in order to acknowledge and validate the trauma experience, before exploring it within the safety of the therapeutic relationship and in doing so, the trauma is made sense of, before being integrated into the client's experience.

Silberg (2022) suggests successful processing involves activating multiple brain functions originally associated with the traumatic event, under new calmer circumstances, providing desensitisation to this originally overwhelming material. Perry (2020) suggests traditional talking / cognitive therapies may not activate the necessary brain areas required for successful processing. Haslar and Hendry (2017) emphasise the importance of creative therapies in trauma processing with children, describing creative therapies as 'brain wise interventions'.

Blaustein and Kinniburgh (2010) emphasise that for a child to safely explore memory, they must be sufficiently able to regulate their affects and physiology, feel safe enough within the therapeutic relationship and have relative stability in their wider life circumstances.

Silberg (2022) summarises the components therapy should attend to during the processing of traumatic material, within the context of a validating relationship either with the therapist or jointly with a loving caregiver.

- Content of the traumatic event
- Sensorimotor experiences associated with the event
- Exploring the event's meaning for the child
- Affects such as anger, shame, fear, sadness, abandonment and loneliness
- Mastery experiences that counter feelings of powerlessness.

> '*As we began to trust we tested how safe our therapist was by asking him to hold our doll/baby. He carefully and genuinely sat cradling her in his arms for months. We were terrified at the start but gradually, very little ones felt safe enough to come and talk. It was because he was kind. Eventually we trusted our therapist enough to go to the very darkest places which meant we had to let go, but we knew he could keep us safe and get us back when it was time to go home. It took a long, long time but we can all still feel that trust, it was new to us.*' **Expert-by-Experience**

b) **Working with Dissociative States or Parts.** Identifying the dissociative 'states' or 'parts' within the child is integral to successful therapy, since they developed in response to trauma and often hold the unbearable pain of these experiences. During assessment, a child may give verbal information about their 'dissociative system,' as in the vignette about Alice; or they may convey this more behaviourally, for example switching between states or parts. The clinician should remain alert, curious and non-judgemental to these signs, aware this process will be gradual and depend upon the child's perceived safety with them.

During Phase 1: Stabilisation, a shared language will develop around parts of the self, e.g., 'I hear that part of you needs to… stay awake at nighttime… hide food in your wardrobe…. hit and kick your brother' etc. Often children reveal parts over time. Alice initially disclosed three 'friends inside', that no one else knew about. Each part had helped her at the time of the abuse and continued to help her in the present. She later revealed several other parts that held different experiences and had different roles. One acted as an 'internal mother' who created a barrier to repairing Alice's attachment with the external 'real life' mother who inadvertently had not protected her daughter from the abuse. It is important to be aware of such potential roles and their impact on progress in therapy.

Waters (2016) suggests 'self-states may be formed depending upon the nature of the traumatic events and the psychological impact on the child. Some of the more common self-states are helpers / rescuers or hero figures, maternal figures, affective states…' (p.182). She also quotes Vogt's (2012) description of perpetrator introjects as, 'complex psychological models that were formed when the child was forced to manage boundary violations by an aggressor, and unconsciously internalised the toxic information contained in the violent scene' (p.180).

Therapy needs to understand the child's dissociative system and accept and work with all parts of the child. Twombly (2000) suggests that dissociative parts may perform in 'scripted ways' which helped the child survive traumatic experiences. Understanding this can help therapists maintain their curiosity and compassion when horror and dismay may be their more natural response.

Once the internal system is identified, the child's awareness is encouraged while working to foster internal cooperation between parts. Tools which can help include the Fraser Table Technique (Fraser, 2003). This involves creating a meeting place for the various parts of the self to present safely. Scenarios may be created using sand tray miniature figures, soft toys placed around a table, drawings, or using metaphors such as of a football team or dance group.

Therapeutic stories may also be utilised (Naish et al., 2017; Sunderland & Hancock, 2003). Van der Hoech's (2022) story, *Beastie, Baby and the Brand New Mummy / Daddy*, gives meaning to the experience of dissociation in children, as does Schofield's (2021) *Our House*, an illustrated storybook using the metaphor of a house to demystify DID.

As the child connects the characters within these stories to their own personal experiences, they may begin co-creating their own story. These stories may include the 'telling' of their own traumatic experiences which have become 'stuck' inside their brains and bodies. This process of becoming 'unstuck' is not necessarily verbal, and stories can be spoken, written with words, or told through pictures, sand play and role play. The use of bilateral stimulation (BLS), www. choosingtherapy.com/bilateral-stimulation/, for example using EMDR buzzers (tools providing physical stimulation on alternating sides of the body) alongside 'telling', can aid the integration of affective and reflective experiences.

Case Example: Simon had no words to describe his traumatic experiences. Removed from his birth family at 10 months, his experiences of abuse and neglect were stored as non-verbal implicit memories, with feelings and sensory experiences stored within his body / nervous system. Asking him questions about 'what happened?', he could give no verbal response. However, asking Simon to draw his experience, to not think too deeply but to draw whatever came into his mind, he was able to produce highly detailed images which he could then find the words for. From the many pictures he drew, along with the reports in Social Work files, we could create a story which made sense to him, and the deeper processing of these experiences could then begin.

Events happening in the present may also hold clues to past traumatic events and exploring these may provide a 'door' to the past event. Often children are referred to services due to 'symptoms' or 'behaviours', which are actually rooted in past events, the imprints of which are making life difficult in the present for the child or those around them. A case example of how this manifested and was treated in the trauma processing phase, incorporating creative methods, body work, EMDR, and consolidating stabilisation, is given below. Please note this example is a brief 'snapshot', taken within a child's therapy journey and as this work is often complex and multi-layered, it gives only a small insight into how early trauma can continue to interfere with a child's present and future development.

Case Example: Trauma Processing. 10-year-old S was having difficulty in school and his English teacher had reported 'disruptive' behaviour. Using creative methods and BLS, provided by 'buzzers', S was able to use miniatures in the sand to recreate the English lesson. Using an EMDR technique, 'The Floatback' (Browning, 1999), S was asked, 'When you look at the sand picture, what do you feel now? And where do you feel it (emotions / sensations), in your body? Let your mind go backwards to the first time you felt that'. S then created a new sand scene with himself as a small baby with a powerful large male figure standing over him. This was the identification of a 'touchstone memory', a memory that laid the foundation for the current problem.

Over several sessions and sand trays, S was able to make sense of a pre-verbal experience of verbal abuse and witnessing violence from his birth father to his mother. The loud deep voice of the English teacher had triggered these early memories, eliciting feelings of terror and a flight response in class, a response disruptive in the present, but potentially adaptive in the past.

In addition to the sand tray and BLS, S was encouraged to allow his body to do what it was unable to do at the time – complete the flight response, through running movements (Levine & Kline, 2006). In this multi-modal way, S was able to process this early preverbal trauma and was no longer triggered by the English teacher's voice

Child's voice: *'For a child with lots of unexpressed anger, punching and kicking and movement is helpful. EMDR gets your brain moving and working and it's helpful to get you talking. BLS can be done in lots of ways and walking is something I found helpful.'*

c) **Integration and/or internal cooperation of dissociative states or parts.** If trauma processing is effective, spontaneous integration of dissociative parts may occur leading to observable improvements in symptoms and behaviours (ESTD, 2017). However, integration is not necessarily an intended goal of therapy and may not be the client's wish. In some cases, developing a more cooperative internal system, may be the primary goal.

In child and adolescent therapy, integration is part of a complex process which includes internal co-operation, gratitude to the parts, trauma processing and integration in the true sense involving incorporating those part's skills and resources into the whole child. This

process is never about dismissing, diminishing or 'getting rid' of parts - which is indeed not possible, as the 'part' is essentially 'part' of the child.

Case Example: *Child L who engaged in therapy from the ages of 3–7 years, had multiple parts whose roles were to protect her, either by fending off others or by keeping her hidden from danger. One part who had been instrumental in keeping her safe in the abusive home, named 'Fighty', represented her much needed armour, underneath which lay multiple sexual abuse experiences. Once this abuse had been processed, over many therapy sessions and several years, 'Fighty' was integrated, given the new role of being calm and renamed, 'Chill'.*

10.8. Phase 3: Recovery / integration

> **Child's voice:** '*Finding out who you are is a big part of therapy, you may have been made to be someone you're not or told lies. Therapy has helped me to understand how and why I reacted and behaved in some situations. I can now be me – the me I was born to be.*'

This phase of trauma work also needs careful attention. Children who have bravely processed their trauma and integrated their dissociative parts, need time to adapt to their new reality, catch-up developmentally, practise new skills, build on their strengths, reinforce positive beliefs and develop a 'post-trauma' identity.

> '*I do not think enough credence is given to this stage. The further away we got from being traumatised most of the time, it became an alien landscape. Me, as the outside part, had to learn not to wait to be told from inside what to do. I had to become assertive while also checking in if it was OK. It was a major shift from being a relatively passive passenger to becoming the main driver. The high adrenaline levels had kept us moving at a rapid pace without having to push ourselves, a bit like free fall; now I have to check energy levels: are we tired? Can we do this? It is a completely new way of being for all of us. I am the main part with a complete supporting cast that trusts me and only needs me to internally support them at times of great distress or uncertainty. We are whole, not integrated. Now we have the ability to think things through, not be a reaction, this is so good, normal and makes us all happy.*'
> **Expert-by-Experience**

When trauma is processed, significant shifts in a child's behaviours and symptoms may be noticed. However, as with each phase in trauma work, the final phase does not always run smoothly. The child may need additional help to catch up academically and with missed developmental stages. They may need scaffolding to build new relationships or redefine old ones. Attachment work with caregivers may need to continue. Opportunities should be sought to assist the child to make peer relationships and build skills in areas previously not possible.

One major consequence of trauma can be avoidance – of affect, of trauma triggers or reminders, and of interpersonal relationships. The human cost of this is immeasurable and the child's world shrinks accordingly in order to survive. In this way, trauma may be seen as a 'thief', stealing joy, time and the child's innate capacity to connect and experience reward in relationships. This may not spontaneously reverse when trauma is processed and therefore needs actively addressing, at the child's pace and with support from the child's significant adults. Caregivers may also need help adjusting to this new world.

Case Example: Josie, 11 years old, was a very 'frozen' child prior to therapy and perceived as shy and quiet. However, after her trauma had been processed, she found her true voice and revelled in using it! This was not always received well by the adults in her world, who had become used to her (trauma-based) compliance. They needed help to recognise that this change was positive, that she was now able to express her needs and wants, and that they had a new role to assist her to do so appropriately and to then ensure those needs were met in healthy ways.

The frequency of therapy sessions may be reduced as the ending approaches, to empower the child to try out new skills and gain confidence. This should be negotiated in flexible and child-centred ways, which respects the child's needs may fluctuate over time.

Case Example: Jessica, 15 years, was reluctant and afraid to end therapy. The analogy of taking off the stabilisers when learning to ride a bicycle made sense to her. The time had come for the stabilisers to be removed, to test how she would manage. There might be some 'wobbling' initially, but with practice, her confidence and skills would improve until she no longer needed her therapist.

Child's voice: You can't do it (therapy), by yourself, but no one can do it for you so take the opportunity.

---

11. Practitioner Care

Working therapeutically with children who have experienced developmental trauma and present with complex trauma and dissociation, can be challenging and requires particularly robust scaffolding and support. One difficulty is knowing which part of the child is showing up to therapy, which parts are engaged in the process and which are not (Fisher, 2017).

Some practitioners may feel drawn to this work through their own experiences of trauma, attachment and healing, and can feel triggered or re-traumatised. Ongoing personal therapy may help protect the therapeutic process from unresolved trauma.

Additional risks for practitioners include lack of support and dysfunction within the work environment. The term 'blocked care' (Hughes, 2011) can apply to professionals as well as caregivers. The most compassionate, sensitive, committed professionals with high expectations (both of themselves and their clients), may be particularly vulnerable to painful feelings of failure. Good self-awareness and self-care, supported by clinical supervision and continuing professional development, are essential.

Not every clinician can at all times work with trauma and dissociation, for a range of valid reasons. Each therapist has their unique skills and strengths, as does each child. One clinician strength is recognising when to refer on to another service / clinician.

Research Question: What personal and professional factors enable clinicians to work effectively with child trauma? Are there factors which make it more difficult for clinicians to undertake this work?

Despite the challenges, this work also offers hope, immeasurable reward, and the potential for vicarious resilience (Killian et al., 2017) – 'The positive effects on helping professionals who witness the healing, recovery, and resilience of persons who have survived severe trauma in their lives.' (Schwartz, 2021, p.32).

12. Summary

Dissociation is an amazing, adaptive strategy that serves a vital purpose in enabling humans to survive traumatic experiences. For a child who has experienced developmental trauma or chronic adversity, the most adaptive response may be dissociation, particularly when their early developmental stage means active survival responses, such as fight and flight, cannot be mobilised.

The chapter has summarised definitions, origins, myths, theories, research and guidelines pertaining to child dissociation. It has outlined pathways for screening, assessment and treatment. The three-phased model of trauma treatment has been emphasised as the overarching structure, and key concepts have been highlighted and explored, including: the importance of therapeutic relationships, working with the child's external system, establishing safety, psychoeducation, emotional regulation, the child's voice, trauma processing, working with dissociative parts, recovery and therapist care. The authors are grateful for the brave contributions allowing the inclusion of clinical vignettes, the child's voice and the voice of the experts by experience, to illustrate the complex range of theories and concepts.

Moving forward, questions for further research have been proposed. The limitations of the cultural bias of the authors and the field in general, is acknowledged, with a call for perspectives that address this.

Child dissociation remains an emerging field in terms of recognition, research and practice. However, dissociation is becoming increasingly accepted and studied, with effective treatment interventions emerging. This work will be needed as long as childhood trauma remains a fact. We should acknowledge the bravery and resourcefulness of traumatised children and young people. We should advocate for the provision of timely, effective care and therapy, to provide the means for their recovery, to lead integrated, fulfilling lives.

Finally, we offer a humble reminder that a clinicians' education about trauma and dissociation is never complete and every client teaches us something new. We are privileged to walk the healing journey alongside children and adolescents who have survived life changing, life threatening, traumatic experiences. A child may be trusting us with their life stories and so with their lives, and nothing is more important or powerful. Hope does exist for real change and improvement and this chapter has aimed to provide a summary and starting point for clinicians to grow their confidence in engaging in this meaningful, rewarding work, discovering the joy of vicarious resilience.

Acknowledgements

With grateful thanks to Dr. Stuart Mitchell for his comments on an earlier version of this chapter.

Chapter 6

Establishing Safeness

Working with Safety Concerns and Trauma-Related Dissociation

Paul Langthorne and Richard Barber

Working with safety concerns is often an integral component of working with people who experience trauma-related dissociation. Safety concerns can be wide-ranging; of varying levels of intensity and severity; and may include self-harm and suicidality or harm to others. The high prevalence of safety concerns, likely explain the high rates of people with complex dissociative difficulties accessing acute-care and inpatient mental health services (Simeon & Putnam, 2022).

1. Common Forms of Safety Concerns Associated with Trauma-Related Dissociation

1.1 Self-harm and Suicidality

People who present with trauma-related dissociation are more likely than other groups to present with self-harm and increased suicidality. Up to 86% of people meeting criteria for a Dissociative Disorder (DD) report a history of non-suicidal self-injury (Foote et al., 2008) and engage in such self-injury more often, with more methods and an earlier age of onset than other psychiatric groups (Saxe et al., 2002). Regarding suicide attempts, several studies have shown trauma-related dissociation predicts suicide attempts (Brokke et al., 2022; Rabasco & Andover, 2020) and that the presence of a DD is a greater predictor of multiple suicide attempts than other psychiatric diagnoses, including PTSD and Emotionally Unstable Personality Disorder (Foote et al., 2008).

1.2 Harm to Others

Sensationalist media portrayals depict people experiencing trauma-related dissociation as a risk to the public. As well as creating stigma (Snyder et al., 2024), such stereotypes can compound people's own fears about their internal world (e.g., *'my anger is dangerous'*).

The evidence suggests the general risk of harm to others is not raised in people presenting with trauma-related dissociation. In a sample of people meeting criteria for a DD, lifetime prevalence of perpetration of sexual coercion or assault towards

DOI: 10.4324/9781003625650-8

a partner were reported by only 2% of clinicians and 4–7% of patients (Webermann et al., 2014). Likewise, Webermann and Brand (2017) did not find raised rates of criminal justice contacts over a preceding 6-month period.

2. Safeguarding

Safeguarding concerns can be a major factor for people who experience trauma-related dissociation. Such concerns may be current and/or historical in nature and when present may need to be prioritised as part of any treatment plan.

2.1 Ongoing Abuse

> *'It's so difficult for people who have experienced childhood trauma to know if their adult intimate relationships are normal, good or not. I had been married for 18 years and was only when I was talking to a friend who happened to be a clinical psychologist about a difficulty in my marriage that she was able to point out I was being financially, emotionally and sexually abused. I thought it was normal to be raped every night, my salary siphoned into his account, to be kept away from friends and not allowed to get my hair done. And once someone provides this perspective, another set of traumas then need to be processed!'* **Sally Adams, Expert-by-Experience**

Survivors may require significant levels of support to be effectively safeguarded from ongoing abuse. Clinicians should be aware of the nuances of coercive control (Hill, 2020; Salter, 2012) and traumatic bonding (Doychak & Raghavan, 2023) and the multiple barriers people face when attempting to extricate themselves from abusive relationships (Miller, 2018).

The rates of revictimisation in adult intimate partner relationships is high for people who experience trauma-related dissociation. For example, Webermann et al. (2021) reported most people meeting criteria for a DD had experienced emotional (60.8–75.6%), physical (26.1–48.9%) or sexual (35.9–44.4%) abuse in the context of such relationships.

Survivors from marginalised communities may face specific issues. For example, individuals from a South Asian background who report ongoing abuse occurring from family or community members risk alienation from their community, or consequences that will befall their whole family or community (Payton, 2014; Sawrikar, 2020). Survivors of abuse from Black or Afro-Caribbean backgrounds may be less likely to disclose abuse due to a legacy of systemic neglect from authorities or due to awareness of being disbelieved due to cultural stereotypes (Goff et al., 2014; Hurcombe et al., 2023).

Some people who have been exposed to familial and/or organised childhood sexual abuse may continue to be at risk in adulthood of ongoing abuse from the same individuals (McMaugh et al., 2024; Salter, 2017). McMaugh et al. (2024) found therapists working with survivors of such abuse reported that the abuse was characterised by its sadistic nature; often involving multiple perpetrators; and links to organised abuse. Factors such as enmeshed and disorganised attachment to the perpetrator; symptoms of severe dissociation; having absent, abusive or non-protective mothers; and social isolation were all found to impact on a person's ability to seek help for ongoing abuse in adulthood (McMaugh et al., 2024).

Perpetrators of such abuse may deliberately use tactics to maintain a state of entrapment and silence (Epstein et al., 2011; Hanson, 2025). Such tactics may include:

- 'Conditioned' loyalty to the group, including the use of extreme forms of abuse/torture to enforce compliance
- Threats/acts of further harm should the person speak out (Miller, 2018)
- If the person has been coerced to harm others, the person may view the group as their only source of 'belonging' (Miller, 2018). The moral injury this creates for the victim coerced into actions that go against their own personal values is very significant (Hanson, 2025)
- Reliance on group members for financial/social support.

'We experienced ongoing abuse for an incredibly long time, despite being in therapy and starting to learn about how we are part of a system. There are strong amnesic barriers between some parts in our system; and, unbeknownst to us, these parts were being triggered into old roles of compliance, submission and participation in our abuse. Whilst some younger parts would insist it was still happening; it was not clear to anyone whether what they were saying related to the present time; or whether they were stuck in 'trauma time' and things just felt like they were happening now.

A few years ago, there was a very violent incidence of sexual abuse by one of our perpetrators... Fortunately, some parts were able to tell our therapist what had happened, and she was able to make the mental health team aware. This prompted a slow realisation within our whole system that things had to change and that it was not safe for anyone in our system to see our family. It also triggered greater support from mental health services around safeguarding and meant we were able to change our name and find new accommodation that was safe.

We hope our story opens people's eyes to the possibility of ongoing abuse that is very likely to be unknown to most of a system that is experiencing it. Please pay close attention whenever a person you support with DID accesses

> *healthcare, they may be trying to tell you or those treating them something that is not immediately obvious; or the primary need for treatment.'* **Liv et al., Expert-by-Experience**

Within the context of ongoing organised abuse there are also reports of threats being made to clinicians (Miller, 2018; Salter, 2012). Working with people who are entrapped in such abusive situations can be very distressing and isolating for clinicians (McMaugh et al., 2024). Access to appropriate professional support, training and supervision is essential for people working with such abuse.

Expectations of society for adult children to offer care or support for elderly family members can also make it difficult for people to step away from harmful relationships.

> *'My mother abused me and took me to be ritualistically abused from a baby to a teenager. Over my adulthood she continued to control me coercively whilst the other parts of me were in constant terror mode, frozen in silence and be a good girl modality. Therapy for me came late in life and as we were able to process and break free from the shackles of heinous abuse, she got an early diagnosis of Alzheimer's, and social services requested I take over as Legal Power of Attorney (LPA). The legal system, alongside our own desire to be a kind daughter keeps us locked in an abusive relationship until she dies.'* **Sally Adams, Expert-by-Experience**

2.2 Non-recent Abuse

People who experience trauma-related dissociation have typically been victims of very serious criminal offences by people who may continue to pose a risk to children, and the public at large. When disclosures are made regarding ongoing or non-recent abuse, there can be safeguarding implications. Tensions regarding the need to share information to protect the public, whilst protecting the needs and wishes of the person are commonplace and important to navigate sensitively. It is important that professionals follow best-practice recommendations in relation to such dilemmas (Rouf & Waites, 2023) and that limits of confidentiality are clearly discussed with the person.

2.3 Safeguarding Children

> *'It is important to recognise ... the positives that [people with] DDs can bring to parenting or at least that it is possible to parent well with a DD ... it*

is very easy to see parents with any mental health issue as being detrimental to children.' **Liv *et al.*, Expert-by-Experience**

Many people who experience trauma-related dissociation offer excellent parenting to their children. Indeed, parenting can be supported by dissociative parts of their personality that ensure that children's needs are met fully and consistently irrespective of what is happening for the person. At times, however, trauma-related dissociation can interfere with a person's ability to parent (Benjamin et al., 1998; Kluft, 1987). The extent to which dissociation impacts on the capacity to parent requires careful assessment.

'I think we need to encourage more open channels of communication for the children who have a parent/carer who has a dissociative disorder to more actively engage in mental health teams discussions regarding their loved one. My three children under the age of 18 were my carers, they knew when I was well and they knew when I needed support, they had all the information on my parts and how they impacted on all of our lives positively and negatively. Yet no one ever asked their opinion or what they needed and when my 17-year-old son who was my main carer asked to attend a professionals meeting or a meeting on if I was to be sectioned, he was refused, because he wasn't seen in law as an adult. So much really helpful information to support the child(ren) and the dissociative parent/carer is lost when mental health teams do not actively seek their views and engage them in the process.

After every emergency admission to hospital after a part had tried to take our life (of which there were many), it would be the local GP that would raise a safeguarding. As a parent I felt terrible shame and guilt that I was hurting my children. I actively encouraged social services involvement, but the children did not receive any tangible support and my son always said 'It's because they don't get your condition'. I think it's so important that social workers receive more knowledge about dissociative disorders, so they can support children more specifically.' **Sally Adams, Expert-by-Experience**

Some people who experience trauma-related dissociation may benefit from additional support regarding parenting (see also Chapter 10, Perinatal). There are examples of structured psychoeducational groups for parents who experience trauma-related dissociation to help them understand and manage the impact of dissociation on parenting (Ruismaki et al., 2014). Some parents may need support to protect their children from harmful others (ISSTD, 2011). Clinicians should be aware of the potential impact dissociation may have on parenting and follow safeguarding advice and policies when concerns are present.

Case Example: A male single parent was struggling with alcohol misuse, their young child deemed 'at risk' by Children's Social Services. They were referred to a local MDT with a remit to support the mental health of families at risk of care proceedings. This team developed a good working relationship with the parent, and significant dissociation began to be disclosed, leading to a diagnosis of DID. Services assumed parenting would be unsafe and the child should be removed. With dissociation-informed supervision, the MDT slowed down the decision-making process to assess the person's dissociative system and impact on parenting. This led to a more formulation-driven and nuanced understanding of the person's strengths and struggles, and an individualised plan was developed to support them and their child.

---

3. Barriers to Addressing Safety Concerns

Any of these safety needs will often need to be addressed as a priority within any treatment, indeed safety concerns may act as a significant barrier to change (ISSTD, 2011). Several factors can make exploration and collaboration on safety concerns a difficult process.

3.1 Factors for the Person Engaging in Unsafe Behaviours

Shame and guilt can make it difficult for people to be able to feel safe to raise or work collaboratively on safety concerns. In addition, behaviours such as self-harm or aggression, have represented an important coping strategy for many people and as such there can be fears that these resources will be 'taken away' (Steele et al., 2017). For some people safety concerns may be driven by dissociative parts for whom they have minimal awareness of.

The need for change must therefore be balanced with attunement, sense-making and consensus building (Brand et al., 2022; Loewenstein, 1993; Nijenhuis, 2015). Creating a safe relationship that helps to de-shame safety concerns and grow resources to work towards replacing unsafe behaviours can aid both disclosure and collaboration in working towards change. This may need time to develop across the person's dissociative system.

3.2 Factors for Clinicians

There can be several factors that interrupt this process for clinicians. Working with safety concerns in general can feel very threatening for professionals and the wider organisational system in which they work. This is particularly the case for people presenting with dissociative difficulties whereby the person's responses may not make sense to themselves, professionals, or the wider organisation.

Case Example: *'Mary' experienced a hostile and angry part who could gain executive control and harm the body through serious cutting, something she would often have no conscious awareness of. 'Mary' was very fearful of the part and had feelings of hatred towards it, due to the emotional and physical harm it had caused.*

The professionals and wider system of care reflected and reinforced this message; and various interventions were offered with the intention of suppressing or eliminating the part (e.g., prescription of anti-psychotic medication, techniques to help distract from, controls, or ignore the part).

This led to a vicious cycle of escalating risk followed by ever increasing desperate attempts to control or eliminate the risk. 'Mary' and the professionals and system of care supporting her were at 'war' with the part responsible for self-harm...all in the name of safety.

This scenario can lead to threat-focused responses aimed at removing 'the problem' such behaviours may pose. This can inhibit compassion (Liotti & Gilbert, 2011) and the capacity to empathise and mentalise (Mitchell & Steele, 2021).

The potential for traumatic re-enactments and power struggles is high in such a context. The person, clinical staff and the wider system may all shift into different roles within such re-enactments. For example, professionals may view the person as *'too fragile'* requiring increasingly restrictive environments to maintain safety. Alternatively, the person may be labelled as the cause of the problem and blamed or rejected for *'not taking responsibility'*. At other times, professionals may appear to miss clear signs that things are not safe.

'I think there are also times that things are ignored or explained away by professionals. I was recently told you've been given the tools to manage self-harm, but what the psychiatrist failed to understand is the part that was hurting us would not engage with the taught strategies. I felt I was being abused by both my self-harming part and an organisation or system that didn't want to help.' **Sally Adams, Expert-by-Experience**.

These responses may mirror internal dynamics within the traumatised person and those that were present in the original traumatising context. A framework that specifically aims to understand and address these re-enactments can be especially important (e.g., Karpman's drama triangle; Karpman, 1968) to help regain a more helpful relational frame (Brand et al., 2022; Turkus & Kahler, 2006). The iatrogenic harm that can be caused by re-enactments should not be underestimated.

> *'It's so frustrating when we are told to reach out for support, something that we may find difficult to do, yet when we do we are rebuffed ... Issues arise when professionals either can't or don't want to understand the patient's issues and blame the patient, rather than look at what is going on inside them, to think someone is being manipulative or attention-seeking ... sometimes I might be seeking some attachment or support, but that's a different entity!'* **Sally Adams, Expert-by-Experience**

> **Case Example:** *During an admission to an inpatient unit the validity of the diagnosis of Dissociative Identity Disorder (DID) was questioned and the work the psychologist had done with the person in the community received some criticism. This impacted on the psychologist's psychological safety in working with the person, they began to feel professionally isolated and as though they were working outside of the acceptable remits of the system in which they worked.*
>
> *At the next session the psychologist noticed an urge to change the focus of the session away from the person's experience of dissociation and towards something that would be more acceptable to the wider system.*
>
> *The person with whom they were working noticed the psychologist's anxiety and reservation to engage with their internal system. They felt that they must have done something wrong, and they began to attack and criticise themselves and their dissociation internally.*

When working with safety concerns it is important for the person experiencing trauma-related dissociation, carers, professionals, and the multidisciplinary team to feel that they are working to a shared understanding and shared goals. At times of high threat different polarised perspectives can emerge. Creating contexts of psychological safety that allow for different perspectives whilst helping to build a shared understanding and treatment plan can be particularly important within and between different services supporting a person experiencing trauma-related dissociation (see Chapter 3, The Multidisciplinary Context of Care).

4. Important Considerations

Key steps for working with safety concerns in trauma-related dissociation have been outlined by the ISSTD (2011), as well as other valuable texts (Brand, 2001; Loewenstein, 2006; Steele et al., 2017). Although presented in a linear fashion, these should be used flexibly in collaboration with the person and alongside wider safeguarding, organisational and professional frameworks.

Practice Point: Key Therapeutic Steps in Working with Safety Concerns

Step 1: Outline the need for safety for treatment to be successful.

Step 2: Determine whether the behaviours that generate safety concerns are occurring outside of the person's awareness.

If so, then an initial task is to increase awareness of the dissociative parts that are responsible for the behaviour. This can be developed either through asking the person to begin to dialogue or 'ask inside' or if not possible then the therapist can communicate directly with the dissociative part. Gradually building an alliance with both the dissociative part(s) and the person as a whole represents a key part of this step once identified.

Step 3: assess the function served by the behaviours that generate the safety concern or the conflict that is giving rise to the behaviours.

Step 4: (if possible) negotiate a truce on the behaviours that generate risk, this may involve safety planning and must involve the perspective of the dissociative parts involved.

Step 5: resolve the underlying conflict between dissociative parts, and/or build adaptive coping skills and resources (e.g., psychoeducation, grounding, targeted use of medication), with the engagement of the parts involved, that reduce the need for the safety concern.

The TOP DD Network study demonstrated that an approach that involved the steps above was effective in reducing non-suicidal self-injury for 69% of the sample over a two year period, with the most dissociative individuals demonstrating the most significant impact (Brand et al., 2019), helping reduce inpatient admissions and associated costs of care (Myrick et al., 2017).

4.1 Safety Concerns that Take Place Outside of the Person's Awareness

Nester, Brand et al. (2022) explored reasons for suicidal self-injury in 156 people who had a DD diagnosis. Over 90% of the sample reported being at least partially unaware of what led them to self-injure. When safety concerns, such as self-harm or violence to others, are happening outside of the person's awareness then it is important to assess why.

It may be that the person has moved outside of their window of tolerance and there are difficulties in encoding of the available information at the time. Alternatively, it may be that the safety concerns are driven by specific dissociative parts to which the person has minimal or no access. In such situations, addressing the safety concern will likely entail making therapeutic contact with the involved dissociative parts.

> *'I am not always sure that professions really get how challenging imple-
> mentation of the intervention is. The effort and the challenge I have when
> dialoguing with parts that want to hurt or kill me is massive.'* **Sally Adams,
> Expert-by-Experience**

The basic assumption in working with parts that drive safety concerns, is that they serve a protective survival function for the whole system (Fisher, 2017; Schwartz, 2021). Such dissociative parts have typically been negatively evaluated both in the internal and external world and as a result experience themselves as very iso-lated (Brand, 2001). Building communication and rapport with these parts and using this to begin to understand and validate their protective function is a key step towards change. Clinicians should not underestimate how polarised such parts can be and the rules, or degree of phobia, that can exist to prevent such parts being seen or known.

Attempts at imposing change by force, are likely to be at best unsuccessful and at worst harmful (Chu, 2011). Indeed, Schwartz (2021) warns of the 'backlash' that can occur when change is imposed rather than consensually agreed. Such efforts can be challenging to uphold, particularly when there is considerable internal pres-sure from the person or external pressure from the wider system to ostracise parts that are perceived as causing harm (Brand, 2001). In this sense the five princi-ples of trauma-informed care (*safety, choice, collaboration, trustworthiness, and empowerment, see* Chapter 1) are important guides for the relational context needed in this work.

4.2 Functional Analysis

Identifying the meaning of any behaviour in the context it takes place is a key part of assessing, understanding, and working with safety concerns. Functional analysis (Ferster, 1973) is one way to guide this. Exploring the context, triggers and conse-quences of safety concerns can help guide long-term efforts to reduce risk, as well as understand immediate safety concerns.

Empathically asking dissociation-informed questions such as: *'What were you (or that part) thinking and feeling before you hurt yourself?'*, *'What would be your (or their) concern if you didn't hurt yourself in that moment?'*, *'What did you (they) hope would happen as a result of hurting yourself?'* or *'what was helpful (for any part of you) about self-harming then?'* can help to elicit the triggers and the functions of behaviours that pose safety concerns (Brand, 2001; Brand et al., 2022).

In the case of structural dissociation of the personality, where interactions between different dissociative parts drive the safety concern, Nijenhuis (2015) recommends the following question be considered as part of any functional analysis:

*'**Who** does **what** and **why?**'*.

This understanding helps inform a formulation regarding safety concerns and steps that can be taken to mitigate, and over time reduce risk. Approaches to formulation, including the Internal Family Systems model (Schwartz, 2021) and Structural Dissociation Model (Fisher, 2017), can help make sense of how one dissociative response impacts another, and inform subsequent safety planning.

Case Example: *'Jane' began to work with a therapist who created a different type of relationship with the part that cut. The therapist accepted the part and offered curiosity about its experience and role.*

The part began to share its role within the internal system. He (the part identified as male) told the therapist he used cutting to ensure Jane was never powerless or silenced again. Cutting made sure his voice was heard, and power exerted within the system. He shared that he didn't want to hurt 'Jane' but felt he had no other way of achieving his goals. He also shared that 'Jane' would often ignore her own needs or feelings, feeling powerless and without a voice as a result. The part described sadness at how misunderstood he felt by Jane and others.

This understanding was shared with Jane who began to be able to develop a different relationship with the part, and the underlying problem he solved. The part agreed to work with Jane on this issue and agreed for a 'pause' between the urge and action of self harm, so that 'Jane' could begin to use this as a prompt. Jane began to use the part as an important guide, signalling her own discomfort with certain situations and using it as a cue to assert herself.

As the part felt more connected and understood, the need and risk of cutting reduced.

As noted above, often the person, or dissociative parts, may have significant phobic avoidance, dissociative amnesia or shame attached to these questions and as such, it may require repeated exploration over time and considerable validation and normalisation of the issues involved.

Functional analysis of risk needs to be culturally competent and consider how distress is expressed and understood culturally, such as: somatic complaints instead of emotional language, religious or spiritual explanations for dissociative episodes, collectivist values influencing help-seeking behaviours. The wider context of historical trauma, systemic racism, and migration-related stress also needs careful consideration in risk assessment and any subsequent functional analysis (Şar, 2022).

4.3 Common Functions Associated with Behaviours that Pose a Safety Concern

Brand (2001) and Nester, Brand et al. (2022) have noted the different general functions served by behaviours that pose a risk to self. These include:

- *Attempts to manage overwhelming affect*
- *Attempts to manage traumatic material*
- *Attempts to manage relational needs for closeness (e.g., to access forms of connection) and/or distance (e.g., to assert boundaries).*

Research Question

What are the common functions served by other risk behaviours, such as violence to others or safeguarding issues?

The escape and avoidance of aversive states of being appears a common denominator across these behavioural functions (Baumeister, 1990).

Case Example: Differing Functions of Safety Concerns. 'Sarah hated the voices she heard. She experienced them as not belonging to her and something she felt disgusted by. She was desperate to get rid of them. She tried lots of ways to do this: medication, keeping busy, self-harm, psychological therapy but nothing worked. The harder she tried to get rid of them, the louder and more insistent the voices became. She became increasingly hopeless, and suicide became the one solution she had to the problem that living with the voices posed for her.'

'John wanted to talk about some of the experiences he had growing up. Every time he tried to talk to his Community Psychiatric Nurse (CPN) about this he experienced a tightening around his throat. The more he tried to "push through" this then the tighter and more forceful the grip became. As John battled to share some of his experiences, he found that he self-harmed prior to and after meeting his CPN. He had no recollection of this and struggled to understand how it had happened. The CPN and John identified that self-harm was being driven by a part that was very angry with John for trying to share this information and breaking rules that had always been important for safety.

'Mary would tie ligatures when on an inpatient ward. Staff and Mary were confused as to why. Using the Structural Dissociation Model (as adapted by Fisher, 2017), staff were able to help Mary recognise that ligaturing was a "Fight" response and through gentle exploration they were able to discover that this was being activated to manage parts stuck in "attachment cry" who were fearful of being trapped on the ward, felt powerless to escape and alone in their distress. The ward staff helped Mary to call the nurse in charge who would spend time with her at times when panicky feelings emerged. This reduced her ligaturing, and time could be spent during the admission growing her own ability to help these parts upon discharge.'

4.4 Dilemmas with 'Safety Contracts'

Chu (2011) outlines the importance of working towards developing a 'truce' in relation to safety concerns; this may take the form of encouraging the person to agree to pause the behaviour, so the underlying issue can be explored. The use of safety contracts is commonplace in certain therapeutic approaches and has been advocated in relation to working with trauma-related dissociation (Kluft, 1983; Putnam, 1989).

Brand (2001) outlines the pros and cons of such safety contracts. On the one hand they can convey caring boundaries to the person and provide containment over the treatment frame; on the other hand, they can create a false sense of security and as such do not replace the need for safety evaluation, crisis intervention or wider treatment planning. Brand (2001) also notes the importance of attending to power dynamics that are likely heightened in both developing a safety contract, but also in crisis intervention, more generally. Maintaining attunement and acknowledging the power of the person is a key part of maintaining a therapeutic alliance when working with safety concerns (Brand et al., 2022).

'Not all parts will sign up to safety contracts. This ... can cause further disagreements within the system and lead to increased risk.

I always felt that if I failed to keep the safety contract I was even more of a failure, letting everyone down. I think safety contracts have to be carefully constructed, so that the patient is clear on what other activities they can engage with safely to avoid for example self-harm and my experience of contracting these with professionals is they miss that really important part out.'
Sally Adams, Expert-by-Experience

As Chu (2011) notes, it is ultimately the responsibility of the person who experiences trauma-related dissociation to choose safety. The task of the clinician is to help facilitate a genuine choice. The aim then is to promote collaboration, empowerment and choice. Developing clear safety plans that detail the steps and resources available to the person to manage the underlying issue may help empower the person, whilst also reducing the level of risk. As Judith Herman (1992) notes '*trauma robs the victim of a sense of power and control; the guiding principle of recovery is to restore power and control (p.159)*'.

4.5 Addressing Underlying Issues and Building Alternative Skills

Helping to grow resources that can address the issues that create the need for the safety concern is key (Schielke et al., 2022). Such skills may include:

- Grounding
- Separating past from present
- Getting healthy needs (such as the need for connection, the need for assertiveness) met safely
- Recognising early warning signs
- Developing care or compassion to self
- Mindfulness, mentalising and curiosity regarding trauma-related reactions
- Celebrating progress.

In addition to skill development, ensuring key physical and relational needs are met are important resources to grow as part of addressing safety concerns.

There can be internal (and external) barriers to navigate when growing such resources.

Internal barriers may include common trauma-related beliefs (Brand, 2001) that may need addressing as part of addressing safety concerns:

- Fear of being hurt by others (i.e., '*I must self-harm and if I do not then I will be hurt by others*')
- A belief in the need for self-punishment (i.e., '*I am bad and deserve to be punished*')
- A belief that a part of the person themselves is the abuser and re-enacts abuse ('*I am the abuser and continue to cause harm*')
- A belief in the separateness of dissociative parts (i.e., '*I can kill the child parts and still survive*')
- A fear of annihilation (i.e. '*You threaten my existence, I will show you who's boss!*')
- Talking about the abuse may lead to actual harm from the abusers (i.e., '*if you tell then they will know, I'll hurt you to stop you from telling*').

Additional complicating factors can involve unresolved fears of attachment and attachment loss in relation to perpetrators and ongoing victimisation in adulthood.

External factors may include a family system that does not support therapeutic change.

4.6 Safety Planning and Thresholds for Additional Containment/Support

Safety planning represents a key task for the management of safety concerns. Turkus and Kahler (2006) provide an outline of the Triangle of Choices for Safety as one approach to safety planning for people experiencing trauma-related dissociation. Such approaches involve acknowledging and encouraging things the person can do themselves and recognising when wider supports may be needed.

As part of safety planning there are situations where the degree of risk means professionals have a duty to act, through crisis intervention, safeguarding or inpatient admission for example. At times such clinical decisions may be against the person's wishes.

Recognising and acknowledging the impact of clinical decisions that remove power from the person (through an involuntary admission for example) is important. Increased acute care support may help to clarify an understanding of the person's clinical presentation and needs (ISSTD, 2011). Acute care services should consider how support can be provided in a person-centred, trauma and dissociation-informed way.

If there are community care professionals already in place, then issues of continuity should be considered. This includes transfer of knowledge (sharing formulations, crisis plans and what helps) with acute care staff; also consideration of how existing therapeutic relationships can be maintained.

In some cases, the increased staffing in inpatient settings can facilitate therapeutic work that seems too dangerous in an outpatient (such as planned work on traumatic memories and/or work with aggressive and self-destructive parts and their behaviours). The pros and cons of inpatient settings should be considered. Many features of inpatient settings, including use of seclusion and restraint, are distressing and potentially retraumatising.

If inpatient admission is necessary, the use of advanced statements for symptom management, and collaboratively developed personal safety plans will be important. The NHS Long Term Plan (2019) emphasises the value of less restrictive settings such as a crisis house as alternatives to admission.

> '*I have found these [crisis house] to be a really helpful alternative to maintaining safety and being able to engage in more advanced work.*' **Sally Adams, Expert-by-Experience**

The provision of specialist inpatient units dedicated to the assessment and treatment of trauma and dissociation is so far limited within the UK.

Key considerations for acute care services should be to:

- Identify precipitating factors that have served to drive the safety concern
- Identify next steps to help to reduce the level of risk
- Use a crisis to provide an opportunity to develop or consolidate the person's resources.

Psychological practitioners may support dissociation-informed multidisciplinary work in acute care settings either directly by working with the person or indirectly through the provision of team formulation, reflective practice, training and supervision of staff (see Chapter 3, The Multidisciplinary Context of Care).

People from minoritised communities may have face additional barriers to crisis care due to:

- Language barriers
- Fear of coercive psychiatric interventions
- Immigration status concerns (e.g., fear of deportation).

It is important that cultural needs are considered for the person as part of any crisis response and the merits of alternative supports be considered with the person (Şar, 2022).

5. Additional Complications

5.1 Ritualised and Organised Abuse

Some people who experience trauma-related dissociation are likely to have been subjected to particularly extreme abuse from a very early age. This may have been from organised groups practising what has been termed 'ritual abuse' or 'mind control'. Such abuse may entail the use of specific classical and operant conditioning methods (Epstein et al., 2011; Miller, 2018) to:

- Instil terror in victims, to further satisfy sadistic perpetrators
- Better embed psychological control over victims through the threat that abusers are 'capable of anything'
- Contribute to a state-of-mind where abusers feel emboldened to perpetrate especially abhorrent acts of abuse
- Discredit victims by making them appear delusional or otherwise unreliable when disclosing abuse, with the overarching aim of perpetrators avoiding detection by safeguarding and/or criminal justice systems and
- Seek, as part of a sophisticated methodology, to condition particular responses and behaviours in victims.

'There came a time in our life when we had to tell our sister and her husband what had happened to us as a child so that she could have the information she needed to protect her newborn son. There is a part in our system, whose role is to end the body's life if any part tells the truth about what happened to us. This part's role was "inserted" into our system using mind control techniques. It was hard for us to believe that this could possibly be the case. The use of mind control seemed too fantastical, something that was limited to the realms of science fiction. Our experiences with this part have taught us otherwise ... All that part knew was that, if we told our sister (or anyone), they had to end the body's life – this was their sole reason for being, it completely absorbed them and their need to end our life could be best described as a compulsion – no other alternative could be conceived of or considered...

This part became activated as the rest of our system made preparations to tell our sister and her husband what had happened to us. It resulted in this part making attempts to end the life of the body on two occasions within a week. During this period, our system was engaged with mental health services. We tried to impress upon them the risk that we were at, but they seemed unable to understand this, offering no extra support. The mental health team in the hospital couldn't/refused to understand the attempts to end the body's life as anything other than attention seeking and manipulation - us trying to force them to give us help. We were repeatedly told to take more responsibility, ring for help and use emotional regulation strategies, as if these were things, we would be able to do when another part intent on ending our life was in control of our body and the actions it took. They couldn't understand that we, as other parts in our system, were pleading for help from them because we knew that our body was not safe from the part that was trying to end our life.

We survived this period because a close friend and our therapist stepped in when it was clear that we were not being taken seriously or going to receive any extra support from mental health services.' **Liv *et al.*, Expert-by-Experience**

This can impact on a person's safety through the activation of dissociative parts that have been deliberately conditioned by perpetrator groups with the primary objective being to ensure a compliant 'member' of the group (Breitenbach et al., 2015). Such conditioning ensures that specific dissociative parts carry out specific tasks or functions, which may include attempting suicide if the person attempts to disclose the abuse. Similar methods may also have been used to increase the probability of other risks, including ongoing victimisation and contact with perpetrators and harm to others.

Clinicians may well need additional help and support to understand the complexities of organised and ritualised abuse, the way this can manifest, and the implications for support.

5.2 Attachment Dilemmas

Sometimes, a person, despite best efforts, does not feel able to accept responsibility for staying safe. Such scenarios require a review of treatment plans and the experience and boundary setting capacity of the treatment offered (Steele et al., 2017).

For a minority of people with trauma-related dissociation, the increased care associated with behaviours such as self-harm or suicidality can dysregulate and inadvertently increase rather than reduce risk. This 'excessive dependency' (Steele et al., 2001) may prompt an escalating cycle of crises and hospitalisations. Equally, for other people counter-dependency, or attachment avoidance, may pose a barrier to working on safety issues and the person may need to work on increasing their reliance on, and sharing of difficulties with, the treatment team (Steele et al., 2001).

These patterns can lead clinicians to either offer more contact (further undermining the person's self-efficacy and capacity to cope) or dramatically distance themselves from the person. Teams should recognise the pull to each of these poles and work to regain a balanced position (Steele et al., 2001).

In scenarios where treatment appears to be escalating the level of safety concern, and where best practice has been followed, then the treatment plan should be reviewed, asking what internal (or external) problem increased contact with services meets; and whether the person wishes to explore alternative ways of meeting this need within the boundaries of what can be offered. If the answer to this is 'no', therapeutic work may for a time be at an impasse (Steele et al., 2017).

6. Applying the Integrated-Motivational-Volitional Model to Trauma-Related Dissociation

Best practice approaches towards working with safety concerns can be adapted to the needs of people with complex dissociative difficulties. By way of demonstration, in the following section the a general evidence-based approach to understanding and intervening with suicidal behaviours is applied to people with complex dissociation. Suicidal ideation is predicted by psychological or social entrapment (O'Connor & Portzky, 2018). The *Integrated-Motivational-Volitional Model* (IMV model; O'Connor, 2011) is one of the dominant current approaches to understanding suicidal behaviours (See Figure 6.1).

6.1 Pre-motivational Phase

Within the IMV model the ***pre-motivational phase*** describes the predisposing and precipitating factors from which suicidal ideation and behaviour subsequently emerge.

For example, in the current context this could entail traumatic experiences, such as abuse, combined with disorganised attachments, which have led to a structural dissociation of the personality to adapt and survive. Such a vulnerability remains dormant until there is a trigger that activates the underlying issue, such as abuse in adulthood, or becoming a parent for the first time.

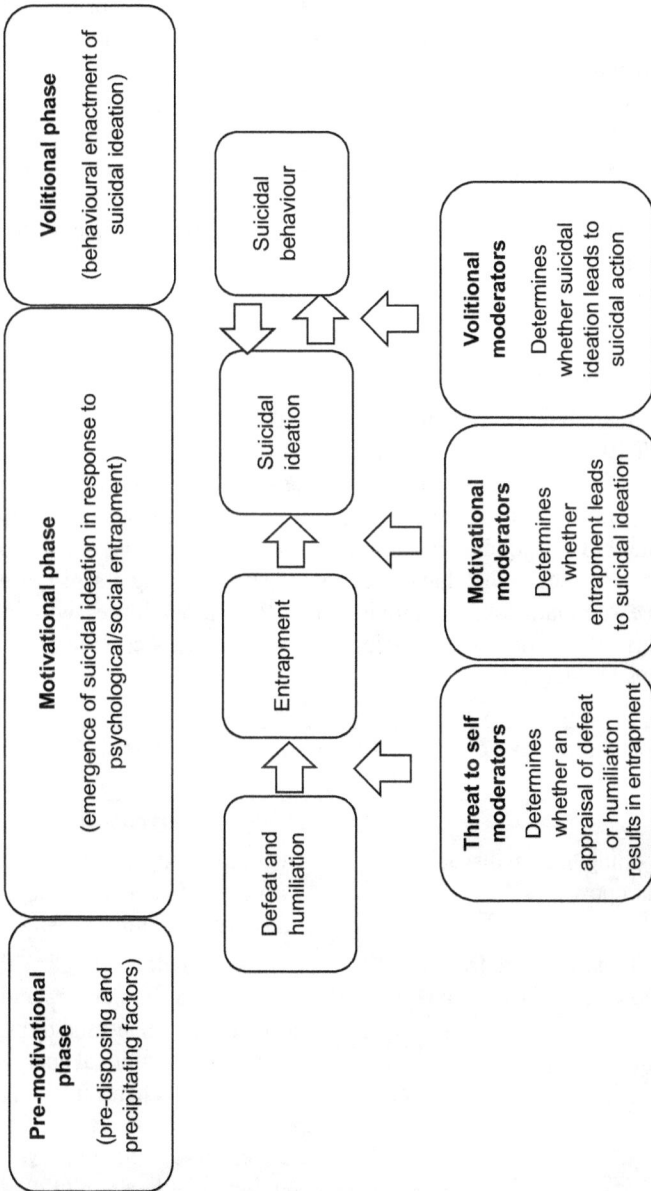

Figure 6.1 The Integrated Motivational-Volitional (IMV) Model of Suicidal Behaviour (O'Connor, 2011)

6.2 Motivational Phase

The **motivational phase** of the IMV model describes the emergence of suicidal ideation. A key assumption is that suicidal ideation is predicted by psychological or social *entrapment*, specifically appraisals of defeat and/or humiliation from which there is no perceived escape.

In relation to trauma-related dissociation, this might involve sudden intrusions of trauma-related dissociative parts into awareness, and the resulting 'breakdown' of dissociative barriers, leading to a sense of defeat for the person (e.g., 'I thought I'd put those experiences behind me, it feels like I've failed').

Alternatively, specific trauma-related dissociative parts may experience defeat or humiliation in relation to the specific motives they pursue, for example feeling they will never be acknowledged by the person orientated to daily life.

6.2.1 Threat to Self-moderators

The extent to which someone can manage appraisals of defeat or humiliation is influenced by the level of resource they have available to them. Within the IMV model these resources are termed 'Threat to Self Moderators' (TSMs) and influence whether an appraisal of 'defeat' or 'humiliation' results in a sense of entrapment or not.

For example, having good social problem solving and coping skills represent a resource that will reduce the chances of someone developing a sense of entrapment; negative ruminations and autobiographical memory biases will increase someone's sense of entrapment. Growing internal resources can therefore be an important focus of intervention.

Practice Point: Examples of Intervention with *'Threat to Self' Moderators to Reduce Entrapment States*

Example	*Possible Intervention*
'I can't do anything to stop dissociative flashbacks. I am powerless'	Begin to teach skills to help with grounding, containment of trauma-related intrusions.
'I can't stop this angry voice from telling me I deserve to die; it takes me over and hurts me'	Engage in dialogue work with the angry voice to understand the problem that the person dying is a solution to (functional analysis). Voice shares it hates it when the person doesn't assert their needs. Person agrees with angry voice that they will begin to find other ways to address this issue (e.g., building assertiveness).

(Continued)

Practice Point: Examples of Intervention with *'Threat to Self' Moderators to Reduce Entrapment States*

'It's not possible to live a meaningful life with trauma-related dissociation. I give up'	Begin to share stories of recovery to generate hopefulness.
'I must be crazy; people will think I am a freak if I told them about how I experience the world'	Connect with others to normalise the experience of trauma-related dissociation.

6.2.2 Motivational Moderators

The final part of the motivational phase is the transition from entrapment to suicidal ideation. Motivational moderators (MMs) influence whether entrapment gives rise to suicidal ideation. Protective MMs include an ability to see a more hopeful future, reasons for living, connectedness, and goal pursuit. MMs such as feeling a burden, lack of social support will increase the likelihood of entrapment leading to suicidal ideation.

Practice Point: Examples of Intervention with *'Motivational' Moderators to Reduce Suicidal Ideation*

Example	*Possible Intervention*
'I can't experience trauma-related dissociation and be a safe parent. It's best if I'm no longer here for the sake of my family'.	Consider family intervention to explore and mitigate any concerns. Encourage belonging and connectedness.
'I am numb, nothing matters, I have no purpose, this is worse than death, I will end it'	Help person recognise depersonalisation/derealisation states. Help validate and normalise. Provide resources to connect with knowledge that these states pass and consider fears attached to 'grounding'.
'She will never accept us...we will make her pay'	Explore the costs of experiential avoidance. Seek to agree graded ways of working with dissociation.

6.3 Volitional Phase

Practice Point: Examples of Intervention with *'Volitional' Moderators to Reduce Suicidal Action*

Example	*Possible Intervention*
'I am 5 years old and back with my father ... if I kill myself, I will be safe from him ... it's my only choice'.	Help the dissociative part orientate to the time, place, and present safety.

'I will kill the 'child parts'… that will stop the crying'	Identify who wants to kill the 'child parts'. Explore whether it is understood that all parts share the same body. Challenge 'delusional separateness'. Consider why the child parts crying is so aversive and whether there are ways of mitigating this. Collaborate to find ways to help reduce the child parts distress.
'I will use suicide to get away from this stuff'	Explore what overwhelms the person, consider how steps forwards towards engaging with dissociation can be taken.
'I forget my coping skills when I dissociate, suicidal feelings emerge, and I am desperate to act'	Create clear '*if-then*' safety plans with the person that are specific to the needs of the person as a whole (including dissociative parts) and are easily accessible at times of high distress. Include threshold for additional support and ensure this support is available and accessible at times of need.

The volitional phase of the IWM model accounts for behavioural enaction of suicidal ideation, this transition to action is governed by what are termed volitional moderators (VMs).

Examples of VMs include capability for suicide (e.g., fearlessness about death; increased tolerance of physical pain); environmental VMs (e.g., access to means of suicide); and social VMs (exposure to suicidal behaviour of others). Additional VMs include clear plans (if-then contingencies), impulsivity, mental imagery and cognitive rehearsal of suicide, history of self-harm or suicide attempts.

6.4 Implications of the IWM Model

The model above has some important implications for working with someone with trauma-related dissociation.

First, it indicates that risk management for people requires both general risk management strategies (e.g., reducing access to means of suicide), but also dissociation-specific risk management strategies (e.g., engaging with trauma-related parts who believe that they do not share the same body and can therefore 'kill' and survive themselves).

Second, the model aids risk assessment and helps to identify factors that may be accelerating risk, as well as how such factors may dynamically change.

Third, the model implies intervention and suicide prevention strategies be tailored to the phase of the model that the person is presently in.

For example, if a person is in an entrapped state regarding dissociative experiences, then interventions that help to reduce entrapment will likely be important, building and growing hope.

If a person is actively suicidal then interventions that reduce the chances of acting on these thoughts are important, this may involve targeting volitional moderators in the first instance before targeting the underlying conflict helping to sequence risk-mitigation strategies (for example, challenging the belief that a dissociative part can 'kill' another without killing the whole may be an initial intervention that could target a strong volitional moderator).

Safety planning around specific dissociative symptoms may help to create new 'if-then' contingencies for the person or identify situations where additional support in the form of crisis supports or inpatient admission is required.

Finally, it directs attention to the issue of psychological entrapment in guiding assessment and intervention strategies. The use of clinical interview or specific assessment resources, such as the four-item entrapment scale short-form (De Beurs et al., 2020) may be beneficial to help identify the presence of entrapment, its relation to trauma-related dissociation and develop collaboration on alternative solutions.

7. Mental Capacity and Trauma-Related Dissociation

Case Example: A young transgender male under the community mental health team (CMHT) received a diagnosis of DID. The date for life-changing gender reassignment surgery came through. CMHT staff were anxious that DID might impact their capacity to give informed consent for the procedure. Senior safeguarding professionals in both hospital trusts became involved.

With dissociation-informed supervision, the decision-making process was slowed down and the views of all parts were sought. Through this the person reached their own unique decision, delaying the procedure (which they still wished to have), while they worked on building up the support they would need post-operatively.

A common consideration when working with safety concerns is whether someone has capacity to make decisions regarding their behaviour and choices.

7.1 Complexities Regarding Capacity

This can be a complex process to assess and determine within trauma-related dissociation and can prove difficult for the person and professionals to navigate together and will typically need to be assessed over time (Sachs, 2015).

Questions regarding capacity addressed in UK case law demonstrate the complexity of this process with trauma-related dissociation. Such examples and the rulings of the court can highlight some of the key considerations that may be encountered in clinical practice.

Case Law Example: Leicestershire County Council v 'P' [2024] EWCOP 53 (T3)

'P' was seen for specialist therapeutic support in relation to trauma-related dissociation. During a therapy session 'P' disclosed that at times where a specific dissociative part was in executive control, she met with a perpetrator group where she was subject to serious sexual abuse. 'P' had numerous significant injuries consistent with these reports. 'P' was clear she wanted this to stop but reported actions such as leaving the property or telling her carers to leave the property were directed by specific dissociative parts of the personality over which she had little influence.

- 'P' took the position that she lacked capacity at such times, and required a crisis plan that could be implemented regardless of her objecting at that point in time. An 'anticipatory declaration' was sought from the court to confirm the legality of this care plan and offer clarity to carers
- The Local Authority took the position that 'P' had capacity regarding her care, support and contact with others and argued against an 'anticipatory declaration' to govern the best interests of a person with capacity for a time where they may lose capacity.

7.2 Mental Capacity Act ('Mental Capacity Act', 2005)

Within England and Wales, the Mental Capacity Act (2005) provides the legislative framework for capacity. Under this framework, capacity is assumed, decision- and time-specific. If there are doubts regarding capacity relating to an 'impairment of mind', then an assessment process must be followed:

- Capacity is demonstrated by:
  - An ability to understand the relevant information related to a decision
  - An ability to retain this relevant information for long enough to make a decision
  - An ability to weigh up the relevant information to make a decision
  - An ability to communicate this decision.
- Trauma-related dissociation may interfere with each aspect of the above. Clinicians may need to have an awareness and assess the different ways in which trauma-related dissociation impacts on someone's mental capacity
- In such a scenario, clinicians have a duty to offer reasonable adaptations to help facilitate capacity, with suggestions summarised in Table 6.1.

Particular challenges regarding capacity often become apparent when someone has significant experiences of identity confusion and alteration.

Table 6.1 Impacts of and Adaptations for Dissociation in Relation to Mental
Capacity Decision Making

Example of impact of trauma-related dissociation on capacity	Example of reasonable adaptation to support capacity
Depersonalisation and derealisation may make it difficult for someone to understand the decision.	Ensuring that someone is in a grounded state before being asked to understand what is being asked of them.
Amnesia and amnesic barriers may make it difficult to retain information.	Ensuring the person can have a record of information, either written or recorded to reduce the impact of amnesia.
Identity confusion may lead to significant conflict relating to decisions and opposing pros and cons.	Ensuring that the pros and cons are considered for each dissociative part of the personality.
Identity alteration may make it difficult for someone to express their decision.	Ensure that different forms of communication are available so that someone can adequately express themselves.

When someone has the experience of multiple dissociative parts of the personality each with their own felt sense of 'I' (first-person perspective), then it can be
practically and ethically challenging to assess capacity.

Case Law Example Continued

Expert witnesses disagreed on clinical diagnosis for 'P'. One argued that 'P'
met criteria for DID; another argued that 'P' met criteria for 'Complex PTSD
with dissociative characteristics' and expressed some doubt on the validity
of DID as a diagnosis.

It was agreed by the court that regardless of diagnosis, it was the presence
of trauma-related dissociative states that took executive control of behaviour which represented the 'impairment of mind'. In this sense diagnosis was
immaterial to the question of capacity.

7.3 Taking the Whole into Account

Sachs (2015) encourages following a democratic process whereby all dissociative
parts of the person are deemed to hold important and valid information relating
to a decision. The aim then is understanding the different positions of each dissociative state and working towards a decision that serves the whole. Sachs (2015)
suggests professionals determine the 'internal logic' of the person's dissociative

system, asking questions similar to those posed by Nijenhuis (2015) above, 'who does **what** and **why?**'.

Case Law Example Continued

In clinical cases (such as the case described above) this would involve exploring with all relevant parts of the personality what underlying motives drive their behaviour and are relevant to the decision at hand at a given point in time.

For example, for some people there may be a conflict between (i) a need to be safe, and (ii) a need to belong. They may feel the perpetrator group is the only source of belonging, or that they would be in great danger if they did not comply with demands from the group.

This may lead to consideration of alternative ways that the need to belong can be satisfied, or specific safeguarding actions may be needed to manage current threat or work on specific barriers (such as conditioning of certain parts of the personality to follow 'commands').

Understanding the 'why' can help to identify the commonality between parts in what is longed for and ultimately sought. Sachs (2015) advises that the route to the development of fully informed decision-making and increased safeness lies in the recognition that all parts are part of an overarching system that has its own internal logic.

7.4 What About Cases Where the Above 'Democratic' Process Is Not Possible and There Are Ongoing Concerns Regarding Capacity?

Whilst a desirable therapeutic goal to work towards there are situations where the above is not yet possible for a decision to be made in a specific context at a specific time.

For example, in situations where a specific dissociative state is fixed on an action that has the potential to be harmful and is not in accordance with the otherwise expressed wishes of the person (e.g., dissociative parts may differ regarding whether a time-sensitive life-saving intervention, such as a blood transfusion, is acceptable or not). Such issues may be more complicated if there is limited internal awareness of dissociation (Ashburn, 2023).

Case Law Example Continued

All parties agreed that 'P' had capacity when she was not dissociating.

An expert witness argued that the capacity of 'P' was binary and that in the presence of any dissociative state she lacked capacity.

The court instead ruled capacity was present in some dissociative states but not others (i.e., some dissociative states could *understand, retain, weigh up* and *express* information relevant to the decision).

Therefore, capacity fluctuated when 'P' dissociated, and the assessment of this was considered in relation to both the person orientated to daily life ('P') and according to the specific dissociative state in executive control at any point in time.

7.5 Weighing Up the Right to Autonomy Vs Safety

Responses to safety concerns when the person is thought to lack capacity also need to be considered against the person's rights for autonomy.

If capacity is not deemed present, then a best-interest decision takes place.

Case Law Example Continued

The court ruled that a best-interest decision was only required in situations where:

(i) a contemporaneous capacity assessment of a specific dissociative state indicated a lack of capacity *and*
(ii) 'P' was not able to manage this using her typical coping strategy (going to her room) and was taking actions likely to lead to harm (such as contacting members of perpetrator group or leaving the property).

The court recommended a clear crisis plan be developed with 'P' for such scenarios that allowed for a best interest decision (including care staff disabling the Wi-Fi or following 'P' if she left the property). The court ruled that an '*anticipatory declaration*' to confirm the legality of a best-interest decision whilst possible in this case was not necessary.

In addition, the court requested that local community mental health team support (which had been reduced to an annual psychiatric review) be reinstated to increase support for 'P'.

This provided the 'least restrictive' response to fluctuations in capacity and provided a balance between the need for safety and the need for autonomy.

- The person to whom the decision relates should remain involved as much as possible, decisions must be in their best interests and should be the least restrictive option. Section 4 of the Mental Capacity Act (2005) outlines what should be considered before making a decision whilst someone lacks capacity

- At times, a best interest decision may lead to restrictions being placed on a person and include a range of restrictions from restraint to a deprivation of liberty
- Deprivation of liberty safeguards (DoLS) provides a legal framework under which the conditions that amount to a deprivation of liberty can in certain settings be legally authorised for a person who lacks capacity.

It may be important for clinicians to consider with the person in advance how their wishes and wants can be considered at times when they lack capacity (in the form of an advanced statement or decisions, for example). This allows the person to put forwards their point of view at a point of relative stability in preparation for a period where this may not be able to be accessed or expressed.

7.6 Wider Considerations

Sachs (2015) emphasises the long-term therapeutic process involved in supporting someone with such decisions and recommends that clinicians:

- Ensure a safe physical and relational environment in which capacity can be assessed and considered
- Ensure that assessments regarding capacity are dissociation-informed (e.g., the assessor is aware that relationships between dissociative parts of the personality may be very hostile, that some dissociative parts may be inaccessible to the person and the assessor, that amnesic barriers may lead to a disjointed account and that one event may have different meanings to different dissociative parts) and
- Understand the longitudinal importance of working towards consensus of views to address safety concerns.

Often questions regarding capacity can lead to a discussion of who is the 'true' or 'core' self to whom 'decisions' ultimately relate and whether dissociative parts can make decisions for the whole. Such discussions are apparent in UK Case Law (e.g., *A Health and Social Care Trust v P and R* [2015] NIFam 19). Sachs (2025) argues that the core self represents the whole of the person, rather than being held by a single dissociative part, and that there is a 'wisdom of the system' that determines the 'decision' to switch or not to switch, with parts united in the wish to ultimately preserve the underlying Self.

8. Concluding Comments

People who experience trauma-related dissociation are likely to encounter a range of safety concerns and threats. A key task of any treatment is to create safety in the here and now. People should be able to access dissociation-informed and dissociation-specific support with safety concerns; this will be critical in helping develop a genuine sense of autonomy, choice, power and control.

Chapter 7

Dissociation and CoMorbid Complexity

Psychosis, Autism and OCD

Angela Kennedy, Emma Černis, Ruth Leaper, Darren James, Paul Langthorne, Helena Crockford, Vivian Okoye and Anthony Redhead

1. Introduction

Comorbid mental health difficulties are common among individuals experiencing trauma-related dissociation (Loewenstein, 2018). Such comorbidity can create significant complexity. This chapter begins by considering a transdiagnostic approach to formulation to help clinicians understand the influence dissociation may have within and across different comorbid clinical presentations. Three common conditions associated with dissociation (and with one another) are explored in further detail: psychosis, autism, and obsessive-compulsive disorder. Conceptual and clinical overlaps with dissociation are then explored, with a summary of the literature, practice guidance and clinical and lived experience examples. Through this, general considerations for addressing the broader range of comorbid and co-occurring difficulties experienced by people with complex dissociation, are illustrated.

2. An Integrated Model to Enhance Understanding of Dissociation as a Transdiagnostic Process

Formulation plays a key role in guiding an understanding of comorbid conditions. Understanding the relationship between trauma-related dissociation and other comorbid clinical presentations is likely to require the integration of different theories. Integrative approaches such as the *Levels of Dissociation Model* (Kennedy et al., 2013) and *Social Mentality* theory (Gilbert, 2020) that can capture the interaction between dissociative and non-dissociative processes may be particularly important in helping clinicians to formulate the interaction between comorbid conditions and subsequently guide intervention. For example, in psychosis, dissociative processes (such as intrusive tactile hallucinations), may interact with 'new-brain' meaning making and mentalising capacities, leading to the development of unusual beliefs or delusions and generating an escalating sense of threat or paranoia (Liotti & Gilbert, 2011). Culturally informed perspectives highlight that dissociative experiences often emerge within complex intersections of identity and cultural meaning-making (Krüger, 2020). For example, possession states or somatic dissociation may reflect adaptive meaning making (Seligman & Kirmayer, 2008).

DOI: 10.4324/9781003625650-9

Integrating sociocultural frameworks alongside biopsychosocial models allows for a more nuanced formulation of how dissociation interacts with comorbidity (see Chapter 15 for further discussion).

> '*As someone who received traditional psychosis care for many years, before my complex dissociation was recognised and appropriate long term therapy received, acceptance and environmental adaptations would have made my life easier prior to, during and after I received the long term therapy that enabled internal change.*' **Expert-by-Experience**

3. Dissociation and Psychosis

Historical conceptualisations of psychotic disorders are closely linked to that of dissociation (Moskowitz & Montirosso, 2019). This overlap in presentation but difference in conceptualisation has been an area of importance for many people with lived experience who have felt wrongly 'diagnosed'. Dissociative difficulties are often mistaken for psychosis, because the outward presentation overlaps the symptoms of psychosis. Whilst both ICD-11 and DSM-5 diagnostic frameworks consider dissociative symptoms to be psychologically caused, the same does not hold for psychosis, with implications for practice. Deville et al. (2014) commented, 'Neurosis and psychosis are precarious terms, as the boundary between both is becoming increasingly blurred' (p.5).

3.1 Epidemiology of Comorbid Psychosis and Dissociation

Accumulating evidence suggests dissociative experiences are found at high rates in people presenting with psychosis. Sun et al. (2019) found that of 66 young people with a first episode of psychosis, 36.4% also had clinical levels of dissociation. A meta-analysis of studies using the DES (Carlson & Putnam, 1993), found significantly elevated levels of dissociation in people with a diagnosis of schizophrenia in comparison with the general population (Lyssenko et al., 2018). Černis et al. (2014) found experiences of depersonalisation were reported by 60% of a sample diagnosed with non-affective psychosis with a persecutory delusion. In a systematic review Renard et al. (2017) concluded people diagnosed with a 'schizophrenia spectrum disorder' experienced high levels of all major symptoms of dissociation (amnesia, depersonalisation, derealisation, identity confusion and identity alteration). Likewise, Longden et al. (2020) found strong associations between dissociation and individual psychotic symptoms, particularly 'positive' psychotic symptoms such as hallucinations, delusions, paranoia and disorganised thinking. Such research demonstrates a clear comorbidity between dissociative and psychotic phenomena.

> '*Psychosis with a traumatic basis may be understood as resulting from elements of experience, which are dissociated, and which remain divided in some way from the core self. In this context, dissociation is also, concurrently, caused by trauma, and is understood to be an active process of organising experience in the face of integrative failures resulting from uncontainable affect, which impacts on the experience of the "self".*' **Angela Kennedy, Consultant Clinical Psychologist**

3.2 The Role of Traumatic Experience

Converging evidence has found significant comorbidity between PTSD and psychosis. In a prospective study of 4000 children, those experiencing severe abuse were 48 times more likely to develop psychosis as adults (Janssen et al., 2004). A meta-analysis of links between childhood adversity and psychosis found people with a psychosis diagnosis were 2.8 times more likely to have suffered childhood trauma (Varese et al., 2012). The estimated population risk was 33%, implying without such childhood adversity the number of people with psychosis would be reduced by one third. Such studies confirm that trauma represents an important etiological factor in the development of psychosis.

> '*A "mis-diagnosis" of psychosis can occur even if attempts to consider trauma history are made, because of the presence of unidentified dissociative amnesia for the trauma. This can be especially true when the trauma is ongoing at the time the person is assessed by mental health services. This is the understanding I came to about my own long journey through the mental health system, during which I was misdiagnosed as psychotic for many, many years before my DID was eventually recognised and I was fortunate enough to receive appropriate and effective long-term psychotherapy.*' **Expert-by-Experience**

Often the themes evident within 'psychotic' experiences have a meaning that directly or indirectly relates to traumatic experience. Hardy et al. (2005) found over 50% of a sample of people experiencing non-affective psychosis reported a trauma-history. 45% had psychotic symptoms that contained themes consistent with their trauma history, but without specific content. 12.5% had both themes and trauma-related content in their hallucinations. Less than half had no observable associations between trauma-meaning and psychotic symptoms. These findings suggested trauma may influence psychotic themes, sometimes through characteristics that have personal rather than obvious meanings.

One reason the relevance of traumatic dissociation is missed for people diag-nosed with schizophrenia, is because they themselves are less likely to link their symptoms and history. As Morrison et al. (2003) note, 'the transparency of the links between symptom content and life events to both patient and professional may determine the diagnosis received' (p.342).

A culturally informed awareness of intersectional identity-based sources of dis-advantage is important here. Systemic oppression, racism, intergenerational trauma and migration-related stressors may increase dissociation and psychosis in minori-tised groups (Pierorazio et al., 2023; Liu & Le, 2024). Chronic inequality may reinforce dissociative coping, interacting with psychosis vulnerability.

Case Example: Yvonne. After her first year at University Yvonne began to experience tactile hallucinations of spiders crawling over her body at night-time. This led to significant fear and beliefs that the spiders were being sent by someone who wanted to hurt her. She would hear voices that would angrily tell her that tablets and injections were being given to poison her.

Yvonne was deemed to lack 'insight' and diagnosed with a delusional dis-order and paranoid schizophrenia. She was seen by the Assertive Outreach Team to ensure compliance with a regime of anti-psychotic medication.

She attended a Hearing Voices group and gradually explored the meaning and context of these experiences. It became apparent that such symptoms were meaningful in the context of her previously undisclosed early traumatic experiences. Yvonne had never seen the connection between her current experiences and past experiences and was surprised to see the parallels in the themes of her life experience and her 'psychotic symptoms'. This helped to identify alternative options for recovery.

3.3 Different Labels for the Same Phenomena?

Current diagnostic systems make a clear distinction between dissociation and psych-osis diagnostic categories, contributing to the systematic under-recognition by ser-vices of dissociation (Bailey & Brand, 2017; Steinberg & Siegel, 2008). As Brand (2024) notes many assessment methods for the diagnosis of psychosis include poten-tially dissociative items, including experiences of depersonalisation and derealisa-tion, suggesting a large conflation between the two categories. Historically, Bleuler formulated *dementia praecox* (the pre-cursor to what is now known as schizo-phrenia) in ways which parallel modern descriptions of DID. Schneiderian first-rank symptoms, considered critical features for the diagnosis of schizophrenia – such as 'made' feelings, thoughts and actions; voice hearing; thought insertion and with-drawal – are highly prevalent in dissociative disorders (Kluft, 1987).

Some theorists (e.g., Moskowitz & Corstens, 2007) argue auditory verbal hallu-cinations (AVH) should be re-categorised and considered dissociative. This follows evidence that AVH occur outside psychosis in a manner indistinguishable from schizo-phrenia, and sometimes at higher rates. Hallucinations occurring 'outside of the head' or talking in the third person, have been considered 'first rank' schizophrenia symp-toms, however Moskowitz and Corstens (2007) summarise numerous studies showing the perceived voice location does not seem relevant to diagnosis or prognosis, and thus cannot be considered highly indicative of schizophrenia. Similarly, research does not support the oft-quoted diagnostic distinction between 'pseudo-' and 'true-' hallucina-tions. These authors therefore dispute the current diagnostic boundaries.

Some have argued that a 'fuzzy' boundary exists between dissociation and psychosis (Renard et al., 2017), suggesting it is difficult, even impossible, to make clear categorical distinctions between the two. Cultural frameworks may also influ-ence whether certain dissociative or psychotic experiences are interpreted as patho-logical. For example, auditory or visual phenomena may be understood as spiritual encounters, ancestral communication, or culturally normative possession states in some non-Western or faith-based communities (Krüger, 2020; Sar, 2022). Without culturally attuned formulation, these experiences may be misclassified as psychosis or classified in a way that does not align with the client's lived experience.

It is worth highlighting here also the clinical experience of some people with com-plex dissociation and identity alteration who describe having specific dissociative parts who 'are psychotic' – for example believing their TV is spying on them – when other parts do not experience or believe this. Consistent with a network approach to psychopathology (Borsboom, 2017), this again highlights the artificial nature of current diagnostic distinctions in general. This suggests increased flexibility is required, as encapsulated by experience-based formulation approaches, including in research, to advance understanding of the clustering of these experiences.

Contrastingly, others have highlighted important differences between dissoci-ation and schizophrenia. Laddis and Dell (2012) compared 40 people diagnosed with schizophrenia to 40 people diagnosed with a dissociative disorder. Dissociative disorders were associated with more first rank symptoms, fewer delusions and more child, angry, commenting and persecutory voices than schizophrenia. First rank symptoms and hallucinations therefore seemed more related to dissociative disor-ders and trauma than to schizophrenia. People with a dissociative disorder diagnosis scored higher on dissociation than people with a schizophrenia diagnosis, and the dissociation experiences in the schizophrenia group appeared less clearly related to abuse history. The authors concluded that dissociation in the context of a schizo-phrenia diagnosis may be phenomenologically different to that within a dissocia-tive diagnosis. In an earlier study Dell et al. (2006) noted that certain Schneiderian symptoms, such as thought broadcasting and delusional perceptions did not typ-ically occur in DID, except in the context of a 'psychotic episode' and were more highly indicative of schizophrenia. Bogar and Dora (2007) found that amongst people with a psychosis diagnosis, those with primarily negative symptoms were a less traumatised population. Steinberg and Siegel (2008) suggested people with schizophrenia had more flattened affect, more loosening of associations and more generalised impairment in their functioning lasting longer than 6 months, than those with dissociation. Figure 7.1 provides an outline of commonalities and differences

Factor/Symptom	Trauma-Related Dissociation (e.g., DID/OSDD)	Schizophrenia/psychosis
Early trauma	Typical higher disclosure of early, chronic trauma (e.g., Boon, 1993).	May be less likely to disclosure early trauma.
Onset of voices	Onset of voices typically in childhood (Brand, 2024).	Onset of voices typically after 18 (Brand, 2024).
Trauma intrusions	High traumatic intrusions on Rorschach (Brand et al., 2009).	Fewer traumatic intrusions on Rorschach (Brand et al., 2009).
DES-II scores and reality testing	High dissociative experiences on DES-II with intact reality testing (Lyssenko et al., 2018).	Moderate dissociative experiences on DES-II with poor reality testing.
Amnesia, identity	Report amnesia and identity alteration.	Lack of amnesia (unless associated with psychotic state) and any identity confusion is associated with delusional beliefs.
First-rank symptoms	Higher levels of Schneiderian 'first-rank symptoms' present.	Schneiderian first rank symptoms present, more often associated with delusional beliefs; lack of awareness of hallucinatory quality of auditory voices; lack of elaborate internal communication associated with voices (Brand, 2024).
Voices	Voices may be internal or external.	Voices may be internal or external.
Affect	Emotional dysregulation/shifting states of self in response to internal and external triggers.	Chronic flat affect.
Cognitive organisation	Thinking/perceptions organised when not experiencing traumatic intrusion (Brand et al., 2009).	Disorganised thought/perception/'loosening of associations'.
Relationships	Internal approach-avoidance conflicts evident in relationships (Brand 2024).	Greater prevalence of avoidant attachment patterns in relationships.

Figure 7.1 Overlaps and Differences Between Factors Associated with a Dissociation vs Psychosis Diagnosis.

between dissociative presentations and schizophrenia spectrum disorders. The interested reader is directed to Brand (2024) for a full discussion of differential diagnosis between schizophrenia and dissociative presentations.

3.4 Dissociation as an Important Mechanism in the Development of Psychosis?

Dissociation has been highlighted as playing a key role in the development of psychotic experiences. Discussing post-traumatic stress in the context of psychosis, Hardy (2017) suggested dissociation can perpetuate psychosis, by influencing stress sensitivity, trauma-related intrusions, and coping responses. The exacerbation of these processes maintains the sense of threat integral to both post-traumatic stress and psychosis. Others have proposed that misinterpreted trauma-based dissociative experiences produce psychotic symptoms (as outlined in the Case Example: Yvonne, described above); or that dissociation employed as a coping strategy maintains the sense of threat and therefore the post-traumatic and psychotic symptoms (Morrison et al., 2003; Newman-Taylor & Sambrook, 2013).

Psychological models of 'positive' psychotic symptoms have also suggested dissociation may be instrumental in forming and maintaining psychotic experiences. For example, Garety et al. (2001) outlined a cognitive-behavioural model of psychotic symptoms where anomalous experiences – including dissociative experiences – cause a 'search for meaning', and the adoption of unusual explanatory beliefs, forming the basis for hallucinations, delusions, and fixed ideas. The search for meaning arises when anomalous or dissociative experiences are mistakenly attributed to external factors and interpreted as significant (or threatening). This interpretation is influenced for example by information processing biases and pre-existing beliefs about the self, world, and others, within the context of genetic and environmental risk.

One implication of these models is the possibility that reducing dissociation may alleviate psychotic symptoms. Interventions being developed to address dissociative experiences in the context of psychosis include the Talking with Voices (TwV) programme (Longden et al., 2022); case studies by Varese et al. (2021) which suggest beneficial effects for targeting dissociation in people presenting with psychosis and trauma; additionally, Farrelly et al. (2024) explored interventions specifically for depersonalisation-derealisation in the context of psychosis; finally Černis et al. (2022) report the development of interventions for transdiagnostic dissociative experiences in the context of psychosis.

3.5 Psychosis and Dissociation: Practice Recommendations

Summarising the practice implications of this discussion, the following points emerge:

- Dissociation is an important consideration when working with psychosis. Clinicians should routinely screen for dissociation when working with clients presenting with psychotic symptoms, particularly where there are positive symptoms

- Accurate assessment will require time, collateral information and a trauma-informed lens
- Irrespective of whether the person has disclosed a trauma history, clinicians should hold in mind the possibility that the person's symptoms could represent an adaptive response to trauma
- At times the person may not recognise any connection between their experiences and trauma, due to amnesia, or other avoidant/defensive processes such as an automatic turning away from adverse experience (Corrigan et al., 2025)
- A psychotic 'symptom' may initially appear devoid of sense of self or wider meaning, because it is being experienced through a single sensory modality (e.g., a voice or bodily state). Alternatively, there may be discrete behavioural states (Loewenstein & Putnam, 2023) that have become functionally disconnected from one another operating with their own first person perspective. Such experiences may interact with 'new brain' meaning-making competencies leading to 'delusional beliefs' in an attempt to account for the distressing experience of intrusion
- The unique way that multiple elements of self develop and relate to each other, may determine the person's clinical presentation. A person-centred, formulation-driven approach may therefore be the most useful way forward to guide support and intervention
- Cultural context, systemic oppression, intergenerational trauma and intersecting identities should all be considered for their role in shaping both the development and expression of dissociation and psychosis, while a culturally informed formulation will explore the personal, spiritual, and sociocultural meanings someone assigns to their experiences.

3.6 Psychosis and Dissociation: Further Research Questions

Future research could help to answer:

- Which of the proposed relationships between dissociation and psychosis (or dissociation subtypes and specific psychotic symptoms) discussed in the section above are most likely?
- What contexts may be relevant?
- Are there particular mechanisms or mediators which are important?
- How can improved understanding of these relationships contribute to better treatment pathways and improved outcomes for those with overlapping presentations?

3.7 Psychosis and Dissociation: Summary

Many people with a diagnosis of schizophrenia or psychosis are likely to also be experiencing forms of trauma-related dissociation. Some experiences that were previously considered highly indicative of schizophrenia (such as Schneiderian first rank symptoms) are a common feature of dissociative presentations. It appears that some pervasive negative symptoms, for example ongoing flattened affect, and ongoing delusional beliefs, may be more differentially distinguishing of schizophrenia. The mechanisms theorised in the development of psychosis may also, at least in part, involve dissociative processes. Comprehensive assessment and psychobiosocial formulation are key to guiding intervention.

4. Dissociation and Autism

> 'We are isolated and on our own. Even since coming to the service, it's better here, but people still don't really get us like. We are constantly trying to fit into society in a way and stopping ourselves doing or saying things, and it's difficult. We are always internally fighting with ourselves. Because we over-analyse everything, and over-focus and it keeps the trauma going. We over analyse everything and have a fear of being judged, that's the autism but the voices amplify it.' **Simon, Expert-by-Experience discussing his experience of trauma, autism and psychosis**

Despite a higher vulnerability to recurring relational trauma, it is likely that levels of trauma in neurodivergent people are underestimated due to a lack of adaptation of current trauma models to this population. Neurodivergent people may be disproportionately exposed to trauma (Kerns et al., 2022). With dissociation a common survival response to interpersonal, pervasive, or inescapable adversity and abuse, then neurodivergent people may also be disproportionately susceptible to dissociation as a means of coping. Recurrently traumatising or perpetually threatening social contexts increase the need for immobilisation survival strategies, such as dissociation. As well as disproportionate trauma exposure, it should be considered whether an autism phenotype includes inherent proneness to dissociation. Dissociation may therefore be an important consideration when working with people with autism, with implications throughout the process of assessment, formulation and intervention.

4.1 Trauma and Autism

Autistic children experience significantly higher rates of Adverse Childhood Experiences (ACEs), being twice as likely to experience four or more ACEs (Berg et al., 2018), particularly family income insufficiency (40% compared to 23% for peer controls); parental divorce (28% compared to 20%); household mental ill health (18% compared with 7%), and household substance use (14% to 10%). The experiences of families and carers are multi-layered and complex, and interactions with services (e.g., health, social care and education) add to the collective trauma context for the child, with 10% of parents or carers subsequently meeting the criteria for complex PTSD (Baker et al., 2021).

Research Question: Does autism interact with a chronic stress context and attachment relationships in a way that increases vulnerability to dissociation? How does the stress context impact on attachment?

Teague et al. (2017) in a systematic review, highlight the role of attachment relationships for autistic children. The authors reference early ruptures in the interaction between the autistic child and caregiver but describe a paucity of data regarding the predictors, correlates, and outcomes of attachment in this population. They suggest the need for longitudinal research to explore this further.

Evidence suggests those with neurodevelopmental difference, including autism, are disproportionately exposed to trauma with ongoing exposure to trauma across the lifespan. This involves a vulnerability to recurring relational trauma, polyvictimisation within immediate and wider interpersonal systems (Baladerian et al., 2013; Hellström, 2019) and traumatisation within care settings and environments which do not understand, and are not designed to meet, autistic people's needs (Kerns et al., 2022).

Rumball et al. (2021) argue this cumulative trauma accounts for the heightened risk of PTSD in autistic populations. Testimonies of autistic people refer to dissociation as a risk factor for further victimisation by reducing capacity to maintain awareness of needs and boundaries in social relationships (Reuben & Parish, 2022). The stress and distress of struggling with social demands, social isolation, discrimination, stigma, and being overwhelmed by the sensory environment, may all form a common part of the experience of autistic people.

'When I'm anxious about something I just like zone out, and don't realise and you forget about your surroundings – an example is when I was in a walking group, I'd still be walking but I'd be gone in my head, in a world of my own.'
Stephen, (28)

4.2 How Common is Dissociation in Autistic People?

There are challenges to determining the prevalence of dissociation in autistic people. There are significant overlaps between autistic experience and dissociation leading to a higher risk of false-positive and false-negative diagnoses. This may mean that many people who are experiencing trauma-related dissociation are incorrectly diagnosed with autism and likewise that many people who are experiencing autism may be incorrectly diagnosed with a dissociative condition (Reuben,

2023). As such issues of comprehensive formulation and differential diagnosis are of particular importance. More stringent definitions of dissociation (as proposed by Nijenhuis, 2015 and outlined in Chapter 1) could help to increase specificity but may come at a cost to sensitivity in this population.

The quote below, reported by Reuben and Parish (2022), from a person with autism who also reported dissociative experiences, provides valuable insight into the stress arising from difficulties navigating social situations. It also highlights the need to explore the underlying meaning and function of specific symptoms.

> I believe my alters experience my autism to different degrees and in different regards. For instance, one alter may be nonverbal and stim by chewing and pulling hair and rocking, while another alter may be very charismatic, abnormally intelligent, and only do small stims (like playing with a spinner ring). Usually, I switch whenever a specific alter seems better fitted to a task, so one alter might be great for managing emotional distress, while another one is better for socialising with peers, while another one is better for socialising with family.

Clinicians working therapeutically with autistic people report dissociation as a common experience for the people they work with (Reuben & Parish, 2022). Reuben et al. (2021) in a survey of 687 autistic people, found evidence for high levels of somatoform dissociation (32%). Some 94% also had one or more clinically elevated subscales on the Multiscale Dissociation Inventory (Briere et al., 2005) with 85% reporting symptoms of emotional disengagement, 72% experienced depersonalisation, 59% derealisation, 53% endorsed dissociation with an amnesic component and 26% rated the most severe dissociative experiences relating to identity. The above study also highlights the potential difficulty in differentiating between autism and trauma-related dissociation. Experiences such as 'emotional disengagement' could be driven by trauma-related avoidance, or by differences in emotional processing, high prevalence of co-occurring alexithymia (Kinnaird et al., 2019) or social communication. An experience such as derealisation could relate to a trauma-based dissociative response or be secondary to autism-related anxiety. As such high scores on specific subscales may not reflect the presence of trauma-related dissociation.

Assessment measures and approaches to formulation that help clinicians to determine the function of such symptoms are key in facilitating an understanding of presenting problems for autistic people and whether they represent a trauma response, feature of autism or indeed are an inter-play between the two.

Lived Experiences of People with co-occurring Autism and Dissociation:

'We are constantly trying to fit in and not seem different to people, so we are always trying to watch what we are doing and saying, and it's hard and tiring. It's like we are always on guard, thinking, analysing, coz people will judge us.' **Ben (27)**

'*I was in music group and I didn't understand why nobody else was bothered by the cymbal crash. I noticed nobody else cared, but I did! It made me feel different.*' **Angela (19)**

'*Most people don't get it, when you've got autism, your cup is already full, it doesn't take much for it to overflow.*' **Stephen (28)**

4.3 What Is the Relationship Between Autism and Dissociation?

The relationship between autism and dissociation may take many forms.

First, core aspects of autism may be misinterpreted as 'dissociation'. For example, Reuben and Parish (2022) described a predisposition to absorption in internal imagination. Although lacking strong evidence, early research shows association between autistic traits and absorption in the form of 'maladaptive daydreaming' (West et al., 2023). Kinnaird et al's (2019) systematic review found that alexithymia, with its decoupling of emotional and physiological experience from conscious awareness (Silani et al., 2008), is common in autism. Experiences of burnout, inertia, meltdown, and shutdown are common in social media narratives and discourse within the autistic community. As highlighted in Figure 7.2 below, these experiences may have phenomenological overlaps with dissociative responses. There can also be significant social drivers that lead people to seek community and connection through social media, something that can lead people to incorrectly self-diagnose DID often driven by a sense of confusion regarding identity (Salter et al., 2025).

Case Example: Lizzy (19), diagnosed with ASD, gave birth to her baby daughter whilst living with her mum, dad, brother, and sister. Her Auntie Margarette lived opposite and spent much time in the family's home. Lizzy had experienced regular dissociative episodes for several years during a turbulent, abusive relationship with her ex-partner. Recovering from an episode of psychosis an 'Open-Dialogue' approach was used, with each family member reflecting on how Lizzy's condition affected them and influenced their thoughts, feelings and behaviour towards her. It emerged how each person was unclear how the others were feeling and how, in trying to be caring and helpful, they were causing Lizzy to feel disempowered and 'worse'.

Auntie Margarette: '*We're all just trying to help, we don't want you to get upset and stressed, with everything you've been through, we don't want to make you worse.*'

Lizzy: '*But you don't understand, it makes me feel stupid and useless and like you don't trust me and that I can't do anything, and that makes me feel worse.*'

Embodied experiences of autism	Key characteristics from the current evidence-base
Burnout	3+ months of persistence: • Chronic exhaustion • Loss of skills (thinking, planning, social, creative) • Reduced tolerance to sensory stimulus and associated avoidance. Some conceptual overlap with depersonalisation (e.g., numbing), memory problems and social withdrawal. (Raymaker et al., 2020; Higgins et al., 2021)
Inertia	Persisting state of being 'stuck' associated with: • Loss of physical capacity to engage in desired activities • Loss of conscious control of planning, initiating, stopping, and transitioning between activities • At times so profound, inability to initiate simple actions suggestive of movement disorder. (Welch et al., 2021; Buckle, 2021)
Meltdown	A phenomenon related to the cumulative stress of social, sensory and emotional experiences that can vary in its expressions: • Complete overwhelm associated with a lack of control • Overt anxiety, frustration, anger and energy outpour • Loss of reflective capacity and memory • Possible aggression or self-injurious repetitive behaviour. (Schaber, 2014; Welch et al., 2021; Lewis & Stevens, 2023)
Shutdown	Inward expression of cumulative response to social, sensory and emotional overload: • Attentional withdrawal from surroundings • Unresponsive to communication • Physical paralysis • Heightened sensory response (e.g., low threshold for overwhelm) • Fluctuating level of functioning, at most profound feeling detached from limbs and assuming foetal position. (Belek, 2019; Phung et al., 2021)
Alexithymia	Decoupling of emotional and physiological experience from conscious awareness associated with difficulties: • Identifying emotions • Distinguishing between emotions and bodily sensations of arousal • Describing emotions to others • Identifying facial expressions • Identifying and remembering faces • Diminished awareness of the emotions of others. (Berthoz & Hill, 2005; Silani et al., 2008; Bird & Cook, 2013)

Figure 7.2 Embodied Experiences of Autism with Similarities to Dissociation.

Auntie Margarette: *'Oh, my darling girl, I am so sorry, I had no idea you felt that way.'*

Mum: *'Oh babe's I'm sorry, we didn't know, we would never have known, we would never want to make you feel like that.'*

Following this curious, non-judgemental approach, family members reported talking more openly and recognising how much stress had been taken out of the family situation as a result.

Second, there can be an interaction between autism and trauma-related dissociation. For example, experiences that are related to autism (such as facial agnosia) may occur alongside and interact with trauma-related dissociative experiences, such as experiences of derealisation and depersonalisation (Minio-Paluello et al., 2020; Reuben et al., 2021). Identity confusion in autistic populations (perhaps secondary to the use of masking as a social survival strategy) may be a possible risk factor for more severe forms of dissociation (Reuben & Parish, 2022) following an early traumatic experience.

Case Example: Gareth (24) was an inpatient in a mental health unit with longstanding diagnoses of Autism, ADHD and Psychosis. To cope with early abuse and neglect, Gareth retreated into the safety of his own mind, constructing an imaginative world comprised of 'multiple levels, a bit like a computer game'. During acute phases of psychosis, the internal world took on a more sinister feel, leading to Gareth acting aggressively, multiple in-patient admissions, and being treated with antipsychotic medication. This reduced his distress from the persecutory elements of his belief system. However, his tendency to retreat into his multi-layered fantasy world remained.

Through ongoing assessment, a psychological formulation was collaboratively developed. Gareth, his family and the team reached a shared understanding that his internal world was part of his neurodivergent thinking style *and* a helpful coping strategy. Gareth had invested time and energy developing and embellishing his internal world and it was something he did not want to lose. All involved agreed it was a well-rehearsed fantasy world providing retreat during times of distress. This helpful coping mechanism was not amenable to change, with or without antipsychotic medication.

The psychological formulation of Gareth's presentation changed the team's understanding and treatment plan. The MDT stopped trying to modify his belief system, which reduced Gareth's distress and his aggressive responses to staff. Instead, Gareth was supported to express his feelings and concerns during times of stress. He acquired new psychological skills, acknowledging and expressing his feelings in a non-threatening way. Gareth continues to function well in the community with his belief system and internal world unchanged.

The case examples above highlight the complexity of overlapping symptoms of neurodivergence and dissociation, as well as psychosis. They highlight the importance of continued assessment, and the value of collateral information from supporters. Time and compassionate attention are needed to discern:

- What might be individual coping styles, particularly in response to trauma?
- What do changes in presentation, levels of distress and ability to function mean?

Third, people with autism may also experience a range of dissociative experiences in similar ways to neurotypical populations (Reuben & Parish, 2022).

Case Example: Charlotte, aged 22, suffered early childhood sexual abuse by her biological father. She also witnessed her father physically and emotionally abusing her mother and remembered feeling terrified and unable to help. The terror continued as she witnessed her alcohol dependent and emotionally unavailable mother develop relationships with a number of aggressive, abusive men. Feeling unloved, terrified, powerless, and unable to help or escape, Charlotte unconsciously developed a strategy to protect herself. She described how now when feeling overwhelmed or frightened, *'This strange feeling covers over me, sometimes it starts with me seeing shadowy figures or things on the wall, my skin prickles and my hairs stand on end. Then this thing, like a dark cloud, comes and wraps around me, it completely covers me and I just like, stop feeling, and then I'm just gone, for ages'.*

Research Question: Identify and explore experiences of trauma-related dissociation – those arising from being autistic in a neurotypical world, and experiences that may be secondary to autism.

At a conceptual level, some cognitive and emotional processes often associated with autism have historically been described in terms of differences in 'new brain competencies' (Gilbert, 2020), such as theory of mind, mentalising or the capacity to identify and communicate emotions. However, more recent evidence suggests that these patterns are frequently linked to co-occurring alexithymia rather than autism itself (Bird & Cook, 2013; Kinnaird et al., 2019). Similarly, what has been framed as a theory of mind difference may in fact reflect relational dynamics, as highlighted in the 'double empathy problem', where misattunements occur across neurotypes rather than within autistic people alone (Milton, 2012). Within such socially complex and sometimes invalidating environments, autistic people may experience uncertainty or confusion about aspects of identity, as a response to conflicting feedback and difficulties in mutual understanding. Alongside these interpersonal factors, sensory differences can create contexts in which withdrawal or detachment is a protective and adaptive response.

4.4 Autism and Dissociation: Practice Recommendations

There are several important considerations for clinical practice, outlined below (Reuben, 2023).

a) Awareness.

- The service in which a client is seen may shape the lens through which the person is understood. If a client is seen for assessment/treatment of trauma, then their experience of autism may be missed, and the same may be true in reverse
- Biological sex and gender can influence the lens through which clinicians interpret a person's presenting difficulties; with males being more likely to be viewed through an autism lens and females through a trauma/dissociation lens
- When autism and trauma are present it is equally important to recognise both, and to consider the interplay between them
- While autistic people may 'mask' and experience identity confusion this may be phenomenologically different from trauma-related structural dissociation of the personality.

b) Assessment and formulation.

- Routine screening for trauma and dissociation should be part of standard assessment when autistic people access the mental health system
- There are factors that could increase the risk of *false negatives* for autistic people (trauma-related dissociation being incorrectly missed when it is present)
    - For example, existing screening measures have accessibility issues for autistic people. Emerging research is working to delineate complex trauma and autism and develop appropriate measures (Cox et al., 2018).
- There are steps that can reduce the risk of such *false negatives* for autistic people
    - Non-adapted screening measures should be used with an awareness of autistic social communication differences and the need for reasonable adjustment and adaptation, e.g. processing and understanding questions about dissociation in literal ways. Assessment questions should be straightforward, precise, well-organised and asked in a range of ways

- Clinicians should be mindful that autistic people may 'mask' to protect themselves, particularly when discussing emotions and emotional experiences
- It is helpful to acknowledge and validate individual's neurodivergent methods of processing and dealing with difficulties, avoiding making assumptions or pathologising what may in fact make sense to the person
- Gather collateral information where possible, including historical information.
- There are also factors which could increase the risk of *false positives* for autistic people (trauma-related dissociation being incorrectly diagnosed when it is not present). As noted by Salter et al. (2025) self-identification could complicate this picture
- There are steps clinicians can take to reduce the risk of *false positives*
  - Clinicians should be well informed about the differing presentations and ensure approaches to assessment, and formulation can facilitate differentiation
  - The endorsement of a symptom is insufficient to determine the underlying function or mechanism
  - Tools that help to assist in the differentiation of trauma-responses, autism, and non-trauma related sources of identity confusion, such as the Coventry Grid (Cox et al., 2018) and the TADS-I (Boon, 2023), should be considered to help determine the relative contribution of autism and trauma-related dissociation and formulate the underlying function of symptoms

- Psychobiosocial formulation provides a tool to explain the relative contributions, functions and origins of symptoms related to autism, trauma-related dissociation or the interaction between the two

c) Treatment

- Treatments need to be informed by a psychobiosocial formulation and matched to the underlying mechanism driving a difficulty. Failure to do this risks iatrogenic harm
- Treatments for trauma-related dissociation will need adaptation around the specific needs of the autistic person, for example their social and sensory needs, as part of a person-centred approach to treatment
- Attention should be given to potentially stressful experiences of social interaction and how a neurodivergent individual may attempt to manage this through complex and well-developed ways of relating to themselves and others, including stimming and complex ordered rituals. Others may retreat into an internal world where they feel safe or powerful. While these 'rehearsed strategies' may seem different, they can be compassionately understood as helpful self-management strategies, not an indication of illness or disordered thinking.

d) Policy and service development.

Health and social care policy related to services for autistic people should consider the following recommendations:

- Early identification and support for autistic children and their families would help to mitigate the consequences of lifelong experiences of polyvictimisation and relational trauma from an early age, preventing the long term consequences of trauma symptoms including dissociation
- Interventions delivered at the level of the wider system should be considered, regarding how services are designed, commissioned, and delivered to meet the mental health needs of autistic children and adults, and improving system health around them (Mevissen et al., 2020)
- Autism, including lived experience voices, should have more prominence in national policy, guidelines and research in relation to trauma and dissociation. This should ensure that new and adapted frameworks for understanding, assessing and intervening, are inclusive of autism and other forms of neurodivergence.

4.5 Autism and Dissociation: Questions for Future Research

Some suggestions for possible areas of future research are as follows:

- Include the autistic experience and perspective in research, through collaboration and coproduction
- Consider a bottom-up, qualitative approach to exploring the phenomenological similarities or differences between dissociation and embodied autism experiences
- Define trauma and its expression, including dissociation, in autistic people, leading to research of new models and frameworks for assessment and intervention.

4.6 Autism and Dissociation: Summary

To summarise, the literature suggests that neurodivergent people experience higher levels of traumatic experience and widely described phenomenological experiences with significant overlap with the function and nature of dissociation. Nonetheless, there are challenges in being able to determine the presence and relative contribution of trauma-related dissociation in autistic people. A range of practice recommendations have been suggested to increase awareness, improve assessment processes, develop appropriate formulations, adapt interventions, influence service development, and consider future research.

5. Dissociation and Obsessive-Compulsive Disorder (OCD)

'For as long as I can remember I've been batting the voices away, trying to quieten them – it's been a daily fight. Since starting therapy, I have realised

that fighting with them does not work. Now we are listening to each other. I have never felt such peace.' **Expert-by-Experience**

Dissociative experiences are often considered psychological defences triggered by external traumatic events, while obsessions and compulsions are commonly viewed as responses to internal distressing thoughts. While they are distinct constructs, research has consistently shown overlap between OCD and dissociation. The clinical management of people with both areas of difficulty requires nuanced understanding, thorough assessment, and integrative treatment approaches that address both trauma and anxiety-related features.

Case Example: Christos, aged 62 and diagnosed with DID, presented in a multidisciplinary Pain Clinic with increased pain and overactivity linked to compulsive cleaning behaviours. In therapy, these behaviours were traced to a dissociative part named Billy, who sought to 'make things right' and was linked to childhood sexual abuse. During abuse episodes, Christos had been forced to clean sheets, and Billy's behaviours were attempts to maintain safety through cleanliness. Through trauma-informed work, Billy was helped to understand the origin of his OCD and began communicating with other parts. Internal collaboration led to reduced compulsions, better pacing and lower pain levels. Exposure and Response Prevention (ERP) was gradually introduced following establishment of grounding techniques, and Billy accepted help from other parts in reducing harmful behaviours.

5.1 The Intersection of Dissociation and OCD

The co-occurrence of OCD and dissociative symptoms is historically well-documented. Shorvon (1946) noted an 88% prevalence of obsessive personality traits in patients with depersonalisation. However, the precise relationship between the two remains unclear. Recently, Soffer-Dudek (2023) proposed five conceptual models to explain the connection between OCD and dissociative experiences, although these models focus primarily on obsessive-compulsive symptoms (OCS) and dissociative experiences, rather than diagnosed dissociative disorders.

Recent research highlights that about 5.1% of individuals with OCD also meet criteria for PTSD (Sharma et al., 2021). Meta-analyses support the relationship between childhood trauma, insecure attachment, and increased OCS severity (Destrée et al., 2021; Miller & Brock, 2017). Furthermore, Belli et al. (2012) found that 14% of OCD patients had a comorbid dissociative disorder, with depersonalisation disorder being most common, followed by DID and dissociative amnesia.

Clinical studies emphasise that dissociative symptoms may underlie or exacerbate treatment-resistant OCD. For example, Tatli et al. (2018) found obsessive ruminations are more strongly linked to dissociative symptoms than other OCD features. Watson et al. (2004) noted parallels between identity alteration in DID and intrusive thoughts seen in OCD, where people fear they have a 'potential self' capable of harmful actions incongruent with their known self.

Boger et al. (2020) found severity of dissociation correlated with OCD severity. Patients with high dissociation levels often show poor habituation during exposure therapy (Rufer et al., 2006), and high psychoform dissociation predicts resistance to both CBT and pharmacotherapy treatments (Prasko et al., 2009). PTSD and trauma histories also reduce treatment responsiveness (Gershuny et al., 2002), and childhood trauma (especially emotional neglect, abuse, and bodily threat) is consistently associated with more severe OCD (Semiz et al., 2014).

5.2 Assessment Considerations

Steinberg (2023) noted 'when someone suffers from dissociation, it is rarely their presenting complaint' in clinical settings. She emphasised that symptoms of OCD, depression, phobias, anxiety, substance abuse etc may be 'external signs' of underlying dissociation. Therefore, clinicians should explore the possibility of dissociation when standard treatment approaches to OCD appear to plateaux or fail, beginning with screening tools such as DES-II (see Chapter 2). Once dissociation is suspected or confirmed, the way dissociation interacts with OCD symptoms should be explored. Each presentation will vary greatly, so clinicians must gather a thorough psychobiosocial history and maintain a flexible, individualised approach.

> *'I'm leaving notes for Jo-Jo (OCD part), I just say 'my back is bad can you go easy today?- and she is listening! Pacing cleaning! Helping in a good way. It's never been like this before. We are working as a team and I feel at last that the future is hopeful.'* **Expert-by-Experience**

When structural dissociation is identified, the relationship between personality parts and OCD symptoms should be explored. Clients often report specific parts engaging in compulsive behaviours. Assessment should include curious and respectful enquiries into each part's role and experience, which models the style of internal dialogue clients aim for in therapy. A collaborative formulation involving as many internal personality parts as possible can aid trust in the therapeutic relationship.

5.3 Treatment Approaches

CBT is the recognised primary treatment for OCD (Elsouri et al., 2024), but dissociation significantly impedes its effectiveness (Rufer et al., 2006). Therefore, for people with comorbid dissociation, addressing these symptoms must be integrated into the OCD treatment plan. A trauma-informed, phase-based model is often most effective, beginning with stabilisation, safety and grounding, progressing to trauma processing, and culminating in internal reconnection and living a more integrated life (see Chapters 4, 5 and 18).

The presence of dissociative symptoms, particularly structural dissociation, complicates the treatment of OCD. OCD behaviours may serve as attempts to manage internal chaos or maintain a sense of safety. Thus, interventions must be paced carefully to avoid overwhelming the person and worsening either condition.

Case Example: Meena, aged 32 and diagnosed with DID, exhibited contamination OCD that interfered with group living in a residential trauma clinic. Rather than isolate OCD from trauma therapy, the treatment team integrated these through collaborative planning. OCD behaviours were understood as trauma reenactments and efforts to reclaim control.

Staff initially expressed frustration over Meena's inflexible behaviours (e.g., refusing to eat with others, difficulty sharing living space), but the team psychologist helped reframe these as trauma responses. Meena's depersonalisation allowed her to tolerate extreme discomfort (e.g., starvation). This disconnection from her body was explored in therapy.

By developing empathy for her internal processes, the team supported more cohesive treatment. The psychologist alerted the team to the commonly reported experience of mirroring the client's fragmented internal processes, by family/caregivers of people with DID. Multidisciplinary collaboration and a trauma-informed understanding helped reduce conflict, allowing Meena to engage in therapy more safely and consistently.

Grounding and stabilisation are critical first steps. These may include breathwork, sensory grounding (e.g., using objects, sounds, smells), and imagery work (e.g., safe place and internal resources). Internal communication between parts should be encouraged (for example, using a shared communication book, or the 'internal conference table'). Grounding preferences for individual personality parts should be acknowledged, for example, a child part may want a cuddly toy, an older part prefer a stress ball. Acknowledging and recognising differences between internal voices, their beliefs and individual past experiences, is essential to hold as therapy proceeds. As understanding and safety increase, more targeted OCD interventions such as ERP may be cautiously introduced.

Therapists should be flexible, validating, and ready to reformulate treatment as new internal dynamics or trauma material emerge. For example, obsessive number counting may be traced back to a dissociative coping ritual during childhood rape, but in adulthood escalates when a lack of felt sense of safety is experienced. Therapists should expect ambivalence and resistance among dissociative parts, some may be eager for change, while others resist therapy out of fear, loyalty to abusers, or desire to protect the internal system. Where amnesia is a dissociative feature, the felt need to continue rituals in OCD may be strong and resistant to cognitive evidence. There may be difficulty recognising evidence of the present day in some parts if they are stuck in a loop of trauma memories.

5.4 Dissociation and OCD: Practice Recommendations

- **Full Assessment:** Use psychobiosocial models and screening tools to determine the presence and interaction of both OCD and dissociative symptoms
- **Collaborative Formulation:** Create shared formulations with the person (and known parts), ensuring all symptoms and their purposes are validated
- **Stabilisation and Grounding:** Always begin with grounding strategies. Help the person to stabilise before addressing OCD rituals or trauma content
- **Internal Dialogue:** Encourage communication between parts. This fosters internal safety and promotes consistency in therapy
- **Trauma-Awareness:** Assume the likelihood of trauma. Pace discussions carefully, ensuring the person does not become destabilised by premature disclosure or exploration
- **Therapist Flexibility:** Be prepared to revise formulations and adjust treatment according to emerging internal dynamics or new disclosures. Not all sessions will follow a structured agenda
- **Respect the Function of Symptoms:** Understand that both OCD and dissociation serve self-protective functions. Understand and address them as adaptive responses that need safer alternatives
- **Work with Resistance:** Recognise that some parts may fear healing. Validate their roles, build trust, and invite their input into therapy
- **Rule-Based Trauma:** For people with histories of coercive, rule-laden abuse, OCD may be an attempt to regain internal control. Therapy must help the person understand the origin of such rules and gradually enable greater flexibility in coping responses
- **OCD and Self-Responsibility:** Younger parts may obsess over being 'good' to maintain attachment or avoid punishment. Identifying these parts and their developmental needs is key to therapeutic progress.

5.5 Dissociation and OCD: Future Research Questions

Some possible areas for further research include:

- Exploring use of standard tools to identify dissociation in OCD
- Developing and measuring the effectiveness of treatment packages that can address OCD in the context of trauma-related dissociation
- Exploring cultural and diversity needs and issues in people with OCD and dissociation comorbidity.

5.6 Dissociation and OCD: Summary

The comorbidity of dissociation and OCD presents unique challenges but also powerful opportunities for healing. When clinicians adopt a trauma-informed, flexible, and collaborative approach, clients can begin to integrate their experiences, reduce debilitating symptoms, and reclaim a sense of internal safety. Understanding the protective roles of both dissociation and compulsive behaviours is crucial in supporting sustainable change. Grounded in empathy and curiosity, therapy can become a space where fragmented selves are welcomed, heard, and ultimately find ways to live more harmoniously.

6. Conclusion

This chapter has explored issues arising in the complex but prevalent area of comorbid overlap between trauma-based dissociative experiences and a range of other mental health difficulties. The co-occurrence of dissociation with each of these three presentations is considerably under-recognised in practice, and yet has implications for engagement, treatment and outcomes. Screening for dissociation should therefore be routine across these comorbid areas, as should careful developmental assessment. Attempts to resolve diagnostic complexity may risk overshadowing the client's distress and individual goals for recovery. A psycho-biosocial formulation should therefore have a key role in informing the unique understanding of the particular person and their overlapping presentation. This will inform treatment planning, ensuring interventions are individualised and directed towards the key drivers for the person's difficulties. The impact of cultural and diverse sources of disadvantage should inform this understanding.

Dissociation-Informed Care for Specific Populations and Contexts

Chapter 8

Dissociation and Physical Health

*Jo Burrell, Fiona Summers, Paul Langthorne,
Rachel Sabin-Farrell and Elizabeth Gallant*

1. Introduction

The reciprocal relationship between mental health and physical health has long been recognised. Some clinical presentations to physical health care settings, such as functional neurological disorder (FND), functional seizures, medically unexplained pain, sensory loss or paralysis may be dissociative in origin (Nijenhuis et al., 1998). Dissociation and the impact of this on a person's physical health and coping may go undetected, potentially leading to misdiagnosis and inappropriate treatment. This chapter provides an overview of the relationship between dissociation and physical health presentations and provides a range of recommendations to better meet the needs of people who experience trauma-related dissociation in physical health settings.

2. The Relationship Between Trauma, Dissociative Experience and Physical Health

There is a strong relationship between trauma and physical health difficulties (Schnurr, 2015), this has been particularly well studied in the context of adverse childhood experiences (ACEs). Felitti et al. (1998) found that more than half of their 17,000 participants reported at least one ACE and a quarter reported two or more. Conditions such as some cancers, chronic lung disease and ischaemic heart disease were more prevalent when there were a higher number of ACEs reported.

There are a number of pathways by which early trauma may relate to physical illness (Schnurr & Green, 2004), some of which are outlined below.

A systematic review of the evidence regarding ACEs and their impact on health biomarkers found experiencing childhood trauma was related to several physiological changes including an increase in immune, structural, and functional brain changes, as well as genetic and epigenetic markers from childhood and that these changes may influence the development of ill health in later life (Soares et al., 2021). It has been suggested that multidirectional pathways connect dissociation, trauma and poor physical health outcomes via the impact of trauma and dissociation on the responsivity of the catecholamine system, hypothalamic–pituitary–adrenal axis

DOI: 10.4324/9781003625650-11

and immune system (Boyer et al., 2022). The disruption of these systems increases the risk of diabetes, cardiovascular issues and inflammation while reducing an individual's threshold for pain (Kendall-Tackett & Klest, 2009).

Individuals exposed to trauma are also more at risk of engaging in unhealthy lifestyles and risk-taking behaviour, potentially as a way of coping (Shonkoff & Garner, 2012) and therefore may be at higher risk of physical ill health as a result. Conversely, experiences relating to physical ill health, and resulting medical procedures can also be traumatic and lead to trauma symptoms and dissociation as a result (Scaer, 2014).

Trauma survivors can also be re-traumatised by contact with physical health providers, for example by procedures requiring intimate contact. They may also actively avoid seeking help for medical issues for fear of being retraumatised (Haven, 2009), potentially leading to further deterioration in physical health.

People with trauma histories who experience dissociation, may also be less aware of their bodies (Haven, 2009) and may have a higher threshold for pain (Ludäscher et al., 2007), and as such may seek help for physical health difficulties at a later stage than others, potentially meaning that issues can progress further without being detected.

Dissociation may present physically through the body, as somatoform dissociation (as discussed in Chapter 1) and may present as negative or positive symptoms. Somatoform dissociative symptoms often reflect the body's typical response to overwhelming attack. This defensive cascade typically involves initial freezing (i.e., motor inhibition), analgesia in response to imminent strike, anaesthesia with total submission followed by acute pain when the threat has passed to promote behaviours that support healing and recovery (Nijenhuis et al., 1998).

Studies have also shown that somatoform dissociation is predicted by physical and sexual abuse histories (Nijenhuis et al., 1998). Somatoform dissociation is reliably and consistently correlated with psychoform forms of dissociation (Dell, 2002; Nijenhuis, 1999). Studies using the SDQ-20 (Nijenhuis et al., 1996) have shown somatoform symptoms to be characteristic of people meeting criteria for a dissociative disorder (DD) diagnosis, particularly Other Specified Dissociative Disorders (OSDD) and Dissociative Identity Disorder (DID), and a core feature of conversion or somatoform disorders. Psychoform and somatoform dissociation is associated with higher rates of somatic symptoms (Scioli-Salter et al., 2016), various types of chronic pain (Panisch et al., 2023) and functional seizures (Fleisher et al., 2002).

There is currently no available data to demonstrate the frequency with which people experiencing dissociation attend general hospitals. However, studies of prevalence rates of dissociation within populations in physical health settings suggest that consideration should be given to dissociative symptoms.

Levels of dissociation appear to be raised in people who experience functional seizures (Mitchell et al., 2012). Indeed, Bowman and Markland (1996) noted that 90% of individuals diagnosed with functional seizures also met the criteria for a

DD. As functional seizures account for 11–27% of all emergency seizure presentations, for up to 20% of patients in epilepsy clinics and 20–40% of patients in epilepsy-monitoring in-patient units (Cengiz et al., 2024), it is likely that people experiencing dissociation are over-represented in these services. A systematic review by Campbell et al. (2022) revealed that dissociation is frequently comorbid with Functional Neurological Disorder (FND), finding elevated scores on measures of both psychoform and somatoform dissociation. Higher levels of dissociation have also been found in populations presenting with fibromyalgia (Romeo et al., 2022), and chronic pain (Duckworth et al., 2000) when compared to healthy controls or general populations.

I was suffering from seizures, losing time and having marked changes in personality/mood along with suicidality, anxiety, depression and PTSD. By age 9 this had been witnessed by various mental health staff. After having an EEG and MRI I was promptly discharged from all physical and mental health care, as the seizures 'were not epilepsy'. At this point, if only one of the professionals was trauma informed, they could have ended my childhood physical, emotional and sexual abuse and I could have got the diagnosis & treatment I so desperately needed, for the DID I already had, 27 years before I then eventually did, aged 32. This could have allowed me a chance of recovery. Speaking to other systems, our experiences are so similar. After being misdiagnosed, you are then failed by the system, often multiple times, causing secondary or NHS trauma. A double deprivation. This makes the larger, now more ingrained trauma, harder to treat, causing a terminal mistrust of services and the health system that can have tragic consequences. This adds to, compounds & amplifies the effects of the ACE's mentioned, sometimes meaning some patients never seek help again. Of course the healthcare professionals never mean this to be detrimental to the patient but actually I've had so many discussions with other systems where we discuss which is worse, 'more evil' or 'more damaging', the original trauma at a young age, a crime that causes fragmentation of the mind, or the endemic, insidious and multiple failings that compound this trauma over years, embedding it even further and making the resources needed so much more when it comes to finally achieving a diagnosis. This makes the treatment needed so much longer, more intense and resource heavy. Ultimately, in some cases, this can lead to recovery being unobtainable, resulting in a markedly worse quality of life and reduced life expectancy. **Expert-by-Experience and Health Care Professional**

3. The Role of the Psychological Practitioner in Supporting the Treatment of Individuals Experiencing Dissociation in Physical Health Care Settings

It is unlikely that psychological practitioners working within physical health will be providing psychological therapy for complex dissociation, as this is more commonly provided within mental health services (see Chapter 4). However, a significant proportion of the population attending physical health care settings are likely to experience symptoms of dissociation (Cengiz et al., 2024). Therefore, it is important that psychological practitioners working within physical health settings can support individuals experiencing dissociation to access the health care that they need. In addition, psychological practitioners need to support the healthcare system to provide care that meets people's needs and reduces the likelihood of the system being retraumatising.

3.1 Psychological Therapy

Psychological practitioners working within physical health settings support individuals with health conditions that may be causing psychological distress and work to help reduce the impact of psychological factors on ill-health. They may also be involved in providing psychological therapy to people who are struggling to engage in necessary healthcare procedures.

People who experience dissociation and have physical health needs may find the demands of a healthcare setting particularly challenging. It is unlikely that a referral to a psychological service within the health care setting will mention the presence of dissociative symptoms. In part this is due to the under-recognition of dissociation (Loewenstein, 2018). It is also possible that the individual is unaware that they are experiencing dissociation and may be confused and frightened by their experiences. Likewise, some people presenting with functional symptoms will not report a history of trauma and may not view adverse experiences they have experienced as traumatic (see Nijenhuis, 2015 for example). A thorough assessment and collaborative formulation are essential to develop a clear and structured care plan (see Chapter 2) whilst maintaining the therapeutic alliance.

Where an individual is being supported by a mental health team or another agency, collaborating with that team is key, so consent to speak with them should be sought early in the assessment process (see Chapter 3). If psychological therapy is already ongoing the psychological practitioner from the physical health team should discuss the formulation and help to ensure recommended adjustments are made wherever possible. If an individual is experiencing trauma related dissociative symptoms that are triggered by the healthcare environment, then psychological therapy to help address the trauma may be appropriate.

I recently required a colonoscopy for a chronic long-term condition. When admitted I immediately said ... 'I have DID. I know I'm also a senior staff member in the hospital, but I also have complex trauma and younger parts that are hospital phobic and might front in this setting, especially recovery' ... That information was ignored. I become very agitated in recovery, pulling all my lines out, then fell from the bed. This compounded my fear of hospitals, particularly colonoscopies ... I ended up being in recovery far longer, far more distressed and using far more resources. This information should always be listened to – it's also such a difficult thing to disclose! **Expert-by-Experience and Health Care Professional**

3.2 Supporting the System

At a health system level, psychological practitioners in leadership positions should work strategically to support and lead the introduction of trauma-informed care into organisations across medical specialties. Providing information, education and guidance to Integrated Care Boards (ICB) and NHS Trust leadership teams is essential in the development of psychologically-, trauma- and dissociation- informed health care within physical health settings (see Chapter 16 for further discussion).

3.3 Multidisciplinary Teams (MDTs)

In addition to providing formal training, psychological practitioners working within MDTs can help increase dissociation-informed thinking by supporting staff to reflect on their work and formulate during case discussions. These discussions can help inform the development of trauma and dissociation informed care/management plans with the individual which also increase 'buy in' from the health care team (see Chapter 3).

Providing clinical supervision and reflective practice for MDT staff provides another opportunity to support health care professionals in considering what part dissociation may be playing in an individual's engagement with health care.

Good Practice Example: *Cancer Nurse Specialists (CNS) attending group supervision with a Clinical Psychologist brought to supervision a situation where a patient in their care did not seem to always retain information about their treatment. They talked about how it was difficult to know how to manage conversations because 'they sometimes seem like completely different people'. This was causing the staff significant anxiety around the interactions and also led them to question if they were being ineffective in their communication.*

In supervision, the possibility that dissociation may be having an impact on this person's ability to take in and access information was discussed. Ways to support this person to be able to have improved access to information, for example providing a brief written summary of the conversation and encouraging having a supportive friend or relative present were considered.

The CNSs found the practical suggestions useful but also felt that having increased understanding of dissociation allowed them to be more empathic and feel less frustration. In addition, it is likely that the improvement in communication and engagement reduced the sense of threat felt in the interactions and so may have reduced the likelihood of the individual responding with dissociation.

Collaborative working, for me, is vital for any effective professional and patient relationship. True collaboration is similar to trust in any relationship. With trust or true collaboration, the relationship is strong and anything, any problems, can be worked on. Without it, on either side, things can very quickly break down. The respect and trust will be lost and true collaborative working will be impossible. **Expert-by-Experience and Health Care Professional**

Good communication between health care professionals involved in an individual's care is particularly pertinent where dissociation is a factor. This can be problematic when an individual has complex health needs which are being treated across different specialities or organisations. When communication between professionals is ineffective, resulting confusion may lead to raised anxiety and a reduced sense of trust which in turn may exacerbate dissociative experiences.

Case Example: *M had extreme needle phobia associated with traumatic medical experiences as a child. When exposed to hypodermic syringes or any paraphernalia associated with injections, M became extremely distressed. At these times she was generally non-verbal and stated that she felt like a 'feral child'. M was deeply ashamed of this behaviour. As a result, she declined routine blood tests in pregnancy and struggled to develop a birth plan that was safe (requesting a home birth but feeling unable to use an ambulance to attend the hospital in an emergency).*

The clinical team worked closely with M and her partner to develop a clear care plan. This involved talking about scenarios involving the need for injections. There were multiple MDT meetings to support M's care over the course of her pregnancy. Plans were made to ensure that exposure to feared stimuli was removed or minimised wherever possible. Management plans were also developed to support M in situations where injections became unavoidable. Strategies for grounding were developed and practised. In

addition, conversations with the hospital security team offered explanations
about how M would be restrained if the need arose.

The legal services team were also involved in case there was a situation
in which the team had to act in M's best interest, and this was fully discussed
with M. While this was an anxiety provoking situation for all involved the
clear and consistent communication with M and between all involved in her
care supported a positive outcome.

Where possible, continuity of care with a trusted health care professional can help
contain anxiety, and promote collaboration and consistency.

3.4 Supporting Adjustments to the Health Care Setting

Psychological professionals within physical health care settings are uniquely
placed to support individuals who experience dissociation and their care teams to
work collaboratively to make formulation-driven adjustments that enable the individual to access care in a way that minimises distress.

Ensuring that any adjustments are person-centred is essential. Without this,
well-intentioned adjustments in approach or the environment, risk inadvertently
increasing anxiety and distress for the individual.

Case Example: *A clinical psychologist was asked to assess a man who was*
on a surgical ward having been treated following an industrial accident in
which he had suffered a crush injury and had been trapped for some time.
When attending the ward the patient was on a bay with other patients with
the curtains drawn around him. He explained that when he experienced
intrusive images and relived the traumatic events the staff would draw the
curtains around his bed space. However this led to an intensification of his
dissociative symptoms. Staff were subsequently advised to keep the curtains
open except when providing personal care.

3.5 Advocating for a Shared Care/Management Plan

Psychological practitioners support good care by developing formulation-driven,
individualised, dissociation-informed care plans collaboratively with the individual, which can then be shared with the health care team. In addition to being
shared and placed on the individual's health record, the individual can have copies
of this document to take with them to appointments creating empowerment in the
interaction with potentially busy treating clinicians.

When a care plan is provided by the individual, the treating clinician should read this respectfully or provide reassurance if they have already read and understood the information from the notes.

> '*I gave him (Consultant Oncologist) the care plan we developed but he just glanced at it and put it on the table. I immediately knew he was not going to understand me so I just shut down.*'

This contrasts with a positive experience in Day Surgery:

> '*The nurse read my care plan and asked me about bits to be sure she understood, it really helped to know they would take the time to help me.*' **JC, Expert-by-Experience**

Care plans should be brief and clear to allow treating clinicians to read and understand them in the limited time available.

4. Recommendations for Primary Care and Outpatient Settings

Elmore (2000) describes the support of people experiencing complex dissociation in primary care settings, using what they term the SELF approach. This consists of:

- *Symptom Recognition*. This relies on clinicians in primary care settings being able to recognise dissociative symptoms accurately
- *Education of the Patient and Family*. When dissociative symptoms are noted then the patient and the family are educated about the symptoms to reduce the fear and shame attached to experiences. The role of medication is considered
- *Learning New Skills*. Emphasis is given to learning to identify the triggers for dissociative experiences and develop more adaptive coping skills that reduce the need for dissociation, including relaxation and assertiveness skills
- *Follow Up*. Follow up contact entails brief sessions to determine impact of any medication and review of assertiveness and relaxation approaches to stress management.

Indeed Elmore (2000) notes that for some people presenting with dissociative difficulties, support from a trusted primary care practitioner who has good links with mental health clinicians, may be more effective than referral to specialist services due to the pre-existing therapeutic alliance. He provides three case studies (all of whom had declined group therapy) demonstrating this approach to the management of people within a primary care setting.

Some general principles can also be very important in providing dissociation informed support which are outlined below.

4.1 Prior to the Appointment

- Health care staff should enquire if an individualised care plan has been developed. If available, they should read and follow the recommendations where possible
- Provide details of appointments in writing and, where possible, support with text reminders to scaffold amnesia
- Consider the layout of the clinic room, with reference to any information in the care plan, and where possible make adjustments in collaboration with the person
- Posters and other displays should be considered for potential trauma triggers.

4.2 In the Waiting Area

- Waiting areas should be welcoming and feel safe
- Tools to support distraction may be helpful, such as magazines or colouring materials
- Some individuals may find it helpful to wait in a quiet area nearby or in their car and be called on their mobile phone to return for their appointment
- The person should be asked if they wish to be accompanied by a friend or relative.

4.3 In the Appointment

- Efforts should be made to ensure the person feels **relationally safe** in the appointment:
  - Staff introduce themselves
  - Wear a name badge
  - Ask the person's preferred name and pronouns
  - Seek permission for medical students to attend
  - Explain the purpose of the procedure
  - Continually review consent steps, to encourage informed consent should be followed (see Chapter 6, Safety Concerns for guidance)
  - Ask what they would like to happen if dissociation occurs
  - Not all people who experience dissociation will understand their experience or have a care plan to support them. They may be frightened, confused and

ashamed if dissociation occurs in the appointment. Clinicians should respond in a trauma-informed way with support and compassion, seeking understanding for how the situation could be made easier in future, and adapting the care plan to accommodate this new information

- Some patients may ask to audio-visually record the appointment to help support their recall (see www.bma.org.uk/advice-and-support/ethics/conf identiality-and-health-records/patients-recording-consultations for guidance from the British Medical Association)
- Where it is routine practice to copy letters to patients, it is helpful to amend letters to reduce medical jargon
- Longer clinic sessions may be required to help an individual who presents with dissociation to manage the consultation and receive the needed care
- Check back with the individual on their understanding of the consultation and its outcome. Put key points arising from the consultation in writing, particularly any actions for the individual, to scaffold amnesia.

- Efforts should be made to ensure the person feels **physically safe** in the appointment:

  - Removal of unnecessary objects or items related to trauma history
  - If not possible explaining the purpose of such equipment
  - Seek consent for all physical touch (including concerns relating to male/ female touch)
  - Explain reasons and processes for any examination/procedure
  - Take into account their care plan and required adaptations (Royal College of Obstetricians and Gynaecologists, 2022 guidance for trauma-informed smear tests)
  - Ask if they would like the process to be explained as it is happening
  - Some hospital settings may mean that people are alone in a windowless room. Reassure the individual that they can be heard, and staff will respond if needed
  - Some procedures require restraints in order to ensure the person remains still for treatment. On occasion medication to support with this process may also be helpful
  - During online consultations it is important to consider how to respond should dissociation, or a functional symptom such as a seizure, occurs. Discussion of this risk should be completed prior to the first online consultation and included in a care plan (e.g., having a trusted person nearby, agreed communication for when the individual is dissociating but still managing and safe, threshold for seeking additional medical help such as an ambulance if there is risk of harm).

5. Recommendations for Inpatient Settings

Additional to the above recommendations in-patient settings may require further adjustments. Across all healthcare settings it is essential to enable staff to recognise dissociation when it occurs.

5.1 Emergency Department

Emergency Departments (EDs) have the almost unique challenge of individuals arriving without prearranged planning. As a result, easy access to any existing care or management plan is essential.

Care plans for people with FND or dissociation should cover the possibility of presenting at the ED for these symptoms and other health reasons, such as accidents or medical emergencies.

Waiting areas can be busy with other attendees expressing high levels of distress. This may be perceived as threatening and increase the risk of dissociation. Providing access to a quiet place to wait or allowing people to wait elsewhere and calling them when they can be seen, can help someone tolerate a longer wait. However, some people may feel safer in a busy area with other people around them.

Dissociation can be confused with delirium (Wilson et al., 2021) which can result in unnecessary admission and intervention. This likelihood can be reduced if a care plan is in place and followed.

Providing as much clarity about the care that may be needed can help the individual feel more in control. However, if the individualised care plan states that the person would prefer to have limited information this should be respected where possible.

5.2 Intensive Care

The severity of illness associated with admission to an intensive care unit (ITU), the treatments used and the highly unusual environment are commonly associated with anomalous patient experiences. There is limited research that considers the impact of pre-existing dissociative experiences on individuals admitted to ITU. However, it has been noted that pre-existing psychological difficulties predict post ICU PTSD symptoms (Hatch et al., 2018). It is reasonable to hypothesise that pre-existing dissociative experiences may be exacerbated by the ITU environment and treatment.

Clear communication with patients, even when the individual is not fully conscious is recommended. Trusted family members or friends may also help support the individual to feel safer in a frightening context. On ITUs there are often noticeboards that provide important information about the patient where the care plan can also be displayed.

Some ITUs offer follow-up clinics, an ideal opportunity to help an individual contextualise their experiences and note the impact that dissociative experiences may have had. ITUs often keep diaries of individuals' time on the unit, which will be offered to patients, although they may choose not to accept them. These can be helpful in making sense of the ITU experience, however the process of reading the diaries should be managed sensitively and it may be appropriate for a psychological practitioner to support the individual in this process.

5.3 The Ward Environment

When there is a planned admission, the care plan should be discussed with the treating team and ward staff prior to admission. This will support the team to understand and clarify the plan and reduce the likelihood of miscommunication, particularly if the individual receiving care struggles to communicate when anxious or experiencing dissociation. The care plan should help guide decisions such as whether the individual would prefer to be accommodated in a bay or side room.

The care plan can support staff to understand that the ward environment may present potential triggers so unexpected responses can be understood and managed with this in mind.

Extended visiting can be helpful to allow trusted friends or family to be present particularly at times when there may be experiences that increase the likelihood of a dissociative response.

Unfortunately, pressured hospital environments may not always be able to accommodate all adjustments, however, effective communication with the individual to explain why this is the case will help.

5.4 Day Surgery/Theatres

Careful consideration of the care plan and excellent communication is again key. Consideration may be given to positioning on theatre lists and the communication of last minute changes that may occur.

Medications routinely used in anaesthesia can induce dissociative states. Case studies have reported the experience of identity alteration during the perioperative and post operative period both in an individual with a pre-existing diagnosis of DID (Kuroda et al., 2022) and someone with no reported history of dissociation (Kirschen et al., 2023).

6. Conclusion

Individuals presenting with dissociative symptoms are likely to be overrepresented in physical health care settings, due to the wide-ranging long-term impacts of early trauma and adversity. Ensuring universal respect and compassion for all patients will improve the care of all, including individuals who experience trauma-related dissociation.

Chapter 9

Dissociation in the Perinatal Context

Meeting the Needs of Mothers and Babies

Janice Rigby

1. Introduction: The Perinatal Context

The perinatal period covers the span from conception to one-year post-partum. It is a time of massive change and transition for women, considering the biological, hormonal, psychological, emotional and social upheaval which accompanies pregnancy, birth and caring for a newborn baby. It is a time which may be anticipated as a time of joy and fulfilment, but may also be fraught with anxiety, uncertainty and increased scrutiny by the multiple professionals involved. Childbearing places great demands on women's resources. Good social support is vital, but even so, many women struggle with lack of sleep, or time for themselves, and often previously used ways of managing stress such as socialising, or exercise may be difficult to access due to childcare responsibilities. Reliance on coping strategies such as substance misuse or self-harming behaviours become especially problematic.

It is known that maternal mental health difficulties may have an impact on child safety and development, with significant long-term consequences. This includes the antenatal period, where the foetus can be affected by factors including maternal cortisol levels and substance misuse (Lewis et al., 2015). It has been estimated that nearly a quarter of children under the age of 2 have been exposed to maternal mental illness in the UK (Abel et al., 2019) and that the costs of untreated maternal mental illness for each 1 year cohort in the UK totals £8.1 billion, mostly related to the adverse impact on the child (Bauer et al., 2014). For these reasons, maternal mental health has been a priority for NHS service development and NICE (2020) guidance has recommended timely access to psychological therapy.

This chapter considers the significance of the perinatal period in the development or exacerbation of maternal dissociative difficulties, their impact on the infant and safeguarding issues. We offer an overview of research highlighting the significance of dissociation during the perinatal period. We explore the varieties of dissociative experiences and how they may manifest in a perinatal context. We illustrate these with clinical examples, highlighting the importance of risk formulation. Finally, we discuss the unique assessment and treatment considerations when working with women experiencing dissociation at this time.

DOI: 10.4324/9781003625650-12

While it is acknowledged that the perinatal period is also an important time for fathers and partners, it is beyond the scope of this chapter to also consider implications for their mental health.

These guidelines have been compiled in the context of a paucity of clinical research in this area, and are intended as a framework to inform clinical practice as opposed to a definitive guide for the assessment and treatment of dissociative difficulties as they manifest in the perinatal period.

2. Maternal Mental Health in the Perinatal Period

The perinatal period is associated with increased risk of the development or exacerbation of mental health problems, including all severe and common mental health difficulties (Jones et al., 2014; Gavin et al., 2005; Brandes et al., 2004). Of relevance to dissociation, difficulties associated with a history of trauma are likely to be experienced in the perinatal period. Birth trauma is unique to the birthing experience, and studies suggest around 3% of women develop post-traumatic stress disorder (PTSD) following traumatic birth. A combination of vulnerability factors, including previous trauma, depression or anxiety during pregnancy, combined with the birth experience, may be causal. Dissociation during childbirth is identified as an important risk factor (Ayers et al., 2016).

Many women with histories of complex trauma, such as childhood abuse, experience traumatic memories being reactivated in the perinatal period. Women's own experiences of being parented become highly valent as they transition to parenthood. Difficulties associated with diagnoses of personality disorder or complex PTSD (C-PTSD) may be exacerbated. Clinical experience also suggests many women with underlying difficulties with emotion regulation or developmental trauma present to mental health services for the first time in the perinatal period.

3. Dissociation in the Perinatal Period

Clinical experience suggests that dissociation is not uncommon in the perinatal period, although it may not be the main initial presenting problem (see Case Example 1: Jane's Story). The literature specifically on this is sparse and as such prevalence rates remain unclear; however, prevalence studies of developmental trauma, such as childhood sexual abuse, which are associated with dissociation, suggest the prevalence might be high in perinatal populations (Cortizo, 2020). Marysko et al. (2010) found a history of childhood abuse was associated with increased maternal dissociative experiences in a group of new mothers compared with peers. The literature on PTSD following birth trauma (Ayers et al., 2016) identifies dissociation during delivery as a risk factor for PTSD.

Research on maternal dissociation and parenting has rarely involved clinical populations. Kluft (1987) studied a sample of mothers diagnosed with 'Multiple Personality Disorder'. A total of 38.7% were judged to be 'competent or exceptional parents', 16% to be 'grossly abusive' and 45.3% to be 'compromised or impaired' as parents. Other studies have sampled from non-clinical populations using dissociation screening questionnaires. Chu and DePrince (2006) found maternal dissociation was associated with dissociation in the children, aged 7 to 11. Hulette et al. (2011) investigated intergenerational relationships between trauma and dissociation and found high betrayal trauma (i.e., abuse perpetrated by a close relative) was associated with higher levels of dissociation in both mothers and their children. Results were consistent with hypotheses that dissociation functions to maintain the relationship with the abuser and that parents with such histories may have greater difficulty detecting relational threats, such as relationships which have the potential to become abusive. This could leave women vulnerable to retraumatisation and their children vulnerable to being abused.

Regarding dissociation and its impact on parenting styles and behaviour specifically in the perinatal period, the literature is even more sparse. Williams et al. (2022) studied maternal dissociation in the perinatal period and used both self-rated measures and behavioural observations of parenting styles. Dissociation, as rated by questionnaire, was associated with reduced maternal sensitivity during mother-child observations, and mediated the relationship between maternal early life maltreatment and self-reported parenting. However, the study recruited from nonclinical populations, and the sample was described as low risk. The authors cautioned that results were not clearcut and further research is needed.

Other research, while not directly focussing on dissociation, nevertheless sheds light on the likely impact of maternal dissociative behaviours on early child development. The attachment literature has studied parent-infant dyads over time, identifying parental behaviours associated with particular outcomes for children, both positive and negative. For instance, Hesse and Main (2006) described maternal behaviours observed during the Strange Situation Procedure which were rated as 'frightened' or 'frightening' and related to the development of disorganised attachment in the infant. They described maternal behaviours which appeared dissociative, such as trance-like behaviour or anomalous facial and vocal expressions. They theorised that such behaviours arose from the parent's internal state and therefore were not contingent on the infant's cues, and so disrupted the regulated functioning of the infant's attachment behavioural system.

Research using the 'still-face paradigm', in which the parent interacting with her infant is instructed to alternate normal, contingent responding to the child with a blank, unresponsive face, has found that infants are regularly observed to become distressed and dysregulated, during the still-face episode (Tronick et al., 1978). The still-face paradigm could be considered analogical to the impact of trance-like dissociation.

Cultural contexts in relation to parenting practices should be considered and how these shape the expression of attachment patterns, for example alloparenting (parenting by multiple caregivers) (Bakaraki et al., 2024). Cultural factors may also influence how much mothers feel able to acknowledge their mental distress, for example within collectivist cultures where this may be experienced as family shame, possibly contributing to dissociative coping (see Chapter 15, Cultural Considerations).

In summary, though limited, research suggests dissociation has significant implications for the perinatal period. It may be relatively common, particularly in women with histories of childhood abuse and trauma. It is one factor amongst several predictive of PTSD developing following a traumatic birth. There is some agreement that dissociation is related to parenting difficulties and contributes to the intergenerational cycle of abuse, although the mediators of this may not necessarily be dissociation per se, but other co-occurring difficulties such as emotional dysregulation or depression. The hypothesis that mothers who dissociated in the context of childhood abuse may have more difficulty in perceiving current relationship threat and may inadvertently expose themselves to retraumatisation as adults and their children to abuse, is worthy of note in this respect. Dissociation may also impact infant development through the disruption of the developing attachment system.

However, it should be noted that most research cited so far has not included clinical populations and may be of limited applicability.

4. Case Examples of Dissociation in the Perinatal Period

Dissociation takes many forms, and implications for the full range of presentations need consideration. The clinical significance of dissociation depends on its manifestation and potential to impact on the mother's and baby's safety and wellbeing. An individual case formulation approach is essential to understand the impact and risks. In this section, case examples are offered to illustrate the variety and complexity of dissociation in the parenting context. The cases have been reported by a group of clinicians working within a perinatal service and represent the clinicians' perspectives. Cases have been anonymised, with potentially identifiable information removed or altered.

The additional stresses associated with the perinatal period can exacerbate pre-existing dissociative difficulties or trigger new-onset difficulties. Many women may have successfully suppressed memories of abuse or trauma for years, only for these to resurface in the context of caring for a baby. The baby's needs may be overwhelming. The baby's need to be soothed or comforted may be especially triggering of dissociative responses. Regulating oneself whilst needing to regulate the baby's emotions is one of the most difficult caregiving tasks (see below Case Example 2: Melanie's Story).

For some women, such as Jane who ran onto the road (Case Example 1), the dissociation may be dramatic, with immediate implications for the mother's and baby's safety. For others, such as Louise (Case Example 2), the dramatic manifestation of dissociation with head banging was a risk more to the mother than the baby. For others again, dissociation may take the form of being 'somewhere else' and therefore unavailable to the baby (see Case Example 6: Anna's Story). Although this may not pose an immediate threat to the baby's safety, the long-term implications may be significant, with possible impact on attachment, as discussed above.

Dissociative seizures pose a particular challenge for women caring for young babies. A seizure may result in a mother being physically and emotionally unavailable, and could result in physical harm to the baby, if she were carrying the baby at the time (see Case Example 5: Ayesha's Story).

Case Example 3: Tracey's Story illustrates how dissociation in the context of a traumatic delivery can trigger difficult emotions, impacting the development of a sense of connection with the baby.

Case Example 1: Jane's Story

Jane was a 30-year-old mother born in the UK of Black African heritage. She had no history of mental health difficulties prior to her pregnancy with her second child. She experienced a suicidal crisis when her new baby was just a few weeks old and was admitted to a psychiatric Mother and Baby Unit (MBU) with her baby. She engaged well with individual psychology sessions. Following a meeting with a social worker, Jane misunderstood a communication to mean that social services wanted to remove her baby. She became highly distressed, throwing herself onto the floor. She later reported having no recollection of this incident. Further episodes of erratic behaviour were observed. In one instance, she perceived some other patients in the hospital grounds as 'ghosts' and fled with her baby in a pram. She ran onto a busy road without regard for the traffic, and only narrowly avoided serious injury to herself and her baby. Again, she reported no recollection of this incident.

Further assessment by the psychologist revealed a history of serious sexual assault as a teenager which left her feeling highly distressed. She told her parents, who took a traditional cultural view of mental distress as being due to spirit possession, and they organised for Jane to undergo an exorcism at her local church. Jane experienced both the assault and the exorcism as so traumatic she resolved never to speak about her mental health again. She disclosed that, additionally to the gaps in her memory, she saw 'auras' around trusted members of staff. At times when highly distressed, she expressed a belief she was possessed by the Devil and became highly agitated.

Jane benefitted from psychoeducation about trauma and its effects and learnt some simple grounding techniques which she was able to use to prevent further episodes of dissociation. Her mental state improved as she developed trust in the staff, and was reassured her care of her daughter was excellent. Her parents and partner engaged with the MBU team and developed a different understanding of her mental health and support needs. Jane was discharged from the MBU with no social services involvement and access to ongoing mental health support in the community.

Case Example 2: Melanie's Story

Melanie was a 35-year-old white British first-time mother. She experienced severe emotional abuse from her own mother, from whom she was estranged. During therapy prior to her pregnancy, Melanie started to dissociate and behave and think as a 6-year-old child. When her baby was born, dissociation was triggered in the context of caring for her baby. Her husband overheard Melanie shouting and swearing at the baby and needed to intervene. Melanie was able to work with a new therapist who helped her to understand how her previous experience of abuse had impacted on her ability to show love to her baby, through resentment at having to provide what she had not experienced herself. Melanie was able to process these difficult emotions and to be present and loving towards her baby.

Case Example 3: Tracey's Story

Tracey was a 30-year-old white British woman. She experienced a traumatic birth with her first child due to an emergency caesarean with inadequate pain relief. She described an 'out of body experience' in which she saw herself shouting and crying and none of the professionals responding to her. She subsequently developed symptoms of PTSD, and beliefs she had been 'at fault' for having the out of body experience. She experienced difficulties connecting with her baby as she had not felt fully present for the birth. She felt guilty and had thoughts about being a 'bad mum'.

Tracey underwent cognitive-behaviour therapy (CBT) for PTSD, which helped with her symptoms. However, she became extremely anxious during her second pregnancy with catastrophic fears that she and her baby would die during the delivery. With psychological support, and a trauma-informed birth plan discussed with her midwife, she delivered her second baby without dissociating and was able to form a positive bond with her.

Case Example 4: Louise's Story

Louise was a 35-year-old white British mother of two. She experienced extreme sexual abuse throughout her childhood, and had been diagnosed with C-PTSD. Her symptoms included flashbacks, which triggered episodes of dissociation during which she would start head banging and was at risk of serious injury. Despite this, Louise could maintain apparently normal functioning at work and with her family, who were not aware of her difficulties.

Her mental health deteriorated following the birth of her second child and she was admitted to an MBU. During the admission, her trauma symptoms were prominent. Louise experienced feeling safe on the MBU, and her mental state started to stabilise. She was offered sessions of EMDR therapy, and was able to process two memories, resulting in them no longer triggering severe distress, and raising her hope that she could overcome her difficulties in the future. Although her trauma symptoms and dissociation were very marked, they were not observed to impact on her care of her baby, and Louise appeared able to ground herself when caring for her baby. She was discharged from the MBU with a plan for further therapy in the community.

Case Example 5: Ayesha's Story

Ayesha was a 35-year-old North African mother of two, with a son aged 10 and a newborn daughter. Ayesha had divorced her first husband and remarried. Her second husband was living overseas. She had a long-standing history of severe depression and dissociative seizures. She had not accessed treatment for her seizures, and they had the potential to impact on her capacity to care for her new baby. She became agoraphobic, and on one occasion fell downstairs whilst having a seizure and her 10-year-old son had to call for an ambulance.

Due to concern about Ayesha's capacity to meet her new daughter's needs and to care for her safely, the local authority instigated care proceedings and commissioned a residential parenting assessment. The assessing team found Ayesha was providing excellent care for her baby, but needed more social support than was available to her. Her ex-husband, who had been caring for their son came forward to offer to live with Ayesha and her daughter. It was also recommended that Ayesha be referred for therapy for her dissociative seizures, which she was able to access. The Family Court decided the arrangements for the family were sufficient to meet the needs of Ayesha's daughter, and mother and baby were enabled to remain together.

Case Example 6: Anna's Story

Anna was a white British mother of two. She experienced a still-birth prior to having her first live baby and developed severe obsessive-compulsive difficulties related to this experience. Following the birth of her second child, these difficulties continued, alongside pseudo-hallucinations in which she saw a dead baby in a cot. She also reported a history of experiencing and witnessing severe physical abuse from her father and experienced flashbacks related to these events. She feared she would not be able to keep her children safe and be a 'good enough' parent. She was diagnosed with C-PTSD and accessed psychological therapy via her local perinatal mental health team. At times of heightened social and family stresses, she presented with dissociation in her therapy sessions, typically adopting the voice of a young child. This affected her ability to meet the needs of her baby beyond basic caring, feeding and changing. However, she was able to maintain safe parenting practices with the help of her partner and family and had only brief involvement from social services. Anna benefitted from CBT for trauma and was referred on to a specialist trauma service for further therapeutic input.

5. Assessment of Dissociation in the Perinatal Context

Women who experience mental health difficulties in the perinatal period may delay seeking help due to stigma and fear of consequences, or may minimise or fail to disclose risk issues for the same reason. Clinicians should bear this in mind when assessing and formulating risk and severity. A mental health assessment in the perinatal context must consider not only the woman's mental health and assess this as in any other context, but also how this interacts with her pregnancy, how she will cope during the delivery and the care of the infant in the post-natal period. Maternal mental health may impact on all of these factors, and, in turn be affected by them.

5.1 Pregnancy

The circumstances of the pregnancy can impact the woman's adjustment to being pregnant and her mental health. Areas for exploration include:

- Whether the pregnancy was planned or unplanned (including being the result of sexual assault)
- Whether the woman was aware of the pregnancy or even concealed it
- The woman's feelings about being pregnant
- Her expectations of parenthood
- Her physical health during pregnancy, which may impact significantly on her mental health, as will concerns about the progress of the pregnancy
- Previous histories of miscarriage, stillbirth or neonatal loss
- A history of trauma, which may impact on how the woman feels about the approaching delivery of the baby
- Lack of trust of professionals, fears about being out of control, and the potentially invasive nature of the delivery itself, all of which may raise anxiety levels during pregnancy
- Triggers for dissociation, including how much the woman is aware of changes in her mental state and able to self-monitor signs of distress

- How dissociative symptoms may impact on the woman's capacity to keep herself safe or care for herself appropriately, including a sensitive discussion about the use of maladaptive coping skills.

5.2 Giving Birth

It is important to consider the possibility of dissociation during delivery of the baby. It is considered good practice to develop a psychologically and trauma-informed birth plan to be shared with the maternity team. This could include psychoeducation for the maternity team, and identify possible triggers for dissociation which may be inherent to the birthing process, along with ways of managing these.

5.3 The Postnatal Period

Assessing the impact of dissociation in the postnatal period should cover short-term immediate risks as well as the cumulative impact of lower grade risks over time. Jane's case illustrates the potential for dissociation to lead to behaviour which places the mother and infant in immediate danger. Lack of continuous ongoing memory is therefore a red flag for clinicians and will need a response which ensures the safety of both mother and baby. In Jane's case, she was placed on 1-1 in-patient observations following the dissociative episode until clinicians were assured she could notice shifts in her emotional state and employ grounding techniques. In the community, safety plans may involve family members being present until the situation has stabilised.

Melanie's case illustrates how the care-giving context in itself can trigger dissociation, impacting the expression of emotions towards the baby which over time could impact negatively on the baby's development of security and trust. Again, the importance of family support was crucial as part of the safety plan.

Anna's case illustrates how dissociation could leave the mother unavailable to provide responsive emotional care, and family support was also crucial.

The importance of having opportunities for direct observation of the mother with the baby cannot be overstated. For instance, how does she manage her own needs versus the baby's needs? How does she cope if the baby cries or is restless and unsettled? Anna's case illustrates how important it was for the therapist to observe directly the impact of dissociation on her interactions with the baby.

If possible, and with the mother's consent, assessment should also involve the father/partner or other family members, who may have observed the dissociative behaviours and how they manifest. Provision of psychoeducational materials for family members is important.

6. Treatment Considerations

The perinatal period involves specific timescales causing natural constraints on timing of interventions. **NICE Guidance (2020) recommends that treatment**

should begin without delay. The baby, whether born or unborn, should not be exposed to the mother's mental ill health for longer than absolutely necessary. On the other hand, beginning therapy close to the arrival of the baby, or within the first few weeks, may not make sense, unless the therapy is directly relevant to the birthing process (e.g., birth anxiety) so that the mother-to-be can prepare herself for the delivery and the needs of the new born baby.

Clinicians have debated how safe it is to undertake exposure-based interventions during pregnancy (e.g., for trauma). Specific recommendations do not yet exist, but neither is there evidence to suggest exposure-based interventions are inherently harmful (Arch et al., 2012). Conversely, the pregnant woman who is not accessing treatment will still expose her foetus to her anxiety. **Pregnancy per se should therefore not be a reason to exclude women from appropriate psychological treatment.**

Similarly, historically, women in the perinatal period have had difficulty accessing therapy for longstanding psychological problems, the rationale being that the woman is focusing on her new mothering role. Some specialist perinatal services have excluded women being offered psychological therapy unless the mental health difficulty actually arose in the perinatal period (such as birth trauma or perinatal OCD). However, the main rationale for the expansion of perinatal mental health services was in order to mitigate the impact of maternal mental health problems on the child. **Therefore, whether or not the difficulties arose in the perinatal period should not be relevant.**

This issue is particularly relevant for women with longstanding psychological difficulties who find themselves in care proceedings due to their mental health. A report by Pause (2022), a charity working with women who have experienced or are at risk of experiencing removal of their children, highlighted how recommendations from expert witnesses for women to access therapy for their difficulties are not translated into access to therapy. In the case example of Ayesha, she was extremely lucky to be able to access psychological therapy in the context of care proceedings. Therapists may be wary of taking on cases where there is active social services involvement. **It is recommended that social services involvement should not be a barrier for women to access psychological therapy, although the delicate issue of confidentiality and expectations from social workers that updates are provided needs careful consideration.**

On the other hand, a woman's caregiving role and lack of access to childcare may be a barrier to accessing treatment in the community. The risks associated with dissociation in the community may necessitate admission to an MBU for treatment. An MBU is a specialist mental health facility for women to receive treatment for their mental health while remaining with their baby. MBUs are resourced to offer a full range of psychological and psychosocial interventions, providing an opportunity for women with severe dissociative difficulties to access treatment in a highly supportive environment, where the baby's needs are also being addressed. In the case example of Louise, the decision to offer EMDR on an MBU was in recognition that Louise required this level of support to undertake trauma therapy safely.

So far, interventions for the mother's mental health have been the focus of discussion. However, the caregiving role may itself give rise to challenges for a woman who experiences dissociation. A baby needs the support of the caregiver to learn how to regulate emotions and learn that emotions can be tolerated. This requires the caregiver to be available, responsive and able to understand the infant's cues. The caregiver needs to be able to regulate her own emotions and understand how past experiences may impair the capacity to respond in the moment to the baby's needs. Interventions which focus on the dyad may therefore also often be indicated.

Several specialist perinatal interventions are designed to support parents to understand and respond sensitively to infants' emotional needs. These include short term interventions such as Video-Interaction Guidance (VIG), where the parent and therapist review clips from a video of the parent playing with her infant. Parent-infant psychotherapy is a longer-term therapy focussing on the parent-infant relationship. Circle of Security is a structured psychoeducational group aiming to support parents in understanding their infant's emotional needs and how parents' own experiences may impact on their capacity to respond to their infant's needs. **Although these interventions are not designed to address dissociation specifically, it is recommended that the clinicians offering them are aware of the possibility of dissociation and agree a care plan to address this.**

7. Safeguarding and Working with Social Services

As highlighted, maternal mental health difficulties in the perinatal period can have significant child safeguarding implications. Clinicians are required to consider and prioritise the needs of vulnerable children in whatever clinical setting they are working. This is a particularly sensitive issue in perinatal mental health, where women may delay seeking help or disclosing the full details of their mental health history for fear of the consequences. In reality most women's concerns about social services are excessive and needless. However for a small but important group of women, their mental health and parenting capacity give rise to legitimate concerns about the safety and wellbeing of the unborn child, infant, and/or other children in the family. This extends to the father/partner or others living in the same household. Vulnerable women may be living in circumstances of domestic abuse or may be unable to protect and safeguard their children from potentially abusive carers including grandparents or other family members.

Perinatal clinicians are therefore required to assess risk in the parent-infant relationship and family context, and to report concerns to social services. This can cause sensitive issues around engagement and the ability to provide a clinical service, where raising child protection concerns risks jeopardising the therapeutic alliance. Perinatal clinicians may often find themselves working closely with social services. Many specialist perinatal mental health teams have social workers within the team, facilitating liaison and information sharing. Safeguarding is however the role of all clinicians.

Psychological practitioners have an important role where there is social services involvement. Children's social workers do not typically have mental health training and rely on mental health professionals to understand the risks of maternal mental ill health on child safety and wellbeing. With dissociation, psychological professionals can provide invaluable education, formulation and advice on the nature of dissociation, how it presents, and the implications within a perinatal context. They may provide a risk assessment for a child protection case conference, or advocate for the mother if the perceived risk is out of proportion to the actual risk.

They are also well placed to advise on the likelihood the mother can benefit from treatment for her difficulties and the likely timescale for this. In the context of Care Proceedings, where the level of concern from the Local Authority that the mother/ parents present such a risk to the infant's health or wellbeing that legal proceedings have been instigated, Family Court judges have welcomed the evidence of perinatal psychological practitioners to facilitate a deeper understanding of the psychological needs of parents and children (Personal Communication).

8. Summary of Practice Recommendations

Summary of Practice Recommendations

Awareness

- Dissociation is likely to be common in the perinatal population
- Dissociation during child birth is a predictor of PTSD relating to the birth
- Pregnancy, childbirth and caring for a newborn have the capacity to reactivate past trauma
- Dissociation may impact on a mother's capacity to meet her infant's needs or to keep herself or her infant safe
- Dissociation may have longer term implications for the infant's emotional development.

Assessment and Treatment

- Assessment of maternal mental health should consider the possibility of dissociation
- Mental health assessments in the perinatal period should carefully assess the impact of maternal mental health including dissociation, on the pregnancy, the delivery, the infant and other children in the family - and vice-versa

- Consider opportunities for direct observation of the mother with the baby
- Timely access to psychological interventions, with appropriate levels of support, is needed to mitigate the impact of dissociation
- Interventions may focus on the mother's mental health, as well as the developing relationship between mother and baby
- Pregnancy and having a new baby should not be treated as barriers for women to access appropriate psychological treatments for dissociation
- Safeguarding is a crucial responsibility of all clinicians
- Psychological professionals are well-placed to provide advice to social services around understanding, risks and treatment for dissociation.

8.1   Further Research Questions

- What is the prevalence of dissociation amongst women accessing mental health services in the perinatal period?
- What are the experiences of women with dissociative difficulties in the perinatal period?
- What are the short and long term consequences of maternal dissociation on child development?
- What is the efficacy of interventions for dissociation in the perinatal period: impact on the mother, mother-infant relationship and child development.

9. Conclusion

Despite a dearth of clinical research into dissociation and its implications for the perinatal period, perinatal mental health clinicians are likely to encounter people with dissociative presentations at this time. Although the clinical implications, particularly for risk and safeguarding, may seem complex and daunting given the evidence of the intergenerational transmission of abuse and trauma, there are reasons to be hopeful that greater awareness can lead to better outcomes for women and their families.

While women in the perinatal period may be fearful of seeking help or fully disclosing their difficulties, they are also often highly motivated to overcome these for the sake of their children. Recent developments in perinatal mental health services mean women can now hope to access timely and meaningful treatments. Careful trauma and dissociation informed assessment, formulation and appropriate therapeutic input can make a huge difference.

Chapter 10

Dissociation and People with a Learning Disability

Reed Cappleman and Pat Frankish

1. Introduction

Until relatively recently people with learning disabilities were excluded from accessing psychological therapies and there was no acknowledgement that this population experience trauma (Beail et al., 2021; Sinason, 2010). This chapter summarises literature around the prevalence and impact of trauma in people with learning disabilities and highlights that dissociation in this group is a phenomenon that has been relatively neglected. The chapter aims to help clinicians consider the presence of dissociation in people with learning disabilities and outlines how the existing literature might be used to approach assessment and intervention on both an individual and systemic level.

2. Trauma and Dissociation in People with Learning Disabilities

People with learning disabilities are more likely to experience trauma and abuse than the general population (McNally, 2022). For example, within the Canadian Incidence Study's large sample, children with learning disabilities were 2–3 times more likely to experience maltreatment than children without (McDonnell et al., 2019). McGilvery (2018) suggests that people with learning disabilities may be less able to leave abusive environments, potentially due to factors such as cognitive/physical limitations and having been conditioned to be compliant to those in positions of power or authority. They may also be less likely to recognise abusive or traumatic situations, and be less likely to be believed if they do identify them. The experience of having a learning disability in a society that does not tolerate difference can also in itself be traumatic (Shimmens & Skelly, 2023; Sinason, 2010).

People with learning disabilities may also be more vulnerable to the psychological sequelae of traumatic events. Lower intellectual functioning can be a risk factor for developing post-traumatic stress disorder (PTSD) following exposure to traumatic events (Brewin et al., 2000). People with learning disabilities may be less able to understand or articulate what has happened to them, or make sense of their emotional response, negatively impacting their recovery (Skelly, 2020). McNally

DOI: 10.4324/9781003625650-13

et al. (2021) highlight that current diagnostic criteria for PTSD may not capture the manifestations of post-traumatic stress in people with learning disabilities, with difficulties such as re-experiencing or reliving being difficult for individuals to verbally report, leading to distress that is communicated behaviourally. Indicators of trauma in people with learning disabilities may therefore go unrecognised and be misinterpreted as simply 'challenging behaviour'. Following trauma, the stigmatisation and exclusion faced by people with learning disabilities (Scior, 2016) may mean that many have no access to the social support that can be protective after trauma (Calhoun et al., 2022).

Although there has been an increasing number of studies and reviews into the impact of trauma on people with learning disabilities over the last ten years, there is very little literature available on dissociative states in this group. It may be argued that people with learning disabilities are at greater risk of having dissociative difficulties missed or misdiagnosed due to problems with verbalising their experiences and the phenomenon of diagnostic overshadowing (Mason & Scior, 2004), where all difficulties are directly attributed to the person's learning disability.

Case Example: *Gemma was a teenage girl who attended a special school. Most of the time she responded well to the teacher and other staff and appeared to engage well in learning. However sporadically she was unrecognisable as that person. She became argumentative, aggressive and then sexually provocative. When she came back to her old self, neither she nor anyone else could understand what had happened.*

---

3. Models of Dissociation in People with Learning Disabilities

There is little research examining how models of dissociation which have been applied to the general population (see Chapter 1) may apply to people with learning disabilities. For example, little is known about whether there may be differences in how dissociation manifests in this population as a result of difficulties with attention, memory and language (Hronis et al., 2017). Sinason's (2010) psychoanalytic work suggested that people with learning disabilities may split off parts of the self as a defence against pain, and in order to present parts of the self that others around the person find more acceptable. This perspective would predict that structural dissociation may be prevalent in this population. From the point of view of the physiological model, McGilvery's (2018) suggestion that people with learning disabilities are less able to leave traumatic situations would also predict greater levels of dissociation in this group, as the dorso-vagal response of shutdown and immobilisation may be the only coping strategy remaining if an individual with a learning disability does not have the ability or power to escape a perpetrator.

3.1 Attachment

Chapter 1 highlights that complex dissociative difficulties may arise from a combination of disorganised attachment strategies followed by subsequent trauma and abuse. The British Psychological Society's (2017) guidance on incorporating attachment theory into learning disability practice highlights specific challenges for this population in being able to develop secure attachment relationships, including:

- Some children with learning disabilities showing less obvious emotional cues and attachment-seeking signals, making it more difficult for parents and caregivers to recognise and respond to their needs
- Distress experienced by some families upon finding their child has a learning disability or chronic health condition could make it harder for them to offer a secure attachment relationship (though this is not the case for the majority of families)
- Care arrangements in supported living or residential services inadvertently being organised in ways that reinforce insecure attachment strategies.

Assessments of attachment for people with learning disabilities are still being developed and refined (Skelly, 2024). There is therefore limited data as to the prevalence of disorganised attachment in people with learning disabilities. However the aforementioned guidance highlights research that found children with Down's Syndrome presenting with insecure attachment were more likely to have a disorganized style, with the rates being comparable to children who had experienced early trauma or institutionalisation.

3.2 Frankish's Model of Emotional Development

Frankish's (2016) approach to understanding the impact of trauma on emotional development in people with learning disabilities has been applied to people presenting with difficulties meeting criteria for a diagnosis of Dissociative Identity Disorder (DID; Frankish & Sinason, 2017) and therefore by implication can be applied to people with learning disabilities presenting with complex dissociation. Frankish's model was based Mahler Bergman, and Pine's (1979) theories derived from observations of children without learning disabilities and their caregivers in the USA. Mahler et al. described the stages of emotional development traversed from birth through to 'individuation', the point at which the child develops a more coherent sense of self separate from caregivers. They suggested individuation usually occurs between the age of three and four years, and marks the child having internalised a representation of the main caregiver. Mahler described five main stages between birth and individuation: symbiosis, differentiation, practising, early rapprochement, and late rapprochement.

Frankish (2016) applied this theory to understanding the emotional needs of people with learning disabilities who have experienced early trauma and subsequently present with complex behavioural and mental health needs. Frankish's model suggested that if trauma occurs prior to individuation then the person will remain at the stage of emotional development they were in at the time of the trauma, with their emotional and behavioural responses corresponding to this stage. The model aimed to provide those around the person with an understanding of how behavioural and relational difficulties could be understood in the context of early trauma, and suggested interventions based on the person's stage of emotional development.

Frankish and Sinason (2017) applied this model to understanding complex dissociation in people both with and without learning disabilities. They argued that those presenting with complex dissociation are functioning at an emotional developmental stage prior to individuation, as they are not able to hold onto a coherent sense of self. This model therefore understands complex dissociation as the result of severe early trauma that occurs before individuation, often being followed by further severe trauma and abuse.

For each of the theoretical models outlined in this section there is a lack of published empirical research applying the models directly to people with learning disabilities presenting with dissociative difficulties, highlighting that this is an area requiring further research.

4. Assessment of Dissociation in People with Learning Disabilities

There are no formally validated assessments of dissociation in people with learning disabilities. In the authors' experience, assessments developed for general adult populations may be used with some people with mild learning disabilities with careful adaptations to language, but these are only suitable for a minority.

4.1 Adapted PTSD Measures

Trauma measures developed for people with learning disabilities include items that may enable some exploration of the presence of dissociation. For example, the informant scale of the Lancaster and Northgate Trauma Scales (Wigham et al., 2011; Wigham et al., 2014) includes items enquiring about flashbacks and the person 'being in a daze'. The adapted versions of the International Trauma Questionnaire (Langdon et al., 2023) and Impact of Events Scale (Hall et al., 2014) also contain potentially helpful items, however the aim of these assessments is to aid the identification and measurement of experiences associated with PTSD and complex-PTSD rather than to specifically assess dissociation.

4.2 Behavioural Observation

In the absence of specific measures for people with learning disabilities, clinical psychologists providing individual therapy for people with learning disabilities may instead monitor clients' behaviour and the content of verbal material in sessions to ascertain the presence of possible dissociative experiences (Porter, 2022).

> **Case Example**: *In therapy, Susan was talking about her life as a child. She then started to speak as a child, shy and mumbling, saying 'no, no, no'. She didn't respond when the therapist spoke to her and seemed to be no longer present. The therapist waited and she 'came back' into the room after 15 minutes. She was confused and had no awareness of the switch.*

When someone with a learning disability and suspected dissociative experiences is supported by a staff team, they can be asked to include any evidence of dissociation in records of the person's day-to-day behaviour. For example, staff may record verbal statements suggestive of dissociative experiences made by the person and behavioural indicators such as speaking in different voices, suddenly presenting as 'numb' or vacant, or suddenly starting to respond to the people around them as though they are someone else. Staff keeping such records require training and support in identifying possible indicators of dissociation.

4.3 Keeping Dissociation in Mind when Interpreting Other Measures

Given the lack of specific assessments, clinicians working with people with learning disabilities and risk factors for dissociation in their history may at times need to check whether information obtained from assessment tools undertaken in routine practice might indicate the presence of dissociation. For example, a functional behavioural assessment (O'Neill et al., 1997) of an individual presenting with behaviours that challenge in the context of trauma might find that the behaviour seems to be maintained by obtaining or avoiding sensory stimulation. When combined with information about the person's presentation and history, clinicians may consider whether such sensory-focused behaviours may indicate the presence of dissociative phenomena, for example the person attempting to regulate dissociative states through contact with or avoidance of stimuli that provoke a strong sensory response.

> **Case Example**: *Through careful observation and record keeping, Chris's team realised that his incidents of severe self-injury were precipitated by separation from favoured staff, and by the ward becoming busier and noisier. Through further discussion and exploration with Chris the team realised that he self-injured as a way of bringing about a dissociative state that would blunt the pain of separation and help him detach from the flashbacks he experienced when around louder and busier environments.*

5. Intervention Approaches for People with Learning Disabilities

5.1 Direct Interventions

There has been little written about direct intervention with people with learning disabilities presenting with dissociative experiences. Stenfert-Kroese et al.'s (2016) pilot study of a trauma-focused CBT group intervention for people with learning disabilities and complex-PTSD included psychoeducation on dissociation. Participants' scores on a trauma symptom measure showed improvement. Group participants also reported that they felt listened to and found it helpful to be in the presence of others who had experienced trauma, but that being in a group could be challenging.

There are also reports in the literature of dissociation being addressed through adapted ego state work and grounding techniques (see Porter's (2022) review of adaptations to EMDR for this population). Cowles et al.'s (2020) case series, which outlined the use of Compassion-Focused Therapy for people with learning disabilities who had experienced trauma, stated that one participant experienced dissociation. However the paper did not focus on how dissociation was specifically addressed using the approach.

Case studies demonstrating the use of a psychoanalytic model with people with learning disabilities who present with dissociative difficulties (Sinason, 2010; Sinason & Silver, 2008) have described the importance of building trust and safety in the relationship, offering the opportunity for long term work over a number of years, taking an approach that facilitates emotional growth for the individual, and fostering the individual's understanding of their system of alters and what can trigger their emergence.

In summary, there are references in the literature to a variety of approaches being used to address dissociation in people with learning disabilities, though no dissociation-specific outcome data is presented and there is a reliance on case studies and small N designs. Although caution is required in interpreting such a limited evidence base, it may be that as with the general population, a range of approaches may be used to foster the development of skills to manage dissociation, whilst more complex dissociative experiences may require longer term work with a focus on relational safety and supporting the person to integrate their different selves (see Chapter 4).

5.2 Systemic Interventions

McNally (2022) outlined a framework for implementing trauma-informed care in residential and supported living services for people with learning disabilities, much of which may be relevant for people with learning disabilities who present with dissociative experiences. He outlined an approach based on Golding and Hughes's (2012) 'pyramid of need', involving developing safe relationships in which co-regulation can occur, prior to any trauma-focused work. McNally outlined that staff working in such services should have knowledge of the individual's history and an associated formulation which explains how the history has led to the current presentation and difficulties. He also recommended that staff should understand how to develop therapeutic relationships with people they support, how and why transitions such as the ends of shifts can be difficult for those with histories of trauma and disrupted attachment, and how to acknowledge the rights of people with learning disabilities to experience the full range of human emotions (e.g., the 'right to be upset').

As outlined above, Frankish's (2016) model can be used to help carers understand the emotional needs of people with learning disabilities who have experienced early trauma. The model has been applied to people diagnosed with DID (Frankish & Sinason, 2017). When applied systemically, this model leads to four key recommendations:

- A safe place to live with a tenancy that is not dependent on the person's behaviour (to reduce anxiety and facilitate learning that things can be mended)
- The availability of a 'significant other' at all times so the individual does not need to ask who is there for them (or act out to try and find out), replicating the secure base that is a prerequisite for emotional development (Bowlby, 1988)
- Staff must be trained and supported to perform their role and to provide a nurturing emotional environment. They must have an understanding of trauma and its impact, dissociation, and how to avoid retraumatisation or triggering dissociative episodes. They must also understand that punitive approaches need to be avoided at all times
- The availability of long-term individual therapy to support the individual in managing their experiences, integrate the dissociated aspects of the self, and to process trauma.

Case Example: *Assessment of Chris's emotional developmental stage using the FAIT indicated that when he was not dissociating he presented at the 'late rapprochement' stage of emotional development, meaning it was possible for staff who knew him well to gently and gradually share some of their understanding with him and engage in two-way negotiation about how staff should best support him when he was experiencing the flashbacks or unbearable emotional pain that made him want to self-injure in order to bring about a dissociated state. As staff placed more emphasis on two-way interaction and negotiation in Chris's care, aggressive incidents also stopped.*

Case study data has suggested that provision of each of these elements of the model may contribute to a reduction in anxiety, a gradual increase in engagement, and progress towards individuation (McInnis, 2016). Within this model, for staff to be able to understand the person's needs and support their continued emotional development, they must understand the individual's stage of emotional development so they can provide care that corresponds to the developmental needs of that stage. The Frankish Assessment of the Impact of Trauma (FAIT, 2019), is an observational assessment that can be used to identify the stage of emotional development for people with learning disabilities, when it is suspected to have been interrupted due to early trauma. This can be used within the model above. By matching support to the individual's developmental stage, alongside the offer of long-term trauma-informed psychotherapy, the aim is that the person moves closer to the stage of individuation where they can form more secure relationships and feel more able to cope with the world around them.

Frankish (2016) argued that whilst support provided using this model may appear more expensive in the short-term, it may be more cost-effective in the long run than numerous failed placements and inappropriate treatments. Frankish also highlighted risks associated with support being withdrawn once the individual appears to have made some improvement. It is important to highlight to commissioners that if somebody is functioning well with the level of support provided in this model, it is likely that the support is required long-term. Frankish argued that reducing the support may result in activation of past traumas relating to neglect and withholding of care, leading to crises involving deterioration in behaviour and significantly increased distress. This might further damage the individual's trust in others to care for them safely, and require a significant period of time to re-establish the previous gains. The retraumatising institutional responses Frankish identified may also apply to the maintenance of other approaches to trauma-informed care for people with severe trauma, such as McNally's (2022) described above.

6. Best Practice Recommendations

Due to the aforementioned lack of research and evidence in this area, the recommendations outlined here are tentative and require further research and evaluation.

- Clinical psychologists and other practitioners working with people with learning disabilities should familiarise themselves with how dissociation presents in the general population and be aware that it may be under-reported in people with learning disabilities due to the lack of attention the phenomenon has received in this population
- Following assessment, psychological practitioners should work with the system around the person to ensure there is a clear understanding of their needs and how these relate to their trauma history, considering application of the models and frameworks in Section 5.2, Systemic Interventions

- If someone with a learning disability and dissociative difficulties presents with behaviours that challenge, behaviour support plans and intervention strategies might integrate the frameworks suggested by Frankish (2016) and McNally (2022) within a Positive Behaviour Support (Gore et al., 2022) framework. Support plans should focus on establishing physical and relational safety for the individual rather than on elements of PBS such as differential reinforcement schedules (Donnellan et al., 1988) as it may be hypothesised that such interventions may be experienced as confusing, distressing, or withholding when used with individuals who may at times feel they have no control over their actions when they are in dissociative states. For individuals presenting with dissociation in the context of earlier stages of emotional development, the emphasis is likely to be on supporting the system around the person to understand why they need to focus on fostering a sense of trust and safety, and on adapting to the person's needs rather than attempting to teach skills (Hudson et al., 2024)
- Systemic interventions will require significant training and support for carers to enable them to understand the links between complex presentations and past trauma, and to support them in managing their own emotional reactions. Carers may need help to understand why even warm, nurturing approaches might trigger traumatic memories of being abused for some people (Johnson, 2001)
- Any systemic interventions should be coproduced with the person themselves as much as they are able to manage. This is to foster a sense of trust with the care team, to minimise fears associated with people in positions of power talking about them, and to reduce the risk of feelings of powerlessness and being 'done to' triggering memories of abuse
- If the person has little support (e.g., people with mild learning disabilities who have been assessed as having low needs for practical support) it is still important to work with the network that does exist around the person (e.g., family, other professionals, third sector organisations that the person accesses) in the first instance, again with the person's consent, and to consider how the principles of approaches such as those outlined by Frankish (2016) and McNally (2022) can be adapted to the person's particular context. If there is very little or no network, the focus initially may need to be on individual work that prioritises helping the person to build a sense of safety and develop more of a social support network where possible
- It is likely that clinical psychologists and other psychological practitioners working in this area will also need to educate commissioners of services around the needs of people with learning disabilities who present with dissociative difficulties, the application of trauma-informed approaches, and the long-term support needs of those who present with complex dissociation
- Individual therapy should be offered, though following assessment, the collaborative formulation might indicate the need for systemic work first. When providing individual work, psychological practitioners working in this area should consider the application of the approaches outlined in Chapter 2 and 4, i.e.,

initially focusing on engagement, safety, and psychoeducation about dissociation, prior to helping the person learn how to manage dissociative episodes and, when they are ready, processing the trauma that is at the root of the dissociation

- People with learning disabilities are likely to need even more time to build trust in the therapeutic relationship due to information-processing difficulties and previous experiences of shame and rejection
- Direct therapy should utilise the general adaptations that are useful to make psychological interventions accessible for people with learning disabilities (Jahoda et al. 2017). Upton (2009) illustrates how creative approaches can be used to facilitate communication and expression for people with learning disabilities accessing psychotherapy for trauma
- Research in this area should prioritise the development of tools to assess dissociation, as this may aid further research into the prevalence of dissociation in this population and support outcome measurement of interventions in order to be able to develop the evidence base.

7. Conclusion

In summary, there is little published literature addressing dissociation in people with learning disabilities despite the increased rates of trauma in this population. Literature that is available indicates that a trauma-informed and relationally oriented approach to formulation and intervention, focusing on both the individual and systemic levels, is required. Further research is required to aid understanding of how dissociative experiences present in people with learning disabilities, and clinical interventions for this population require further evaluation.

Chapter 11

Dissociation in Older People

Claire Lee

> '*Look at me now … if I don't sleep this is a trigger, but I know I'll sleep at some point. If I have a nightmare or setback it's ok as I'm in a different place now. Yes, I do take myself off to bed to cope but I'll get up again. Keep to your routines Rose, do go when I've said I'm going to go, and get booking more holidays.*' **Rose the Explorer, Expert-by-Experience**

1. The Relevance of Dissociation to Older People

Between 30–50% of older adults may have experienced significant trauma (Cook et al., 2017), yet complex dissociative difficulties are rarely recognised (Hayward, 2019). Trauma-related experiences, such as dissociation, are often explained away as a 'normal' part of ageing (Cook et al., 2017; Pless Kaiser et al., 2019). Dissociation may be misidentified as delirium, dementia, substance misuse, side effects of medication or physical health conditions (Kluft, 1988; Kluft, 2007; Loewenstein & Putnam, 2004).

Studies suggest that severe dissociative identity disorder (DID) symptoms can persist or appear in later life (Kluft, 1985; Kluft, 1988; Kluft, 2007; Smith, 2023).

Overt signs of trauma-related dissociation in older people include signs of identity alteration (e.g., the person insisting that their name is different or presenting in a child-like state) and episodes of amnesia (Kluft, 1988). Clinicians must also recognise non-verbal signs and shifts of dissociation. For example,

- 'Attention should be given to body posture, dress, fixed eye contact, eye fluttering, alterations in speech and cognitive abilities' (Hayward, 2019, p.36).
- More subtle signs of dissociative switching may include blinking or drooping of eyelids, changes in body posture (Fisher, 2017).

DOI: 10.4324/9781003625650-14

Practice Points: How Dissociative Experiences May Manifest in Older People (from Kluft, 1988, 2007):

- Decrease in number of dissociative parts of the personality with one predominant dissociative part
- Manifestations of dissociative parts of the personality more subtle
- Other dissociative parts of the personality may have atrophied or been dormant for years
- Less frequent switching
- Older people may present to services with anxiety, depression and 'inner voices without signs of a chronic psychotic disorder'
- New dissociative parts of the personality may emerge to manage different life stressors (e.g., end of life, Fan, 2024)

2. Models to Understand Trauma-Related Dissociation and Older People

2.1 Precipitating Events for Later Onset Presentation

The appearance of dissociative symptoms in later life is often triggered by traumatic, stressful or overwhelming life events. The impact of such events can undermine the ability to maintain trauma-related avoidance or may present new challenges to the person requiring additional resource.

Stressors linked to transitions and 'age-related experiences' in later-life, offer a broad range of predisposing factors for older people to navigate. Recent experiences involving physical harm or threats to life, attachment loss or betrayal are more likely to be traumatising and potentially act as precipitating events (Van der Hart et al., 2006).

An accumulation of such events may make it harder over time for people to avoid trauma-related stimuli. Focusing on activities of daily living may be harder to pursue due to needing to receive or give care, separation or loss. Concurrently, distress held by trauma-related dissociative parts of the personality may intrude on the person due to increased feelings of vulnerability, helplessness and fears associated with ageing (Poon, 2014). By way of example, Fisher (2017) described a 70-year-old woman whose ability to function deteriorated after 'the empty house and the loneliness triggered the young traumatized parts she'd been able to ignore for so many years' (Fisher, 2017, p. 53).

Hearing or visual loss may put the older person at increased risk of hearing voices, visual hallucinations or dissociation associated with PTSD (Crompton et al., 2017; Longden et al., 2012). Older people who have been living symptom free for decades after experiencing trauma may develop PTSD symptoms in the early stages of dementia (Johnson et al., 2020).

When considering potential precipitating events clinicians should consider

- Potential retraumatisation that contact with services may evoke
- There may be new trauma or retraumatisation through hospitalisation, moving into care or other institutional settings
- There may be cohort differences related to the societal and political context such as significant historical events, medical treatments, or impact of economic recessions and international conflicts.
- Difficulties associated with trauma-related dissociation are unlikely to resolve without treatment (Brand et al., 2016).

Case Example: *Piotr a retired hospital worker suddenly became flooded with memories of deceased people coming back to life, yet during his working life reported that this never bothered him. As his physical health declined, he started to see a dark shadow (past abuser who was deceased) at night when he was on his own.*

2.2 Threats to Physical, Relational and Psychological Integrity

For older people there may be differences in what is experienced as a 'threat to life'. Older people may experience significant internal threats and uncertainties related to ageing bodies and minds that may increase feelings of vulnerability and a heightened awareness of their own death. A serious fall or health event may be particularly traumatic especially if the older person is on their own.

Self-harm may resemble attempted suicide, as physical frailty results in self-harm or overdose causing greater harm (Patel et al., 2024). In some cultures, harming the self intentionally is considered a sin, prohibited or an offence to God. Risk to self may manifest in physical neglect or refusing medical treatment so this may need to be explored sensitively with older people.

Clinicians should consider more subtle potential precipitating events such as neglect through absence of physical or emotional care, continuous abuse, experiencing intense feelings of loneliness and lack of restorative experiences from others.

There is an increased risk of developing dementia following traumatic life events (Severs et al., 2023), with the brain being particularly sensitive to the effects of trauma (exposure to stress hormones) as it ages (Lupien et al., 2009). The effects of dementia on memory may reveal well-hidden trauma (Craftman et al., 2020), while other factors associated with loss and ageing may destabilise internal structures and mobilise threat systems.

'I find myself now once again not mentioning DID ... This was after I was seeking reassurance about cognitive changes and mentioning I was naturally concerned what part being DID might play in these situations. I was really taken aback as this person had been really helpful with my husband and I risked trusting her enough to share my fears, never again, DID has had to go underground yet again, I no longer have the energy to fight this battle.'
Melanie Goodwin, Expert-by-Experience

2.3 The Role of Loss for Older People and the Impact on Dissociation

Real and symbolic loss is often a key challenge facing older people (Hayward, 2019). Such life changes may evoke a sense of 'loss of control' associated with past trauma (Pless Kaiser et al., 2019). Losses undermine safety strategies that previously helped to contain traumatic material and could activate an underlying dissociative response to past traumatisation. For example, some people may have maintained distance through being highly self-reliant; loss of independence suddenly places the person in a position of needing care (Smith et al., 2017), potentially reactivating traumatic memories and increasing dissociative symptoms.

Age-related losses of social connectedness and resources may impact the experience of dissociation. Older people are more likely to experience the death of significant others, role changes or caregiver trauma related to caring for someone with dementia (Breslau et al., 1998; Cooper et al., 2010; Pless Kaiser et al., 2019). Losses may trigger fears of abandonment and loneliness or create new dependencies (often on services), increasing fears of attachment and loss. Loneliness is also associated with sleep problems in older people which may increase complex PTSD symptoms (Fox et al., 2022).

Older age is often a time of reflection on the life the person has led. This can be challenging for older people who experience trauma-related dissociation. There may be increased awareness and grieving for the childhood or parent they never had, and for the multi-faceted ways that trauma has impacted on their adult life.

How the older person manages and tolerates these losses and transitions will depend on their internal resources (e.g., Erickson, 1997). This may be aided by having a sense of purpose in life, a sense of self as strong and resilient, ability to function independently, positive social support, a perspective to compassionately challenge unhelpful beliefs, acceptance, spirituality and meaning making (Kadri et al., 2025; Prati & Pietrantoni, 2009; Rea et al., 2022).

2.4 Formulation

Formulation with the older person involves understanding how trauma has affected their relationships with self and others, as well as the meaning and inner resources they have or may develop. Exploration of early history and life events can be an important part of the formulation, although, it will likely be most helpful to focus on the meaning older people have made of their experiences and what helped them cope. This may help facilitate a 'sense of coherence' and 'meaning making', which is important during the third and final phase of trauma interventions (Antonovsky, 1987; Herman, 1992). For others, not exploring the past until sufficient stabilisation has been reached may be critical.

Case Example: *The legacy of childhood trauma lingered in Mavis's interactions with self and others. Cumulative trauma strengthened her belief that other people were a threat, and she was to blame. To protect Mavis an angry part had withdrawn from relationships, but now Mavis felt isolated. A depressed part wanted to sleep and not wake up. Exploring her inner resources helped her consider what each part did to survive (reframed as trauma-responses).*

What haunted her most were flashbacks of finding her son dead. An angry part wanted to die to end her suffering, with 'death' whispering to her; but after an overdose Mavis felt ashamed. Her son's death led to loss of 'purpose and meaning in life,' and exacerbated her isolation. An old wound of feeling 'unable to protect others' resurfaced. This mirrored pain she felt in discovering that her 'sacrifices' to a childhood abuser had not protected her siblings from abuse.

---

3. Barriers to the Recognition of Dissociation in Older People

---

Case Example: *Carole had never spoken about childhood abuse or abandonment by her mother. As an adult she successfully managed her own business but struggled in relationships and experienced 'breakdowns' when these ended. She struggled to recall these episodes, although her history showed patterns of hospital admissions following an overdose.*

Carole had many years of wellness until a stroke resulted in her needing to rely on other people. She developed non-epileptic seizures, 'blank spells on a daily basis, sometimes preceded by uncomfortable feelings in body and head'. Carole was not aware of triggers, but behavioural charts indicated these episodes followed situations when she was asked to do something she found difficult or when others provided care.

3.1 Individual, Service and Societal Barriers to the Recognition of Trauma-related Dissociation in Older People

Temporary coping strategies for surviving earlier trauma may become habitual ways of living, resulting in different diagnoses. Dissociative symptoms such as flashbacks, suddenly becoming aware of voices, and paranoia may lead to misdiagnosis, for instance, symptoms being attributed to late onset psychosis or dementia (Kluft, 2007; Bruneau et al., 2020).

When services are not dissociation-informed, misdiagnosis is more likely. This may lead to neglecting or not recognising trauma-related reactions, retraumatising or inadvertently triggering the service user:

- The shift into dissociative parts may be missed and instead labelled as 'personality' or 'behavioural'
- Addressing substance misuse behaviours can become the focus, with underlying trauma responses being unaddressed
- Switching off from reality with unusual experiences may be labelled psychosis.
- Flashbacks may be seen as hallucinations in dementia.

(Adapted from Clarke & Nicholls, 2018).

As well as service-related barriers, older adults may have their own barriers. They may be reluctant to disclose dissociative symptoms and underlying abuse or mistreatment due to safety fears for themselves and others; they may not recognise certain behaviours as abusive, or experience embarrassment, stigma, uncertainty about their future, lack of independence, and cultural or generational preferences for privacy (Cations et al., 2022; Dong et al., 2009). Older people are also:

- Fearful of being labelled 'mad', having hidden trauma for decades (Hayward, 2019)
- Less likely than younger cohorts to connect their symptoms to traumatic events (Pless Kaiser et al., 2019)
- More likely to report physical health problems, pain, sleep difficulties or cognitive difficulties rather than emotional difficulties and less likely to seek mental health support (Pless Kaiser et.al., 2019)
- Older adults who have been in and out of mental health services for many years may have internalised a double stigma of different or multiple diagnoses combined with a sense of hopelessness about change associated with ageing (e.g., 'it's a longstanding problem', 'it's not a new behaviour').

Past trauma may be hidden behind amnesic barriers or may have been repeated across many previous re-enactments of prior abuse. The older person's experiences of abuse may also be disbelieved and dismissed by their adult children who may know the abuser as a beloved grandparent (Kluft, 2007). This may mirror similar responses older people received as a child from a non-abusing parent or family member.

It is also possible older adults may not be experiencing trauma-related dissociation as frequently or severely. As the person ages there may be a pattern of 'relapsing and remitting' in which they either 'mask or suppress' symptoms for periods of time (Loewenstein & Putnam, 2004). Time elapsed may act as a buffer, with age leading to the development of more control over dissociative symptoms, increased resilience over time or less severe dissociation (Connor, 2015; Pless Kaiser et al., 2019). Through reminiscence or life review in later life older people may work through experiences they have previously avoided (as fewer distractions) to find meaning and coherence (Pless Kaiser et al., 2019).

A final thought is whether older people who experience trauma-related dissociation are less likely to present to services due to the higher mortality rates associated with early traumatisation than non-dissociative counterparts (Hiroeh et al., 2001; Johnson et al., 2020).

4. Special Issues in Older People's Services and Trauma-Related Dissociation

4.1 End of Life Care

The capacity for dissociation may continue into the very last stages of life with new dissociative parts being created to manage specific issues. For example, DID has been documented during end-of-life care for a 77-year-old woman (Fan, 2024). Different dissociative parts lay dormant for years, becoming activated when she was bed-bound, receiving palliative care. A new dissociative part developed to manage the stress of the situation.

Narratives around death and end of life vary across cultures and religions which may contribute to how end of life is experienced. For instance, the later stages of life can be accompanied by heightened spiritual reflection particularly within Muslim communities and other religious traditions that emphasise beliefs about the afterlife (Gatrad & Sheikh, 2001). Individuals may experience increased anxiety around the concept of Judgement Day, questioning whether they will pass this divine test, and whether they will be granted entry into paradise or face punishment in the afterlife based on the way they have lived their life on Earth. These concerns may be particularly salient in the context of unresolved trauma or dissociative experiences, which may be interpreted through a religious lens as moral or spiritual failings (Koenig, 2018). End of life care should be approached with cultural sensitivity.

4.2 Attachment and Dependency

The challenges of older age can activate underlying attachment systems and threat-related systems. A common clinical presentation may involve the high proximity seeking associated with the 'attachment cry'. Service contexts can focus on finding a 'quick fix', inadvertently contributing to a 'culture of dependency, rejection and abandonment' (Seagar, 2014, p.222). Such clinical presentations can be common in older people and are important when working with safety concerns (see Chapter 6 Working with Safety Concerns). Steele et al. (2001) outline ways of working with such relational patterns; these should be considered alongside the specific needs and context of the older person.

For example, encouraging the person's social support is important, rather than the therapist or service becoming a substitute. Being able to 'step back' from strong reactions requires people to have the support of others or the ability to develop new coping skills (Byng-Hall, 1995). This may be challenging for some older people with unmet needs for social connection and reduced ability to develop new skills.

Case Example: *Working with Dorothy's 'cry for help' part involved understanding its function, making connections with past experiences and validating her need for connection. We tracked triggering situations and explored what the therapeutic relationship evoked (e.g., how her wish to be taken care conflicted with my attempts to develop her coping skills and autonomy).*

We developed strategies for managing the loneliness and increasing her tolerance (e.g., helping her feel connected with different parts and other people, exploring what she valued about solitude and developing a 'safety net approach' [Fisher, 2017]). We mapped her support network and considered who else she could hold in mind (including different parts and deceased people) to feel less alone

---

Some people, due to changes in needs and functioning, may need regular support and/or function better in a supported living environment with boundaried responses from staff. In addition, emphasising the narrative that older people can live healthy, active and independent lives, countering discourses of this population as frail and dependent, can offer hope and empowerment.

4.3 Dissociative Amnesia vs Dementia

'I also would like those working with DID to understand about trauma responses that may become more extreme as the fears of aging hit and anxiety levels naturally become more pronounced and the horror suggesting memory tests raises in many of us with DID. I probably could never do many of the things they ask but have learnt a way of managing. Yet again I often feel worthless, a waste of space or that I am over dramatising a situation

> *that I am risking sharing, trying to have an adult conversation.'* **Melanie Goodwin, Expert-by-Experience**

Suspected dementia and trauma-related dissociation may both lead people to report memory problems and marked changes in behaviour and personality.

Identity alteration and amnesia in DID can be misidentified as 'time-shifting' in dementia (experiencing a different reality and recalling memories from earlier in life). With dissociative amnesia the person may lack awareness of their memory loss (Kluft, 1988) also common in some types of dementia. Traumatic experiences impact the processing of memory, especially the encoding stage. Vascular/subcortical vascular dementia also affects encoding, with Alzheimer's disease affecting the memory storage system (Lezak et al., 2012). Smaller hippocampal and amygdala volumes have been reported in people with DID (Vermetten et al., 2006).

Interactions between dissociative responses and organic difficulties can also occur. For example, a previously contained dissociative system may break down when the older person develops cognitive impairment. This may mean the person presents with an increase in trauma-related symptoms as a result of the cognitive impairment (Martinez-Clarvera et al., 2017). PTSD may also accelerate cognitive decline and increase risk of developing dementia (Lapp et al., 2011; Roberts et al., 2022).

How to Identify Dissociation, Dementia or a Combination of These?

Investigations should rule out organic causes (e.g., no abnormalities on brain scans, blood tests clear, no neurological problems on examination). No single neuropsychological test distinguishes if 'a memory disorder is dissociative, organic, malingered, or of mixed etiology' (Loewenstein & Putnam, 2004, p. 16). Screening tools and more in-depth assessments supports the process (see Chapter 2) with formulation being key in aiding differential diagnosis.

Case Example: *Frank's previous neuropsychological assessments failed to distinguish between frontotemporal dementia (FTD) or mood disorder. Brain scans showed mild ischaemic changes. He continued reporting memory problems leading to referral to older adult services. Other concerns included self-neglect, anger outbursts and impulsivity.*

Repeated neuropsychological scores remained stable with difficulties in attention and executive function (difficulty inhibiting responses, mental inflexibility). During assessment Frank suddenly reported he 'didn't know where he was but felt it was far from home'. Inclusion of DES-II indicated a high probability of a potential dissociative disorder.

Detailed trauma history revealed extensive childhood and adult trauma resulting in 'multiple overdoses,' 'relationship breakdowns' and 'episodes of wandering'. He disclosed suicidal thoughts and a disregard for his own safety.

Frank was diagnosed with a Dissociative Disorder (DD), with small vessel ischaemia, which seven years later had not progressed to FTD.

5. Clinical Recommendations for Improving the Quality of Care in Older People's Services

'Older people deserve the same respect whether Dissociative Disorder (DD) or not, being listened to and given realistic hope. TIC could play such a big part when working with this age group.' **Melanie Goodwin, Expert-by-Experience**

5.1 Service-level Recommendations

The following suggestions for improving access to dissociation-informed care for older people are offered:

- Improve multidisciplinary staff recognition of dissociation and how it may present in older people. This includes:
  - Improve awareness of different types of dementia and dissociation to aid differential diagnosis
  - Addressing myths, for example that 'older people do not experience dissociation'
  - Support service implementation by developing 'complex trauma and dissociation' supervision/consultation groups.
- Older people may be less likely to connect their symptoms to trauma:
  - Services should be alert and assess because trauma-related dissociation is unlikely to resolve without treatment
  - Physical health including pain and delirium should be addressed quickly to reduce distress.
- Foster more positive attitudes towards ageing, by challenging perceptions of older people being unable to change.

5.2 Considering the Therapeutic Relationship

Older people 'experiencing DDs need time to trust and reveal the hidden parts of themselves to clinicians' (Hayward, 2019, p.36). Careful attunement, the development of shared meaning and consensus building within the therapeutic relationship may be of great importance.

> **Case Example**: *Rose was initially very unresponsive but over time responded to my gentle invitations and validation of her emotions (empathic attunement). When she did start talking she was flooded by memories and vividly recalled traumatic events. The challenge was slowing her down and 'putting on the breaks'* (Rothschild, 2017) *until she had the coping skills in place to work with the trauma.*

Clinicians may need to be mindful of how age, hierarchy and respect are negotiated in the therapeutic relationship. In many cultural contexts elders are afforded a position of high status, often seen as the most respected members of the family or community with authority over key decisions (Sung & Kim, 2003). Within these frameworks, a younger clinician may be perceived as lacking sufficient life experience or authority, which could impact the therapeutic alliance. Furthermore, older adults may be unaccustomed to being invited to explore their own internal world or express vulnerability with someone younger or of a different background.

5.3 Holding Hope for Change

It is important for clinicians to validate natural responses to loss, challenging dominant ageist beliefs about being too old to change, and exploring reasons to live and die which parts may feel differently about.

> *'I would have died long ago, you gave me hope, when I had none.'* **Gita, Expert-by-Experience**

5.4 Dissociation-informed Therapy Recommendations (see Chapter 4, Therapy) Adapted for Older People

The key steps to therapeutic change (outlined in Chapter 4) need some adaptation for the specific needs of older people.

Older people may feel unsafe in their bodies, unsafe with other people and unsafe in their environments (e.g., if in a care home or living alone). Connection with the body and five senses as an anchor for grounding and 'being present' (not dissociated) may need careful consideration.

Difficulties in relationships and changes in roles that develop as the person ages can provide an opportunity to explore cycles of interaction, what drives or motivates them to maintain contact with perpetrators, or triggers to their distress.

6. Conclusion

Older people may present with dissociative experiences across many different older adult services. There are many barriers to recognising trauma-related dissociation in older people, contributing to misdiagnosis, inappropriate treatment and retraumatisation. Psychologists working with older people have an important role in recognising, responding and leading the development of multidisciplinary trauma and dissociation-informed responses adapted to the unique needs of older people. This includes developing cultural sensitivity and attending to loss, loneliness, increased feelings of vulnerability and psychological safety.

Chapter 12

Dissociation and Eating Disorders

Hannah Wilson, Caroline Wyatt and Melanie Bash

'*People wouldn't keep physically harming their body with an eating disorder if there wasn't something very bad that they were escaping. Dissociation wouldn't be tempting or useful or helpful if you were happy and coping and living an easy life. Really all of it is a symptom of an underlying problem and without addressing the underlying problem it's unrealistic to expect someone to fully recover.*' **Laura, Expert-by-Experience**

1. The Need for Dissociation-Informed Services

Eating disorders and disordered eating are complex mental health presentations characterised by significant distress experienced within someone's relationship with food, weight, eating and/or their body shape/appearance. This may entail the person presenting with one or more of the following behaviours:

restrictive eating, purging, binge-eating and compensatory behaviours such as excessive exercise.

There is a strong link between traumatic experience and the subsequent development of an eating disorder. Eating disorders may often co-occur with trauma-related dissociation. Despite this, clinical guidelines for eating disorders have historically failed to recommend trauma- or dissociation-specific pathways of care.

This can lead to a focus on treating the symptoms of an eating disorder, with insufficient attention to the context in which it has developed, and survival function it continues to play for the person. Likewise, trauma-specific services can overlook the specific needs attached to supporting someone with an eating disorder. Such a service milieu can result in difficulty in accessing support that addresses the full needs of the person.

DOI: 10.4324/9781003625650-15

Zoe, Expert-by-Experience, said that her dissociation and dissociative switching were not picked up for a long time, and not actively enquired about by health care professionals. She noted that professionals in eating disorder services were largely unaware of dissociation or trauma-informed adaptations, even senior experienced staff. Conversely, professionals in trauma services were unable to account for or integrate the eating concerns. She noted that *'sometimes it feels like some professionals get frustrated or annoyed with me'*.

2. Relationship between Trauma, Dissociation and Eating Disorders

Laura, Expert-by-Experience, thought that for her, the eating disorder was *'almost entirely about shutting things off and having a break from everything … you can turn all of your thoughts towards food and stop being worried about other things, and you can become emotionally numb, more emotionally resilient to triggers and take the sting out of memories, feel euphoric and strong and weightless and like you're floating on a cloud'* [by restricting her eating].

[Without the eating disorder] *'everything you weren't thinking about comes back, it's like you fall from your cloud and hit the earth with a thud'*.

2.1 Trauma and Eating Disorders

Traumatic experience appears to play an important role in the development of an eating disorder. For example, studies have shown there to be an elevated prevalence of traumatic experience in adolescents and adults with a diagnosis of an eating disorder (Convertino et al., 2022; Groth et al., 2020). Rates of childhood trauma in eating disorder populations vary from 21%–59% (Molendijk et al., 2017) and over 63% for adult-onset trauma (Trevillion et al., 2012). The level of post traumatic symptomology appears raised in eating disorder populations in comparison to the general population (Brewerton et al., 2020; Scharff et al., 2021).

Several studies have shown a correspondence between the severity of trauma experienced and the severity of eating disorder, as well as the presence of wider difficulties, such as self-harm (Backholm et al., 2013; Brewerton et al., 2020; Kovács-Tóth et al., 2022; Molendijk et al., 2017). Significant trauma histories and the presence of PTSD symptomology in eating disorder populations have been shown to predict a more complex course of illness, higher rates of treatment drop out and poorer clinical outcomes (Convertino & Mendoza, 2023). The presence of significant traumatic experience appears associated with both an increased complexity of clinical presentation *and* difficulties in engaging with 'treatment as usual'.

2.2 Dissociation Plays a Mediating Role in the Relationship Between Trauma and Eating Disorders

Dissociation has been highlighted as one potential mediating variable between childhood trauma and the development of an eating disorder (Everill et al., 1995; Fuller-Tyszkiewicz & Mussap, 2008; Moulton et al., 2015; Palmisano et al., 2018; Rabito-Alcón et al., 2020). In a sample of eating disorder patients, Vanderlinden et al. (1993) found that 25% of the sample reported trauma-related experiences and 12% reported dissociative experiences to a degree as high as in a group of dissociative disorder (DD) patients. Rabito-Alcón et al. (2020) reported significantly higher levels of dissociation in an eating disorder group compared to controls.

3. How Eating Disorders and Dissociation Impact on Trauma-Related Distress

---

Hayley, Expert-by-Experience, shared that both her dissociative experiences and eating difficulties served the same function of '*protecting from overwhelming pain and feelings*'. Dissociation was the only option for her when she was '*little and overwhelmed*', as she couldn't get out of the situations that had put her into 'fight or flight'. She described dissociation then becoming her '*go-to strategy*' before she developed difficulties with eating.

3.1 An Escape from Self

Fisher (2017) draws a link between eating disorders and the evolved 'flight' response, noting:

> '*[dissociative] parts driven by the flight response tend to engage in eating disorders that result in numbing or addictive behaviour that alters consciousness, allowing distance from unbearable feelings and flashbacks.*' (p.29).

There are common functions to both dissociation and eating difficulties. For example, both dissociation and eating disorders can provide a powerful way to cope with overwhelming emotions, trauma, or stress and can serve a very powerful avoidance and/or escape function for the person (Heatherton & Baumeister, 1991).

There can also be similar formulations regarding the need for control. The achievement of this can generate significant positive affect and 'euphoria'. It is thought that the powerful influx of positive affect overwhelms the information processing system in a similar way to the negative affect of a trauma memory. When this is repeated time and again it can become embedded in implicit memory and become an 'automatic response'.

Dissociation may also be somatic in origin, helping the person to disconnect from the awareness of the physical body. For example, Orbach (1994) describes how early traumatic events can lead to defensive dissociative reactions, which can increase detachment from the body and pain tolerance. Lewis et al. (2021) considers how this may apply to individuals with an eating disorder which inherently entail some disconnect from bodily experiences. This may be of particular significance when working with people from certain cultures for example there is evidence that distress may manifest more often through somatic dissociation in Eastern cultures than in Western ones (Şar, 2022).

3.2 Dissociative Mechanisms Associated with Eating Disordered Behaviours

Some common ways in which dissociation can influence and be influenced by eating disorders include:

> For **Laura, Expert-by-Experience,** dissociation in response to emotional stressors felt *'like the world wasn't real, like you were in a simulation. Sometimes it felt like there was a fog, or like I was standing a step back from a window looking at the world. Sometimes I would feel like I was looking down on myself. I felt detached from everything and physically/emotionally numb. I couldn't concentrate on anything or think clearly or remember much. I felt lost. It often felt uncomfortable and was something that I wanted to stop.'*
>
> In contrast, Laura described dissociation from restrictive eating as *'more of a gentle slide'* into a dissociative state, rather than the *'jarring'* experience of non-eating related dissociation. Laura also reflected that she felt *'in control'* in this space, and *'protected'* from the world.

- Restrictive eating can slow cognitive processing and often results in people reporting a 'disconnection' from their body and a 'numbing' of emotions (Fisher, 2017). To restrict food intake significantly, an individual also needs to disconnect or dissociate from their physical sensations of hunger (and/or thirst). This can result in a greater sense of control over experiences of depersonalisation or derealisation

- Binge eating can also lead to increased parasympathetic hypo-arousal, leading to increased relaxation, disconnection from the body, and drowsiness (Fisher, 2017). People often report experiences of depersonalisation and derealisation both before and during binge eating episodes (Vanderlinden & Palmisano, 2019). There can also be experiences of amnesia and timelessness following a binge (Abraham & Beumont, 1982). Binge eating can act as a distraction from other thoughts and feelings, and some individuals report binge eating in an almost 'trance-like' state. This detachment during binge eating is regarded as particularly significant by some service users

---

Laura, Expert-by-Experience, spoke about using binge eating to '*force so much sugar into my body to force a shift into a different state, or to feel so sick that I felt something*'. She recalled '*almost waking up from a daze*' to find lots of food eaten. She also spoke about sometimes '*watching myself binge*' as if outside the body and feeling '*horrified*' but unable to stop it.

- In both the binge and purge stages of bulimia there is a reduction in hyperarousal and increased dorsal-vagal activation (Faris et al., 2008). Purging, for example by self-induced vomiting can result in disconnection from bodily sensations. Vomiting over time is also reported to release opiates/endorphins which can leave someone feeling 'spacey' (Abraham & Joseph, 1986). State dissociation in response to threat cues have been found to precede bulimic eating behaviors, further supporting the link between dissociation, and eating disorders (Hallings-Pott et al., 2005)
- Compensatory behaviours such as excessive exercise can lead to the release of endorphins and subsequently alter the mood or enable someone to disconnect from the present moment. It also typically requires someone to dissociate from their physical sensations of pain, as excessive exercise often involves pushing the body well beyond physical comfort.

Zoe, Expert-by-Experience, explained that '*it makes sense to me that as parts of me fragmented and split in order to cope with that [childhood] trauma, different ways of managing food became trapped in those new parts*'.

Zoe described how it could be '*as if I'm merely watching myself buy and eat or purge or whatever*' and that it can '*feel as if my body has been hijacked and that I'm just bearing witness to whatever the eating disorder behaviour may be*'.

> She described how '*the eating disorder alone feels like a demon and a dictator tormenting me and then on top of that other DID parts are shouting at me or hurling abuse about how out of control or pathetic I am or controlling food/ eating without my control. It is so hard to explain just how powerless and out of control of my own head I feel and how trapped and hopeless it all can make me feel. It isn't that I don't try or that I don't want things to be different. It is just hard to see a way though without too much fallout or distress.*'

4. Eating Disorders and Dissociative Parts of the Personality

For some people presenting with eating disorders, the eating disorder represents one manifestation of a wider trauma-related structural dissociation of the personality. Several clinical investigators have emphasised the importance of recognising and treating trauma related structural dissociation for people presenting with an eating disorder (Berger et al., 1994; McCallum et al., 1992; Tobin et al., 1995). Indeed, people can experience dissociative parts that use eating disordered behaviors; such parts may operate largely outside of the person's awareness and be relatively inaccessible to the person.

In support of this, a number of people with eating disorders describe experiencing an 'eating disorder voice'; 'a second- or third-person commentary on actions and consequences relating to eating, weight, and shape' (Pugh & Waller, 2016, p.622). Pugh, Waller and Esposito (2018) demonstrated a link between childhood trauma, dissociation and such internal voice(s). They found that the 'relative power' of the 'eating disorder' voice was related to experiences of childhood *emotional* abuse more than other early traumas, and that the association was partially mediated by dissociation.

For people who experience an eating disorder driven by trauma-related structural dissociation it is hard to see how the eating disorder (and the function it serves) can be effectively treated without addressing the underlying structural dissociation. Indeed, there is evidence to suggest that neglecting the role of trauma-related dissociation may limit the effectiveness of approaches that aim to target eating disorder symptomology (Brewerton et al., 2024; Longo et al., 2020; Serra et al., 2020). For example, Serra et al. (2020) reported that dissociation partially mediated the negative relationship between 'trauma impact scores' and symptom remission after 6 months of CBT for binge-eating disorder (i.e., higher levels of dissociation was associated with lower levels of remission).

5. Unhelpful and Helpful Service Responses to Dissociation and Eating Disorders.

5.1 Treating Individual Symptoms or Whole People?

People who experience eating disorders will typically access support from specialist eating disorder services. Such services are typically guided by NICE guidance and as such are focused on the treatment of the eating disorder symptomology, such as CBT-E. Given that people often struggle to understand or relate to the eating disordered parts of their personality, cognitive models often only resonate to a certain extent. Organising services by clinical presentations can limit their ability to recognise or support the needs of the person as a whole or the wider trans-diagnostic factors that can be key in the development and maintenance of an eating disorder.

Hayley, Expert-by-Experience, spoke about the tendency for ED services to treat the ED as '*some sort of devil*' that needs to be resisted and '*cast out*'. She felt that this created a barrier to accessing help for her, as there was little recognition of the protective nature of her ED. She also explained how this was particularly difficult when there are dissociated parts involved, as the suggestion to '*get rid of the ED*' meant '*getting rid of a part of her*'. As this part had developed eating difficulties as a way of managing difficult memories and feelings of shame, this focus on '*casting it out*' reinforced the belief that other parts were disgusting or shameful.

This can lead to a focus on targeting the eating disorder whilst neglecting the context in which it has developed and the wider function it serves for the person. When the eating disorder has developed as part of a wider trauma-related structural dissociation this service-response risks neglecting a key driver for the eating disorder. Indeed, attempts to 'remove' the eating disorder without addressing the protective need it meets can not only be ineffective but could also lead to iatrogenic harm. Eating disorder clinicians often learn to externalise the eating disorder and encourage patients to see it as 'not them' and something to rid themselves of (Voswinkel et al., 2021). For those patients for whom the eating disorder is held by a dissociative part, this can create intense inner conflict and is contrary to trauma-informed approaches of working compassionately with parts, acknowledging their function and roles (e.g., Schwartz, 2021).

Zoe, Expert-by-Experience, said that '*some staff underestimated the intensity/severity of the restrictive eating disorder voice*', especially because she '*wasn't as underweight as the other patients*'. Zoe also commented on how weight '*really isn't the best indicator of severity, especially somebody who dissociates; there is definitely more mental risk if the person feels out of control of their actions*'. Zoe also cautioned against professionals assuming that '*once the trauma is addressed the eating disorder won't serve a purpose and will sort itself out*', highlighting this may be '*naive*' when it has become so ingrained or part of someone's life.

People with complex trauma often present with a range of eating disordered behaviours which do not fall neatly into the diagnostic categories of 'anorexia nervosa' or 'bulimia nervosa'. This can then be viewed as 'disordered eating' and seen to not be the remit of specialist eating disorder services, particularly if they have received other diagnoses, such as 'Emotionally Unstable Personality Disorder'. Given that these diagnoses are often indicative in themselves of structural dissociation, this leads people who dissociate to struggle to access eating disorder services in the first place. For people not able to access specialist eating disorder support, there can be a significant risk of failing to provide adequate support in relation to the eating disorder symptomology, in terms of health checks and nutritional support for example.

In treating the whole person, it is also imperative that we consider the wider socio-cultural context within which they exist, and within which the eating disorder developed. Professionals should hold a curious stance towards understanding broad-ranging socio-cultural factors. For example, it may be that the function of an eating disorder is to manage a dissociative part's gender dysphoria (Banasiak, 2022), or due to a part's desire to delay body maturation (Levinson & Brosof, 2016).

5.2 Joined Up Care and Developing a Shared Understanding and Language

> **Zoe, Expert-by-Experience,** also noted how unhelpful it is for people to be '*debating which issue is primary and what to sort first (trauma/eating), with nobody wanting to take charge for ages and being passed back and forth like a ball in a game of ping pong between services. Treatment worked best when it was collaborative or when one team took charge*'.

Service responses that can meet the person's needs as a whole person are therefore essential. This means being able to integrate the specialist needs posed by both trauma-related dissociation and eating disorders. Without this, services run the risk of offering a fragmented response from a dissociated system of care.

One barrier to providing joined up care lies in the lack of shared language and understanding of eating disorders that is related to dissociation. This understanding could be facilitated by the adoption of trauma and dissociation-informed models of eating disorders (Brewerton, 2023; Brewerton et al., 2024) and mental health conditions more generally (Johnstone & Boyle, 2018; Schwartz, 2021). Recent work by Brewerton et al (2023, 2024) has articulated a trauma and dissociation-informed model of eating disorders and advocated adopting a phased approach to the treatment of eating disorders that have developed as a trauma-related response.

The adoption of such models of formulation would bridge the divide between specialist and generic services and help to provide a consistency in the understanding of someone's difficulties.

5.3 Relational Models of Care

The core conditions of the therapeutic alliance are particularly important factors in peoples recovery journey; a service response that is trauma and dissociation-informed prioritises a relational approach based on the foundations of safety, empowerment and connection (Herman, 1992). This is particularly important given the high level of shame that can exist in relation to both trauma-related dissociation and the experience of an eating disorder.

Hayley, Expert-by-Experience, shared that in her experience services are wary of people building attachments with professionals, but that this needs to happen in order for 'recovery' to begin. She shared that you need to be able to trust the professional more than the eating disorder, so that you can 'hand them your trust and have it handed back to you when you have the skills'.

Without this people may find it hard to be open about the extent of the difficulties they experience in relation to their eating disorder or the role trauma-related dissociation plays in this. This could be exacerbated by service responses that fail to address peoples' needs in an integrated way.

In this sense, it is important for professionals to respect and empathically understand the function served by an eating disorder and its association with trauma-related dissociation, as well as the struggles people may experience with letting go of this as a survival strategy.

Laura, Expert-by-Experience, emphasised the importance of acknowledging both the advantages and disadvantages of eating disorders, not just the latter. She also wanted to ensure that professionals bear in mind that there may often be some ambivalence to change if their difficulties are also serving a helpful purpose, but that doesn't mean that they don't want or need help. Laura emphasised the importance of taking a person-centred approach and recognising that change or recovery may happen at different paces for different people.

5.4 Dissociation-Informed and -Specific Pathways of Care

> **Laura, Expert-by-Experience,** suggested professionals working with people experiencing eating disorders, especially if there is a trauma history, should 'assume dissociation until proven otherwise'. This is perhaps a very important consideration for professionals to note.

It is important that specialist eating disorder services can *recognise* when an eating disorder forms part of a wider trauma-related structural dissociative system and *respond* appropriately, rather than viewing this as 'not their business'. As Finlay (2019) states: '*unless the trauma and the eating disorder are treated simultaneously, treatment becomes futile at best, fraught with multiple relapses, behavioural substitutions, feelings of hopelessness, and premature termination*' (p.42).

With regard to recognising the presence of trauma-related dissociation, the routine use screening tools can be a helpful way of opening a conversation about wider trauma-related and dissociative experiences (see Chapter 2).

> **Hayley, Expert-by-Experience,** shared how completing a dissociation screening tool was the first time that she thought 'oh yeah, that's what happens to me'. She had never previously found a way to put these experiences into words, and found it helpful to know that others experienced them. The conversations that she was then able to have as part of this assessment allowed her to realise that she is not 'broken' or 'fundamentally flawed', but has a different way of experiencing and coping with the world both due to neurodiversity and trauma.

Treatment approaches for this group therefore need to meet the specific needs posed by both the eating disorder and the underlying trauma-related dissociation. Such approaches would be based on the assumption that eating disorders may serve to manage the emotional consequences of trauma, and in this sense are aimed at survival (Rabito-Alcón et al., 2020).

Many aspects of dissociation can interfere with someone's ability to be sufficiently present to make use of treatment. Professionals understanding this and creating relationships that are sufficiently safe for the person to share blocks and barriers to treatment, can be important to promote collaborative problem solving and find a dissociation-informed way of helping the person to make use of the support.

Hayley, Expert-by-Experience, described '*appearing to be following a meal plan or attending a therapy session but I wasn't actually connected to any of it and didn't work through any of the emotions*'. This led to it appearing to professionals that she was 'stuck' or 'not applying the skills she had'. She shared a recent example of having to tell a professional that going out for lunch together wasn't helping her, and '*We had to step it right back to doing what I was able to manage without detaching and work on tolerating that first. It felt like a step back but at least I was then able to work through the thoughts and feelings and reflect on it.*'

For some people presenting with an eating disorder, dissociation-specific support will likely be critical. Brewerton (2024) reported a case series outlining beneficial clinical outcomes for 15 inpatient participants with a comorbid diagnosis of Dissociative Identity Disorder and eating disorders. Treatment was informed by ISSTD (2011) guidelines and therefore followed a phased approach which targeted both structural dissociation and the eating disorder. This treatment approach included during stage 1, eating disorder-specific nutritional and psychoeducational support as part of a wider-trauma and dissociation-informed stabilisation phase; stage 2 in addition to the treatment of traumatic memories, involved developing an understanding of the links between the adaptive functions served by eating disorder functions and the traumatic context in which they have developed.

6. Conclusion

Eating disorders/disordered eating, trauma and dissociation are commonly found clustering together and may be both inter-related and inter-dependent. Professionals should routinely enquire about dissociative experiences. Both eating disorders and dissociation serve a function in helping the person to manage intolerable feelings and experiences. When people experience an eating disorder *and* dissociation it is unhelpful to the individual to attempt to treat these separately and this can be experienced as invalidating by the person. It is unhelpful to assume that the eating disorder will self-remit following trauma treatment. In addition, the absence of low weight does not rule out a very serious eating disorder.

Acknowledgements: We would like to give special thanks to Hayley, Laura, and Zoe, three experts by experience who kindly gave us their time, insight and reflections, which helped to shape and structure this chapter.

Chapter 13

Dissociation, Harmfulness and Violence

Altered States of Consciousness as Offence-Related Factors

Jon Taylor

1. Introduction

Identity, a Hollywood blockbuster, portrays a fictitious account of Dissociative Identity Disorder (DID). As the story unfolds, ten people gradually realise they are being systematically murdered. One of the travellers, a driver called Ed, seeks to determine the murderer's identity. Little do we know until the plot is revealed that Ed is one of ten self-states, one of whom is systematically killing his fellow travellers.

Identity, alongside other Hollywood depictions of trauma-related dissociation, allows the casual observer to believe that the presence of a harmful self-states is a common feature of DID. As has been clear throughout this book, there is little evidence to support such a suggestion, with evidence repeatedly indicating that the experience of trauma-related dissociation is not associated with an increase in criminality (Webermann & Brand, 2017; Webermann et al., 2014). Indeed, people experiencing complex dissociative difficulties are much more likely to be a victim than a perpetrator of crime.

Despite this, the experience and significance of trauma-related dissociation has become an area of interest in forensic settings. The chapter aims to explore the significance, prevalence and influence of dissociative phenomena amongst forensic populations. The role of adversity amongst people who are justice-involved will be considered before moving on to the explore how differing manifestations of dissociation may influence the risk of offending. The chapter concludes with practice recommendations in light of these findings.

> **Practice Point**: It is not uncommon for people who commit violent offences to deny memory of their actions (Bourget et al., 2017) and such denials are often assumed to be malingering. However, studies suggest that dissociative states may play a mediating role between exposure to childhood trauma and subsequent serious violent offending (e.g., Moskowitz, 2004; Quimby & Putnam, 1991).

DOI: 10.4324/9781003625650-16

2. Childhood Adversity and Offending

Trauma plays a recurring and significant role in the development and maintenance of dissociation (see Chapter 1). Studies indicate that forensic service users experience childhood adversity at significantly higher rates than the general population. Reavis et al. (2013) found four times as many adverse childhood events (ACEs) in a population of men with a range of convictions than are found in men without convictions. A similar picture of early adversity is found amongst those people who commit sexual offences (Jespersen et al., 2009; Reavis et al., 2013) who are found to have generally high rates of ACEs (Levenson et al., 2016). Levenson et al. (2016) found that both men and women who commit sexual offences were almost twice as likely to have experienced four or more adverse events than are found in the general population, while Taylor (2021) found that men with sexual convictions had typically experienced over seven of the original ten ACE items. Systematic reviews similarly highlight an association between early trauma and convictions (Graf et al., 2021; Malvaso et al., 2022), suggesting that ACEs are associated with justice system contact in a dose-response fashion.

Furthermore, Karatzias et al. (2018) found that multiple experiences of trauma amongst imprisoned women were associated with the severity of offending, while Fox et al. (2015) found an association between chronic exposure to childhood adversity and extreme violence.

While there has undoubtably been a significant shift in the awareness of the presence of trauma that permeates the lives of people who commit serious offences, there has been less acknowledgement of the impact of such adversity on the developmental trajectory and subsequently on the acquisition of factors that are associated with risk of causing harm to others.

While the repercussions of trauma and adversity are somewhat individual, a number of recurring themes have been identified in the literature (see for example Maté, 2022), including

1. A disruption to the experience of attachment, including the reciprocal nature of proximity seeking, a secure base and the experience of a safe haven.
2. An alteration to neuro-biological development that may interrupt the growth of mirror neurones, the development of mentalisation and the learning of competencies that facilitate emotional regulation.
3. A disruption to learning processes, including a sensitisation to the presence of threat in the social environment and reduction in the ability to anticipate rewarding outcomes.
4. A rehearsal of threat-based survival strategies as key protective strategies.

In terms of dissociative processes, there are a number of implications of such defensive responses to threat. First, the inability to form affiliative relationships undermines the core human need to form bonds and experience a sense of belonging. Second, the lack of opportunity to form a reciprocal connection, combined with the lack of opportunity to develop emotional regulation creates a vulnerability to experience heightened emotional states in the context of ambivalent or anxious attachment relationships. Third, some people may have been 'coached' throughout their early lives to anticipate threat (rather than detect threat) and miss cues that signal positive outcomes, and therefore have a perceptual bias that creates a vulnerability to re-experiencing and re-enacting past traumatic experiences. And finally, psychological flight strategies (depersonalisation, derealisation) may represent an effective defence mechanism. When these states are experienced repeatedly as an individual navigates through further adverse life events the initially temporary nature of dissociation may lead to a more enduring manifestation and identity alteration could emerge.

Childhood adversity is a recurrent theme in the histories of people who cause harm to others. The immediate repercussions of adversity stimulate a range of protective strategies which, whilst effective in the moment, may become embedded over time and leave people vulnerable to latent misrepresentations of experiences in the moment. This learning, that allows people to detach from the fear and threat of early life adversity may subsequently create a disposition towards an ability to dissociate from the present and respond to the present with a perceptual filter from the past. The potential for these responses to stimulate dissociative states would therefore seem to be an important area for assessment within forensic contexts.

Furthermore, forensic populations often reflect broader social inequities. The overrepresentation of racially minoritised and marginalised groups in forensic settings may, in part, reflect gaps in how mainstream services recognise and respond to trauma-related dissociation in culturally sensitive ways (Lammy, 2017). Cultural stigma, mistrust of mental health services and diagnostic overshadowing may further reduce recognition of dissociation in these populations (Pierorazio et al., 2023).

With this in mind, we will briefly consider the prevalence of trauma responses in forensic settings before moving on to consider the potential influences of dissociation (as a trauma response) on risk of harm to others.

3. Trauma-related Responses, Dissociation and Altered States of Consciousness amongst Forensic Populations

The relationship between adversity and subsequent psychological distress is well established and the presence of two discrete trauma responses (PTSD and CPTSD) in contemporary diagnostic systems is perhaps testament to the significant impact of such life experiences. Both DSM V and ICD 11 definitions of PTSD clearly reference the presence of experiences that indicate dissociative phenomena; re-experiencing represents a shift in conscious awareness (and therefore a discontinuity in integration), while a heightened perception of threat represents a disturbance in sensitivity to environmental cues.

People who are detained in forensic services are typically viewed through a lens that highlights their harmfulness and the distress that their actions have caused to others, often with little regard to the distress that they may have experienced across their lifetime. However, with the growth of trauma-informed forensic practice (Willmot & Jones, 2022), there has been an increased willingness to consider the presence and functional significance of trauma responses.

3.1 Post-traumatic Stress Responses

Post-traumatic responses have been explored in offending populations with considerable evidence that PTSD is over-represented amongst people in custody. Baranyi et al. (2018) found the prevalence of PTSD was 6.2% and 21.1% for men and women in prison respectively, while Karatzias et al. (2018) found that over half (58%) of female prisoners met the criteria for DSM-5 PTSD.

PTSD has been identified as a precursor to offending (Wojciechowski, 2020), as an autogenic consequence of an offence (Soh et al., 2023) and as a consequence of incarceration. Facer-Irwin et al. (2022) found that prisoners who met current criteria for PTSD were more likely to engage in violent behaviour during the first three months of imprisonment, and that exposure to interpersonal trauma and violent behaviour in custody was mediated by total PTSD severity. Similarly, Silva et al. (2001) identified four factors associated with violence; flashbacks, sleep disturbance, mood lability and combat addiction.

Given the prevalence of PTSD and the relationship between PTSD and institutional violence, the potential role of dissociation becomes a significant area of concern in forensic services.

3.2 Autogenic Post-traumatic Responses

Traumatic reactions to one's own behaviours has also received attention (e.g., Soh et al., 2023), with studies indicating that a person's index offence is often described as a traumatic event (Kerig, 2019; Payne et al., 2008). Badenes-Ribera et al. (2021) found the prevalence of PTSD following a homicide to be 42.6%, and offending-related trauma symptoms have been found to remain long after the offence (Welfare & Hollin, 2015). Furthermore, the presence and the persistence of trauma symptoms may be mediated by the nature of the relationship with the victim, with people who have killed or harmed family members or friends experiencing more severe and persistent trauma responses (Ternes et al., 2020). Critically, PTSD, untreated, arising from offending behaviour may increase the risk of reoffending (Fleurkens et al., 2018).

With this in mind, the significance of PTSD and the individual experience of PTSD phenomena as mediating and/or contributory factors to risk becomes an important consideration.

3.3 Complex Post-traumatic Stress Responses

The prevalence of ACEs that are typically a prominent feature in the lives of people who offend would suggest that CPTSD may have a significant presence in offending populations.

In the only large-scale study to date, Facer-Irwin et al. (2022) found 7.7% of the male sentenced prisoners met diagnostic criteria for ICD-11 PTSD and 16.7% for CPTSD. A diagnosis of CPTSD was associated with complex trauma exposure antecedents (developmental, interpersonal, repeated, or multiple forms), and comorbid with anxiety, depression, substance misuse, psychosis, and ADHD.

Given the core diagnostic criteria for CPTSD, which includes the primary symptoms of PTSD alongside disturbances in self-organisation, it is likely that a proportion of people in custody or secure care will experience dissociative states.

3.4 Trauma-related Altered States of Consciousness within PTSD and Complex PTSD

As is outlined in Chapter 1, dissociation represents a disruption in the normal integration of different states of consciousness. This can manifest as post-traumatic and complex post-traumatic responses to stress. A recurring theme of these diagnoses concerns trauma-related altered states of consciousness (TRASC), dissociation being a particular example of such an altered state. Thompson and Zahavi (2007) have outlined four dimensions of TRASC; time, thought, body and emotion. Frewen and Lanius (2014) have elaborated on this further by exploring a spectrum of dissociation across these four dimensions.

On this basis, traumatic responses that may manifest as PTSD, CPTSD or altered states of consciousness, would seem to be prevalent within prison and wider forensic settings. Given the earlier review of trauma responses and the prevalence of adversity in the lives of people with convictions, it would seem reasonable to suggest that people in contact with the justice system are highly likely to present 'symptoms' associated with dissociation. The association(s) between dissociative phenomena and offending is therefore an important area for research and it is this research that we now turn towards.

4. Trauma, Dissociation and Offending

While it has been argued that people who have been convicted of serious offences may have ulterior motives for the denial of their actions, dissociative experiences remain a possible explanation for reports of amnesia, depersonalisation and derealisation before, during or after the offence. The possibility of dissociative experiences occurring at various stages of an offence pathway points towards the potential role of altered states of consciousness as a factor that may contribute to risk of offending, risk management, the salience of protective factors, and ultimately the successful reintegration of people into the community. In this section, we review the literature that explores the presence of dissociative states amongst people who commit a range of offences. Although dissociation is the focus of the review, it is again important to recognise that dissociative states only represent One component of a complex interaction of factors that lead to serious offending. The reader is directed to the work of Bethany Brand and colleagues (Brand, 2024; Brand, Schielke, & Brams, 2017;

Brand, Schielke, Brams, et al., 2017; Brand et al., 2016) for further discussion of the relationship between dissociation and offending behaviours.

4.1 Sexual Offending

In a review of dissociative experiences amongst adolescents with sexual convictions, Friedrich et al. (2001) found 14.3% were identified as meeting criteria for a Dissociative Disorder (DD) diagnosis compared with 4.2% of psychiatric in-patients. Cumulative trauma did not differ significantly between the two groups, but physical abuse was related to a DD diagnosis. Similarly, in a study of men convicted of sexual offences two thirds had histories of 'spontaneous self-hypnotic' experiences (dissociations); seven of these would have met the diagnostic criteria for a DD, while six demonstrated some evidence of a DD. The authors concluded that dissociative experiences, when interacting with other factors, contributed to the perpetration of the crimes in many of these cases (Bliss & Larson, 1985).

In a unique study into the prevalence of dissociation amongst men convicted of sexual offences, Becker-Blease and Freyd (2007) found a strong relationship between dissociation during victimisation and dissociation during perpetration. Similarly, people who reported dissociation when offending and in their everyday life were more likely to report amnesia for their offence. The authors propose a number of processes that may mediate the presence of dissociative experiences, including prior traumatisation, fantasy absorption, depersonalisation and derealisation and identity alteration or compartmentalisation.

Case Example: *Mark was chronically sexually abuse throughout his early school years by his stepfather. His dominant memory of the abuse was that he noticed his stepfather approaching him while he was washing himself in the bathroom sink.*

Mark has some vague memories of his stepfather's actions but reports having learned to focus on the water in the sink, the bubbles and the texture of soap on his skin. He feels that these sensory experiences enabled him to 'escape' from the actual events that took place, though simultaneously became linked to involuntary sexual arousal.

Whilst at a student party (which included public sexual acts and was fuelled with alcohol), Mark recalls being in the bathroom and washing his hands as another person entered the room. Mark believed that he had locked the door and experience the arrival of the other person as intrusive. He remembers experiencing sexual arousal and reports feeling that he had no control over his physiological reaction. He remembers feeling an intense and overwhelming urge to act on his arousal and forced the other person (a young man) to perform a sex act on him. While Mark remembers the act itself, he does not recall the person involved and describes his victim as his stepfather. Mark did not deny his offence.

Although not directly linked to sexual offending, Katehakis (2016) describes the way that individuals describe their mind being 'hijacked' by what he describes as 'dissociative fantasy states' when experiencing sexual arousal and considers that fantasy can actively shift the state of consciousness based on anticipatory craving. Whether this shift would constitute a dissociative process is not clear. However, the role of sexual fantasising (the repeated visualisation of sexual activity, as opposed to sexual fantasy (brief sexual thoughts) has been identified as a key consideration for risk of sexual offending (Bartels, 2021).

Leibowitz et al. (2011) explored relationships between dissociation, victimisation, and juvenile sexual offending. Self-reported data on dissociation and five types of abuse were collected with significant correlations between all types of child abuse and dissociation with the exception of emotional neglect. Dissociation, sexual victimisation and physical abuse showed significant effects in predicting sexual offending. It is important to note, however, that dissociation alone does not predict sexual offending, but rather may interact with a range of other factors (including paraphilias, sex drive and trait factors) to increase the probability that a sexual offence may occur.

Nevertheless, people with sexual convictions have reported significantly more frequent experiences of dissociation than people without convictions, though describe comparable levels of dissociation with people convicted of violent offences (Baker & Beech, 2004).

4.2 Intimate Partner Violence

While the links between dissociation of sexual offending maybe somewhat tentative, there is an established body of literature that cites an association between altered states of consciousness and intimate-partner violence (IPV). Dutton et al. (2006) noted that some men were able to recall events leading up to and following the violence but were unable to remember the actual incident itself despite acknowledging their responsibility. Furthermore, a number of men were unresponsive to environmental cues (including visible harm and distress) and persisted with violence until the point of exhaustion. Dutton and colleagues speculated that amnesia and a lack of responsiveness to environmental cues may represent a dissociative state (Dutton et al., 2006).

More systematic investigations continue to highlight the association between IPV and dissociation. Cuartas (2002) examined dissociative experiences amongst men attending an IPV intervention and found that 46% experienced some dissociative experiences during the commission of violence. Similarly, Simoneti et al. (2000) found that exposure to IPV as a child was significantly related to greater IPV dissociation. A unique component of this study was that it also controlled for impression management, thus reducing the potential that men were claiming amnesia due to shame. More recently, LaMotte and Murphy (2017) found that almost a quarter of participants in a large scale study of an IPV intervention reported one or more dissociative episodes during IPV, that the frequency of dissociative IPV correlated with exposure to traumatic events and that PTSD symptoms mediated the relationship between exposure to trauma and dissociative IPV. Conversely, Webermann et al. (2014), reporting on an analysis of associations between childhood maltreatment, IPV and dissociation, did not find dissociation to be a mediator between early adversity and IPV. They did, however, find that certain types of childhood abuse (physical and emotional abuse) were associated with physical and emotional IPV amongst individuals with a diagnosis of a dissociative presentation. Finally, in a systematic review of IPV and dissociation, Tschoeke et al. (2019) concluded (albeit somewhat tentatively) that pathological dissociation may contribute to enduring violence.

Overall, then, dissociative experiences seem to have a role in IPV, albeit mediated by exposure to ACEs and/or PTSD. However, as the Weberman study indicates dissociation does not simply predict IPV and a range of additional factors are likely to influence the link between the two.

4.2 Homicide and non IPV Violence

The relationship between dissociation and more general violence has been apparent in the literature for some time. Tanay (1969) proposed that a significant proportion (70%) of men were in a 'dissociative reaction' when they committed murder, suggesting that they experienced an altered state of consciousness in the moments before they killed. While Tanay's work was somewhat speculative, more recent systematic studies have been undertaken across the spectrum of dissociative presentations. In a study of women with a diagnosis of DID, Kluft (1987) found that 16% had acted violently (causing serious bodily harm) towards their children, while Dell and Eisenhower (1990) reported that a third of adolescents with DID had committed or threatened acts of aggression. In a study of adult men with DID more than 40% had convictions for murder, while a study of in-patient behaviour found a relationship between scores on the Dissociative Experiences Scale (Bernstein & Putnam, 1986) and physical aggression (Quimby & Putnam, 1991).

In a particularly comprehensive review of dissociative experiences and violence, Moskowitz (2004) proposes four types of (non-exclusive) dissociation-based homicide (see Table 13.1). As is apparent below, Moskowitz proposes contrasting ways in which dissociation may mediate serious acts of violence, though recognises that despite long-term depersonalisation, people who present with psychopathy would be unlikely to meet the diagnostic threshold for a DD.

Table 13.1 Four Types of Dissociation-Based Homicide

DID	Identity alteration, amnesia before, during and after offence.
Fantasy driven	Temporary identity alteration, depersonalisation and amnesia.
Over-controlled	Environmental trigger leads to a splitting off from rage.
Psychopathy	Chronic depersonalisation but no change at time of offence.

In summary, trauma-related dissociation would seem to have a potential role in various types of offending and in various ways. While this is not meant to suggest that the experience of dissociation represents a risk of harm per se, is does indicate the need for forensic practitioners to be mindful of the potential role of dissociation and plan assessments and interventions accordingly.

Research Question

How can we understand the different developmental trajectory for the sub-group of people who go on to cause harm to others? What is different from those who do not harm others?

With this in mind, and before we turn to practice recommendations explicitly, it is important to consider the concept of offence-related altered states of consciousness that has gained increased traction in forensic practice.

5. Offence-related Altered States of Consciousness

First described by Jones (2022), offence-related altered states of consciousness (ORASC) refer to the capacity of an individual to experience a shift in conscious awareness in response to threat-based contexts that are reminiscent of previous harm/trauma. These shifts stimulate evolved responses that can detach an individual from the function of an emotion or heighten an emotion stimulating an approach orientated threat response (fight). Similarly, other people can become less important (have reduced survival gains) and thus lose their significance as social contacts.

Although a much broader concept than dissociation, ORASC includes dissociative components which can be triggered by traumatic events. While it is beyond the scope of this chapter to do justice to the integration of theories that are captured within the concept of ORASC, three specific processes are highlighted by Jones (see Table 13.2).

Jones (2022) suggests that the influence of triggers is often non-specific but rather act as setting conditions that increase the possibility of offending. Further, unlike trait characteristics (e.g., recklessness, impulsivity), posttraumatic risk-seeking refers specifically to the emergence of these behaviours following exposure to trauma. Finally, Jones highlights that triggers might not be directly related to the eventual reaction(s), emphasising the need for careful functional analysis (see Chapter 6).

6. Practice Recommendations

The preceding discussion raises several practice points for forensic services linked to the experience of trauma and adversity and the human responses that can arise in

Table 13.2 Key Processes Stimulating ORASC

Trauma Triggers	Experiences that evoke a trauma-based memory	Urge to act in a way to avoid an aversive state
		Altered consciousness; increased capacity (e.g., impulsiveness) or reduced capacity (e.g., reflectiveness)
Post-traumatic risk seeking	The active pursuit of experiences that can cause harm to self or others.	Intentionally motivated actions with a functional link to trauma.
Trigger chaining	Response to an event triggers a memory of another similar response, in turn triggering another response which triggers an action.	For example, shame triggers memories of abuse-related shame which triggers memories of a response which generates feelings from that response.

response to such experiences. Based on the evidence summarised above, a number of recommendations for future practice can be offered.

6.1 Assessment

- Given the evidence linking early life adversity and dissociation, screening for ACEs would seem to be an imperative component of reception into secure settings
- Assessment should consider the repercussions of adversity including the learning from traumatic events, personal meanings that are ascribed (for example, 'I deserved it') and the specific strategies employed to manage the experience of harm (e.g., dissociation from the experience)
- Given the potential links between dissociative experiences and violence formal assessment of dissociation should be considered. While many acts of violence are instrumental in nature, acts of violence that are extreme, frenzied or out of character may indicate some degree of dissociation before, during or after the violent act
- The reader is directed to the work of Bethany Brand and colleagues (Brand, 2024; Brand, Schielke, & Brams, 2017; Brand, Schielke, Brams, et al., 2017; Brand et al., 2016) for further discussion of the relationship between dissociation and offending behaviours

6.2 Formulation

- Identification of criminogenic factors should identify the developmental contexts that trigger areas of risk, including (when appropriate) dissociative states and altered states of consciousness

- Where dissociation is assessed to have been present during early life trauma, the salience of contexts that may stimulate current dissociative states should be considered in the context of harmful behaviours
- The suggestion that traumatic experiences contribute to risk of harm without a hypothesis that links trauma to risk is both unethical and potential retraumatising; the link needs to be made explicit
- The significance of dissociative states and altered states of consciousness and risk of harm should be made explicit.

6.3 Risk Management

- Structured Professional Judgement tools (SPJs) need to include a consideration of the role of dissociative experiences as an idiosyncratic components of risk formulation
- SPJ scenarios need to incorporate identified risk factors into risk scenarios explicitly. Where dissociative experiences contribute to risk either directly or when operating in tandem with other risk factors this should also be made explicit in risk management scenarios.

6.4 Intervention

- Treatment protocols for individuals whose offence was driven by trauma-related dissociation are likely to require interventions that address the dissociative response and those stimuli likely to induce dissociative states
- Interventions that focus heavily on offence accounts need to consider the possibility of dissociative amnesia and acknowledge that an inability to provide details of an offence is caused by this process rather than by attempts to conceal
- For individuals who have experienced autogenic PTSD as a consequence of their own offence(s), care needs to be taken when reviewing offences
- Strengthening the self may be central to the development of a mental 'time traveller' (Lanius, 2015) and thus facilitate mindful awareness and the promotion of safe relationships
- Chronic exposure to early trauma can undermine access to executive functions, thereby challenging the utility of interventions based solely in the cognitive domain. Multi-modal and integrative psychotherapies that have an explicit trauma focus would therefore seem more appropriate intervention approaches
- Access to trauma- and dissociation-informed interventions should be culturally responsive. Services should account for mistrust stemming from historical and ongoing systemic harm experienced by racialised communities and should adapt interventions to reflect culturally meaningful healing practices when appropriate (see Chapter 15).

7. Conclusion

From the outset of this chapter it has been clear that dissociative states do not explain offending and do not stand alone as primary areas of criminogenic need. However, the prevalence of dissociation amongst forensic populations points towards the ways in which dissociative states may act as mediating factors, either to enhance the salience or presence of other areas of risk, or to inhibit the capacity to contain and manage risk factors.

Chapter 14

Working with Trauma-based Dissociation in Independent Practice

Andrew Rayner, Mike Lloyd, Remy Aquarone and Melanie Goodwin

1. Introduction

> '*This chapter highlights all the relevant and very important areas that will lead to successful outcomes. I think it is essential to be open and honest and engender a feeling of working in partnership, a sharing of overall responsibility while being aware for some parts this can feel like abandonment. Feelings of abandonment may be relevant to your relationship with the client but also the relationship between the funders and you. At times very difficult conversations become necessary. Maybe your circumstances have changed. It is so important to continue being open and honest, tough but real. So much for us as children was unreal that this is a gift you can give under all circumstances.*' **Sonia, Expert-by-Experience**

Psychological practitioners increasingly work in a range of settings outside the public sector. These include working for independent care providers (many who see NHS clients under specialist commissioning arrangements) in a variety of settings such as hospitals, rehabilitation or supported living services. Many practitioners have split working arrangements, working both independently and within the NHS, possibly offering different services in each role. Within the independent sector practitioners may also work across a variety of different contexts simultaneously; for example, having their own out-patient practice and being employed by an organisation in a hospital or rehabilitation setting. This means the issues faced by independent practitioners in relation to clients who dissociate, will vary, with much information in other chapters being relevant.

This chapter will therefore focus primarily on independent psychological practitioners working on a self-employed or limited company basis, effectively as lone workers. It builds on general guidance (Bor & Stokes, 2010) to explore some unique opportunities and challenges for working with complex dissociation in independent practice.

DOI: 10.4324/9781003625650-17

2. Meeting the Person who Dissociates in a Lone Worker Context: Opportunities and Challenges

Working in isolation as opposed to within an organisation, means no management structure and relatively little externally imposed bureaucracy. Adherence to the codes of conduct of relevant professional and regulatory bodies and the legal requirements of business remain essential; however, aside from this, there may be greater freedom to shape practice according to values and preferences. This can facilitate effective practice in working with complex trauma and dissociation in several ways. These same freedoms can however lead to significant challenges. Some of the key issues are outlined, in the following sections.

2.1 Developing a Robust and Stable Framework for Practice

In most mental health organisations, psychological practitioners work alongside other MDT members, are line-managed and have a ready-made peer network of other psychological practitioners. A general framework for practice is set and referenced in policy and guidance documents. These professional support structures can prove particularly helpful when working with more severe and complex presentations due to the need to consider safety planning and safeguarding issues. A diverse MDT can also support clinicians in reflecting on issues of diversity that could impact on the work. NHS or other organisational contexts provide robust learning opportunities, from which adaptations for independent practice can be considered.

2.2 Setting out Professional Boundaries in Guidance, Policies and Procedures

Independent practitioners may not have developed specific policies or guidance documents beyond the strictly necessary. However, developing these to share with clients can be helpful in clarifying parameters of the work, from the outset of engagement. With people who dissociate this is particularly recommended, as professional boundaries may be subject to greater pressure (Steele et al., 2017). As ISSTD (2011) highlights, *'clinicians need to be exceedingly prudent, cautious, and thoughtful about the issue of boundaries, including the need to clearly define roles, rules, expectations, rights, and other elements of the treatment frame and the therapeutic relationship' (p.164).* Some form of agreement or contract that sets out important aspects of the treatment boundaries may be very helpful. This may cover duration, location and frequency of sessions, therapist availability between sessions, acceptable methods of communicating and time frames for response, crisis resources, the policy on fee payment, missed appointments, and confidentiality (Brand et al., 2022).

Challenges to professional boundaries are potentially exacerbated when working outside the structures of an organisation. For instance, independent practitioners may be more likely to use **direct means of communication**, such as mobile phones and email, to arrange and cancel appointments. This needs careful consideration, as for some people this may activate dissociative parts in different ways. For example, parts that are seeking care may yearn for more support and time from the therapist via these means. Parts seeking control may wish to undermine the relationship and send abusive messages. Therapist responses to these messages could reinforce the behaviour or trigger a rupture in the therapeutic alliance.

There may also be benefits to messages between sessions, such as establishing engagement with dissociative parts who do not communicate in sessions or articulating something that may have felt impossible in the session and 'breaks the ice' for the person or part. Some people with amnesia find it helpful to capture their reflections soon after the session and send this to the therapist to hold for them. However, reading and responding to messages outside of sessions can pose difficulties, especially if these are lengthy and / or contain sensitive disclosures. Therefore, best practice may be to agree that anything non-urgent will be read at the beginning of the session (and therefore this time is already accounted for and paid for). Whether a practitioner can provide an urgent response and what form this can realistically take should also be clearly communicated (See Chapter 14, Online Resource: 'Guidance on email use').

Some people who dissociate may also have **difficulty ending and leaving sessions on time** and this can be stressful to negotiate, especially when working alone in offices without the back-up of other clinical staff available. These kinds of boundaries may need bluntly reinforcing. Messages can easily be miscommunicated and misinterpreted, and intense conflicts within the person's attachment system – intense approach / proximity seeking versus intense avoid / defend (Liotti, 2017; Steele, 2018) – may mean ruptures are challenging to work through.

This can therefore be a field which can attract a high number of complaints and **having clear contracts, complaints procedures, suitable professional indemnity and professional supports** are important elements of the practice framework.

2.3 Developing Support Networks

Joining peer networks and special interest groups (See Chapter 14, Online Resources (www.routledge.com/9781041038450)) can be helpful in addressing the need for connection with other professionals. Another option is to work with associates, affiliates or become an associate of another established practice.

2.4 Advertising

How services are advertised to the person who dissociates needs careful thought. The term **'Specialist'** denotes several years of experience with a number and range of clients with dissociative diagnoses / presentations, and specialist training and supervision.

'**A special interest in**' would be a more suitable term for someone earlier on in their development of competencies and experience in this area. This denotes a commitment to working with people who dissociate, and to developing a specialist level of competency.

2.5 Choice of Therapy Space/Consulting Room

Independent psychological practitioners may have greater control and choice over their physical working environment than within many public sector organisations, where clinical space may be shared. Generally, within psychological practice, great value is placed on having '**stable and personal consulting rooms that permit them to adapt to the needs of the clients, be attentive, and avoid disturbances**' (Punzi & Singer, 2018, p.1).

When working with a person who dissociates, key issues are **stability and having control over the room and booking arrangements**. Access to the same space over time (and this may be a long period) facilitates predictability and security. There is also value in being able to leave personal items in the room, like drawings, toys or colouring implements, so that in each session the client can access them. Access to familiar grounding objects (Lucre & Clapton, 2021) and having consistency in the layout and objects within a room can all be helpful, especially for people experiencing derealisation, and those with comorbid complexity, such as being on the autistic spectrum. For someone with complex trauma who dissociates, changes in meeting rooms and unpredictable exposure to new objects may take on even greater importance, due to the potential for trauma triggers.

Independent practitioners are likely to have to consider health and safety concerns around **lone working in non-clinical environments**, important regardless of the nature of their work (Health and Safety Executive, 2020).

Online working is possible and acceptable for some clients who dissociate; however, this is a general matter to consider rather than being particularly relevant to independent practice.

2.6 Length and Course of Treatment

Psychological practitioners in the public sector often have resource limitations placed on their services, as organisations manage high demand and limited budgets. Clients with complex trauma and dissociation may therefore be offered less time in therapy than can be offered in the independent sector. The relative freedom for longer treatment frames, as well as the flexibility to increase or decrease the frequency of sessions to respond to client needs can be beneficial for working with complex dissociation, where longer-term therapy is recommended (Corrigan & Hull, 2015; International Society for the Study of Trauma and Dissociation, 2011). In the absence of significant financial limitations for the client, the practitioner has the advantage of being able to commit (as far as possible) to see treatment through to the end, working at the client's pace.

Reviewing literature on the impact of time limits on therapy suggests this is a complex and under-researched issue. However, some evidence suggests a time limit exerts pressure on the therapy process, creating an expectancy effect, with both positive and negative consequences. These include acceleration in symptom improvement (although how well this is maintained is questioned) and the therapist becoming more directive at the expense of client empowerment (De Geest & Meganck, 2019).

For people who dissociate, having a sufficiently long-term commitment may provide more opportunity to build the therapeutic relationship and create safeness (especially for dissociative parts who may take longer to trust). Also to build the capacity to address aspects of their traumatic experiences and attachment dilemmas that they may particularly fear or feel ashamed of. Too short a timeframe may pressure clients to tackle issues before they are ready and risk destabilising their mental health, or alternatively, may make it more likely they avoid complex issues completely (perhaps wisely).

More open-ended arrangements, on the other hand, could also facilitate avoidance as tackling feared issues can be put off indefinitely. Deciding how much therapy is sufficient is a complex matter and the ending itself may be feared and avoided. The freedom of independent practitioners may allow more looseness around setting and working through the end of therapy and could facilitate greater avoidance. A further consideration with dissociation is where people have some parts who feel more dependent on the therapist. If not managed well, this risks unhelpful dependency (Steele, 2018).

In sum, the flexibility regarding treatment length places more personal responsibility on both clinician and client to consider these decisions. Good practice may be to build in regular reviews and consider an ending frame from the outset. If this is to be extended, the rationale for this and the pros and cons of doing so should be considered carefully with the client, and in supervision. This collaborative stance is likely to be beneficial in itself, although the therapist may need to take ultimate responsibility for the decision, having sensitively and openly discussed the client's viewpoint.

3. Funding Issues

People seeking treatment for complex dissociation in the independent sector may be funding this from their own resources, or via a funding package from their local health services budget.

3.1 Self-funding

For self-funding clients, the number of sessions depends on their financial resources, and this can lead some people into difficulties. People with dissociative difficulties may have experienced a long journey and many obstacles in order to receive an accurate diagnosis or formulation, and specialist treatment. This arises when public sector services have significant gaps in provision or where appropriate provision exists, but waiting times are significant. Therefore, independent practitioners may meet people desperate for treatment without necessarily having the means to pay. Funding can therefore be an ethical consideration for starting or continuing therapy, especially given the often long-term nature of the work. Psychological practitioners should enquire about the ability to pay from the outset, check on this over the course of the therapy and tune into any changes of circumstances or other signs the client may be struggling. This is a complex issue, however, and financial feasibility may be difficult to judge. In an understandable attempt to reduce their considerable suffering, clients may go to extreme lengths to pay for their therapy, including amassing large debt. The client may justifiably argue that on balance the stress of incurring debt is secondary to the suffering caused by the trauma and dissociation. Of course, this decision is their right to make. Open discussion about the pros and cons of this will be helpful.

3.2 Public Sector Funding

'If you are receiving NHS funding, be absolutely clear on all aspects of the contract. I know of so many people who had very harmful experiences. Some funders asked for a review every few weeks. For these clients so little progress was made as they spent much time working towards the assessments and the fallout afterwards, often with therapy then seen as failing. This is so frustrating for both you and your client as every moment of good therapy feels so precious.' **Sonia, Expert-by-Experience**

In some cases, a practitioner might be treating someone with funding commissioned through their local NHS Integrated Care Board (ICB). Treating clients under this kind of arrangement will involve setting up a contract which should specify the minimum number of sessions envisaged, the frequency of sessions (weekly or twice weekly), a reasonable number of sessions to be completed within a calendar year, how progress will be reported on and when.

It is recommended in this context, to set a specified treatment length, probably between 2–4 years depending on the severity and prognostic indicators and sticking to that ending where possible. Renegotiating further funding can be complicated and not always beneficial (see Case Example 2). Furthermore, the catastrophic unmet needs and trauma from early childhood, in contrast to what is often the first caring secure attachment experienced in therapy, may contribute (at least at an unconscious level) to destabilisation and crises as the ending approaches. Responding to this by extending the treatment time could be unhelpful and just move the problem further on. Working through the ending as agreed can be the first experience for the person of a secure finishing without something going wrong.

Case Example 1: A client self-referred to an independent psychologist, believing they experienced dissociation after gaining information and resources online. Initial screening, including questionnaires, indicated treatment might be suitable. Assessment and treatment costs were discussed with the person who felt unable to afford such a commitment over time. With the person's consent, the provider contacted the GP to discuss whether all local mental health (NHS) resources had been attempted. The person had been discharged from local mental health services as there were no specialist therapies available to manage their level of dissociation. With this information, the GP applied for funding from the local ICB, based on information from the provider about costs, processes and outcome measures, the local ICB reviewed the application, agreeing that the lack of local services meant an initial assessment should be funded. This assessment resulted in recommendations for a 'treatment package', agreed between the provider, GP and person involved. The ICB approved funding for the package, with an annual review including outcome measures and key performance indicators. **Dr Mike Lloyd, Consultant Clinical Psychologist**

Where MDTs are involved, the funding process may reflect the medical model, requiring approval from a Consultant Psychiatrist. This is complicated when different views are presented in relation to diagnosis and subsequent treatment plan (see Case Example 2).

Case Example 2: A client in a rehabilitation placement was diagnosed with DID and funded for psychological treatment. Treatment was successful in improving her functioning such that she moved out of this service. Some follow up sessions were funded on an independent basis.

This worked until the client needed a further period of therapy. She had moved into another area, and therefore a different care team. The same ICB requested the application for further treatment to be approved by the new psychiatrist, who did not know the client. Previous reports were shared showing detailed assessment and evidence of significant improvements during therapy, prior to which there were years without change. Despite this, the psychiatrist took a different view, gave the client a diagnosis of emotionally unstable personality disorder, and did not approve the funding request. The client requested a second opinion which had a similar outcome. Her treatment for DID was interrupted, a battle she continues to fight. **Dr. Andrew Rayner, Consultant Clinical Psychologist**

4. Developing Skills, Competencies and Experience to Treat Dissociation in Independent Practice

Personal and therapeutic competencies needed in work with dissociative diffi-culties (such as the ability to notice and respond effectively to transference and countertransference experiences and to be able to tolerate and skilfully explore ruptures in the therapeutic alliance in a non-defensive manner and to repair them) are outlined in Chapter 17 (Training). However, some which bear particularly on the independent practice setting are considered further here.

4.1 Ability to Do Long-term Work

Psychological therapy for more severe dissociation is ideally carried out over a minimum of two years and may, in many instances require over double this time. Independent practitioners are more likely to be able to offer this kind of in-depth work. Developing and maintaining therapeutic relationships and deliver-ing interventions over several years comes with unique challenges. It can be an important area of self-discovery, as longer-term therapeutic work may reveal one's own unconscious attachment issues. Due to the short-term nature of pre-training employment and training placements, psychological practitioners are unlikely to experience longer-term work until post qualification. Working with dissociation may not be the ideal context to discover these insights!

4.2 Complex Case Management Issues

Complex trauma and dissociation work throws up challenging dilemmas and responsibilities relating to safeguarding issues and risk (see Chapter 6, Safety). Containing and managing these different aspects of the work in lone practice can be challenging. Learning these skills is perhaps ideally undertaken within the NHS, or another organisational context where there is support, advice, and an umbrella of teams, structures and processes to enable careful management of these issues. In the absence of this opportunity, it would be recommended to have such casework closely supervised by someone highly experienced in this type of work, who could be responsive as and when these situations arise.

4.3 Post-qualification Experience

Given the need to develop competencies to work with people who dissociate, newly qualified practitioners would not be advised to actively seek work with people with complex dissociation in an independent practice setting. This advice should not dampen anyone's enthusiasm for working in this area, because as pointed out elsewhere, there is huge unmet need. The attraction to undertaking this work is understandable as the potential rewards are considerable. For instance, there are likely to be deep relational dynamics and real potential for transformational change, and this can lead to some of the most meaningful and joyful experiences that one can have as a therapist.

Clients with severe dissociative difficulties also become therapists, strongly motivated to help people like themselves. This of course could be a wonderful way to find purpose and meaning, to draw on the hard-earned wisdom of one's own recovery and to share it with others. In some respects, this might represent an act of triumph over the considerable suffering experienced. However, good intentions can have the potential to create unintended negative consequences. Whatever the motivations, the concern is that practitioners may be pulled into advanced practice before their skills and experience are robustly established. In doing so they may cause harm to the client and themselves. Compassionate behaviour needs to be guided by wisdom so that it is competent, safe and helpful, rather than harmful (Gilbert, 2022). Therefore, in the best interest of both parties, practitioners should consider carefully, when competencies, setting and general therapeutic experience combine to safely undertake work with people with complex trauma-based dissociation. Two to three years post-qualification is a likely minimum, however the issue is less about 'time served' and more about developing the competencies required.

4.4 Conscious Incompetence: To Treat or Not to Treat?

Finding oneself unintentionally working with severe dissociation may be a common experience. This may arise from the lack of training on dissociation across core mental health professional training. However, it may also arise because many aspects of dissociative experience are hidden, even from the person themselves, and the true nature of the person's difficulties may emerge only gradually during therapy. Whilst good screening and assessment processes exist (see Chapter 2), these take experience and skill to interpret well and even then, are not guaranteed to identify significant dissociation. Thus, it is possible, even for highly experienced practitioners, to suddenly become aware of being outside one's competence. when identifying complex dissociation for the first time.

If discovered at an early stage of therapy, it may be relatively straightforward to decline the work and refer on. However, if the discovery comes after a working relationship has developed, this can pose significant ethical dilemmas that should be shared with the client and considered carefully. On one side of the dilemma, a useful, safe, collaborative therapeutic relationship may already have developed within which the client has chosen to disclose aspects of their experience for the first time. This may already be of significant therapeutic value, achieved with real effort, time and courage and therefore not to be dismissed lightly. On the other hand, without the specialist theoretical knowledge, treatment skills and frameworks, a psychological practitioner can cause iatrogenic harm to a client with complex dissociation. This may lead to therapeutic impasse with wasted time, money and effort, and prolongation of suffering. It may lead to destabilisation, including increased risks and deterioration in everyday functioning. For clients with a significant history of risk to themselves or others, particularly when linked to the actions of a dissociative part (for which standard safety planning approaches are less likely to be effective, see Chapter 6, Safety), this must be a major consideration in the decision.

A compromise position may be to offer short-term stabilisation and psychoeducation work (see Chapter 4, Psychological Therapy), with a view to referring on to someone with the necessary competencies to continue the work. This may be a particular challenge for the independent practitioner who may not have established relationships with other practitioners and might find it more difficult to advise the client on suitable options.

A minimum requirement is always to access specialist supervision to support the work. Accessing appropriate training and reading materials will also be essential. For the independent practitioner, the time and financial costs of this will need to be considered. Figure 14.1 summarises this advice.

- Articulate and share the dilemma with your client to think and work it through together, rather than taking the decision yourself. This collaborative stance is likely to be experienced as an empowering and authentic exchange
- Be honest about your limitations and fears, and about what the literature says
- Explore as fully as possible all treatment options and their implications
- Discuss your dilemmas in supervision
- Consider what continuing with treatment would really mean, including formulating and executing a plan to address the need to be competent enough; accounting for the financial and time costs of this, and whether you can fully commit to these actions at this point in your practice
- Consider the merits of offering short-term educational and stabilisation work and referring on
- Consider carefully with the client the possible consequences of ending the work and referring on and what would contribute to a smooth and contained transition.

Figure 14.1 'To Treat or Not to Treat?'

5. Liaising and Joint Working with the Public Sector

Given the complexity and severity of some dissociative difficulties, it is reasonably common for clients to have independent psychological practitioner as a therapist but also receive NHS mental health services. At a minimum, the person will have a GP, and considering sharing information with them may be invaluable. Seeking the client's consent to liaise with the network of care with which they are involved is strongly recommended. If the client does not consent, this requires thorough discussion and may give rise to concerns and consideration for whether the work can be undertaken safely at that time. Good communication between all parties is needed. However, in practice this may be difficult, partly due to differences in the culture of independent and statutory services.

> *'In many situations a therapist needs to have a good understanding of their local mental health team. This can play such a vital role in times of crisis. It might be one psychologist has an 'interest' in DID so make sure you work with them and not allow your client to be further traumatised through ignorance within the service in a time of crisis.'* **Sonia, Expert-by-Experience**

5.1 Service Culture Differences

Aquarone and Hughes (2006) helpfully summarised the history of these two cultures in relation to work with dissociation in the UK, describing a segregated situation with suspicion, resentment and hostility on both sides. The independent sector was viewed by the NHS as an indulgence for wealthy clients and lacking in credibility and accountability, whereas the independent sector was critical of the over-medicalised and politicised NHS with an emphasis on public protection, where inappropriate interventions could have harmful and retraumatising consequences, often failing to consider trauma and dissociation as relevant to the diagnosis. The independent sector then, were doing most of the therapeutic work in this area and had developed a perspective on their clients that was based on their clinical experience, wisdom and knowledge of the literature. The NHS of course would be called upon for some of these same clients in times of crisis to offer an urgent response to significant risk and bore the huge responsibility and pressure of public protection.

Although the public sector has moved gradually towards offering more trauma-informed care, and the number of psychological practitioners having experience of both practice settings has grown, elements of these distinct cultures may still persist, and be obstacles to effective communication and collaboration.

5.2 Good Collaborative Practice

Aquarone and Hughes (2006) offered suggestions for good practice between all parties which they termed the 'Positive Family Model'. In essence, this involved being mindful of different transference and counter-transference reactions, the strong pull for 'splitting' and resisting this by maintaining an open and collaborative approach. Their suggestions are expanded here:

- Understand the language of the client and the NHS. Using the framework of psychiatric diagnosis may facilitate understanding. The use of SCID-D assessments (Steinberg, 2023), clearly setting out how a client meets criteria for a dissociative disorder diagnosis, may be necessary before psychological formulations are considered
- Decisions should ideally be taken at care network meetings with the client present.
- Problems with the care provision should be 'owned by the whole group' and resolved together through collaborative exploration and negotiation, working to empower the client wherever possible
- Formulate and share how and why the client's behaviour might change during an emergency admission or crisis team involvement. For example, this might trigger compliance by some parts of their dissociative system but fighting for control by other parts
- During inpatient admissions, consider remaining involved rather than withdrawing. Therapy may be on hold but retaining a continuity of connection with the client and the care team may be beneficial. Continuing therapy may help to formulate what has triggered the crisis and the person can negotiate with the internal system and diffuse any unsafe urges. As above, this decision should be taken together after discussion with all parties
- Plans for future admissions can be made proactively by learning from the crisis experience, for example avoiding unnecessary changes to diagnosis or medication, and understanding the role different dissociative parts have played in the crisis.

In independent practice this need for collaboration raises issues of potentially considerable time the practitioner must spend outside of the contracted therapy sessions. The question of if, when and how this is charged for should be discussed and considered carefully as part of treatment planning, whether the person is self-funding, or has a funded package.

6. Summary

This chapter focuses on the dilemmas and pragmatic considerations for psychological practitioners in independent practice who work in relative isolation and are providing treatment for people with complex dissociation. Their relative freedom to operate gives rise to some important opportunities, but also to some challenges.

- Independent practitioners should develop a stable and robust framework for their practice. This could include developing professional support networks, setting out professional boundaries in Guidance, Policies and Procedures (e.g., around the use of text messaging and emails), advertising appropriately, choosing consulting rooms which offer consistency and control, and having careful consideration and collaboration around the length and course of treatment
- Where clients are self-funding, open discussion around feasibility (especially where treatment may be long term) is needed at the start and over the course of the therapy. There may be ethical dilemmas to explore
- Public sector funding arrangements may be possible and require a contract to specify a realistic treatment length (minimising the need to reapply), the frequency of sessions, a reasonable number of sessions to be completed within a calendar year, methods for evaluating progress and a reasonable schedule for progress reports
- Practitioners will ideally have already developed the necessary skills and competencies to treat complex trauma and dissociation in independent practice. These include the ability to carry out long-term work, to tolerate the distress entailed in the work (both client and therapist), to handle complex case management issues and to work with multiple and shifting transference and counter-transference dilemmas
- Practitioners may however find themselves working with people with complex trauma and dissociation without intending to. This situation raises important dilemmas around the wisdom and ethics of continuing. This situation requires open, honest, direct and collaborative discussions with clients about the likely pros and cons, especially where there are significant risk issues. A compromise position may be to offer short-term stabilisation and psycho-education work before referring on to someone with the necessary expertise
- Finally, the complex task of liaising with wider care teams in the public sector is discussed with consideration of the different working cultures and how they might conflict. It is always important to develop good collaborative practices.

Figure 14.2   Summary of Recommendations

Developing a stable and robust practice frame, acquiring dissociation-specific competencies, having ongoing support, addressing funding dilemmas, and negotiating links with the person's public sector care networks have all been considered. Figure 14.2 provides a summary of the offered guidance.

Dissociation-Informed Practice

Consolidating Change

Cross-Cultural Considerations and Culturally Informed Practice with Trauma-Related Dissociation

Kiki Hassen

1. Introduction

Trauma-related dissociation manifests in diverse ways across cultures. While historically conceptualised through Western psychiatric frameworks, research increasingly demonstrates that dissociation is a universal response to developmental trauma and stress, expressed through varying cultural idioms, spiritual beliefs, societal narratives and symbolic languages (Krüger, 2020; Şar, 2022). Clinicians working in increasingly multicultural contexts need to understand dissociation through a culturally informed lens for ethical and effective care. This chapter offers a brief overview on cross-cultural manifestations of trauma-related dissociation and adaptations for intervention.

2. Cultural Contexts to Mental Health

Cultural contexts, including collective historical traumas, political conflict, colonial oppression, systemic racism, migration and acculturation stress, all significantly shape how trauma is expressed and experienced. These legacies of intergenerational trauma can affect attachment relationships and familial mental health in subsequent generations, contributing to the development of dissociative coping (Krüger, 2020). Furthermore, systemic oppression, ongoing discrimination and persistent experiences of racism and structural inequity create psychological stress which accumulates over time (Pierorazio et al., 2023).

> **Case Example: Amina**, a 28-year-old British-Pakistani woman, presented with frequent daydreaming, identity confusion, and memory gaps; feeling like she became 'someone else' at work by acting more confident and Westernised. At home she reverted to a quieter, more compliant version of herself. Amina's parents migrated during political conflict, and her upbringing was characterised by themes of obedience, sacrifice, and family honour. She feared discussing her mental health would bring shame to her household. Amina's internal fragmentation mirrored the tension between conflicting

DOI: 10.4324/9781003625650-19

cultural expectations, individual and social identity. Structural dissociation may have emerged as an adaptive means to manage these tensions.

Racial trauma contributes to internalised racism, which, while under-researched in relation to dissociation, has been linked to disrupted self-identity, self-perception and increased psychological distress (Willis et al., 2021). Migration and acculturation (adapting to a dominant culture) are additional culture-related risk factors. Migration and adjustment to a new culture constitutes a form of collective and identity-related trauma (Aydin & Kolburan, 2024). Migrants face internal conflict when self-perception clashes with perception of them by the dominant culture, necessitating identity fragmentation (Krüger, 2020). Therefore, the nature of lived experience as a first- or second-generation migrant may reinforce the use of dissociation as an adaptive coping strategy.

3. Definitions of Dissociation across Cultures

Dissociative-like phenomena are observed across cultures, reflecting diverse definitions, expressions and experiences of dissociation (Şar, 2022). Presentations include medically unexplained somatic symptoms (e.g., seizures, chronic pain, fainting) or culturally normative and non-pathologised experiences such as spirit possession, trance states, or ancestral communication (Lewis-Fernández et al., 2007). While dissociative experiences universally involve disconnection, detachment and lack of agency, cultural frameworks shape how this is understood – viewed as pathological in Western contexts, but as spiritual or meaningful in many non-Western cultures (Seligman & Kirmayer, 2008). Therefore, pathologising dissociation, without understanding its sociocultural meaning, can be harmful, invalidating and misleading.

Case Example: Linh, a 40-year-old Vietnamese woman, reported recurring chest pain, 'empty head', and exhaustion, with no medical cause identified. In therapy, she described a family history marked by war, displacement and loss. Linh believed she was carrying ancestral pain and that her spirit had become imbalanced. Her distress was expressed through somatic language rooted in cultural beliefs about energy and harmony. Exploring these somatic symptoms through both ancestral lenses helped Linh feel validated. Psychoeducation was adapted using metaphors of ancestral burden and energetic balance, rather than terms like 'dissociation' or 'conversion'.

Dissociative experiences cannot be universally understood without examining how different cultures define selfhood (Krüger, 2020; Seligman & Kirmayer, 2008; Şar 2022). Western, individualistic contexts assume a unitary, coherent, and autonomous self, which pathologises dissociative shifts in identity, amnesia, or altered consciousness. In non-Western collectivist societies, the self is often viewed as relational, multiple, and context-dependent, thus experiences such as spirit possession or trance states may be understood as meaningful, valued expressions of the self. The novel, Freshwater by Akwaeke Emezi (2018) offers an artistic portrayal of these concepts through Ada, a Nigerian woman, whose identity is shaped by ogbanje spirit beings from Igbo cosmology. In such cultural contexts, identity can be temporarily displaced by spirits in spiritually sanctioned ways, as the self is collective, allowing multiple influences (human or supernatural) to coexist without violating cultural norms.

4. Culturally Specific Experiences and Expressions of Suffering

In many cultures, psychological trauma and distress is not openly discussed due to stigma or differing beliefs. Instead, distress is voiced, experienced and understood through cultural scripts, somatic or spiritual language involving dissociative features (this chapter's Online Resources (www.routledge.com/9781041038450) provide specific examples). In collectivist cultures which prioritise social harmony, open displays of individual suffering may be discouraged and channelled through such idioms. Western psychiatry may define trauma through life-threatening events or prolonged exposure to stress, whereas some cultures broaden this to include experiences such as spiritual violation (e.g., a curse), family shame, sin, or spiritual trials (Hinton & Lewis-Fernández, 2011). Trauma is also subjective and relative, so individuals and societies exhibit varied thresholds for types of traumas, the severity of trauma and its subsequent impact (Gilmoor et al., 2019).

5. The Function of Dissociation across Cultures

DSM-5 (APA, 2013) diagnostic categories now include 'possession-form identities' and 'dissociative trance', recognising that what may be viewed as pathological in one culture can be normative in another, cautioning against diagnosis when such experiences align with cultural or religious practices. However, the Western pathologisation of dissociation has often failed to recognise its cultural significance. *Sinbyeong*, a spiritual sign of being called to become a shaman in Korean culture, is characterised by dissociative phenomena and resolved through ritual initiation rather than psychiatric intervention (this chapter's Online Resources (www.routledge.com/9781041038450) provide further examples). Socially sanctioned dissociative states enable people to reenact or symbolically resolve trauma in culturally resonant ways, reclaiming identity through collective healing (Hegeman, 2013). Dissociation may function as a culturally mediated coping strategy, serving a protective or regulatory role (Douglas, 2009). For instance, in collectivist cultures which emphasise emotional restraint and compliance, dissociative phenomena serve an adaptive purpose, detaching someone from emotional distress to promote outward conformity (Lewis-Fernández et al., 2007).

6. Intersectionality

Case Example: Rafael, a non-binary person raised in a conservative Christian Latina family, presented with dissociative fragmentation. Different parts held conflicting roles – one deeply rooted in faith, another rebellious and angry, and a third compliant with their family's views that they must remain presenting as their gender assigned at birth to avoid bringing shame to their family. Rafael's dissociation developed as a survival strategy in a household where queerness was silenced and punished. From an intersectional lens, therapy focused on building compassion and internal cooperation between parts. Unfortunately for Rafael, this involved leaving their family community. The therapist supported Rafael to grieve the loss of their family community and develop an internal and external community where both their faith and queerness could be celebrated.

A person's cultural heritage and background cannot be understood without exploring their particular intersectional factors (Crenshaw, 2013). Two people from the 'same' broad cultural background can have very different dissociative profiles and needs. Intersectionality refers to overlapping social identities (e.g., race, disability, age, ethnicity, gender, class, sexuality and immigration status) which intersect to shape unique experiences of oppression and privilege. Thus, UK ethnic minority populations experience their cultural heritage differently to similar populations in their country of origin. Women have different experiences of cultural values and norms compared to men, compounded further for gender diverse, transgender and non-binary individuals. Minoritised people from low-income socioeconomic backgrounds experience more community violence than those from affluent areas (Carter, 2007). Contrastingly, intersectional identities also provide resources and strengths, potentially reducing dissociation, such as protective religious beliefs or possessing an age or gender that provides cultural sanction and protection (Pierorazio et al., 2023). Applying an intersectional lens to understanding dissociation involves paying close attention to how traumatic stress operates within systems of power and understanding the role of dissociation in survival.

7. Adapting Psychological Assessment and Formulation

Ethnic minority client groups are often under-represented in UK mental health services. The dominance of Western psychiatric models may deter engagement by not aligning with culturally diverse forms of healing such as ritualistic or religious practices. In culturally sensitive practice, denial or defence should not be assumed when the person does not readily acknowledge trauma or dissociation. Clinicians should explore whether experiences are interpreted through spiritual or cultural frameworks, revealing what might otherwise remain undetected (Lewis-Fernández et al., 2010), avoiding misdiagnosis and better distinguishing between the pathological and non-pathological.

An overrepresentation of white professionals may also deter some minority clients from therapeutic engagement, concerned their needs will not be understood (Meyer & Zane, 2013). Practitioners should assess their own cultural biases and acknowledge how their services may represent governmental authority or symbolise structural oppression. Minoritised clients may harbour mistrust due to legacies of systemic racism. Asylum seeker and refugee populations may fear personal information being shared with immigration authorities. Clients may fear how accessing mental health care could affect their family's wellbeing or reputation, particularly if abuse disclosures lead to shame, criticism, or isolation (Sawrikar, 2017).

Clinicians working with culturally diverse clients must consider the sacrifices made regarding familial harmony, and barriers and fears overcome to access psychological support.

Case Example: Maz's Story. *'As part of my religion and culture, I was taught that we can never go against the teachings of God and that I needed to respect my elders, be obedient and comply, do not question authority and tolerate all that was expected of me as a South Asian woman. My role in my family was to serve my parents and grandparents. The expectation to be obedient was greater for women, therefore I was taught that I was not entitled to as much freedom as men. I had stricter rules to follow and was not able to do anything that would impact the reputation of my family. The most difficult part of suppressing myself was in relation to my gender and sexuality, as I did not have a space I could explore this. In my culture, being gay was not acceptable and I was told that I must marry a man for the reputation of my family. Being gay was also deemed a sin religiously, so I had to hide it from others as well as myself. In therapy, I have learnt that my mind's use of dissociation enabled me to comply to these demands and maintain my role within my family despite my anger, pain, grief and frustration. This led me to become so used to suppressing my emotions that I lost the ability to be aware of when I was not feeling okay. Since starting therapy, I have been on a journey to rediscover my identity, to choose what kind of life I want to lead and what kind of person I want to be. This has caused tension in my relationship with my parents. When they found out my therapist was a White female, they assumed that me not following rules and not obeying was her fault. They told me that as she is not from the same cultural background as us, she will not understand our obligations, duties, ways of life and expectations. As it was unacceptable to behave any differently, they encouraged me to stop therapy as they felt I was being negatively influenced.'* **Maz, Expert-by-Experience**

> **Online Resource provides further detailed guidance on adapting assessment, formulation and interventions across cross-cultural contexts.**

8. Adapting Psychological Interventions

Clinicians should integrate the client's spiritual, symbolic or cultural frameworks into the therapeutic process to validate the client's experiences and enhance engagement. Some clinicians may worry that validating cultural frameworks could reinforce dissociative coping. However, these frameworks often mirror the therapeutic goals of trauma work: understanding inner experiences, gaining agency over dissociative processes, fostering internal collaboration, and building compassionate internal relationships (Emezi, 2018). Even when cultural narratives are experienced as distressing (e.g., demonic possession), the client's meaning making should not be dismissed or invalidated. These understandings often carry deep cultural, spiritual, or familial significance. Instead, clinicians can gently explore alternative frameworks, while affirming that all explanations can hold meaning. The goal is not to replace the client's beliefs, but to expand the ways in which they can make sense of their experiences with compassion and choice.

9. Research Questions or Areas for Further Exploration

This section suggests possible research questions for further exploration of cultural and intersectional diversity factors in relation to dissociation:

- Qualitative research looking into how culturally diverse clients in the UK make meaning of their dissociative experiences
- In what ways do culturally informed healing practices interact with or complement psychological interventions for trauma-related dissociation?
- How can existing screening tools for dissociation (e.g., DES-II, SDQ-20, SCID-D) be culturally adapted and validated in non-Western populations?
- What is the impact of intersectional oppression on the development of dissociative coping?
- How do cultural factors and experiences influence the functioning and development of parts/alters in complex dissociation?
- To what extent do cultural idioms of distress or culturally specific ways of understanding distress overlap with diagnostic categories for dissociative disorders?
- How do culturally specific understandings of selfhood shape the experience and expression of multiplicity and dissociative parts/alters?

10. Conclusion

In summary, this chapter has offered an initial foundation to deepen understanding of dissociation as a culturally embedded response. Trauma-related dissociation is shaped by cultural, spiritual, and intersectional contexts, which calls for thoughtful and respectful clinical engagement. Clinicians should remain curious and attentive to diverse experiences of dissociation to deliver inclusive therapeutic care. As this chapter offers only a brief overview, readers are encouraged to review the accompanying online resource, which provides additional culturally specific examples and offers detailed practical guidance on adapting assessment, formulation and intervention practices to respect and integrate clients' cultural narratives.

Chapter 16

Considerations for Service Leads, Commissioners and Organisations

Paul Langthorne and Helena Crockford

1. Introduction

> *'My experiences of trauma growing up included being told that what was happening wasn't happening, that I was wrong, making things up, that the problem was me. I learnt that to survive and be accepted I had to pretend certain things weren't happening and most of all I must not talk about it. Sadly, my experience of accessing mental health services has been similar.'*
> **Jill, Expert-by-Experience**

Trauma-informed care is a key driver for service transformation within healthcare (NHS England, 2019; SAHMSA, 2014); however, organisations have typically failed to incorporate dissociation into trauma-informed care (Salter, 2023).

This is particularly problematic given the widespread prevalence of trauma-related complex dissociative difficulties. The prevalence of Dissociative Identity Disorder (DID) in the general population for example is estimated to be 1.1–1.5% of the population (Simeon & Putnam, 2022; Sar, 2011), suggesting between 761,530 to over 1 million people within the UK would meet criteria for the most severe of the dissociative disorders (DDs).

To be truly trauma-informed services need to:

- *Realise* the prevalence and impact of trauma-related dissociation
- *Recognise* trauma-related dissociation and how it impacts on the person and their interaction with services
- *Respond* to the person's needs in a way that is *dissociation-informed* (e.g., adapting routine aspects of care), and *dissociation-specific* (providing support around specific dissociation-related needs)
- *Resist-retraumatisation* by creating policies, practices, and procedures that support people to heal, rather than create further harm
- *relationships matter* (NHS Education for Scotland, 2023) when working with people who experience trauma-related dissociation; support and interventions

DOI: 10.4324/9781003625650-20

should be provided in relational contexts which offer safe, empowered forms of connection (Herman, 1992).

This chapter summarises the costs of inappropriate care for people with trauma-related dissociation, the benefits of adapting services around people's needs and offers recommendations to achieve this.

2. The Case for Change

2.1 What Are the Costs of Failing to Meet the Needs of People with Trauma-Related Dissociation?

> 'I have felt that service providers have needed me to fit with their understanding of mental health and to keep quiet about the parts of my experience which don't match their labels. I have been told by a staff member that my experience of dissociation wasn't happening, that I could not have my diagnosis of DID written in my discharge notes as it wasn't a valid diagnosis for payment purposes, and I have learnt to keep quiet rather than have my experiences rewritten as something I knew they weren't.' **Jill, Expert-by-Experience**

For the **person experiencing trauma-related dissociation and their family/support system** the human cost is significant. Meeting criteria for a DD diagnosis is associated with:

- Higher rates of attempted suicide and self-harm (Foote et al., 2008)
- High rates of adult revictimisation (Webermann et al., 2014)
- Disability and multiple long-term health conditions, at higher rates than other psychiatric groups (Langeland et al., 2020)
- A higher rate of hospital admissions and being over-represented in the most restrictive settings (Şar, 2011).

The evidence-base and existing best practice guidelines suggest failing to take account of trauma-related dissociation is likely to result in ineffective interventions (ISSTD, 2011).

For **healthcare staff**:

- Professional training across all disciplines has failed to equip staff to work safely and effectively with trauma-related dissociation (Bestel et al., 2024; Kumar et al., 2022)
- Staff may experience working with high levels of risk and complexity without access to adequate supervision or support (Edwards et al., 2006)

- This contributes to staff burnout, and vicarious traumatisation (Prosser et al., 1996).

For **healthcare organisations**:

- Poor **cost-effectiveness**. Failing to provide effective pathways of care results in poor outcomes. The effective diagnosis and treatment of complex dissociative difficulties is associated with cost savings of between 25-64%, with reduced treatment length, emergency, and inpatient care utilisation, suicidality and self-harm (Lloyd, 2016; Myrick et al., 2017)
- Negative impact on **staff well-being and retention**. Ensuring the workforce is adequately trained and supported to work in dissociation-informed and specific-ways should support staff well-being, reducing absence rates and improve retention
- **Reputational harm.** The association with risk and high levels of relational re-enactments (Steele et al., 2001) mean a significant proportion of serious unto-ward incidents, unresolved complaints and breakdowns in the relationship with a service, may be associated with complex trauma and dissociation (Pierorazio et al., 2024). This has additional financial and human costs
- **Social inequality and social injustice.** People who experience trauma-related dissociation are a marginalised group, experiencing significant health inequal-ities and barriers to accessing services (Herman, 2023; Nester et al., 2022).

2.2 What Are the Potential Benefits?

The development of services that can sustainably meet the needs of people experi-encing trauma-related dissociation should:

- Reduce harm and suffering for the person and their families/carers. Increase successful outcomes for people experiencing complex dissociation and other clinical presentations where trauma-related dissociation is a key factor
- Aid the development of evidence-based practice to improve clinical outcome
- Reduce staff burnout and vicarious traumatisation
- Improve costs of care provision, staff morale, sickness absence and retention, and organisational reputation
- Address health inequalities and social injustices for survivors of relational trauma and abuse.

3. Putting this into Practice

3.1 Realisation

Staff, organisations and society need to *realise* the prevalence of trauma-related dissociation and the multi-faceted impact it has on health. There is no part of healthcare where trauma-related dissociation does not either impact on someone's presenting difficulties or ability to access a service.

This means making the following **realisations**;

- The extent and true prevalence of childhood abuse and neglect
- How dissociation is a hallmark survival response for children who have been harmed by trusted adults or people on whom they depend
- The scale of betrayal blindness (Freyd, 1996) shown by society to survivors of various forms of childhood abuse and neglect
- The moral and legal responsibility of the NHS to commission services that meet the reasonable needs of people who experience trauma-related dissociation ('National Health Service Act', 2006)
- The responsibility of services to ensure staff are well-trained, well-supported and well led
- The limits of our existing dominant frameworks and pathways of care and how this intersects with other forms of marginalisation (see Chapter 15)

What Can Be Done to Achieve this Level of Realisation?

- Addressing training and supervision needs for the workforce (see Chapter 17, Training)
- Many NHS care pathways are based on NICE guidelines for specific diagnostic categories (e.g., OCD, depression, Emotionally Unstable Personality Disorder). A wider understanding of evidence-based practice that goes beyond the limits of short-term randomised controlled trials (APA Presidential Task Force on Evidence-Based Practice, 2006) is required to inform evidence-based practice for complex clinical presentations such as trauma-related dissociation. Services need to realise the need for pathways that address needs associated with trauma-related dissociation
- Addressing stigma associated with dissociation and childhood experiences of abuse and neglect, and challenge societal messages that have created and compounded shame.

3.2 Recognition

With such realisations, improved recognition becomes possible. A dissociation-informed service would **recognise**:

- The variety of ways trauma-related dissociation manifests across a range of individual, cultural and intersectional contexts
- The importance of a response that validates, 'I see you; *and* I believe you'
- The importance of shared language and communication regarding dissociation
- How terrifying and isolating it can be for people to have trauma-related dissociation needs recognised.

What Can Be Done to Improve Recognition of Trauma-related Dissociation?

- Health professionals need to be able to understand the impact of dissociation on a person to deliver routine aspects of care (e.g., developing care plans, risk assessments) and consider key dissociation-related factors (see Chapter 3, and Chapter 6).
- In some contexts, using dissociation-specific assessment and diagnostic tools will be important to identify the extent of someone's needs (see Chapter 2) and provide support.

Case Example: *'Alex' worked in a crisis setting as a manager; and oversaw work with several people who were highly dissociative as a result of past (and in one case ongoing) organised sexual abuse. 'Alex' worked directly with these survivors, as well as dealing with the safeguarding issues; and supervising other staff.*

Despite access to high quality internal/external supervision and an effective reflective practice space, 'Alex' became vicariously traumatised. They began to worry about being followed home by members of a perpetrator group; and to experience intrusive imagery about physical and sexual abuse. At no point did 'Alex' stop enjoying the rewarding nature of supporting people, and nor did they experience burnout or compassion fatigue. Nevertheless, the vicarious trauma quietly took hold.

'Alex' did eventually realise what was happening; and took steps to counter it. They reached out to practitioners working elsewhere in this field. They limited time spent researching organised abuse; instead using the extra time on non work-related areas that brought them satisfaction... 'Alex' felt like they had 'repaired' the damage wrought.

- Health professionals should have support to reflect on and manage relational challenges (see Chapter 2, and Chapter 3), whilst working in services that are committed to understand and, whenever possible, repair relationships
- Professionals and services should recognise that minoritised and racialised groups may experience additional barriers to care due to systemic such as the legacy of systemic racism, cultural stigma, mistrust of services, and culturally incongruent explanatory models of distress (Pierorazio et al., 2023; Meyer & Zane, 2013).

3.3 Response

When someone's needs related to trauma-related dissociation are recognised, this should guide the service response. A dissociation-responsive service would **respond** by:

- Offering 'hope for healing' and clearly convey '*if it felt safe enough for you, we could help you with these needs*'
- De-shaming needs related to trauma-related dissociation
- Adapting routine aspects of care around these needs when required
- Provide specific, sustainable, evidence-based therapeutic support that directly addresses the needs of the person's trauma-related dissociation.

What Can Be Done to Improve Responses to Trauma-related Dissociation?

- Routine aspects of care should be adapted to the needs of the individual. For example, safety planning should include consideration regarding the needs of all parts of the person. Policies, processes and procedures should support this
- Peer-support options may help de-shame and reduce stigma; reduce alienation, build community
- People should have access to treatment pathways that address needs associated with trauma-related dissociation
  - For some this may be psychologically informed interventions delivered by members of the MDT (see Chapter 3)
  - For others this requires access to longer-term and highly specialist phase-based individual psychological therapy (see Chapter 4)
  - Such pathways should be support by a robust training and support framework (see Chapter 17)
  - The commissioning of appropriate interventions requires dedicated budgets
- When service gaps exist, this should be openly acknowledged. Options for specialist commissioning of private providers should be actively considered in such circumstances
- Services should have ways of detecting if the service offer is meeting peoples' needs and reflect and respond when unmet needs are apparent.

3.4 Resist Retraumatisation

'As a service receiver I don't hold the power to argue against professionals who have insisted that my experiences were something different, something which didn't match my reality, but which matched their training or their drop down menus for funding purposes. And so the cycle of trauma, of being told

it isn't really happening, that you are being difficult, that you are the problem, that cycle continues.' **Jill, Expert-by-Experience**

A dissociation-informed service would **resist retraumatisation** by;

- Recognising policies, processes and procedures that cause harm to the person experiencing trauma-related dissociation or dismiss their lived experience
- Taking action to address these when possible
- Acknowledging aspects of service delivery where harm is inherent within the intervention (e.g., involuntary admission)
- Monitor meaningful progress using audit tools
- Examining which communities and groups remain inadvertently excluded from dissociation-informed services.

What Can Be Done to Resist Retraumatisation for People who Experience Trauma-related Dissociation?

- Gather regular feedback on the experience of receiving care from people with complex dissociative difficulties. Ensure this feedback is regularly reviewed and, where possible, acted upon
- Include people with lived experience of trauma-related dissociation in planning and reviewing the design and delivery of services
- It may be helpful embed mechanisms to consult with diverse lived experience groups to inform culturally responsive service development and to ensure that groups are not inadvertently excluded from dissociation-informed and specific services
- Ensure staff have access to sufficient support to work safely and effectively with people experiencing trauma-related dissociation.

4. Conclusion

The costs of failing to meet the needs of people who experience trauma-related dissociation are high. Once this is realised, organisations can take practical steps to address this by:

- Improving the ability to recognise someone's needs
- Developing sustainable, dissociation-informed and -specific care that addresses these needs
- Resist practices, policies and procedures that cause further harm.

If such care is provided in relational contexts that provide safe, empowered connection, it is likely the costs and harms associated with trauma-related dissociation would reduce and would promote wider efforts to create a more socially just society.

Chapter 17

Towards a Training and Competency Framework for Mental Health Professionals Working with Trauma-Based Dissociation

Helena Crockford, Paul Langthorne and Melanie Goodwin

> *'I think if my dissociation had been picked up sooner, I would have received the correct treatment and therefore my recovery could have been so much faster.'* **Becci, Expert-by-Experience**

1. Introduction

This book has highlighted the historic lack of core mental health training about trauma-related dissociation, particularly relative to other serious mental health difficulties. Dissociation is a relatively common experience, particularly for people presenting to mental health services. The costs of not providing dissociation-informed interventions have been outlined (see Chapter 1, Chapter 16). As summarised in Figure 17.1 below and outlined in Chapter 16, dissociation should be an integral component of trauma-informed care.

This chapter provides a framework of core competencies, training and support aiming to equip professionals to better meet the needs of people with trauma-based dissociation as part of their presentation, wherever they present to health and social care services. This framework is consistent with national and international movements towards health and care services becoming trauma-informed, and specific international guidance where this exists (Maves, 2024; Richardson, 2018).

2. Trauma-based Dissociation Training Levels

The proposed framework suggests all staff should have access to training and ongoing support (consultation or supervision) but require different levels of knowledge and skill depending on their role. The Scottish Framework (NHS Education for Scotland, 2017) described four incremental levels for trauma-informed care training. This is extended here to incorporate trauma-based dissociation (see Figure 17.2 below).

Realise the prevalence of trauma-related dissociation

Recognise trauma-related dissociation and how it impacts a person and their interaction with services and staff

Respond to someone's needs in dissociation-informed (adapting routine aspects of care) and dissociation-specific ways (supporting dissociation-related needs)

Resist retraumatisation by creating policies, practices and procedures that support people to heal, rather than create further harm

Relationships matter by providing support and interventions through relational contexts which offer safe, empowered connections

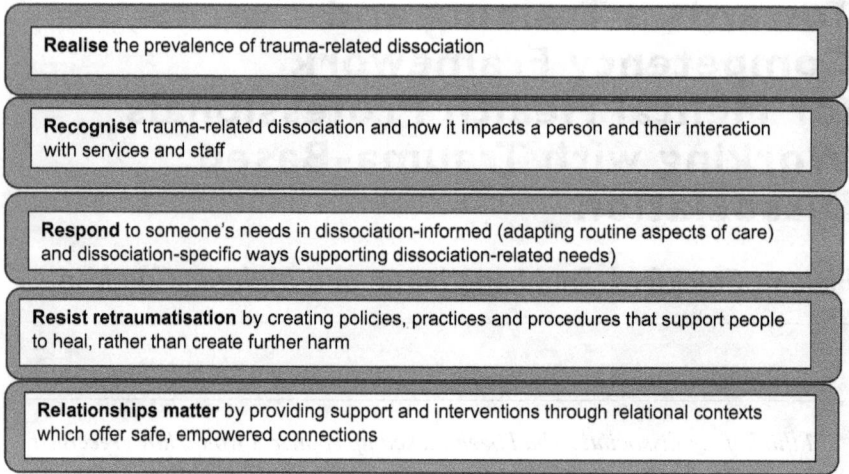

Figure 17.1 The 5 R's and Trauma-Related Dissociation.

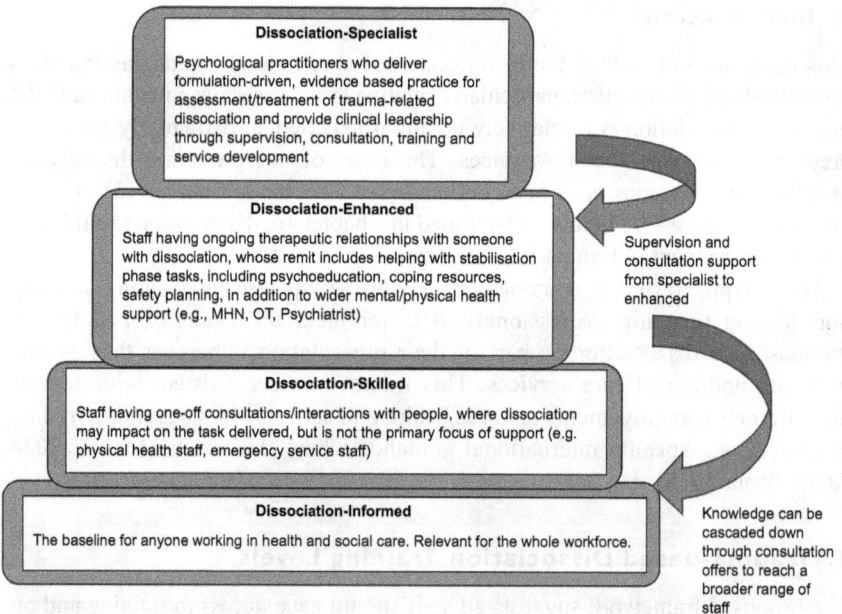

Dissociation-Specialist

Psychological practitioners who deliver formulation-driven, evidence based practice for assessment/treatment of trauma-related dissociation and provide clinical leadership through supervision, consultation, training and service development

Dissociation-Enhanced

Staff having ongoing therapeutic relationships with someone with dissociation, whose remit includes helping with stabilisation phase tasks, including psychoeducation, coping resources, safety planning, in addition to wider mental/physical health support (e.g., MHN, OT, Psychiatrist)

Supervision and consultation support from specialist to enhanced

Dissociation-Skilled

Staff having one-off consultations/interactions with people, where dissociation may impact on the task delivered, but is not the primary focus of support (e.g. physical health staff, emergency service staff)

Dissociation-Informed

The baseline for anyone working in health and social care. Relevant for the whole workforce.

Knowledge can be cascaded down through consultation offers to reach a broader range of staff

Figure 17.2 Levels of Practice and Support Needs for Staff Supporting People with Dissociation.

3. Content of Training

The first four dissociation-related competency areas set out in Figure 17.1 above are elaborated below for each of the staff skill levels set out in Figure 17.2. The fifth area – relational skills – is woven throughout.

'Dissociation was a survival strategy when I was younger, it enabled me to go to school and carry on with life, meanwhile living a very scary life at home. Whilst dissociation helped me then, it isn't so helpful as an adult. I have parts stuck in time still thinking and behaving like a frightened young child, not realising they are safe now.' **Becci, Expert-by-Experience**

3.1 REALISATION of Trauma-related Dissociation

All staff with some interface to mental health require baseline knowledge about trauma and dissociation, wider understanding of the prevalence and impact of abuse and coercive control (Hill, 2020), and core relational skills to facilitate compassionate, collaborative interactions with people, whatever their role or task. Training should be contextualised within wider trauma-informed training and culturally sensitive practices, supported with consultation as required.

To increase **realisation**, **Dissociation-Informed competencies** include:

- Awareness of:
  - The five symptom areas of dissociation
  - Somatic presentations
  - Prevalence, comorbidity and interaction with intersectional identities
  - Cultural variation in expression and understanding of dissociation

- Understanding the origins of dissociation in:
  - Traumatic experiences and relationships
  - Disrupted attachment histories.

- Understanding of:
  - Dissociation as trauma and threat survival responses
  - How dissociation might impact the task in hand (e.g., engagement with a medical procedure)
  - Core relational skills, remaining curious, collaborative, compassionate and non-judgemental
  - Where to signpost for more information and help
  - The importance of prevention and early intervention.

> **Good Practice Example**: In Cheshire, short talks on dissociation were arranged within GP Practice training. Relative informality allowed for questions on the nature of dissociation, referral pathways, barriers to service delivery and outcomes. Staff reported these were helpful to develop general understanding of trauma-related mental health and implement simple screening tools.

- **Dissociation-Enhanced and Specialist staff** require more detailed knowledge of:
  - Developmental origins of dissociation
  - Neurobiological underpinnings
  - Cultural diversity in trauma experiences, selfhood and dissociation
  - Models of dissociation.

- **Specialist staff** require:
  - Understanding of the prevalence, impact and clinical implications of ritual and organised abuse (Miller, 2018).

3.2 RECOGNISING Trauma-Related Dissociation

Staff similarly have a range of needs regarding **recognising** trauma-related dissociation.

Dissociation-Skilled staff require competencies to:

- Identify if someone experiences dissociation, using basic screening questions (Chapter 2, Section 4) and recognising non-verbal signs

> *'For me, diagnosis is critical, I received an incorrect diagnosis, and the treatment not only didn't work it sadly was retraumatising and caused more problems than it solved. I wished someone had followed up on the initial screening tool I completed that scored highly for dissociation.'* **Becci, Expert-by-Experience**

- Signpost someone to further information, resources, and treatment.

Dissociation-Enhanced staff require training to:

- Administer screening assessment tools, with Dissociation-Specialist support for scoring and interpretation
- Understand diagnostic categories
- Support guided self-help and psychoeducation about dissociation, including understanding a diagnosis
- Support with developing culturally informed psychobiosocial formulations of presenting experiences, for example identifying triggers for someone's depersonalisation/ derealisation experiences.

Dissociation-Specialist staff require training in:

- Diagnostic interviews (e.g., SCID-D training) and other assessment and formulation processes
- Adapting assessment protocols for cultural and intersectional identities (see Chapters 7, 14, 18).

All levels require **access to supervision or consultation** to support with complexity in screening, assessment, diagnostic and formulation processes (see Chapter 2).

3.3 RESPONDING to Trauma-Related Dissociation

> *'All my parts have different likes and dislikes and different ideas of what they want, just deciding what we're going to have for dinner can be a complex decision, so it makes sense that giving consent for a procedure can be very challenging.'* **Becci, Expert-by-Experience**

Dissociation-Skilled and Enhanced staff need to adapt routine aspects of care **to respond** to and accommodate.

Dissociation-Skilled staff need to:

- Take dissociation into account when delivering routine tasks such as:
  - Giving someone more time to complete a form if dissociating in response to stress
  - Understanding it may be complex for someone to reach internal consensus on consent for a procedure, if negotiating with conflicting internal viewpoints from dissociative parts

- Have access to additional supervision or consultation regarding clinical dilemmas
- Understand local referral routes for assessment and treatment of dissociation.

Dissociation-Enhanced staff should understand adjustments for dissociation when delivering routine tasks (see Chapters 3 and 6), for example:

- Developing a plan of care, goals for treatment and how these progress
- Managing a therapeutic relationship, including hostile/protective dissociative parts
- Assessing risk and developing a safety plan
- Prescribing medication
- Giving treatments, including psychological therapy, for other mental health difficulties (see Chapters 7 and 12).

Dissociation-Enhanced and Specialist staff need to offer specific, evidence-based, culturally relevant responses to help someone manage trauma-related dissociation, based on the phase-based approach (see Chapters 2, 4, 5, 15).

Dissociation-Enhanced staff need role-relevant skills in safety and stabilisation phase tasks, including psychological intervention techniques, for example:

- Staying curious
- Monitoring their own and client's window of tolerance
- Developing personalised emotional regulation strategies, including grounding, breathing or mindfulness exercises.

Dissociation-Specialist staff require specialist therapeutic training and supervision to provide best practice, evidence-based and culturally informed treatments adapted specifically for trauma-related dissociation.

I see it like putting a plaster cast on an arm for a broken leg. It won't fix the leg! ... I have been in the mental health system a very long time and finally the treatment for dissociation is giving me a vision and hope for my future, something I have never dared get excited about before. **Becci, Expert-by-Experience**

Specialist training should cover:

- Detailed knowledge of stabilisation-phase tasks (see Chapters 2, 4, 5)
- Working with dissociative systems, multiplicity and parts in graded and safe ways

- Working with clinical complexities (e.g., disorganised attachment patterns, attachment to an abuser, ongoing abuse, working with hostile/protective or 'installed' dissociative parts)
- Skills and pacing across all three phase-based stages
- Intersectional considerations regarding dissociation in people from minoritised groups (see Chapters 15).

3.4 RESISTING RETRAUMATISATION for People with Trauma-Related Dissociation

Including diverse lived experience perspectives in the development and delivery of all training is integral to **resisting retraumatisation** (Richardson, 2018).

> *'It feels empowering to think I can contribute a small amount to changing the system and ensure no one ever has to go through what I went through.'* **Becci, Expert-by-Experience**

Training feedback shows participants value training being co-designed and co-delivered with lived experience practitioners (Crockford et al., 2019).

Dissociation-Informed practice means all staff should hold awareness of:

- How services or interpersonal interactions could retraumatise
- The risk of secondary traumatisation to staff
- The importance of:
  - Safe and collaboratively agreed boundaries
  - Joined up working across the person's care network
  - Relational repair for working through ruptures, difficulties and harms incurred through receiving care
  - Awareness of intersecting issues of power and privilege (see Chapter 15).

> *'All my parts respond well to boundaries and compassion, they make us feel safe. I have child parts that are desperate to attach and be taken care of, and I have protector parts that explode with anger when they feel like the child parts have been hurt. They all have the same agenda to keep everyone safe.'* **Becci, Expert-by-Experience**

- Appropriate supervision and reflective practice.

Dissociation-Enhanced and Specialist staff require more advanced consideration of:

- Working therapeutically with transference, countertransference, and relational re-enactments
- Supporting other staff through supervision, consultation and training
- Continued training and supervision to support their practice.

3.5 Overarching Training Principles

The training content outlined owes much to past and existing training offers. Summarising these, Richardson (2018) advocated additional general training principles:

- A co-ordinated training strategy to reduce fragmentation
- Addressing different practice contexts
- Accommodating different learning styles, and diversity.

4. Effectiveness of Training

There is limited research on the effectiveness of dissociation training within the wider TIC context. Kumar et al. (2022) found participants attending complex trauma training rated improved levels of knowledge and competence, with information on dissociation cited as particularly valuable. Webb et al. (2025) analysed CMHT staff feedback (N=63) on a two day training, co-designed with a lived experience practitioner. Significant improvements in trauma-informed attitudes, awareness, understanding and skills for working with dissociation were reported. Staff valued combined professional and lived experience perspectives but reported anxiety at changing practice, and system barriers, highlighting needs for ongoing supervision and consultation.

Good Practice Examples

1) Norfolk and Suffolk Mental Health Trust developed a psychology-led strategy, where experienced psychological practitioners trained as Dissociation Champions, supported by external supervision. Champions cascaded Dissociation Awareness Training and case consultation to multi-disciplinary colleagues (Crockford et al., 2019).
2) Experienced psychologists in Derbyshire Healthcare NHS Foundation Trust attended specialist training, supported by external group supervision from a dissociation specialist. They cascaded training, supervision and consultation to local colleagues and early career psychological practitioners. Thematic analysis of supervision feedback identified:

- The benefits of 'speaking the same language' around trauma-related dissociation
- Increased knowledge and confidence working with dissociation
- Challenges to implementing change, through MDT constraints.

(Choksi et al., 2025)

5. Supervision and Consultation

Dissociation-Enhanced and Specialist staff require access to clinical supervision of sufficient quality and expertise to meet the *normative, formative* and *restorative* functions of clinical supervision (Proctor, 2010). Without ongoing support, training is unlikely to translate into maintained changes in practice.

Dissociation-Enhanced staff need support from a **Dissociation-Specialist,** but can cascade advice and consultation to **Dissociation-Informed and Skilled staff**. NHS Scotland modelled Trauma Champions, and Dissociation Champions have been modelled in some UK mental health services, supporting colleagues and cascading expertise (see examples above).

Dissociation-Specialist staff require specialist supervision from someone with expertise and experience in trauma-related dissociation. Organisations early in developing expertise may require investment in external supervision to support staff and service development.

Organisations should also address system-level barriers to implementing and maintaining practice changes (see Chapter 16).

6. Towards a Competency Framework for Dissociation-Informed and - Dissociation-Specific Care

The training goals set out represent a graded competency framework to equip the health and social care workforce to address the needs of people presenting with trauma-related dissociation, wherever they seek help across the health and social care system.

Future developments should include:

- A nationally agreed competency framework (www.ucl.ac.uk/pals/research/clinical-educational-and-health-psychology/research-groups/competence-frameworks)
- Coordinated and validated training for multidisciplinary staff
- Evaluating the impact of training on:
  - Clinical outcomes
  - The lived experiences of people with trauma-related dissociation and their supporters
  - The wellbeing of staff and organisations (see Chapter 16).

- Embedded systems of staff training, supervision and consultation, for example via Dissociation Champions.

7. Conclusion

This chapter has embedded within the TIC training agenda, a framework for training multidisciplinary staff in trauma-related dissociation. Next steps, co-produced with those with lived experience should include:

- Developing a national competency framework
- Embedding training in dissociation within all core mental health professional trainings
- Organisations investing in staff being trained, supervised and supported to address the needs of people experiencing trauma-related dissociation
- Organisations addressing system-level barriers to implementing changes in practice.

Chapter 18

Epilogue: 'Do No Harm'

An Expert-by-Experience Perspective

Melanie Goodwin

1. Introduction

As someone with DID I have been able to reach a place with good internal communication and a lot of the traumas resolved. This happened over 20 years and involved working very hard with an experienced DID focussed therapist. Many people will sadly not be able to experience this level of resolution, whatever resolution may mean to them. I firmly believe that with DID-informed help, appropriate expectations and supportive containment, changes can happen.

This chapter reflects my experiences both personally and through my work. Some areas I have only been able to touch on briefly.

I co-founded First Person Plural (FPP), a registered charity focussing on DID that closed in 2023 after 26 years. FPP's work included developing resources, raising awareness and providing co-produced training to a wide range of mental health practitioners. Our members received regular newsletters, often contributing articles. In the early days we held Open Meetings and later moved to online groups, with well-established ground-rules playing a vital part.

FPP produced two training DVDs (available at www.mairsinn.org.uk/publicati ons.html). 'A Logical Way of Being', won the 2011 ISSTD media award and continues to be used globally at all levels of training. 'No Two Paths the Same' considers the three stages of therapy. Both films featured EbEs and experienced therapists. Since then, another film 'Dissociative Identity Disorder – Learning From Others' Perspectives' (https://dissociation.co.uk/videos) has been made, many years after ending therapy, involving a reflective conversation about the treatment journey, between myself and my therapist, facilitated by a consultant psychiatrist.

As someone with DID I wanted to fit in and not need any special tweaking. I still hold onto this principle while acknowledging that some DID focused adjustments to services are necessary. Initially, when I began to understand the full reality of my situation, I felt totally isolated. I would ring helplines for people who had experienced childhood sexual abuse, but there was little understanding for how complex it is living with DID. I felt even more isolated. Yet, twice when I rang the Samaritans at my wit's end, they naturally practised trauma-informed care skills, listening and caring in the moment enabling me to get through the next few hours.

DOI: 10.4324/9781003625650-22

The Survivors Trust website (https://thesurvivorstrust.org) sensitively demonstrates how a more general resource for survivors of childhood sexual abuse can feel welcoming and inclusive to people living with DID.

2. What Is Trauma-Informed Care (TIC) and Dissociation-Specific Care?

I think it is important to clarify the difference between TIC and dissociation-specific care.

TIC (UK Government, 2022) provides a framework for working with people who have experienced trauma. It emphasises the need for genuine listening, respect and interest in what is being shared, while having the ability to gently help the person contain the trauma. Many clinicians provide this naturally but sadly this is often not the case.

A word of caution, TIC focusses on what happened rather than what is wrong with you. For many people with DID their survival relies on not knowing what happened to them. I would have been unable to answer this question but there were other indicators that things were not as I, the outside part, presented.

Dissociation-specific care needs more training and a broader understanding of the often life-saving role that dissociation has played. The danger, I use that word quite deliberately, is that it is all too easy to 'open someone up' by bringing abuse into the person's full consciousness too quickly. The clinician's kindness and wanting to help may be the first time someone managing complex dissociation has been in this situation and without the necessary skills may open up traumas before grounding skills have been developed.

Clinicians walk a narrow path between helping the containment of such memories and not engendering old feelings of rejection and abandonment. Being willing to have a conversation about 'why doing deep trauma work too soon is unhelpful', if managed well, can feel empowering for the client. Collaboratively working out what is going to help ensures the client feels part of the process.

> *'I was told, "You are safe", as I was handed over to a paedophile ring on a Saturday afternoon. It took over 50 years before we, working together as a whole, understood what safety meant to us. It is "not being hurt".'*
> **Tamarisk, Expert-by-Experience**

The UK Government (2022) summarises a working definition of TIC with links to further information on developing this in practice. It addresses six core principles: Safety, Trustworthiness, Choice, Collaboration, Empowerment and Cultural Consideration. These are often severely compromised for those experiencing complex dissociation, including those meeting the diagnostic criteria for DID.

TIC acknowledges the need to see beyond an individual's presenting behaviours and to ask, 'What does this person need?' rather than 'What is wrong with this person?' (UK Government, 2022, p.3).

> *'When I was in a situation where the word "safe" was used, we would blank out or become defensive, usually unhelpful in the situation. It was experienced by those around me as odd and if it caused a panic attack and we removed ourselves, confusion and frustration often ensued at what appeared to be a totally unprovoked behavioural reaction.'* **Lucy, Expert-by-Experience**

In a mindful TIC way, a response like 'I can see something has changed, I am not quite sure what is happening but how can I help you?' is appropriate. This encourages the brain to reengage from the default, polarised position and helps stimulate a gentle curiosity in your client about what might be happening.

> *'There were times in a medical situation where a little one's fear of such places meant they came out and took over. To those watching it could be mistaken for psychosis, a young child's voice talking about being abused by her Daddy, but it was me.'* **Little Beth, Expert-by-Experience**

Many similar situations could be managed kindly and effectively with this approach rather than what might feel like criticism or condemnation, even if not actively intended. I have talked to many people who felt misunderstood, leading to hospitalisation and/or over-medication, based on a practitioner's assumption of what they think is happening rather than exploring their client's reality in that moment. Often neither clinical intervention leads to positive, sustainable outcomes, while adding another layer of trauma.

A simple question like, 'I can see this is hard for you, can you tell me a bit about what is happening?' may help defuse the situation. Sadly, driven by risk aversion, inappropriate and unhelpful actions may result instead.

3. The Three-Phased Approach to Trauma Therapy

This section is firmly based on all the parts having the opportunity to be involved in therapy, directly talking with the therapist, or if this feels impossible some parts may communicate through other parts. I am only a part of the whole, so my voice was very limited until it was safe for the amnesic barriers to become less powerful, and I could bear to hear, engage, and grow to love all my many parts. They had different names, ages, genders, likes, dislikes, and even allergies. If a part was not welcomed or felt unheard, they quite rightly made sure this changed, becoming an important member of the whole, once their traumas had been allowed to be explored safely and processed.

Stabilisation is a starting place but is also infinite. Throughout the therapeutic journey this is returned to regularly. As the whole system begins to work together, stabilisation needs may change, requiring old skills to be updated.

A lot may be achieved working within the framework of TIC and an understanding of DID, focussing on developing stabilising techniques. If therapy is short-term this will be the main focus. Therapy should be client-led to avoid retriggering feelings of hopelessness and powerlessness. Through genuine partnership-working and collaboration it is possible to achieve sustainable, positive outcomes.

Therapist-led quick fixes are often unsustainable, undermining the person's ability to find their own way.

Many people with DID will use stabilisation throughout their lives, however well trauma has been processed; the often brutal history remains their experience and cannot be 'therapied' away.

> *'I still need to plan my day so there is time for us all to quietly regroup. If we don't, we become overwhelmed, leading to us being unable to function. With a little thought, we lead a good, and what I would describe "ordinary", life. I find it amazing that with the right help we have been able to achieve this.'*
> **Melanie, Expert-by-Experience**

Processing allows the memory to come into consciousness, maybe initially through body memories (Levine, 1997). A narrative may then become possible, and triggers gradually lose their power. Eventually it becomes a fully processed memory that will not be destabilising if revisited.

Developing a narrative, moving from a body memory to words, was important for my system. I have worked with brutalised animals, and consistently through love and care they have become much happier, but in every case, triggers have retained their power, perhaps because an animal cannot put a narrative to their experiences.

A person's individuality should be respected at all times. Therapists and supporter roles are to listen, allow, help to contain, and celebrate the differences. Comparing or being prescriptive is disempowering.

4. Phase 1: Identifying and Developing Stabilising Techniques and Strategies

Stabilising techniques and strategies will be many, different for every system and different for parts within a system.

4.1 Recognising the Person's Own Resources

It is important to help a client to identify strategies they already use, but may be unrecognised as such. Often a client will say 'Well, I just do that'. Identifying and naming them as coping skills can feel empowering, allowing them to be consciously called upon when required. This begins to move from habitual reactions to a thoughtful, purposeful response.

> *'When life felt too over-whelming, or a memory was surfacing we walked up to 10 miles, fast, before we could stop. I had no words, but walking seemed to work. When I made the link between cause and effect it was like being given a gift. I now had this as part of my grounding folder and could consciously go to it when I began to feel I was not coping. This was my first link in identifying and naming an action that I could use to prevent a full-blown crisis. It allowed us to begin to stay with feelings, understanding they were just that, and we had skills to help us all feel grounded.'* **Lizzie, Expert-by-Experience**

Nature often plays an important role in many people's lives and is something that can be enjoyed by all ages within a DID system. Looking at trees continues to be one of our grounding techniques. We have developed our own simplified version of mindfulness.

As always this may only be possible for some parts, others finding it triggering. Both reactions must be respected and worked with.

4.2 Collaboration Is Key

Working collaboratively within a relationship that models partnership-working allows the client to begin to feel and understand trust. A common thread throughout our journey was understanding the importance of sustainability and foundation building. This may mean work feels as if it is progressing very slowly. I had to learn to trust and respect the process.

There are times you might share things you have heard from others, but offer this as a possibility for consideration, not something you think would be 'good' for them.

For many with DID-type difficulties, the mention of breathing exercises may be met with a look of horror where heavy breathing had accompanied their childhood abuse. Techniques need to be very simple, possibly a single element in the early days. Later on, when revisiting these techniques, they may be expanded.

It is hard to convey how chaotic a DID brain is when in crisis, so grounding actions need to be simple and achievable, stimulating feelings of success and empowerment.

Abused children often carry the message, 'This is your fault', and spend their childhoods trying to make the horror stop. They are set up for inevitable failure. Of course it is never their fault, but this belief has often become organically powerful. Through your relationship, helping someone succeed can play an important role in the brain rewiring.

> *'I believed I caused all the bad things in my family and once this seed was sown it became one of the most powerful, organic beliefs – if I did not cause it then the abusers were choosing to hurt us, and that was intolerable.'* **Lizzie, Expert-by-Experience**

There are so many creative ways people with complex dissociation can learn to feel grounded; each time a chosen strategy prevents a crisis it builds on positive thinking.

4.3 Balancing Communication with Containment

Journalling has definitely been helpful in my journey, but initially it added to us being retraumatised. I read about communicating with my inner child through writing, prior to knowing we are many and without grounding skills in place. The whole system thought it was amazing and different parts started writing about their traumas. Once the trauma is brought into full consciousness too quickly it is very hard to contain it safely.

Later in our journey this became more helpful but we used it to get to know each other better, sharing all our different likes, interests and present day-to-day things, rather than traumas. Journalling helped the little ones develop their own, individual grounding techniques.

Early internal communication, encouraging each part to work out what they like, can help them to develop their own, age-appropriate grounding skills; it may be a story read by the therapist, or quietly sitting doing a jigsaw; they will know. This contains the child's distress safely, enabling the outside part to take over, returning to a calmer body. Like the outside part/s, the child will begin to feel empowered. A residue of their distress may remain throughout the body, but feel more manageable.

It is so important to help the whole system understand the need for this first stage. It is not saying you do not want to hear about their traumas, but it is saying clearly that this first stage is helping them prepare for future work. This information and way of working should be introduced from the very start. Embarking on trauma work too early and then trying to contain it, can feel rejecting; annihilation was the only way we could describe it, and suicidal thoughts became our default position. Clients might feel they have upset you, or it is wrong to talk about trauma, echoing an old message 'It is my fault', and triggering the negative thinking of an abused child. It is a difficult situation to manage, relying on the trust you are building within this relationship.

Time constraints may severely restrict what is achievable. It is important to explain why you will not be addressing the traumas directly, but will work out ways to help them be safely contained. Focus on something that the client chooses and feels will make a difference in their daily lives, and is achievable within the constraints. It must be client-led. It is easy to think you know what is best for this person, but it is about what is important to them. If used well like a single, planned phone call, something positive is achievable.

Traumas will emerge throughout therapy and need handling sensitively. Validate the person's reality and acknowledge how hard it was, while helping to develop containing skills. You may have to explain this many times in different ways, enabling all ages to understand. Handled sensitively this can be empowering, enabling the client to take control of their own journey.

Crisis situations are inevitable. When things have again reached calmer waters, try to work out together why this happened and what would be helpful in the future to prevent the revolving door experience. Collaboration, not criticism or rescuing, is empowering in the longer term.

4.4 Working with Parts that Appear to 'Sabotage' the Work

Some parts may seem very negative, but once you have developed a relationship and understood their roles, their logic within their situation will emerge.

Sometimes there are parts who are detrimental to the whole system and unwilling to engage. Their behaviour, beliefs and roles need gradually understanding to help them engage in different, more adaptive ways of managing. DID-informed supervision is important.

When working with people who have experienced Organised Abuse, specialist literature (Miller, 2018) and DID-focussed supervision will be beneficial.

The reality of living with complex dissociative difficulties is hard to capture. This is beautifully achieved in a short film, 'Petals of a Rose' (Crumpler, 2022).

4.5 Finding a Language and the Power of Curiosity

Often people with complex dissociation have never learnt the names of emotional states. I was told I was a sulky, jealous child, the reality was a very sad little girl who could not make any sense of so much of her life. Part of this first stage is helping all parts to express their feelings using many imaginative ways of doing so and naming them. Different parts will probably hold different feelings and have many ways of expressing them.

It is important to metaphorically hold that the outside part/s are often learning about their reality alongside you.

It can be challenging for someone who is highly dissociative to do 'joined up thinking'. Initially it translates into 'beware danger ahead', triggering old, defensive ways of coping. A therapist being respectfully curious about the person's reactions and gently reflecting, 'I feel something has changed or happened and I am feeling a bit confused; can you help me?' may allow the client to also reflect. A non-judgemental approach may allow the beginning of a narrative. Your curiosity may enable the client to be curious and connect with what other parts are trying to convey. Your thoughtful use of language can help the whole system to remain engaged, preventing a full shut down.

4.6 The Role of Attachment in Working with Guilt and Shame

Viewing DID through the prism of attachment enables an understanding which considers how many developmental stages were missed or contaminated whilst other parts of their brain were activated much too young. This helps both therapist and client to put behaviours within a developmental and trauma context. Gerhardt's (2004) book 'Why Love Matters' captures this area in a humane way which is not depersonalising.

With this understanding, feelings of grief and loss may be triggered. I found this stage extremely hard and had to work on staying connected. In the longer term we all felt more whole, gaining a part of our missed development which has now been sustainably achieved.

> *'It has helped us to understand the full impact of this ingrained belief system by likening it to a religious belief that was fed to the child from their first breath and fully supported by the whole family and actions throughout their childhood. It helped us all to better understand what a big job we had to challenge the organised abuse beliefs and find our truth.'* **Lizzie and Her Internal Family, Experts-by-Experience**

If someone is ready, mentally and physically, to begin the healing process, facilitating internal communication is an important part of your role. DID clients often need to find the exact word that is right for them. There were no words to describe what many survivors experienced. Shame and humiliation play a big role in an abused childhood – 'Guilt is ingrained and often feels personified. I am learning direct links back to childhood, when it was other people's guilt that was imposed on me from a very early age' (Goodwin, 2011).

4.7 Theories that Have Helped

For many people with complex dissociation, psychoeducation is helpful, for others this is not the case. Be aware of these polarities and respect them. There is no one way and no wrong way. I, Melanie found different models helpful at various times although they could also be triggering. I needed to understand what was happening to me/us and that allowed me to begin to connect to my internal family, let go of my iron grip of trying to control everyone and everything. This is different for everyone, we had to learn to trust ourselves.

- *The 'Structural Dissociation' Model (*Boon et al., 2011*).*

Structural dissociation is discussed formally elsewhere (Chapter 1), but I want to reflect on how this model may help those with DID to find a language. In the early days, when first realising and beginning to accept that you have DID. It can feel like it is infinite, no shape or edges, no beginning, middle or end. It can feel out of control, and this can be retraumatising and trigger unhelpful reactions as it reignites similar feelings experienced during childhood. An example is how our anorexic part took control of our body for several years.

In this model the parts are neatly categorised as the outsider, 'apparently normal parts' (ANPs), and the 'emotional parts' (EPs). I found this helpful as I began to understand how limited my role as an ANP was. I was amnesic to my past, emotionless and in many ways robotic. I could begin to take on board how the EPs were usually parts who had managed the abuse, had no time frame and thought the abuse was still happening, stuck in the 1950s and 1960s. Quickly this concept felt too simplistic, even derogatory, but it gave us the beginning of a shape, an edge to the whole. We no longer felt we were drowning, but paddling very fast to stay afloat.

It addressed the terror I was experiencing and explained why I had little influence over so much. What felt like alien behaviours were unfolding, often with no apparent context. Yet I knew these came from the body I inhabited, and so I must take ownership. Learning about amnesic barriers, how some might be slightly permeable while others are impenetrable, did not 'let me off the hook', but helped me to appreciate my powerlessness, until we had more internal communication.

Psychoeducation was so important to us as a whole. I read everything I could and shared it with my therapist. This helped us develop the sense of partnership working.

- *The Motivational Systems Model.*

Linington (2025) extended the model of seven motivational systems, which represent extensions to attachment theory (Heard et al., 2009) – Caregiving, Careseeking, Self-Defence, Interest Sharing, Sexuality, External Environment and Internal Environment.

These categories felt inclusive to us all and evoked a feeling of wanting to explore further rather than triggering the defensive parts. Parts were very enthusiastic about labelling their roles, giving them a framework. Often previous labels had felt disrespectful. We like a sense of shape and this approach allowed fluidity while offering names for roles.

> *'All too often we are castigated with pejorative terms, rather than recognising the various functions of our parts that have enabled us to stay alive and function despite experiencing horrific atrocities.'* **Hannah**

- *Poly-vagal Theory (*Porges, 2011).

> *'Understanding how my brain worked, or in many cases did not work, helped me to come to terms with how immature in so many ways I was at forty. It allowed me to explore myself as the grown up outside part in charge for a lot of the time, and gave me reasons for why at times I felt totally lost about so many areas of life that my friends seemed to understand.'* **Melanie, Expert-by-Experience**

Poly-vagal theory really resonates with many people experiencing extreme levels of trauma and dissociation (Porges, 2022). This model is complex but for clients who want and need to understand what is happening within their brain it can provide neurophysiological answers about the wiring that has been so compromised and depleted throughout childhood. We can understand how safety, co-regulation, and connection are paramount to a healthy human experience, engendering an acceptance and ownership.

- *Attachment-informed Models.*

Sue Richardson (in 'a Logical Way of Being', First Person Plural, 2011) cites the use of the '5 Cs': **compassion, communication, collaboration, co-operation,** and **connection.** She applies this to working with the internal family, external relationships and how they form the platform for supporting people with complex dissociation. Considering these five areas may help someone begin to understand their parts and make connections.

I have used these theories eclectically at different stages of my journey. They allowed us to explore an area of our experience and the behaviours related to it without feeling humiliated or shamed, engendering safe and healthy connections. I was a very grown-up person, a mother of four, holding down a job requiring management skills, but who was so fragile once my surface was scratched. As an outside part, I was hearing things that had happened throughout our childhood for the first time, and also hearing and understanding how depleted my role was on many developmental stages, and this was painful and humiliating.

Therapists risk being 'hoodwinked' into assuming the presenting outside parts are 'more than' their reality. We shared this depleted childhood, where parts learnt how to behave through watching and copying, rather than through core development. My three-year old part's emotional development was shared by us all, there was not a time before when things were good enough and could be revisited. The journey involves rewiring the brain. These changes are stimulated by and within a strong therapeutic relationship.

Books for our whole system included Jade Miller's magical four book series *Dear Little Ones* (Miller, 2021), aimed at younger parts, with simple text and beautiful illustrations. Also, Lindsay Schofield's (2021) books, *Understanding Dissociative Identity Disorder: A Guidebook for Survivors and Practitioners* and *Our House: Making Sense of Dissociative Identity Disorder*.

5. Phase 2: Trauma Work

> *'I guess something that was really helpful to me and the work I did with my therapist at this stage is creating a psychologically safe place for each part to go to when reliving trauma in stage 2. So, my part Little Sally has her Nanna's chair and her teddy, Chipper; Evil has a punchbag and things to be physically active with. This was so helpful.'* **Sally Adams, Expert-by-Experience**

The second stage, trauma work, will be part of the whole journey but usually only fully addressed when someone is resourced with stabilising strategies and techniques and their current life appropriately stable. However carefully stabilisation is addressed, trauma work will be challenging for the therapist and client. Outcomes are built on the trust shared. Trust is a two-way process; the client needs to have learnt that the therapist is trustworthy while the therapist needs to trust the client to use their strengths and ability to access and use their carefully developed resources.

6. Phase 3: Integration

> *'I found I was always waiting to see what might happen or what others wanted, I had to learn to be proactive, this felt scary but also exhausting. In the longer run it has been amazing and allowed me to enjoy my grandchildren*

> *with an understanding that was missing in my own children's childhood, probably my biggest loss.'* **Melanie, Expert-by-Experience**

Integration and reconciliation are in my opinion a core part of the whole journey. At the start it may appear much more chaotic, perhaps inevitably as the amnesic barriers become less rigid, allowing the beginnings of joined-up thinking. Whilst amazing the person is moving towards a level of stability and the changes this allows, living without dissociation as a part of every moment is hard. It is a completely new, alien landscape and change inevitably brings challenges.

Forgiveness will be a very personal thing and may change overtime. If this is not what the person wants however, encouraging them to try to forgive can yet again be a shaming experience.

> *'I have not forgiven my perpetrators. I feel unless they own their actions it is wrong of me to forgive them, it feels patronising. I have let go of what happened to us, I refuse to allow their actions to steal any more of our lives and I know I cannot get anything from them.'* **Melanie and All, Experts-by-Experience**

7. Conclusion

In this chapter, I have tried to capture some of the aspects that have helped us personally. These are also the things we have used in teaching others. My final words of encouragement are to stay alongside your client as they navigate their way through their journey, maybe enhanced by others' experiences, but tailored at all times to their own needs. If you live with complex dissociation, fight to get your needs met, so hard but worth it.

Glossary of Terms

I:I in-patient observations the process within a mental health in-patient ward when a patient is allocated a member of staff to regularly check their safety due to significant concerns of risk of self-harm

ACES Adverse Childhood Experiences are potentially traumatic events, occurring in childhood, age 0–17

ADHD Attention Deficit and Hyperactivity Disorder, a neurodevelopmental diagnostic category

A&E Accident and Emergency Departments, UK hospital term equivalent to ER (Emergency Room) or ED (Emergency Department)

Alters Dissociative parts of the person, with their own sense of identity, memory and subjectivity (see also EPs below)

ANPs Apparently Normal Parts of the personality which carry on with daily life, from the Structural Dissociation Model

ASD Autism Spectrum Disorder, a neurodevelopmental diagnostic category

AVH Auditory verbal hallucinations

BIMS Burnout, Inertia, Meltdown and Shutdown experiences for autistic people

CAMHS Child and Adolescent Mental Health services

CBT Cognitive-Behaviour Therapy

CPN Community Psychiatric Nurse (see also MHN below)

C-PTSD Complex Post Traumatic Stress Disorder, a DSM-5 diagnostic category

DBT Dialectical Behaviour Therapy

DES-II Dissociative Experiences Scale-II, a commonly used and freely available screening questionnaire

DSM-5 Diagnostic and Statistical Manual of the American Psychiatric Association Version 5, published in 2013

EbE Expert-by-Experience

EIP Early Intervention in Psychosis services

EMDR Eye-Movement Desensitisation and Reprocessing Therapy

EPs Emotional Parts, referring to similar experiences as the term Alters, from the Structural Dissociation Model

ESTD European Society for Trauma and Dissociation, with a UK branch, ESTD-UK

EUPD Emotionally Unstable Personality Disorder, an ICD-10 psychiatric diagnosis

FND Functional Neurological Disorder describes problems with how the brain receives and sends information to the rest of the body ('the software'), rather than damage to the structures of the brain ('the hardware')

FPP First Person Plural, a UK national charity for people with complex dissociation which ran between 1997–2023, and now has a legacy website

GP General Practitioner, the primary care doctor within the UK NHS system

IAPT Improving Access to Psychological Therapies services, now known as NHS Talking Therapies, provide NHS psychological therapies to people with mild to moderate mental health difficulties, and long-term physical health conditions

Iatrogenic When an intervention from a health-care professional even inadvertently, causes harm or retraumatisation

ICB Integrated Care Board. ICBs replaced clinical commissioning groups (CCGs) in 2022, to take on NHS planning functions in England. ICBs form part of an integrated care system (ICS), a partnership of organisations that come together to plan and deliver joined up health and care services within defined localities

ICD-11 International Classification of Disorders Version 11 of the World Health Organisation

Intersectionality Intersectionality refers to overlapping social identities (e.g., race, disability, age, ethnicity, gender, class, sexuality and immigration status) which intersect to shape unique experiences of oppression and privilege

IPV Intimate partner violence

ISSTD International Society for the Study of Trauma and Dissociation

MBT Mentalisation Based Therapy

MBU Mother and Baby Unit, an in-patient mental health unit where women are admitted for treatment, with their babies

MDT A multidisciplinary team made up of professionals from a range of backgrounds. In mental health services these often comprise psychological therapy, psychiatry, nursing, occupational therapy, social work and support staff

Mental Health Liaison Team A team of mental health professionals who in-reach to acute (physical health) hospitals; sometimes called Psychiatric Liaison teams

MHN Mental Health Nurse

NDD Neurodevelopmental difference, including ADHD and ASD (see above)

ORASC Offence-related altered states of consciousness

OSDD Other Specified Dissociative Disorder is a diagnostic category within DSM-5, replacing the DSM-4 diagnosis of Dissociative Disorder Not Otherwise Specified (DDNOS)

PTSD Post Traumatic Stress Disorder, a diagnostic category within both DSM-5 and ICD-11

Strange Situation Procedure   A research paradigm used to classify attachment status in young children through their response to reunion with their caregiver after a few minutes of absence

The Survivors Trust   An umbrella body representing organisations in the UK and Ireland who provide specialist support for women, men and children who have survived rape, sexual violence or childhood sexual abuse

TIC   Trauma-informed care is a policy emphasis for health and care interventions, which understands that trauma exposure can impact an individual's development across neurological, biological, psychological and social domains of life

VCSE   Voluntary, Community and Social Enterprise Sector, including charitable and not-for-profit organisations

References

Abel, K. M., Hope, H., Swift, E., Parisi, R., Ashcroft, D. M., Kosidou, K., Su Osam, C., Dalman, C., & Pierce, M. (2019). Prevalence of maternal mental illness among children and adolescents in the UK between 2005 and 2017: A National retrospective cohort analysis. *Lancet Public Health*, *4*, e291–e300. https://doi.org/10.1016/s2468-2667(19)30059-3

Abraham, H. D., & Joseph, A. B. (1986). Bulimic vomiting alters pain tolerance and mood. *International Journal of Psychiatry in Medicine*, *16*(4), 311–316. https://doi.org/10.2190/QG04-42KU-MKVR-CRHT

Abraham, S. F., & Beumont, P. J. (1982). How patients describe bulimia or binge eating. *Psychology Medicine*, *12*(3), 625–635. https://doi.org/10.1017/s0033291700055732

Achenbach, T. M., & Ruffle, T. M. (2000). The child behavior checklist and related forms for assessing behavioral/emotional problems and competencies. *Pediatrics in Review*, *21*(8), 265–271. https://doi.org/10.1542/pir.21.8.265

Akyüz, G., Doğan, O., Şar, V., Yargiç, L. l., & Tutkun, H. (1999). Frequency of dissociative identity disorder in the general population in Turkey. *Comprehensive Psychiatry*, *40*(2), 151–159. https://doi.org/10.1016/S0010-440X(99)90120-7

Al-Shamali, H. F., Winkler, O., Talarico, F., Greenshaw, A. J., Forner, C., Zhang, Y., ... & Burback, L. (2022). A systematic scoping review of dissociation in borderline personality disorder and implications for research and clinical practice: Exploring the fog. *Australian and New Zealand Journal of Psychiatry*, *56*(10), 1252–1264. https://doi.org/10.1177/00048674221077029

Allen, J. G. (2013). *Restoring Mentalizing in Attachment Relationships: Treating Trauma with Plain Old Therapy* (1st ed.). American Psychiatric Publishing. https://doi.org/10.1176/appi.books.9781615378227

American Psychiatric Association. (2013). *Diagnostic and Statistical Manual of Mental Disorders* (5th ed.). https://doi.org/10.1176/appi.books.9780890425596.

Anda, R. F., Felitti, V. J., Bremner, J. D., Walker, J. D., Whitfield, C., Perry, B. D., ... & Giles, W. H. (2006). The enduring effects of abuse and related adverse experiences in childhood. A convergence of evidence from neurobiology and epidemiology. *European Archives of Psychiatry and Clinical Neuroscience*, *256*(3), 174–186. https://doi.org/10.1007/s00406-005-0624-4

Antonovsky, A. (1987). *Unraveling the Mystery of Health: How People Manage Stress and Stay Well*. Jossey-Bass. Hoboken, New Jersey. https://doi.org/10.4135/9781446221129.n9

APA Presidential Task Force on Evidence-Based Practice. (2006). Evidence-based practice in psychology. *The American Journal of Psychiatry*, *61*(4), 271–285. https://doi.org/10.1037/0003-066X.61.4.271

Aquarone, R. (2020). *Dissociative Identity Disorder: Using the Countertransference.* www. pesi.co.uk/blog/2020/october/dissociative-identity-disorder-using-the-countertr

Aquarone, R., & Hughes, W. (2006). The history of dissociation and trauma in the UK and its impact on treatment. *Journal of Trauma Practice, 4,* 305–322. https://doi.org/10.1300/ j189v04n03_07

Arch, J. J. (2012). Are exposure-based cognitive behavioral therapies safe during pregnancy? *Archives Womens Mental Health, 15*(6), 445–457. https://doi.org/10.1007/ s00737-012-0308-9

Armstrong, J. G. (1996). Psychological assessment. In J. L. Spira & I. D. Yalom (Eds.), *Treating Dissociative Identity Disorder* (pp. 3–37). Jossey-Bass: Hoboken, New Jersey.

Armstrong, J. G. (2002). Deciphering the broken narrative of trauma: Signs of traumatic dissociation on the Rorschach. *Rorschachiana, 25*(1), 11–27. https://doi. org/10.1027/1192-5604.25.1.11

Armstrong, J. G., Putnam, F. W., Carlson, E. B., Libero, D. Z., & Smith, S. R. (1997). Development and validation of a measure of adolescent dissociation: The Adolescent Dissociative Experiences Scale. *Journal of Nervous and Mental Disease, 185*(8), 491–497. https://doi.org/10.1097/00005053-199708000-00003

Ashburn, A. (2023). Dissociated decision-making: Contract competency evaluations of individuals with Dissociative Identity Disorder. *Columbia Journal of Law and Social Problems, 56*(2), 195–243.

Aydin, A., & Kolburan, S. G. (2024). Dissociogenic effects of migration as a collective trauma on family dynamics. *Turkiye Klinikleri Psychology Special Topics, 9*(2), 122–128.

Ayers, S., Bond, R., Bertullies, S., & Wijma, K. (2016). The aetiology of post-traumatic stress following childbirth: A meta-analysis and theoretical framework. *Psychological Medicine, 46,* 1121–1134. https://doi.org/10.1017/s0033291715002706

Baars, E. W., van der Hart, O., Nijenhuis, E. R., Chu, J. A., Glas, G., & Draijer, N. (2011). Predicting stabilizing treatment outcomes for complex posttraumatic stress disorder and dissociative identity disorder: An expertise-based prognostic model. *Journal of Trauma Dissociation, 12*(1), 67–87. https://doi.org/10.1080/15299732.2010.514846

Backholm, K., Isomaa, R., & Birgegård, A. (2013). The prevalence and impact of trauma history in eating disorder patients. *European Journal of Psychotraumatology, 4,* 22482. https://doi.org/10.3402/ejpt.v4i0.22482

Badenes-Ribera, L., Molla-Esparza, C., Longobardi, C., Sánchez-Meca, J., & Fabris, M. A. (2021). Homicide as a source of posttraumatic stress?: A meta-analysis of the prevalence of posttraumatic stress disorder after committing homicide. *Journal of Traumatic Stress, 34*(2), 345–356. https://doi.org/10.1002/jts.22630

Bae, H., Kim, D., & Park, Y. C. (2016). Dissociation predicts treatment response in eye-movement desensitization and reprocessing for posttraumatic stress disorder. *Journal of Trauma Dissociation, 17*(1), 112–130. https://doi.org/10.1080/15299732.2015.1037039

Bailey, T. D., & Brand, B. L. (2017). Traumatic dissociation: Theory, research, and treatment. *Clinical Psychology: Science and Practice, 24*(2), 170–185. https://doi.org/ 10.1111/cpsp.12195

Bakaraki, M. P., Dourbois, T., & Kosiva, A. (2024). Attachment theory across cultures: An examination of cross-cultural perspectives and alloparenting practices (mini review). *Brazilian Journal of Science, 3*(8), 36–42. https://doi.org/10.14295/bjs.v3i8.616

Baker, E., & Beech, A. R. (2004). Dissociation and variability of adult attachment dimensions and early maladaptive schemas in sexual and violent offenders. *Journal of Interpersonal Violence, 19*(10), 1119–1136. https://doi.org/10.1177/0886260504269091

Baker, P., Cooper, V., Tsang, W., Garnett, I., & Blackman, N. (2021). A survey of complex trauma in families who have children and adults who have a learning disability and/or autism. *Advances in Mental Health and Intellectual Disabilities, 15*(5), 222–239. https://doi.org/10.1108/AMHID-07-2021-0032

Baladerian, N. J., Coleman, T. F., & Stream, J. (2013). *Abuse of People with Disabilities: Victims and Their Families Speak Out.* Spectrum Institute Disability and Abuse Project. https://to mcoleman.us/publications/2013-survey-report.pdf

Banasiak, B. S. (2022). The role of gender dysphoria in the development of an eating disorder. *American Journal of Psychiatry Residents Journal, 18*(1), 6–8. https://doi.org/10.1176/appi.ajp-rj.2022.180104

Baranyi, G., Cassidy, M., Fazel, S., Priebe, S., & Mundt, A. P. (2018). Prevalence of post-traumatic stress disorder in prisoners. *Epidemiologic Reviews, 40*(1), 134–145. https://doi.org/10.1093/epirev/mxx015

Bartels, R. M. (2021). Understanding sexual fantasising: Implications for forensic practice and research. In U. K, W. J. Smid, & K. McCartan (Eds.), *Challenges in the Management of People Convicted of a Sexual Offence: A Way Forward* (pp. 19–33). Palgrave Macmillan: London.

Bateman, A., & Fonagy, P. (2006). Mentalizing and borderline personality disorder. In *The handbook of mentalization-based treatment* (pp. 185–200). John Wiley. https://doi.org/10.1002/9780470712986.ch9

Bauer, A., Parsonage, M., Knapp, M., Iemmi, V., & Adelaja, B. (2014). *TThe Costs of Perinatal Mental Health Problems.* Centre for Mental Health and London School of Economics. https://eprints.lse.ac.uk/59885/1/__lse.ac.uk_storage_LIBRARY_Secondary_libfile_shared_repository_Content_Bauer%2C%20M_Bauer_Costs_perinatal_%20mental_2014_Bauer_Costs_perinatal_mental_2014_author.pdf

Baumeister, R. F. (1990). Suicide as escape from self. *Psychological Review, 97*(1), 90–113. https://doi.org/10.1037/0033-295X.97.1.90

Beail, N., Frankish, P., & Skelly, A. (2021). *Trauma and Intellectual Disability: Acknowledgement, Identification and Intervention.* Pavillion: London.

Becker-Blease, K., & Freyd, J. J. (2007). Dissociation and memory for perpetration among convicted sex offenders. *Journal of Trauma & Dissociation, 8*(2), 69–80. https://doi.org/10.1300/J229v08n02_05

Belli, H., Ural, C., Vardar, M. K., Yesılyurt, S., & Oncu, F. (2012). Dissociative symptoms and dissociative disorder comorbidity in patients with obsessive-compulsive disorder. *Comprehensive Psychiatry, 53*(7), 975–980. https://doi.org/10.1016/j.comppsych.2012.02.004

Benjamin, L. R., Benjamin, R., & Rind, B. (1998). The parenting experiences of mothers with dissociative disorders. *Journal of Marital and Family Therapy, 24*(3), 337–354. https://doi.org/10.1111/j.1752-0606.1998.tb01089.x

Berg, K. L., Shiu, C. S., Feinstein, R. T., Msall, M. E., & Acharya, K. (2018). Adverse childhood experiences are associated with unmet healthcare needs among children with autism spectrum disorder. *Journal of Pediatrics, 202*, 258–264.e251. https://doi.org/10.1016/j.jpeds.2018.07.021

Berger, D., Saito, S., Ono, Y., Tezuka, I., Shirahase, J., Kuboki, T., & Suematsu, H. (1994). Dissociation and child abuse histories in an eating disorder cohort in Japan. *Acta Psychiatrica Scandinavica, 90*(4), 274–280. https://doi.org/10.1111/j.1600-0447.1994.tb01593.x

Bernstein, E. M., & Putnam, F. W. (1986). Development, reliability, and validity of a dissociation scale. *Journal of Nervous and Mental Disease, 174*(12), 727–735. https://doi.org/10.1097/00005053-198612000-00004

Bestel, N. S. A., Williamson, D. C., Tirlea, L., & Mackelprang, J. L. (2025). Dissociation training and symptom identification accuracy among Australian psychologists. *Psychological Trauma, 17*(8), 1707–1716. https://doi.org/10.1037/tra0001717

Binet, E. (2023). *Early childhood crying and dissociative attunement: An alternative approach to our understanding of the emergence of dissociative processes.* 8th ESTD International Conference, 09–11 March, Brussels.

Bion, W. R. (1964). *Learning From Experience.* Karnac Books: Bicester, Oxfordshire. https://doi.org/10.4324/9781003411840

Bird, G. & Cook, R. (2013). Mixed emotions: The contribution of alexithymia to the emotional symptoms of autism. *Translational Psychiatry.* E285. https://doi.org/10.1038/TP.2013.61

Blaustein, M., & Kinniburgh, K. M. (2010). *Treating Traumatic Stress in Children and Adolescents: How to Foster Resilience Through Attachment, Self-regulation, and Competency.* Guilford Press: New York.

Bliss, E. L., & Larson, E. M. (1985). Sexual criminality and hypnotizability. *Journal of Nervous and Mental Disease, 173*(9), 522–526. https://doi.org/10.1097/00005053-198509000-00002

Bogar, K., & Dora, P. (2007). Trauma and psychosis. *Psychiatria Hungarica: A Magyar Pszichiatriai Tarsasag tudomanyos folyoirata, 22*(4), 300–310. https://europepmc.org/article/med/18167424

Boger, S., Ehring, T., Berberich, G., & Werner, G. G. (2020). Impact of childhood maltreatment on obsessive-compulsive disorder symptom severity and treatment outcome. *European Journal of Psychotraumatology, 11*(1), 1753942. https://doi.org/10.1080/20008198.2020.1753942

Boon, S. (2023). *Assessing Trauma-related Dissociation: With the Trauma and Dissociation Symptoms Interview (TADS-I).* W.W. Norton: New York.

Boon, S. & Draijer, N. (1993c). The differentiation of patients with MPD or DDNOS from patients with a cluster B Personality Disorder. *Dissociation, 6,* 2/3, 126–135. https://scholarsbank.uoregon.edu/server/api/core/bitstreams/aadc7c5d-0ad5-4341-8ba2-d09634e5b18e/content

Boon, S., Steele, K., & Van Der Hart, O. (2011). *Coping with Trauma-related Dissociation: Skills Training for Patients and Their Therapists* (1st ed.). W.W. Norton: New York.

Bor, R., & Stokes, A. (2010). *Setting Up in Independent Practice: A Handbook for Counsellors, Therapists and Psychologists.* Palgrave Macmillan: London.

Borsboom, D. (2017). A network theory of mental disorders. *World Psychiatry, 16*(1), 5–13. https://doi.org/10.1002/wps.20375

Bostock, J., & Armstrong, N. (2019). Developing trauma-informed care and adapted pathways using the Power, Threat, Meaning framework (Part 1: Being heard and understood differently). *Clinical Psychology Forum, 314,* 25–29. https://doi.org/10.53841/bpscpf.2019.1.314.25

Bourget, D., Gagné, P., & Wood, S. F. (2017). Dissociation: Defining the concept in criminal forensic psychiatry. *Journal of the Amercian Academy of Psychiatry and the Law, 45*(2), 147–160. https://pubmed.ncbi.nlm.nih.gov/28619854/

Bowlby, J. (1988). *A secure base: Parent-child attachment and healthy human development.* Basic Books: New York.

Bowman, E. S., & Markand, O. N. (1996). Psychodynamics and psychiatric diagnoses of pseudoseizure subjects. *The American Journal of Psychiatry, 153*(1), 57–63. https://doi.org/10.1176/ajp.153.1.57

Boyer, S. M., Caplan, J. E., & Edwards, L. K. (2022). Trauma-related dissociation and the dissociative disorders: Neglected symptoms with severe public health consequences. *Delaware Journal of Public Health*, *8*(2), 78–84. https://doi.org/10.32481/djph.2022.05.010

Bradley, R., Greene, J., Russ, E., Dutra, L., & Westen, D. (2005). A multidimensional meta-analysis of psychotherapy for PTSD. *The American Journal of Psychiatry*, *162*(2), 214–227. https://doi.org/10.1176/appi.ajp.162.2.214

Brand, L., B., McNary, S. W., Myrick, A. C., Classen, C. C., Lanius, R., ... & Putnam, F. W. (2013). A longitudinal naturalistic study of patients with dissociative disorders treated by community clinicians. *Psychological Trauma: Theory, Research, Practice, and Policy*, *5*, 301–308. https://doi.org/10.1037/a0027654

Brand, B. (2001). Establishing safety with patients with dissociative identity disorder. *Journal of Trauma Dissociation*, *2*(4), 133–155. https://doi.org/10.1300/J229v02n04_07

Brand, B. L. (2024). *The concise guide to the assessment and treatment of trauma-related dissociation*. American Psychological Association. https://doi.org/10.1037/0000386-000

Brand, B. L., Classen, C. C., McNary, S. W., & Zaveri, P. (2009). A review of dissociative disorders treatment studies. *Journal of Nervous and Mental Disease*, *197*(9), 646–654. https://doi.org/10.1097/NMD.0b013e3181b3afaa

Brand, B. L., & Lanius, R. A. (2014). Chronic complex dissociative disorders and borderline personality disorder: Disorders of emotion dysregulation? *Borderline Personality Disorder Emotional Dysregulation*, *1*, 13. https://doi.org/10.1186/2051-6673-1-13

Brand, B. L., Loewenstein, R. J., Schielke, H. J., Van der Hart, O., Nijenhuis, E. R. S., Schlumpf, Y. R., ... & Reinders, A. A. T. S. (2019). Cautions and concerns about Huntjens et al.'s schema therapy for dissociative identity disorder. *European Journal of the Psychotraumatology*, *10*(1), 1631698. https://doi.org/10.1080/20008198.2019.1631698

Brand, B. L., Loewenstein, R. J., & Spiegel, D. (2014). Dispelling myths about dissociative identity disorder treatment: An empirically based approach. *Psychiatry*, *77*(2), 169–189. https://doi.org/10.1521/psyc.2014.77.2.169

Brand, B. L., Sar, V., Stavropoulos, P., Krüger, C., Korzekwa, M., Martínez-Taboas, A., & Middleton, W. (2016). Separating fact from fiction: An empirical examination of six myths about dissociative identity disorder. *Harvard Review of Psychiatry*, *24*(4), 257–270. https://doi.org/10.1097/HRP.0000000000000100

Brand, B. L., Schielke, H. J., & Brams, J. S. (2017). Assisting the courts in understanding and connecting with experiences of disconnection: Addressing trauma-related dissociation as a forensic psychologist, Part I. *Psychological Injury and Law*, *10*(4), 283–297. https://doi.org/10.1007/s12207-017-9304-8

Brand, B. L., Schielke, H. J., Brams, J. S., & DiComo, R. A. (2017). Assessing trauma-related dissociation in forensic contexts: Addressing trauma-related dissociation as a forensic psychologist, Part II. *Psychological Injury and Law*, *10*(4), 298–312. https://doi.org/10.1007/s12207-017-9305-7

Brand, B. L., Schielke, H. J., Putnam, K., Pierorazio, N. A., Nester, M. S., Robertson, J., ... & Lanius, R. A. (2025). A randomized controlled trial assists individuals with complex trauma and dissociation in Finding Solid Ground. *Psychological Trauma: Theory, Research, Practice, and Policy*, *2025-02*. https://doi.org/10.1037/tra0001871

Brand, B. L., Schielke, H. J., Putnam, K. T., Putnam, F. W., Loewenstein, R. J., Myrick, A., ... & Lanius, R. A. (2019). An online educational program for individuals with dissociative disorders and their clinicians: 1-year and 2-year follow-up. *Journal of Trauma Stress*, *32*(1), 156–166. https://doi.org/10.1002/jts.22370

Brand, B. L., Schielke, H. J., Schiavone, F. L., & Lanius, R. A. (2022). *Finding solid ground: Overcoming obstacles in trauma treatment.* Oxford University Press: Oxford. https://doi.org/10.1093/med-psych/9780190636081.001.0001

Brand, B. L., Vissia, E. M., Chalavi, S., Nijenhuis, E. R., Webermann, A. R., Draijer, N., & Reinders, A. A. (2016). DID is trauma based: Further evidence supporting the trauma model of DID. *Acta Psychiatrica Scandinavica, 134*(6), 560–563. https://doi.org/10.1111/acps.12653

Brand, B. L., Webermann, A. R., & Frankel, A. S. (2016). Assessment of complex dissociative disorder patients and simulated dissociation in forensic contexts. *International Journal of the Law Psychiatry, 49*(Pt B), 197–204. https://doi.org/10.1016/j.ijlp.2016.10.006

Brandes, M., Soares, C. N., & Cohen, L. S. (2004). Postpartum onset obsessive-compulsive disorder. *Archives of Womens' Mental Health, 7,* 99–110. https://doi.org/10.1007/s00737-003-0035-3

Breitenbach, G., Rabe, M. J., & ProQuest. (2015). *Inside views from the dissociated worlds of extreme violence: human beings as merchandise* (1st ed.). Karnac Books: Bicester. https://doi.org/10.4324/9780429475986

Breslau, N., Kessler, R. C., Chilcoat, H. D., Schultz, L. R., Davis, G. C., & Andreski, P. (1998). Trauma and posttraumatic stress disorder in the community: The 1996 Detroit Area Survey of Trauma. *Archives of General Psychiatry, 55*(7), 626–632. https://doi.org/10.1001/archpsyc.55.7.626

Brewerton, T. D. (2023). The integrated treatment of eating disorders, posttraumatic stress disorder, and psychiatric comorbidity: A commentary on the evolution of principles and guidelines. *Frontiers in Psychiatry, 14,* 1149433. https://doi.org/10.3389/fpsyt.2023.1149433

Brewerton, T. D., Perlman, M. M., Gavidia, I., & Suro, G. (2024). The treatment of dissociative identity disorder in an eating disorder residential treatment setting. *International Journal of Eating Disorders, 57*(2), 450–457. https://doi.org/10.1002/eat.24106

Brewerton, T. D., Perlman, M. M., Gavidia, I., Suro, G., Genet, J., & Bunnell, D. W. (2020). The association of traumatic events and posttraumatic stress disorder with greater eating disorder and comorbid symptom severity in residential eating disorder treatment centers. *International Journal of Eating Disorders, 53*(12), 2061–2066. https://doi.org/10.1002/eat.23401

Brewin, C. R., & Andrews, B. (2017). Creating memories for false autobiographical events in childhood: A systematic review. *Applied Cognitive Psychology, 31*(1), 2–23. https://doi.org/10.1002/acp.3220

Brewin, C. R., Andrews, B., & Valentine, J. D. (2000). Meta-analysis of risk factors for posttraumatic stress disorder in trauma-exposed adults. *Journal of Consulting and Clinical Psychology, 68*(5), 748–766. https://doi.org/10.1037//0022-006x.68.5.748

Briere J., Johnson K., Bissada A., Damon L., Crouch J., Gil E., Hanson R., & Ernst V. (2001). The Trauma Symptom Checklist for Young Children (TSCYC): reliability and association with abuse exposure in a multi-site study. *Child Abuse Negl.* Aug; *25*(8), 1001–1014. doi: 10.1016/s0145-2134(01)00253-8. PMID: 11601594.

Briere, J., Weathers, F. W., & Runtz, M. (2005). Is dissociation a multidimensional construct? Data from the Multiscale Dissociation Inventory. *Journal of Trauma Stress, 18*(3), 221–231. https://doi.org/10.1002/jts.20024

Briere, J. N. (1992). *Abuse Trauma: Theory and Treatment of the Lasting Effects*. Sage: Thousand Oaks, CA.

Briere, John. (1996). Trauma Symptom Checklist for Children (TSCC). Journal of Abnormal Psychology Assessment of family violence: A handbook for researchers and practitioners. 10.1037/t06631-000.

British Psychological Society (2017). *Incorporating Attachment Theory into Practice: Clinical Practice Guideline for Clinical Psychologists working with People who have Intellectual Disabilities.* https://www.rcpsych.ac.uk/docs/default-source/members/faculties/intellectual-disability/bps-attachment-guidelines.pdf?sfvrsn=a83ef76b_2

Brokke, S. S., Bertelsen, T. B., Landrø, N. I., & Haaland, V. (2022). The effect of sexual abuse and dissociation on suicide attempt. *BMC Psychiatry, 22*(1), 29. https://doi.org/10.1186/s12888-021-03662-9

Brown, L. S. (2008). *Cultural Competence in Trauma Therapy: Beyond the Flashback* (1st ed.). American Psychological Association: Washington DC.

Browning, C. (1999, September). Floatback and float forward: Techniques for linking past, present and future. *EMDRIA Newsletter, 4*(3), 12,34. https://emdrtherapyvolusia.com/wp-content/uploads/2016/12/Floatback_and_Float.pdf

Bruneau, M.A., Desmarais, P., & Pokrzywko, K. (2020). Post-traumatic stress disorder mistaken for behavioural and psychological symptoms of dementia: case series and recommendations of care. *Psychogeriatrics*. Sep; 20(5), 754–759. doi: 10.1111/psyg.12549.

Brunner, R., Parzer, P., Schuld, V., & Resch, F. (2000). Dissociative symptomatology and traumatogenic factors in adolescent psychiatric patients. *Journal of Nervous and Mental Disease, 188*(2), 71–77. https://doi.org/10.1097/00005053-200002000-00002

Burton, N., & Lane, R. C. (2001). The relational treatment of dissociative identity disorder. *Clinical Psychology Review, 21*(2), 301–320. https://doi.org/10.1016/s0272-7358(99)00049-5

Byng-Hall, J. (1995). *Rewriting Family Scripts: Improvisation and Systems Change.* Guilford Press: New York.

Bækkelund, H., Ulvenes, P., Boon-Langelaan, S., & Arnevik, E. A. (2022). Group treatment for complex dissociative disorders: A randomized clinical trial. *BMC Psychiatry, 22*(1), 338. https://doi.org/10.1186/s12888-022-03970-8

Calati, R., Bensassi, I., & Courtet, P. (2017). The link between dissociation and both suicide attempts and non-suicidal self-injury: Meta-analyses. *Psychiatry Research, 251*, 103–114. https://doi.org/10.1016/j.psychres.2017.01.035

Calhoun, C. D., Stone, K. J., Cobb, A. R., Patterson, M. W., Danielson, C. K., & Bendezú, J. J. (2022). The role of social support in coping with psychological trauma: An integrated biopsychosocial model for posttraumatic stress recovery. *Psychiatric Quarterly, 93*(4), 949–970. https://doi.org/10.1007/s11126-022-10003-w

Campbell, M. C., Smakowski, A., Rojas-Aguiluz, M., Goldstein, L. H., Cardeña, E., Nicholson, T. R., ... & Pick, S. (2022). Dissociation and its biological and clinical associations in functional neurological disorder: Systematic review and meta-analysis. *BJPsych Open, 9*(1), e2. https://doi.org/10.1192/bjo.2022.597

Carlson, E. B., & Putnam, F. W. (1993). An update on the Dissociative Experiences Scale. *Dissociation: Progress in the Dissociative Disorders, 6*(1), 16–27. https://psycnet.apa.org/record/1994-27927-001

Carter, R. T. (2007). Racism and psychological and emotional injury: Recognizing and assessing race-based traumatic stress. *The Counseling Psychologist, 35*(1), 13–105. https://doi.org/10.1177/0011000006292033

Cations, M., Keage, H. A. D., Laver, K. E., Byles, J., & Loxton, D. (2022). Intimate partner violence and risk for mortality and incident dementia in older women. *Journal of Interpersonal Violence, 37*(5–6), Np2605–Np2625. https://doi.org/10.1177/0886260520943712

Cengiz, O., Jungilligens, J., Michaelis, R., Wellmer, J., & Popkirov, S. (2024). Dissociative seizures in the emergency room: Room for improvement. *Journal of Neurololy and Neurosurgical Psychiatry, 95*(4), 294–299. https://doi.org/10.1136/jnnp-2023-332063

Černis, E., Dunn, G., Startup, H., Kingdon, D., Wingham, G., Pugh, K., … & Freeman, D. (2014). Depersonalization in patients with persecutory delusions. *Journal of Nervous and Mental Disease, 202*(10), 752–758. https://doi.org/10.1097/NMD.0000000000000185

Černis, E., Ehlers, A., & Freeman, D. (2022). Psychological mechanisms connected to dissociation: Generating hypotheses using network analyses. *Journal of Psychiatric Research, 148*, 165–173. https://doi.org/10.1016/j.jpsychires.2022.01.049

Chaturvedi, S. K., & Sinha, P. (2011). Dissociative experiences and somatoform dissociation in non psychotic patients attending outpatient services. *Indian Journal of Social Psychiatry, 27*, 24–31.

Chien, W. T., & Fung, H. W. (2022). Commentary: The assessment of dissociative pathology in culturally and clinically diverse contexts. *Alpha Psychiatry, 23*(3), 104–105. https://doi.org/10.5152/alphapsychiatry.2022.0006

Choi, K. R., Seng, J. S., Briggs, E. C., Munro-Kramer, M. L., Graham-Bermann, S. A., Lee, R. C., & Ford, J. D. (2017). The dissociative subtype of Posttraumatic Stress Disorder (PTSD) among adolescents: Co-occurring PTSD, depersonalization/derealization, and other dissociation symptoms. *Journal of the Amercian Academy of Child and Adolescent Psychiatry, 56*(12), 1062–1072. https://doi.org/10.1016/j.jaac.2017.09.425

Choksi, T., DeBoos, D., & Langthorne, P. (2025). *Exploring changes in clinical practice from attending the complex trauma and dissociation supervision group: A service evaluation.* University of Nottingham.

Christofides, S., Johnstone, L., & Musa, M. (2012). 'Chipping in': Clinical psychologists' descriptions of their use of formulation in multidisciplinary team working. *Psychology and Psychotherapy, 85*(4), 424–435. https://doi.org/10.1111/j.2044-8341.2011.02041.x

Chu, J. A. (2011). *Rebuilding Shattered Lives: Treating Complex PTSD and Dissociative Disorders.* Wiley: New Jersey.

Chu, A., & DePrince, A. (2006). Development of dissociation: Examining the relationship between parenting, maternal trauma and child dissociation. *Journal of Trauma and Dissociation, 7*, 75–89. https://doi.org/10.4324/9781439804384-5

Clarke, I., & Nicholls, H. (2018). *Third Wave CBT Integration for Individuals and Teams.* Routledge: Oxfordshire.

Cloitre, M., Hyland, P., Prins, A., & Shevlin, M. (2021). The international trauma questionnaire (ITQ) measures reliable and clinically significant treatment-related change in PTSD and complex PTSD. *European Journal of Psychotraumatology, 12*(1). https://doi.org/10.1080/20008198.2021.1930961

Connor, T. S. (2015). Dissociation across the lifespan. *Johnson County Community College Honors Journal, 7*(1), Article 2. https://scholarspace.jccc.edu/honors_journal/vol7/iss1/2/

Convertino, A. D., & Mendoza, R. R. (2023). Posttraumatic stress disorder, traumatic events, and longitudinal eating disorder treatment outcomes: A systematic review. *International Journal of Eating Disorders, 56*(6), 1055–1074. https://doi.org/10.1002/eat.23933

Convertino, A. D., Morland, L. A., & Blashill, A. J. (2022). Trauma exposure and eating disorders: Results from a United States nationally representative sample. *International Journal of Eating Disorders, 55*(8), 1079–1089. https://doi.org/10.1002/eat.23757

Cook, J. M., McCarthy, E., & Thorp, S. R. (2017). Older adults with PTSD: Brief state of research and evidence-based psychotherapy case illustration. *Amercian Journal of Geriatric Psychiatry, 25*(5), 522–530. https://doi.org/10.1016/j.jagp.2016.12.016

Coons, P. M. (1996). *Depersonlization and Derealization.* Springer: New York.

Cooper, C., Selwood, A., Blanchard, M., & Livingston, G. (2010). Abusive behaviour experienced by family carers from people with dementia: The CARD (caring for relatives with dementia) study. *Journal of Neurology and Neurosurgical Psychiatry, 81*(6), 592–596. https://doi.org/10.1136/jnnp.2009.190934

Corrigan, F., & Hull, A. (2022). The shadow costs of dissociative identity disorder. *British Journal of Psychiatry, 220*(2), 98–98. https://doi.org/10.1192/bjp.2021.73

Corrigan, F. M., & Hull, A. M. (2015). Recognition of the neurobiological insults imposed by complex trauma and the implications for psychotherapeutic interventions. *BJPsych Bulletin, 39*(2), 79–86. https://doi.org/10.1192/pb.bp.114.047134

Corrigan, F. M., Young, H., & Christie-Sands, J. (2025). *Deep Brain Reorienting: Understanding the Neuroscience of Trauma, Attachment Wounding, and DBR Psychotherapy.* Routledge: Oxfordshire.

Cortizo, R. (2020). Hidden trauma, dissociation and prenatal assessment within the calming womb model. *Journal of Prenatal and Perinatal Psychology and Health, 34*, 1–12.

Cowles, M., Randle-Phillips, C., & Medley, A. (2020). Compassion-focused therapy for trauma in people with intellectual disabilities: A conceptual review. *Journal of Intellectual Disability, 24*(2), 212–232. https://doi.org/10.1177/1744629518773843

Cox, C., Bulluss, E., Chapman, F., Cookson, A., Flood, A., & Sharp, A. (2018). The Coventry grid for adults: A tool to guide clinicians in differentiating complex trauma and autism. *Good Autism Practice, 20*(1), 76–87. https://samsonandbulluss.com/application/files/1016/4799/7666/Cox_Bulluss_et_al_May_19_GAP.pdf

Craftman, Å, G., Swall, A., Båkman, K., Grundberg, Å., & Hagelin, C. L. (2020). Caring for older people with dementia reliving past trauma. *Nursing Ethics, 27*(2), 621–633. https://doi.org/10.1177/0969733019864152

Crenshaw, K. W. (2013). Mapping the margins: Intersectionality, identity politics and violence against women of colour. In M. A. Fineman (Ed.), *The Public Nature of Private Violence* (pp. 93–118). Routledge: Oxfordshire.

Crockford, H., Cairns, P., Kingerlee, R., & Goodwin, M. (2019). 'You have to start somewhere': A service improvement strategy for people with trauma-related dissociation in Norfolk. *Clinical Psychology Forum, 314*, 10–16. https://doi.org/10.53841/bpscpf.2019.1.314.10

Crompton, L., Lahav, Y., & Solomon, Z. (2017). Auditory hallucinations and PTSD in ex-POWS. *Journal of Trauma & Dissociation, 18*(5), 663–678. https://doi.org/10.1080/15299732.2016.1267682

Crumpler, D. (2022). *Petals of a Rose.* www.dylancrumpler.com

Cuartas, A. S. (2002). Dissociation in male batterers. *Dissertation Abstracts International: Section A, 62*, 1–171. https://doi.org/10.1037/e609242012-140

Dalenberg, C. J., Brand, B. L., Gleaves, D. H., Dorahy, M. J., Loewenstein, R. J., Cardeña, E., ... & Spiegel, D. (2012). Evaluation of the evidence for the trauma and fantasy models of dissociation. *Psychological Bulletin, 138*(3), 550–588. https://doi.org/10.1037/a0027447

Dalenberg, C. J., Brand, B. L., Loewenstein, R. J., Gleaves, D. H., Dorahy, M. J., Cardeña, E., ... & Spiegel, D. (2014). Reality versus fantasy: Reply to Lynn et al. (2014). *Psychological Bulletin, 140*(3), 911–920. https://doi.org/10.1037/a0036685

Dana, D. (2018). *The Polyvagal Theory in Therapy: Engaging the Rhythm of Regulation.* W W Norton: New York.

De Beurs, D., Cleare, S., Wetherall, K., Eschle-Byrne, S., Ferguson, E., O'Connor, D. B., & O'Connor, R. C. (2020). Entrapment and suicide risk: The development of the 4-item Entrapment Scale Short-Form (E-SF). *Psychiatry Research, 284.* https://doi.org/10.1016/j.psychres.2020.112765

De Geest, R. M., & Meganck, R. (2019). How do time limits affect our psychotherapies? A literature review. *Psychologica Belgica, 59*(1), 206–226. https://doi.org/10.5334/pb.475

De Jongh, A., Resick, P. A., Zoellner, L. A., van Minnen, A., Lee, C. W., Monson, C. M., ... & Bicanic, I. A. E. (2016). Critical analysis of the current treatment guidelines for complex PTSD in adults. *Depression and Anxiety, 33*(5), 359–369. https://doi.org/10.1002/da.22469

DeAngelis, T. (2007). A new diagnosis for childhood trauma? *Monitor on Psychology, 38*(3), 32. https://doi.org/10.1037/e599682007-021

Dell, P. F. (2002). Dissociative phenomenology of dissociative identity disorder. *Journal of Nervous and Mental Disease, 190*(1), 10–15. https://doi.org/10.1097/00005053-200201000-00003

Dell, P. F. (2006). The Multidimensional Inventory of Dissociation (MID): A comprehensive measure of pathological dissociation. *Journal of Trauma & Dissociation, 7*(2), 77–106. https://doi.org/10.1300/J229v07n02_06

Dell, P. F., & Eisenhower, J. W. (1990). Adolescent multiple personality disorder: A preliminary study of eleven cases. *Journal of the Amercian Academy of Child and Adolescent Psychiatry, 29*(3), 359–366. https://doi.org/10.1097/00004583-199005000-00005

Destrée, L., Brierley, M. E., Albertella, L., Jobson, L., & Fontenelle, L. F. (2021). The effect of childhood trauma on the severity of obsessive-compulsive symptoms: A systematic review. *Journal of the Psychiatric Research, 142,* 345-360. https://doi.org/10.1016/j.jpsychires.2021.08.017

Devillé, C., Moeglin, C., & Sentissi, O. (2014). Dissociative disorders: Between neurosis and psychosis, *Case Reports in Psychiatry, 425892,* https://doi.org/10.1155/2014/425892

Dong, X., Simon, M., Mendes de Leon, C., Fulmer, T., Beck, T., Hebert, L., ... & Evans, D. (2009). Elder self-neglect and abuse and mortality risk in a community-dwelling population. *JAMA, 302*(5), 517–526. https://doi.org/10.1001/jama.2009.1109

Donnellan, A. M., LaVigna, G. W., Negri-Shoultz, N., & Fassbender, L. L. (1988). *Progress Without Punishment: Effective Approaches for Learners with Behavior Problems.* Teachers College Press: New York.

Dorahy, M. J., Brand, B. L., Sar, V., Krüger, C., Stavropoulos, P., Martínez-Taboas, A., ... & Middleton, W. (2014). Dissociative identity disorder: An empirical overview. *Australian and New Zealand Journal of Psychiatry , 48*(5), 402–417. https://doi.org/10.1177/0004867414527523

Douglas, A. N. (2009). Racial and ethnic differences in dissociation: An examination of the dissociative experiences scale in a nonclinical population. *Journal of Trauma & Dissociation, 10*(1), 24–37. https://doi.org/10.1080/15299730802488452

Doychak, K., & Raghavan, C. (2023). Trauma-coerced attachment: Developing DSM-5's dissociative disorder "identity disturbance due to prolonged and intense coercive persuasion". *European Journal of Trauma & Dissociation, 7*(2). https://doi.org/10.1016/j.ejtd.2023.100323

Duckworth, M. P., Iezzi, T., Archibald, Y., Haertlein, P., & Klinck, A. (2000). Dissociation and posttraumatic stress symptoms in patients with chronic pain. *Journal of Rehabilitation and Health, 5*(2), 129–139. https://doi.org/10.1023/a:1012958206465

Dutra, L., Bureau, J. F., Holmes, B., Lyubchik, A., & Lyons-Ruth, K. (2009). Quality of early care and childhood trauma: A prospective study of developmental pathways to dissociation. *Journal of Nervous and Mental Disease, 197*(6), 383–390. https://doi.org/10.1097/NMD.0b013e3181a653b7

Dutton, M. A., Green, B. L., Kaltman, S. I., Roesch, D. M., Zeffiro, T. A., & Krause, E. D. (2006). Intimate partner violence, PTSD, and adverse health outcomes. *Journal of Interpersonal Violence, 21*(7), 955–968. https://doi.org/10.1177/0886260506289178

Edwards, D., Burnard, P., Hannigan, B., Cooper, L., Adams, J., Juggessur, T., ... & Coyle, D. (2006). Clinical supervision and burnout: The influence of clinical supervision for community mental health nurses. *Journal of Clinical Nursing, 15*(8), 1007–1015. https://doi.org/10.1111/j.1365-2702.2006.01370.x

Elmore, J. L. (2000). Dissociative spectrum disorders in the primary care s. *Primary Care Companion Journal of Clinical Psychiatry, 2*(2), 37–41. https://doi.org/10.4088/pcc.v02n0201

Elsouri, K. N., Heiser, S. E., Cabrera, D., Alqurneh, S., Hawat, J., & Demory, M. L. (2024). Management and treatment of obsessive-Compulsive Disorder (OCD): A literature review. *Cureus, 16*(5), e60496. https://doi.org/10.7759/cureus.60496

Emezi, A. (2018). *Freshwater*. Grove Press: New York..

Epstein, O. (2018). From proximity seeking to relationship seeking: Working towards separation from the 'scaregivers'. *Frontiers in the Psychotherapy of Trauma and Dissociation, 2*(1), 290–306. https://doi.org/10.46716/ftpd.2018.0016

Epstein, O. B., Schwartz, J., Schwartz, R. W., & John Bowlby, C. (2011). *Ritual abuse and mind control: The manipulation of attachment needs*. Karnac: London.

Erickson, E. (1997). *The life cycle completed*. W.W. Norton: New York.

European Society for Trauma and Dissociation. (2017). *Guidelines for the assessment and treatment of children and adolescents with dissociative symptoms and dissociative disorders*. www.estd.org/sites/default/files/files/estd_guidelines_child_and_adolescents_first_update_july_2.pdf

Everill, J., Waller, G., & Macdonald, W. (1995). Dissociation in bulimic and non-eating-disordered women. *International Journal of Eating Disorders, 17*(2), 127–134. https://doi.org/10.1002/1098-108X(199503)17:2<127::AID-EAT2260170204>3.0.CO;2-B

Facer-Irwin, E., Karatzias, T., Bird, A., Blackwood, N., & MacManus, D. (2022). PTSD and complex PTSD in sentenced male prisoners in the UK: Prevalence, trauma antecedents, and psychiatric comorbidities. *Psychology Medicine, 52*(13), 2794–2804. https://doi.org/10.1017/s0033291720004936

Fan, J. N. (2024). Caring for a patient with dissociate identity disorder at end of life. *Journal of Pain and Symptom Management, 67*(5), e738. https://doi.org/10.1016/j.jpainsymman.2024.02.229

Faris, P. L., Hofbauer, R. D., Daughters, R., Vandenlangenberg, E., Iversen, L., Goodale, R. L., ... & Hartman, B. K. (2008). De-stabilization of the positive vago-vagal reflex in bulimia nervosa. *Physiology & Behaviour, 94*(1), 136–153. https://doi.org/10.1016/j.physbeh.2007.11.036

Farrelly, S., Peters, E., Azis, M., David, A. S., & Hunter, E. C. M. (2024). A brief CBT intervention for depersonalisation-derealisation disorder in psychosis: Results from a feasibility randomised controlled trial. *Journal of Behavior Therapy and Experimental Psychiatry, 82*, 1–7. https://doi.org/10.1016/j.jbtep.2023.101911

Felitti, V. J., Anda, R. F., Nordenberg, D., Williamson, D. F., Spitz, A. M., Edwards, V., ... & Marks, J. S. (1998). Relationship of childhood abuse and household dysfunction to many of the leading causes of death in adults. The Adverse Childhood Experiences

(ACE) Study. *Amercian Journal of Preventive Medicine, 14*(4), 245–258. https://doi.org/10.1016/s0749-3797(98)00017-8

Ferster, C. B. (1973). A functional analysis of depression. *American Psychologist, 28*(10), 857-870. https://doi.org/10.1037/h0035605

Finlay, H. A. (2019). Recognising the territory: The interaction of trauma, attachment injury and dissociation in treating eating disorders. In A. Seubert & P. Virdi (Eds.), *Trauma-informed Approaches to Eating Disorders*. Springer: London.

First Person Plural. (2011). *A Logical Way of Being*. www.mairsinn.org.uk/publications.html

Fisher, J. (2017). *Healing the Fragmented Selves of Trauma Survivors: Overcoming Internal Self-alienation*. Routledge: Oxfordshire.

Fisher, J. (2021). *Transforming the living legacy of trauma: A workbook for survivors and therapists* (1st ed.). PESI: Eau Claire, WI.

Fleisher, W., Staley, D., Krawetz, P., Pillay, N., Arnett, J. L., & Maher, J. (2002). Comparative study of trauma-related phenomena in subjects with pseudoseizures and subjects with epilepsy. *Amercian Journal of Psychiatry, 159*(4), 660–663. https://doi.org/10.1176/appi.ajp.159.4.660

Fleurkens, P., Hendriks, L., & van Minnen, A. (2018). Eye movement desensitization and reprocessing (EMDR) in a forensic patient with posttraumatic stress disorder (PTSD) resulting from homicide: A case study. *Journal of Forensic Psychiatry & Psychology, 29*(6), 901–913. https://doi.org/10.1080/14789949.2018.1459786

Foote, B., Smolin, Y., Kaplan, M., Legatt, M. E., & Lipschitz, D. (2006). Prevalence of dissociative disorders in psychiatric outpatients. *Amercian Journal of Psychiatry, 163*(4), 623–629. https://doi.org/10.1176/ajp.2006.163.4.623

Foote, B., Smolin, Y., Neft, D. I., & Lipschitz, D. (2008). Dissociative disorders and suicidality in psychiatric outpatients. *Journal of Nervous and Mental Disease, 196*(1), 29–36. https://doi.org/10.1097/NMD.0b013e31815fa4e7

Ford, J. D. (2024). Inequity, intersectionality, trauma, and dissociation. *Journal of Trauma Dissociation, 25*(4), 419–421. https://doi.org/10.1080/15299732.2024.2357846

Forgash, C., & Copeley, M. (2008). *Healing the Heart of Trauma and Dissociation with EMDR and Ego State Therapy*. Springer: New Jersey.

Forner, C. (2023). *Dissociation 101*. International Society for the Study of Trauma and Dissociation. https://cfas.isst-d.org/content/dissociation-101-comprehensive-exploration-field-dissociation-and-complex-trauma-0

Fox, B. H., Perez, N., Cass, E., Baglivio, M. T., & Epps, N. (2015). Trauma changes everything: Examining the relationship between adverse childhood experiences and serious, violent and chronic juvenile offenders. *Child Abuse and Neglect, 46*, 163–173. https://doi.org/10.1016/j.chiabu.2015.01.011

Fox, R., Hyland, P., Coogan, A. N., Cloitre, M., & McHugh Power, J. (2022). Posttraumatic stress disorder, complex PTSD and subtypes of loneliness among older adults. *Journal of Clinical Psychology, 78*(2), 321–342. https://doi.org/10.1002/jclp.23225

Frankish, P. (2016). *Disability Psychotherapy: An Innovative Approach to Trauma Informed Care*. Karnac: London.

Frankish, P., & Sinason, V. (Eds.). (2017). *Holistic Therapy for People with Dissociative Identity Disorder*. Karnac: London.

Fraser, G. A. (2003). Fraser's "Dissociative table technique" revisited, revised: A strategy for working with ego states in dissociative disorders and ego-state therapy. *Journal of Trauma & Dissociation, 4*(4), 5–28. https://doi.org/10.1300/J229v04n04_02

Frewen, P., & Lanius, R. (2015). *Healing the Traumatized Self: Consciousness, Neuroscience, Treatment*. W. W. Norton: New York.

Frewen, P. A., & Lanius, R. A. (2014). Trauma-related altered states of consciousness: exploring the 4-D model. *Journal of Trauma & Dissociation, 15*(4), 436–456. https://doi.org/10.1080/15299732.2013.873377

Freyd, J. J. (1996). *Betrayal Trauma: The Logic of Forgetting Childhood Abuse.* Harvard University Press: Cambridge, MA.

Friedrich, W. N., Gerber, P. N., Koplin, B., Davis, M., Giese, J., Mykelbust, C., & Franckowiak, D. (2001). Multimodal assessment of dissociation in adolescents: Inpatients and juvenile sex offenders. *Sex Abuse, 13*(3), 167–177. https://doi.org/10.1177/1079063 20101300302

Fuller-Tyszkiewicz, M., & Mussap, A. J. (2008). The relationship between dissociation and binge eating. *Journal of Trauma Dissociation, 9*(4), 445–462. https://doi.org/10.1080/ 15299730802226084

Fung, H. W., Ross, C. A., & Ling, H. W.-H. (2019). Complex dissociative disorders in social work: Discovering the knowledge gaps. *Social Work in Mental Health, 17*(6), 682–702. https://doi.org/10.1080/15332985.2019.1658689

Gómez, A., & Hosey, J. (2025). *The Handbook of Complex Trauma and Dissociation in Children: Theory, Research and Clinical Applications.* Routledge: Oxfordshire.

Garety, P. A., Kuipers, E., Fowler, D., Freeman, D., & Bebbington, P. E. (2001). A cognitive model of the positive symptoms of psychosis. *Psychological Medicine, 31*(2), 189–195. https://doi.org/10.1017/S0033291701003312

Gatrad, A. R., & Sheikh, A. (2001). Medical ethics and Islam: Principles and practice. *Archives Disorders Child, 84*(1), 72–75. https://doi.org/10.1136/adc.84.1.72

Gavin, N. I., Gaynes, B. N., Lohr, K. N., Meltzer-Brody, S., Gartlehner, G., & Swinson, T. (2005). Perinatal depression: A systematic review of prevalence and incidence. *Obstetics and Gynecology, 106*(5), 1071–1083. https://doi.org/10.1097/01.aog.0000183597.31630.db

Gerhardt, S. (2004). *Why Love Matters: How Affection Shapes a Baby's Brain* (1st ed.). Brunner-Routledge: Hove, East Sussex.

Gershuny, B. S., Baer, L., Jenike, M. A., Minichiello, W. E., & Wilhelm, S. (2002). Comorbid posttraumatic stress disorder: impact on treatment outcome for obsessive-compulsive disorder. *Amercian Journal of Psychiatry, 159*(5), 852–854. https://doi.org/10.1176/appi. ajp.159.5.852

Gilbert, P. (2020). Compassion: From its evolution to a psychotherapy. *Frontiers in Psychology, 11*, 586161. https://doi.org/10.3389/fpsyg.2020.586161

Gilbert, P. (2022). Introducing and developing CFT functions and competencies. In P. Gilbert & G. Simos (Eds.), *Compassion Focused Therapy: Clinical Practice and Applications.* Routledge.

Gilbert, P., & Leahy, R. L. (2007). *The Therapeutic Relationship in the Cognitive Behavioral Psychotherapies.* Routledge: Oxfordshire.

Gilmoor, A. R., Adithy, A., & Regeer, B. (2019). The cross-cultural validity of post-traumatic stress disorder and post-traumatic stress symptoms in the Indian context: A systematic search and review. *Front Psychiatry, 10*, 439. https://doi.org/10.3389/ fpsyt.2019.00439

Goff, P. A., Jackson, M. C., Di Leone, B. A. L., Culotta, C. M., & DiTomasso, N. A. (2014). The essence of innocence: Consequences of dehumanizing Black children. *Journal of Personality and Social Psychology, 106*(4), 526–545. https://doi.org/10.1037/a0035663

Goffinet, S. J. L., & Beine, A. (2018). Prevalence of dissociative symptoms in adolescent psychiatric inpatients. *European Journal of Trauma and Dissociation, 2*, 39–45. https:// doi.org/10.1016/j.ejtd.2017.10.008

Golding, K. S., & Hughes, D. (2012). *Creating Loving Attachments: Parenting with PACE to Nurture Confidence and Security in the Troubled Child.* Jessica Kingsley: London.

Gómez, A., & Hosey, J. (2025). *The Handbook of Complex Trauma and Dissociation in Children: Theory, Research and Clinical Application.* Routledge: Oxfordshire.

Gómez, J. M., Gobin, R. L., & Barnes, M. L. (2021). Discrimination, violence, & healing within marginalized communities. *Journal of Trauma & Dissociation, 22*(2), 135–140. https://doi.org/10.1080/15299732.2021.1869059

Gonzalez-Vazquez, A. I., Rodriguez-Lago, L., Seoane-Pillado, M. T., Fernández, I., García-Guerrero, F., & Santed-Germán, M. A. (2017). The progressive approach to EMDR group therapy for complex trauma and dissociation: A case-control study. *Frontiers in Psychology, 8,* 2377. https://doi.org/10.3389/fpsyg.2017.02377

Goodwin, M. (2011). The other 8600 hours- everyday societal challenges of living with complex dissociation. *Attachment: New Directions in Relational Psychoanalysis and Psychotherapy, 5,* 70–74. https://pep-web.org/browse/AJRPP/volumes/5

Gore, N. J., Sapiets, S. J., Denne, L. D., Hastings, R. P., Toogood, S., MacDonald, A., ... & Group. (2022). Positive Behavioural Support in the UK: A state of the nation report. *International Journal of Positive Behavioural Support, 12*(1), 4–39. https://kar.kent.ac.uk/93504/

Graf, G. H., Chihuri, S., Blow, M., & Li, G. (2021). Adverse childhood experiences and justice system contact: A systematic review. *Pediatrics, 147*(1). https://doi.org/10.1542/peds.2020-021030

Groth, T., Hilsenroth, M., Boccio, D., & Gold, J. (2020). Relationship between trauma history and eating disorders in adolescents. *Journal of Child and Adolescent Trauma, 13*(4), 443–453. https://doi.org/10.1007/s40653-019-00275-z

Hagan, M. J., Hulette, A. C., & Lieberman, A. F. (2015). Symptoms of dissociation in a high-risk sample of young children exposed to interpersonal trauma: Prevalence, correlates, and contributors. *Journal of Traumatic Stress, 28*(3), 258–261. https://doi.org/10.1002/jts.22003

Hall, J. C., Jobson, L., & Langdon, P. E. (2014). Measuring symptoms of post-traumatic stress disorder in people with intellectual disabilities: The development and psychometric properties of the Impact of Event Scale-Intellectual Disabilities (IES-IDs). *British Journal of Clinical Psychology, 53*(3), 315–332. https://doi.org/10.1111/bjc.12048

Hallings-Pott, C., Waller, G., Watson, D., & Scragg, P. (2005). State dissociation in bulimic eating disorders: An experimental study. *International Journal of Eating Disorders, 38*(1), 37–41. https://doi.org/10.1002/eat.20146

Hanson, E. (2025). *Organised Ritual Abuse and Its Wider Context: Degradation, Deception and Disavowal.* NAPAC and the Hydrant Programme. www.hydrantprogramme.co.uk/assets/NPCC-Organised-ritual-abuse-and-its-wider-context-Degradation-deception-and-disavowal-July-2025-v2.pdf

Hardy, A. (2017). Pathways from trauma to psychotic experiences: A theoretically informed model of posttraumatic stress in psychosis. *Frontiers in Psychology, 8.* https://doi.org/10.3389/fpsyg.2017.00697

Hardy, A., Fowler, D., Freeman, D., Smith, B., Steel, C., Evans, J., ... & Dunn, G. (2005). Trauma and hallucinatory experience in psychosis. *Journal of Nervous and Mental Disease, 193*(8), 501–507. https://doi.org/10.1097/01.nmd.0000172480.56308.21

Hasler, J. (2022). A journey of discovery. In V. Sinason & R. P. Marks (Eds.), *Treating Children with Dissociative Disorders: Attachment, Trauma, Theory and Practice,* (pp. 200). Routledge: Oxfordshire.

Hasler, J., & Hendry, A. (2017). *Creative Therapies for Complex Trauma: Helping Children and Families in Foster Care, Kinship or Adoption*. Jessica Kingsley: London.

Hatch, R., Young, D., Barber, V., Griffiths, J., Harrison, D. A., & Watkinson, P. (2018). Anxiety, depression and post traumatic stress disorder after critical illness: A UK-wide prospective cohort study. *Critical Care, 22*(1), 310. https://doi.org/10.1186/s13 054-018-2223-6

Haven, T. J. (2009). "That part of the body is just gone": Understanding and responding to dissociation and physical health. *Journal of Trauma & Dissociation, 10*(2), 204–218. https://doi.org/10.1080/15299730802624569

Hayward, L. (2019). The legacies of loss, trauma, and the hidden selves. *Faculty of the Psychology of Older People, 146*, 34–48. https://doi.org/10.53841/bpsfpop.2019.1.146.34

Health and Safety Executive. (2020). *Protecting Lone Workers: How to Manage the Risks of Working Alone*. www.hse.gov.uk/pubns/indg73.htm

Health Education England. (2020a). *Multi-professional Approved/Responsible Clinician Implementation Guide*. Health Education England. https://www.hee.nhs.uk/sites/default/files/documents/Multi%20Professional%20Approved%20Responsible%20Clinician%20Implementation%20Guide.pdf

Health Education England. (2020b). *The Competence Framework for Mental Health Peer Support Workers*. Health Education England. www.hee.nhs.uk/sites/default/files/documents/The%20Competence%20Framework%20for%20MMH%20PSWs%20Part%202%20-%20Full%20listing%20of%20the%20competences.pdf

Heard, D., McCluskey, U., & Lake, B. (2009). *Attachment Therapy with Adolescents and Adults: Theory and Practice Post Bowlby*. Routledge: Oxfordshire.

Heatherton, T. F., & Baumeister, R. F. (1991). Binge eating as escape from self-awareness. *Psychological Bulletin, 110*(1), 86–108. https://doi.org/10.1037/0033-2909.110.1.86

Hegeman, E. (2013). Ethnic syndromes as disguise for protest against colonialism: Three ethnographic examples. *Journal of Trauma & Dissociation, 14*(2), 138–146. https://doi.org/10.1080/15299732.2013.724340

Hellström, L. (2019). A systematic review of polyvictimization among children with attention deficit hyperactivity or autism spectrum disorder. *International Journal of Environmental Research Public Health, 16*(13). https://doi.org/10.3390/ijerph16132280

Henrich, J. P. (2020). *The WEIRDest people in the world: How the West became psychologically peculiar and particularly prosperous*. Farrar, Straus and Giroux: New York.

Herman, J. (2023). *Truth and Repair: How Trauma Survivors Envision Justice*. Basic Books: New York.

Herman, J. L. (1992). *Trauma and Recovery*. Basic Books: New York.

Hesse, E., & Main, M. (1999). Second-generation effects of unresolved trauma in nonmaltreating parents: Dissociated, frightened, and threatening parental behavior. *Psychoanalytic Inquiry, 19*(4), 481–540. https://doi.org/10.1080/07351699909534265

Hesse, E., & Main, M. (2000). Disorganized infant, child, and adult attachment: Collapse in behavioral and attentional strategies. *Journal of the American Psychoanalytic Association, 48*(4), 1097–1127. https://doi.org/10.1177/00030651000480041101

Hesse, E., & Main, M. (2006). Frightened, threatening and dissociative parental behavior: Theory and associations with parental adult attachment interview status and infant disorganization, *Development and Psychopathology, 18*, 309–343. https://doi.org/10.1017/s0954579406060172

Higgins, J. M., Arnold, S. R., Weise, J., Pellicano, E., & Trollor, J. N. (2021). Defining autistic burnout through experts by lived experience: Grounded Delphi method investigating #AutisticBurnout. *Autism : The International Journal of Research and Practice*, *25*(8), 2356–2369. https://doi.org/10.1177/13623613211019858

Hill, J. (2020). *See What You Made Me Do: Power, Control and Domestic Abuse*. Hurst: London.

Hinton, D. E., & Lewis-Fernández, R. (2011). The cross-cultural validity of posttraumatic stress disorder: implications for DSM-5. *Depress Anxiety*, *28*(9), 783–801. https://doi.org/10.1002/da.20753

Hiroeh, U., Appleby, L., Mortensen, P. B., & Dunn, G. (2001). Death by homicide, suicide, and other unnatural causes in people with mental illness: A population-based study. *Lancet*, *358*(9299), 2110–2112. https://doi.org/10.1016/s0140-6736(01)07216-6

Hoeboer, C. M., De Kleine, R. A., Molendijk, M. L., Schoorl, M., Oprel, D. A. C., Mouthaan, J., ... & Van Minnen, A. (2020). Impact of dissociation on the effectiveness of psychotherapy for post-traumatic stress disorder: Meta-analysis. *BJPsych Open*, *6*(3), e53. https://doi.org/10.1192/bjo.2020.30

Holmes, E. A., Brown, R. J., Mansell, W., Fearon, R. P., Hunter, E. C., Frasquilho, F., & Oakley, D. A. (2005). Are there two qualitatively distinct forms of dissociation? A review and some clinical implications. *Clinical Psychology Review*, *25*(1), 1–23. https://doi.org/10.1016/j.cpr.2004.08.006

Hornstein, N. L., & Putnam, F. W. (1992). Clinical phenomenology of child and adolescent dissociative disorders. *Journal of the Amercian Academy Child and Adolescent Psychiatry*, *31*(6), 1077–1085. https://doi.org/10.1097/00004583-199211000-00013

Howell, E. F. (2005). *The Dissociative Mind*. Analytic Press: Piedmont, CA.

Howell, E. F. (2011). *Understanding and Treating Dissociative Identity Disorder: A Relational Approach*. Routledge: Oxfordshire.

Howell, E. F., & Itzkiwitz, S. (2016). *The Dissociative Mind in Psychoanalysis: Understanding and Working with Trauma*. Routledge/Taylor & Francis: Abingdon, Oxfordshire.

Hronis, A., Roberts, L., & Kneebone, II. (2017). A review of cognitive impairments in children with intellectual disabilities: Implications for cognitive behaviour therapy. *The British Journal of Psychiatry*, *56*(2), 189–207. https://doi.org/10.1111/bjc.12133

Hudson, M., Skelly, A., & Shimmens, V. (2024). Intellectual disability revisited: The emotional development approach. *The Psychologist, November 2024*. www.bps.org.uk/psychologist-issue/2024/november/psychologist-november-2024

Hughes, D. (2011). *Attachment-focused Family Therapy Workbook*. WW Norton: New York.

Hughes, D. A. (1997). *Facilitating Developmental Attachment: The Road to Emotional Recovery and Behavioral Change in Foster and Adopted Children*. Jason Aronson: Lanham, MD.

Hughes, D. A., & Baylin, J. (2012). *Brain-based Parenting: The Neuroscience of Caregiving for Healthy Attachment*. W. W. Norton & Company: New York.

Hulette, A. C., Kaeler, L. A., & Freyd, J. J. (2011). Intergenerational associations between trauma and dissociation, *Journal of Family Violence*, *26*, 217–225. https://doi.org/10.1007/s10896-011-9357-5

Huntjens, R. J. C., Rijkeboer, M. M., & Arntz, A. (2019). Schema therapy for Dissociative Identity Disorder (DID): Rationale and study protocol. *European Journal of the Psychotraumatology*, *10*(1), 1571377. https://doi.org/10.1080/20008198.2019.1571377

Hurcombe, R., Redmond, T., Rodger, H., & King, S. (2023). Institutional responses to child sexual abuse in ethnic minority communities. In A. K. Gill & H. Begum (Eds.),

Child Sexual Abuse in Black and Minoritised Communities: Improving Legal, Policy and Practical Responses (pp. 217–248). Palgrave Macmillan: Basingstoke.

Implementing Recovery through Organisational Change Programme. (2013). *Peer Support Workers: A Practical Guide to Implementation.* https://static1.squarespace.com/static/65e873c27971d37984653be0/t/668ce1d012bd721c16847151/1720508881816/7-Peer-Support-Workers-a-practical-guide-to-implementation.pdf

International Society for the Study of Trauma and Dissociation. (2004). Guidelines for the evaluation and treatment of dissociative symptoms in children and adolescents. *Journal of Trauma and Dissociation, 5*(3), 119–150. https://doi.org/10.1300/j229v01n03_09

International Society for the Study of Trauma and Dissociation. (2011). Guidelines for treating dissociative identity disorder in adults, third revision. *Journal of Trauma and Dissociation, 12*(2), 115–187. https://doi.org/10.1080/15299732.2011.537247

International Society for Traumatic Stress Studies. (2019). *ISTSS Guidelines Position Paper on Complex PTSD in Adults.* https://istss.org/wp-content/uploads/2024/08/ISTSS-Guidelines-Position-Paper-on-Compex-PTSD-in-Adults.pdf

Jahoda, A., Stenfert-Kroese, B., & Pert, C. (2017). *Cognitive Behaviour Therapy for People with Intellectual Disabilities: Thinking Creatively.* Palgrave Macmillan: Basingstoke.

Janssen, I., Krabbendam, L., Bak, M., Hanssen, M., Vollebergh, W., de Graaf, R., & van Os, J. (2004). Childhood abuse as a risk factor for psychotic experiences. *Acta Psychiatrica Scandinavica, 109*(1), 38–45. https://doi.org/10.1046/j.0001-690x.2003.00217.x

Jepsen, E. K., Langeland, W., & Heir, T. (2014). Early traumatized inpatients high in psychoform and somatoform dissociation: Characteristics and treatment response. *Journal of Trauma & Dissociation, 15*(5), 572–587. https://doi.org/10.1080/15299732.2014.924461

Jespersen, A. F., Lalumière, M. L., & Seto, M. C. (2009). Sexual abuse history among adult sex offenders and non-sex offenders: a meta-analysis. *Child Abuse and Neglect, 33*(3), 179–192. https://doi.org/10.1016/j.chiabu.2008.07.004

Johnson, D. (2001). Trauma, dissociation and learning disability. *Clinical Psychology Forum, 147*, 18–21. https://doi.org/10.53841/bpscpf.2001.1.147.18

Johnson, J., Chaudieu, I., Ritchie, K., Scali, J., Ancelin, M. L., & Ryan, J. (2020). The extent to which childhood adversity and recent stress influence all-cause mortality risk in older adults. *Psychoneuroendocrinology, 111*, 104492. https://doi.org/10.1016/j.psyneuen.2019.104492

Johnson, J. G., Cohen, P., Kasen, S., & Brook, J. S. (2006). Dissociative disorders among adults in the community, impaired functioning, and axis I and II comorbidity. *Journal of Psychiatric Research, 40*(2), 131–140. https://doi.org/10.1016/j.jpsychires.2005.03.003

Johnstone, L., & Boyle, M. (2020). *The Power Threat Meaning Framework.* BPS Books. Leicester.

Johnstone, L., & Dallos, R. (2006). *Formulation in Psychology and Psychotherapy: Making Sense of People's Problems.* Routledge: Abingdon, Ox.

Jones, I., Chandra, P. S., Dazzan, P., & Howard, L. (2014). Bipolar disorder, affective psychosis, and schizophrenia in pregnancy and the post-partum period. *The Lancet, 384*(9956), 1789–1799. https://doi.org/10.1016/s0140-6736(14)61278-2

Jones, L. (2022). Trauma-informed risk assessment and intervention: Understanding the role of triggering contexts and offence-related altered states of consciousness (ORASC). In Wilmot, P. & Jones, L. (Eds.) *Trauma-informed Forensic Practice* (pp. 49–73). Routledge: Abingdon, Ox. https://doi.org/10.4324/9781003120766-5

Kadri, A., Gracey, F., & Leddy, A. (2025). What factors are associated with posttraumatic growth in older adults? A systematic review. *Clinical Gerontology, 48*(1), 4–21. https://doi.org/10.1080/07317115.2022.2034200

Kandeğer, A., Boysan, M., Karaoğlan, G., Tekdemir, R., Şen, B., Tan, Ö., ... & Selvi, Y. (2022). Heterogeneity of associations between dissociation and attention deficit symptoms. *Current Psychology*, *Nov 10*, 1–14. https://doi.org/10.1007/s12144-022-03836-y

Karatzias, T., Power, K., Woolston, C., Apurva, P., Begley, A., Mirza, K., ... & Purdie, A. (2018). Multiple traumatic experiences, post-traumatic stress disorder and offending behaviour in female prisoners. *Criminal Behaviour Mental Health*, *28*(1), 72–84. https://doi.org/10.1002/cbm.2043

Karpman, S. (1968). Fairy tales and script drama analysis. *Transactional Analysis Bulletin*, *7*(26), 39–43. https://karpmandramatriangle.com/pdf/DramaTriangle.pdf

Kate, M. A., Hopwood, T., & Jamieson, G. (2020). The prevalence of Dissociative Disorders and dissociative experiences in college populations: A meta-analysis of 98 studies. *Journal of Trauma & Dissociation*, *21*(1), 16–61. https://doi.org/10.1080/15299 732.2019.1647915

Kate, M. A., Jamieson, G., Dorahy, M. J., & Middleton, W. (2021). Measuring dissociative symptoms and experiences in an Australian college sample using a short version of the multidimensional inventory of dissociation. *Journal of Trauma & Dissociation*, *22*(3), 265–287. https://doi.org/10.1080/15299732.2020.1792024

Kate, M. A., Jamieson, G., & Middleton, W. (2021). Childhood sexual, emotional, and physical abuse as predictors of dissociation in adulthood. *Journal of Child Sexual Abuse*, *30*(8), 953–976. https://doi.org/10.1080/10538712.2021.1955789

Katehakis, A. (2016). *Sex Addiction as Affect Dysregulation: A Neurobiologically Informed Holistic Treatment*. W. W. Norton: New York.

Kearney, B. E., & Lanius, R. A. (2022). The brain-body disconnect: A somatic sensory basis for trauma-related disorders. *Frontiers in Neuroscience*, *16*, 1015749. https://doi.org/10.3389/fnins.2022.1015749

Kendall-Tackett, K., & Klest, B. (2009). Causal mechanisms and multidirectional pathways between trauma, dissociation, and health. *Journal of Trauma & Dissociation*, *10*(2), 129–134. https://doi.org/10.1080/15299730802624510

Kennedy, F., Kennerley, H., Pearson, D., & ProQuest. (2013). *Cognitive Behavioural Approaches to the Understanding and Treatment of Dissociation* (1st ed.). Routledge: Abingdon, Ox.

Kerig, P. K. (2019). Linking childhood trauma exposure to adolescent justice involvement: The concept of posttraumatic risk-seeking. *Clinical Psychology Science Practice*, *26*, e12280. https://doi.org/10.1037/h0101756

Kerns, C. M., Lankenau, S., Shattuck, P. T., Robins, D. L., Newschaffer, C. J., & Berkowitz, S. J. (2022). Exploring potential sources of childhood trauma: A qualitative study with autistic adults and caregivers. *Autism*, *26*(8), 1987–1998. https://doi.org/10.1177/136236 13211070637

Keuroghlian, A. S., Kamen, C. S., Neri, E., Lee, S., Liu, R., & Gore-Felton, C. (2011). Trauma, dissociation, and antiretroviral adherence among persons living with HIV/AIDS. *Journal of the Psychiatric Research*, *45*(7), 942–948. https://doi.org/10.1016/j.jpsychires.2011.05.003

Kezelman, C., & Stavropoulos, P. (2019). *Practice Guidelines for the Clinical Treatment of Complex Trauma*. Blueknot Foundation. https://blueknot.org.au/product/practice-guidelines-for-clinical-treatment-of-complex-trauma-digital-download/

Kezelman, C., & Stavropoulos, P. (2020). *Practice guidelines for identifying and treating complex trauma-related dissociation*. Blueknot Foundation. https://blueknot.org.au/product/practice-guidelines-for-identifying-and-treating-complex-trauma-related-dissociation-digital-download/

Killian, K., Hernandez-Wolfe, P., Engstrom, D., & Gangsei, D. (2017). Development of the Vicarious Resilience Scale (VRS): A measure of positive effects of working with trauma survivors. *Psychology Trauma, 9*(1), 23–31. https://doi.org/10.1037/tra0000199

Kinnaird, E., Stewart, C., & Tchanturia, K. (2019). Investigating alexithymia in autism: A systematic review and meta-analysis. *European Psychiatry, 55,* 80–89. https://doi.org/10.1016/j.eurpsy.2018.09.004

Kirschen, G. W., Shorey, M. E., Han, J., Leppla, I., Masear, C. G., & Robinson, J. (2023). Dissociative identity precipitated by emergence from general anesthesia: A case report and analytical framework. *Psychiatry Research Case Report, 2*(2), 100152. https://doi.org/10.1016/j.psycr.2023.100152

Kleindienst, N., Limberger, M. F., Ebner-Priemer, U. W., Keibel-Mauchnik, J., Dyer, A., Berger, M., ... & Bohus, M. (2011). Dissociation predicts poor response to Dialectial Behavioral Therapy in female patients with Borderline Personality Disorder. *Journal of Personlity Disorders, 25*(4), 432–447. https://doi.org/10.1521/pedi.2011.25.4.432

Kluft, R. (1994). Treatment trajectories in the multiple personality disorder. *Dissociation: Progress in the Dissociative Disorders, 7*(1), 63–76. https://scholarsbank.uoregon.edu/server/api/core/bitstreams/c6bd8346-c819-44dd-9ac1-7ab6253ccb6d/content

Kluft, R. (2005). Diagnosing Dissociative Identity Disorder: Understanding and assessing manifestations can help clinicians identify and treat patients more effectively. *Psychiatric Annals, 35*(8), 633–643. https://doi.org/10.3928/00485713-20050801-05

Kluft, R. P. (1983). Hypnotherapeutic crisis intervention in multiple personality. *American Journal of Clinical Hypnosis, 26*(2), 73–83. https://doi.org/10.1080/00029157.1983.10404147

Kluft, R. P. (1985). *The natural history of multiple personality disorder*. In Kluft, R. (Ed.), *Childhood Antecedents of Multiple Personality Disorders* (pp 198–238). American Psychiatric Press Inc.: Washington DC.

Kluft, R. P. (1987). First-rank symptoms as a diagnostic clue to multiple personality disorder. *The American Journal of Psychiatry, 144*(3), 293–298. https://doi.org/10.1176/ajp.144.3.293

Kluft, R. P. (1987). The parental fitness of mothers with multiple personality disorder: A preliminary study. *Child Abuse and Neglect, 11*(2), 273–280. https://doi.org/10.1016/0145-2134(87)90067-6

Kluft, R. P. (1988). On treating the older patient with multiple personality disorder: "Race against time" or "make haste slowly". *American Journal of Clinical Hypnosis, 30*(4), 257–266. https://doi.org/10.1080/00029157.1988.10402748

Kluft, R. P. (1993). The initial stages of psychotherapy in the treatment of multiple personality disorder patients. *Dissociation: Progress in the Dissociative Disorders, 6*(2–3), 145–161. https://psycnet.apa.org/record/1995-10404-001

Kluft, R. P. (2007). The older female patient with a complex chronic dissociative disorder. *Journal of Women Aging, 19*(1–2), 119–137. https://doi.org/10.1300/J074v19n01_08

Koenig, H. G. (2018). *Religion and Mental Health: Research and Clinical Applications*. Elsevier Academic Press: Amsterdam.

Kovács-Tóth, B., Oláh, B., Kuritárné Szabó, I., & Túry, F. (2022). Adverse childhood experiences increase the risk for eating disorders among adolescents. *Frontiers in Psychology, 13,* 1063693. https://doi.org/10.3389/fpsyg.2022.1063693

Krishnamurthy, K., & Kumar, V. (2023). DID and religion: Possession. In H. Tohid & I. H. Rutkofsky (Eds.), *Dissociative Identity Disorder* (pp. 169–173). Springer: London.

Krüger, C. (2020). Culture, trauma and dissociation: A broadening perspective for our field. *Journal of Trauma & Dissociation, 21*(1), 1–13. https://doi.org/10.1080/15299 732.2020.1675134

Kumar, S. A., Brand, B. L., & Courtois, C. A. (2022). The need for trauma training: Clinicians' reactions to training on complex trauma. *Psychologica Trauma, 14*(8), 1387–1394. https://doi.org/10.1037/tra0000515

Kuroda, I., Hashimoto, M., Sato, A., Tachi, N., Okuni, N., Tashiro, H., … & Okuda, M. (2022). General anesthesia for a dissociative identity disorder patient with 20 personalities: A case report. *Anesthesia Progress, 69*(2), 30–34. https://doi.org/10.2344/ anpr-68-04-04

Laddis, A., & Dell, P. F. (2012). Dissociation and psychosis in dissociative identity disorder and schizophrenia. *Journal of Trauma & Dissociation, 13*(4), 397–413. https://doi.org/ 10.1080/15299732.2012.664967

Lammy, D. (2017). *The Lammy Review: An Independent Review into the Treatment of, and Outcomes for Black, Asian and Minority Ethnic Individuals in the Criminal Justice System.* https://assets.publishing.service.gov.uk/media/5a82009040f0b62305b91f49/ lammy-review-final-report.pdf

LaMotte, A. D., & Murphy, C. M. (2017). Trauma, posttraumatic stress disorder symptoms, and dissociative experiences during men's intimate partner violence perpetration. *Psychologica Trauma, 9*(5), 567–574. https://doi.org/10.1037/tra0000205

Langdon, P. E., Bisson, J. I., Rogers, G., Swain, S., Hiles, S., Watkins, A., & Willner, P. (2023). Evaluation of an adapted version of the International Trauma Questionnaire for use by people with intellectual disabilities. *British Journal of Psychiatry, 62*(2), 471–482. https://doi.org/10.1111/bjc.12421

Langeland, W., Jepsen, E. K. K., Brand, B. L., Kleven, L., Loewenstein, R. J., Putnam, F. W., … & Heir, T. (2020). The economic burden of dissociative disorders: A qualitative systematic review of empirical studies. *Psychologica Trauma, 12*(7), 730–738. https:// doi.org/10.1037/tra0000556

Lanius, R. A. (2015). Trauma-related dissociation and altered states of consciousness: A call for clinical, treatment, and neuroscience research. *European Journal of Psychotraumatology, 6*, 27905. https://doi.org/10.3402/ejpt.v6.27905

Lanius, R. A., Brand, B., Vermetten, E., Frewen, P. A., & Spiegel, D. (2012). The dissociative subtype of posttraumatic stress disorder: Rationale, clinical and neurobiological evidence, and implications. *Depression Anxiety, 29*(8), 701–708. https://doi.org/10.1002/da.21889

Lanius, R. A., Vermetten, E., & Pain, C. (2010). *The Impact of Early Life Trauma on Health and Disease: The Hidden Epidemic.* Cambridge University Press: Cambridge.

Lapp, L. K., Agbokou, C., & Ferreri, F. (2011). PTSD in the elderly: The interaction between trauma and aging. *International Psychogeriatrics, 23*(6), 858–868. https://doi. org/10.1017/s1041610211000366

Leibowitz, G. S., Laser, J. A., & Burton, D. L. (2011). Exploring the relationships between dissociation, victimization, and juvenile sexual offending. *Journal of Trauma & Dissociation, 12*(1), 38–52. https://doi.org/10.1080/15299732.2010.496143

Leonard, D., Brann, S., & Tiller, J. (2005). Dissociative disorders: Pathways to diagnosis, clinician attitudes and their impact. *Australian and New Zealand Journal of Psychiatry, 39*(10), 940–946. https://doi.org/10.1080/j.1440-1614.2005.01700.x

Levenson, J. S., Willis, G. M., & Prescott, D. S. (2016). Adverse childhood experiences in the lives of male sex offenders: Implications for trauma-informed care. *Sexual Abuse: Journal of Research and Treatment, 28*(4), 340–359. https://doi.org/10.1177/1079063214535819

Levine, P. (1997). *Waking the Tiger*. North Atlantic Books: Berkeley, CA.

Levine, P.A. and Kline, M. (2006). *Trauma Through a Child's Eyes: Awakening the Ordinary Miracle of Healing*. USA: North Atlantic Books: Berkeley, CA.

Levinson, C. A., & Brosof, L. C. (2016). Cultural and ethnic differences in eating disorders and disordered eating behaviors. *Current Psychiatry Reviews, 12*(2), 163–174. https://doi.org/10.2174/1573400512666160216234238

Lewis, A. J., Austin, E., Knapp, R., Vaiano, T., & Galbally, M. (2015). Perinatal maternal mental health, fetal programming and child development. *Healthcare, 3*, 1212–122. https://doi.org/10.3390/healthcare3041212

Lewis, Y. D., Kapon, S., Enoch-Levy, A., Yaroslavsky, A., Witztum, E., & Stein, D. (2021). Dissociation and suicidality in eating disorders: The mediating function of body image disturbances, and the moderating role of depression and anxiety. *Journal of Clinical Medicine, 10*(17). https://doi.org/10.3390/jcm10174027

Lewis-Fernández, R., Gorritz, M., Raggio, G. A., Peláez, C., Chen, H., & Guarnaccia, P. J. (2010). Association of trauma-related disorders and dissociation with four idioms of distress among Latino psychiatric outpatients. *Culture, Medicine and Psychiatry, 34*(2), 219–243. https://doi.org/10.1007/s11013-010-9177-8

Lewis-Fernández, R., Martínez-Taboas, A., Sar, V., Patel, S., & Boatin, A. (2007). The Cross-cultural Assessment of Dissociation. Springer Science & Business Media: Berlin. https://doi.org/10.1007/978-0-387-70990-1_12

Lezak, M. D., Howieson, D. B., Bigler, E. D., & Tranel, D. (2012). *Neuropsychological Assessment* (5th ed). Oxford University Press: Oxford.

Linnington, M. (2025). Using an attachment based model to understand and work with people with dissociative identities. In S. Richardson, M. Goodwin, J. E, & M. Jowett (Eds.), *Dissociative Identities: Attachment-based Approaches to Psychotherapy*. Routledge: Abingdon, Ox.

Liotti, G. (2006). A model of dissociation based on attachment theory and research. *Journal of Trauma & Dissociation, 7*(4), 55–73. https://doi.org/10.1300/J229v07n04_04

Liotti, G. (2009). Attachment and dissociation. In P.F. Dell and J. A. O'Neil (Eds.), *Dissociation and the Dissociative Disorders: DSM-V and Beyond* (pp. 53–65). Routledge/Taylor & Francis Group: Abingdon, Ox.

Liotti, G. (2017). Conflicts between motivational systems related to attachment trauma: Key to understanding the intra-family relationship between abused children and their abusers. *Journal of Trauma & Dissociation, 18*(3), 304–318. https://doi.org/10.1080/15299732.2017.1295392

Liotti, G., & Gilbert, P. (2011). Mentalizing, motivation, and social mentalities: Theoretical considerations and implications for psychotherapy. *Psychology and Psychotherapy: Theory, Research and Practice, 84*(1), 9–25. https://doi.org/10.1348/147608310x520094

Lipsanen, T., Korkeila, J., Peltola, P., Järvinen, J., Langen, K., & Lauerma, H. (2004). Dissociative disorders among psychiatric patients. *European Psychiatry, 19*(1), 53–55. https://doi.org/10.1016/j.eurpsy.2003.09.004

Liu, X., & Le, T. P. (2024). Internalized racism, racial collective self-esteem, and Asian American adults' disordered eating: Psychological distress as mediator. *Appetite, 201*, 107623. https://doi.org/10.1016/j.appet.2024.107623

Lloyd, M. (2016). Reducing the cost of dissociative identity disorder: Measuring the effectiveness of specialized treatment by frequency of contacts with mental health services. *Journal of Trauma & Dissociation, 17*(3), 362–370. https://doi.org/10.1080/15299 732.2015.1108947

Lloyd, M. (2019). Living with dissociative identity disorder: A client's and therapist's perspective. *Clinical Psychology Forum, 314,* 5–9. https://doi.org/10.53841/bpscpf.2019.1.314.5

Loewenstein, R. J. (1993). Dissociation, development, and the psychobiology of trauma. *Journal of Amercian Academy Psychoanalogy, 21*(4), 581–603. https://doi.org/10.1521/ jaap.1.1993.21.4.581

Loewenstein, R. (2005). Psychopharmacologic treatments for dissociative identity disorder. *Psychiatric Annals, 35,* 666–673. 10.3928/00485713-20050801-08

Loewenstein, R. J. (2006). DID 101: A hands-on clinical guide to the stabilization phase of dissociative identity disorder treatment. *Psychiatric Clinics of North Amercia, 29*(1), 305–332, xii. https://doi.org/10.1016/j.psc.2005.10.005

Loewenstein, R. J. (2018). Dissociation debates: Everything you know is wrong. *Dialogues Clinical Neuroscience, 20*(3), 229–242. https://doi.org/10.31887/DCNS.2018.20.3/rloew enstein

Loewenstein, R. J., & Putnam, F. (2004). The dissociative disorders. In B. J. Kaplan & V. A. Saddock (Eds.), *Comprehensive Textbook of Psychiatry* (8th ed., pp. 1844–1901). Lippincott, Williams & Wilkins: Philipdelphia.

Loewenstein, R. J., & Putnam, F. W. (2023). Discrete behavioral states theory. In M. Dorahy., S. N. Gold & J.A., O'Neil (Eds.), *Dissociation and the Dissociative Disorders: Past, Present, Future* (2nd ed., pp. 281–296). Routledge: Abingdon, Ox.

Longden, E., Branitsky, A., Moskowitz, A., Berry, K., Bucci, S., & Varese, F. (2020). The relationship between dissociation and symptoms of psychosis: A meta-analysis. *Schizophrenia Bulletin, 46*(5), 1104–1113. https://doi.org/10.1093/schbul/sbaa037

Longden, E., Corstens, D., Bowe, S., Pyle, M., Emsley, R., Peters, S., … & Morrison, A. P. (2022). A psychological intervention for engaging dialogically with auditory hallucinations (Talking With Voices): A single-site, randomised controlled feasibility trial. *Schizophrenia Research, 250,* 172–179. https://doi.org/10.1016/j.schres.2022.11.007

Longden, E., Madill, A., & Waterman, M. G. (2012). Dissociation, trauma, and the role of lived experience: Toward a new conceptualization of voice hearing. *Psychological Bulletin, 138*(1), 28–76. https://doi.org/10.1037/a0025995

Longo, P., Marzola, E., De Bacco, C., Demarchi, M., & Abbate-Daga, G. (2020). Young patients with anorexia nervosa: The contribution of post-traumatic stress disorder and traumatic events. *Medicina (Kaunas), 57*(2). https://doi.org/10.3390/medicina57010002

Lord, C., Kennedy, F., Smart, K., & Maguire, T. (2025). Developing a scale to measure dissociation between self-states (the Dissociation-Integration of Self States scale, D-ISS Scale). *The Cognitive Behaviour Therapist, 18,* e-18. https://doi.org/10.1017/ s1754470x25000042

Lucre, K., & Clapton, N. (2021). The Compassionate Kitbag: A creative and integrative approach to compassion-focused therapy. *Psychol Psychother, 94*(Suppl 2), 497–516. https://doi.org/10.1111/papt.12291

Ludäscher, P., Bohus, M., Lieb, K., Philipsen, A., Jochims, A., & Schmahl, C. (2007). Elevated pain thresholds correlate with dissociation and aversive arousal in patients with borderline personality disorder. *Psychiatry Research, 149*(1–3), 291–296. https://doi.org/ 10.1016/j.psychres.2005.04.009

Lupien, S. J., McEwen, B. S., Gunnar, M. R., & Heim, C. (2009). Effects of stress throughout the lifespan on the brain, behaviour and cognition. *Nature Review Neuroscience, 10*(6), 434–445. https://doi.org/10.1038/nrn2639

Lyssenko, L., Schmahl, C., Bockhacker, L., Vonderlin, R., Bohus, M., & Kleindienst, N. (2018). Dissociation in psychiatric disorders: A meta-analysis of studies using the dissociative experiences scale. *Amercian Journal of Psychiatry, 175*(1), 37–46. https://doi.org/10.1176/appi.ajp.2017.17010025

Mahler, M., Pine, F., & Bergman, A. (1979). *The Psychological Birth of the Human Infant: Symbiosis and Individuation.* Basic Books: New York.

Malvaso, C. G., Cale, J., Whitten, T., Day, A., Singh, S., Hackett, L., … & Ross, S. (2022). Associations between adverse childhood experiences and trauma among young people who offend: A systematic literature review. *Trauma Violence Abuse, 23*(5), 1677–1694. https://doi.org/10.1177/15248380211013132

Mann, B. J., & Sanders, S. (1994). Child dissociation and the family context. *Journal of Abnormal Child Psychol, 22*(3), 373–388. https://doi.org/10.1007/BF02168080

Martin, H., Hillman, S., Cross, R., & Anderson, K. (2022). The manifestations and correlates of dissociation amongst looked-after children in middle childhood. *European Journal of Trauma & Dissociation, 6*(1), 100232. https://doi.org/10.1016/j.ejtd.2021.100232

Martinez-Clarvera, C., James, S., Bowditch, E., & Kuruvilla, T. (2017). Delayed-onset post-traumatic stress disorder symptoms in dementia. *Progress in Neurology and Psychiatry, 21*(3), 26–31. https://doi.org/10.1002/pnp.477

Martínez-Taboas, A., Canino, G., Wang, M. Q., García, P., & Bravo, M. (2006). Prevalence and victimization correlates of pathological dissociation in a community sample of youths. *Journal of Trauma Stress, 19*(4), 439–448. https://doi.org/10.1002/jts.20144

Marysko, M., Reck, C., Mattheis, V., Finke, P., Resch, F., & Moehler, E. (2010). History of child abuse is accompanied by increased dissociation in young mothers 5 months postnatally. *Psychopathology, 43,* 104–109.

Mason, J., & Scior, K. (2004). 'Diagnostic overshadowing' amongst clinicians working with people with learning disabilities in the UK. *Journal of Applied Research in Intellectual Disabilities, 17,* 85–90.

Maté, G. (2022). *The Myth of Normal: Trauma, Illness & Healing in a Toxic Culture.* Ebury Digital: London.

Maves, P. A. (2024). ISSTD' S professional training program: Beginnings and future directions. *Journal of Trauma & Dissociation, 25*(1), 1–5. https://doi.org/10.1080/15299732.2023.2234595

McCallum, K. E., Lock, J., Kulla, M., Rorty, M., & Wetzel, R. D. (1992). Dissociative symptoms and disorders in patients with eating disorders. *Dissociation, 5*(4), 227–235. https://scholarsbank.uoregon.edu/server/api/core/bitstreams/e3e04827-d6ba-4dc6-bea8-602ef3431c69/content

McDonnell, C. G., Boan, A. D., Bradley, C. C., Seay, K. D., Charles, J. M., & Carpenter, L. A. (2019). Child maltreatment in autism spectrum disorder and intellectual disability: Results from a population-based sample. *Journal of Child and Psychology Psychiatry, 60*(5), 576–584. https://doi.org/10.1111/jcpp.12993

McFetridge, M., Hauenstein Swan, A., Heke, S., Karatzias, T., Greenberg, N., … & Morley, R. (2017). *Guidelines for the Treatment and Planning of Services for Complex post-traumatic Stress Disorder in Adults.* UKPTS. https://ray.yorksj.ac.uk/id/eprint/4862/

McGilvery, S. (2018). *The Identification and Treatment of Trauma in Individuals with Developmental Disabilities.* NADD Press.

McInnis, E. (2016). Effectiveness of individual psychodynamic psychotherapy in disability psychotherapy. *Advances in Mental Health and Intellectual Disabilities, 10*(2), 128–144. https://doi.org/10.1108/amhid-09-2015-0047

McMaugh, K., Roufeil, L., Salter, M., & Middleton, W. (2024). Incestuous abuse continuing into adulthood: Clinical features and therapists' conceptualisations. *Journal of Trauma & Dissociation, 25*(5), 535–550. https://doi.org/10.1080/15299732.2024.2341221

McNally, P. (2022). *A Framework for the Implementation of Trauma-informed Care in Residential and Supported Living Services for Adults with a Learning Disability.* Ulster University. https://pure.ulster.ac.uk/files/118300516/jppi.12457.pdf

McNally, P., Taggart, L., & Shevlin, M. (2021). Trauma experiences of people with an intellectual disability and their implications: A scoping review. *Journal of the Applied Research and Intellectual Disability, 34*(4), 927–949. https://doi.org/10.1111/jar.12872

Mental Capacity Act, United Kingdom Parliament c. 9. (2005). www.opsi.gov.uk/acts/acts2 005/20050009.htm

Metzl, J. (2009). The Protest Psychosis: How Schizophrenia Became a Black Disease. Boston: Beacon Press.

Mevissen, L., Ooms-Evers, M., Serra, M., de Jongh, A., & Didden, R. (2020). Feasibility and potential effectiveness of an intensive trauma-focused treatment programme for families with PTSD and mild intellectual disability. *European Journal of Psychotraumatology, 11*(1), 1777809. https://doi.org/10.1080/20008198.2020.1777809

Meyer, O. L., & Zane, N. (2013). The influence of race and ethnicity in clients' experiences of mental health treatment. *Journal of Community Psychology, 41*(7), 884–901. https://doi.org/10.1002/jcop.21580

Miller, A. (2018). *Healing the Unimaginable: Treating Ritual Abuse and Mind Control* (1st ed.). Routledge: Abingdon, Ox.

Miller, J. (2021). *Dear Little Ones (Book 1): Hope, Help and Healing for Your Inner Children.* Multifaceted Press.

Miller, M. L., & Brock, R. L. (2017). The effect of trauma on the severity of obsessive-compulsive spectrum symptoms: A meta-analysis. *Journal of Anxiety Disorders, 47*, 29–44. https://doi.org/10.1016/j.janxdis.2017.02.005

Milton, D. E. M. (2012). On the ontological status of autism: the 'double empathy problem.' *Disability & Society, 27*(6), 883–887. https://doi.org/10.1080/09687 599.2012.710008

Minio-Paluello, I., Porciello, G., Pascual-Leone, A., & Baron-Cohen, S. (2020). Face individual identity recognition: A potential endophenotype in autism. *Molecularr Autism, 11*(1), 81. https://doi.org/10.1186/s13229-020-00371-0

Mitchell, J. W., Ali, F., & Cavanna, A. E. (2012). Dissociative experiences and quality of life in patients with non-epileptic attack disorder. *Epilepsy & Behavior, 25*(3), 307–312. https://doi.org/10.1016/j.yebeh.2012.08.022

Mitchell, S., & Crockford, H. (2019). Editorial. *Clinical Psychology Forum, 314*, 1–2. https://doi.org/10.53841/bpscpf.2019.1.314.1

Mitchell, S., & Steele, K. (2021). Mentalising in complex trauma and dissociative disorders. *European Journal of Trauma & Dissociation, 5*(3), Article 100168. https://doi.org/10.1016/j.ejtd.2020.100168

Molendijk, M. L., Hoek, H. W., Brewerton, T. D., & Elzinga, B. M. (2017). Childhood maltreatment and eating disorder pathology: A systematic review and dose-response meta-analysis. *Psychological Medicine, 47*(8), 1402–1416. https://doi.org/10.1017/s00332 91716003561

Morrison, A. P., Frame, L., & Larkin, W. (2003). Relationships between trauma and psychosis: A review and integration. *British Journal of Clinical Psychology, 42*(4), 331–353. https://doi.org/10.1348/014466503322528892

Moskowitz, A. (2004). Dissociation and violence: A review of the literature. *Trauma Violence Abuse, 5*(1), 21–46. https://doi.org/10.1177/1524838003259321

Moskowitz, A., & Corstens, D. (2007). Auditory hallucinations: Psychotic symptom or dissociative experience? *Journal of Psychological Trauma, 6*(2–3), 35–63. https://doi.org/10.1300/J513v06n02_04

Moskowitz, A., & Montirosso, R. (2019). Childhood experiences and delusions: Trauma, memory, and the double bind. In *Psychosis, trauma and dissociation: Evolving perspectives on severe psychopathology, 2nd ed.* (pp. 117–140). Wiley Blackwell. https://doi.org/10.1002/9781118585948.ch8

Mosquera, D. (2019). *Working With Voices and Dissociative Parts: A Trauma Informed Approach.* INTRA-TP: S.L.

Mosquera, D., Gonzalez, A., & Leeds, A. M. (2014). Early experience, structural dissociation, and emotional dysregulation in borderline personality disorder: the role of insecure and disorganized attachment. *Borderline Personality Disorder Emotional Dysregulation, 1*, 15. https://doi.org/10.1186/2051-6673-1-15

Moulton, S. J., Newman, E., Power, K., Swanson, V., & Day, K. (2015). Childhood trauma and eating psychopathology: A mediating role for dissociation and emotion dysregulation? *Child Abuse and Neglect, 39*, 167–174. https://doi.org/10.1016/j.chiabu.2014.07.003

Mueller, C., Moergeli, H., Assaloni, H., Schneider, R., & Rufer, M. (2007). Dissociative disorders among chronic and severely impaired psychiatric outpatients. *Psychopathology, 40*(6), 470–471. https://doi.org/10.1159/000108129

Music, G. (2024). Unsafe foetuses and risky wombs? Why we need to take prenatal experiences more seriously, especially when working with adoption. *International Journal of Birth and Parent Education, 12*(1), 29–32. https://ijbpe.com/journals/volume-12/83-vol-12-issue-1

Myrick, A. C., Brand, B. L., McNary, S. W., Classen, C. C., Lanius, R., Loewenstein, R. J., … & Putnam, F. W. (2012). An exploration of young adults' progress in treatment for dissociative disorder. *Journal of Trauma & Dissociation, 13*(5), 582–595. https://doi.org/10.1080/15299732.2012.694841

Myrick, A. C., Webermann, A. R., Langeland, W., Putnam, F. W., & Brand, B. L. (2017). Treatment of dissociative disorders and reported changes in inpatient and outpatient cost estimates. *European Journal of Psychotraumatology, 8*(1), 1375829. https://doi.org/10.1080/20008198.2017.1375829

Myrick, A. C., Webermann, A. R., Loewenstein, R. J., Lanius, R., Putnam, F. W., & Brand, B. L. (2017). Six-year follow-up of the treatment of patients with dissociative disorders study. *European Journal of Psychotraumatology, 8*(1), 1344080. https://doi.org/10.1080/20008198.2017.1344080

Naish, S., Jefferies, R., Evans, M., & Well-being, C. (2017). *Charley Chatty and the Disappearing Pennies: A Story About Lying and Stealing.* Jessica Kingsley: London.

National Health Service Act (2006). House of Commons, UK Parliament. https://www.legislation.gov.uk/ukpga/2006/41/contents

Nester, M. S., Brand, B. L., Schielke, H. J., & Kumar, S. (2022). An examination of the relations between emotion dysregulation, dissociation, and self-injury among dissociative disorder patients. *European Journal of Psychotraumatology, 13*(1), 2031592. https://doi.org/10.1080/20008198.2022.2031592

Nester, M. S., Hawkins, S. L., & Brand, B. L. (2022). Barriers to accessing and continuing mental health treatment among individuals with dissociative symptoms. *European Journal of Psychotraumatology*, *13*(1), 2031594. https://doi.org/10.1080/20008198.2022.2031594

Newman-Taylor, K., & Sambrook, S. (2013). The role of dissociation in psychosis; implications for clinical practice. In F. Kennedy, H. Kennerley, & D. Pearson (Eds.), *Cognitive Behavioural Approaches to the Understanding and Treatment of Dissociation*. Routledge: Abingdon, Ox.

NHS Education for Scotland. (2017). *Transforming Psychological Trauma: A Knowledge and Skills Framework for the Scottish Workforce*. NHS Education for Scotland. https://www.nes.scot.nhs.uk/media/rgxngvpv/nationaltraumatrainingframework-execsummary-web.pdf

NHS Education for Scotland. (2023). *A Roadmap for Creating Trauma-informed and Responsive Change: Guidance for Organisations, Systems and Workforces in Scotland*. NHS Education for Scotland. www.traumatransformation.scot/implementation/

NHS England. (2019). *The NHS Long Term Plan*. www.longtermplan.nhs.uk/publications/nhs-long-term-plan

NHS England. (2022). *Psychological Therapies for Severe Mental Health Problems (PTSMHP) Implementation Guidance*. www.england.nhs.uk/long-read/implementation-guidance-2024-psychological-therapies-for-severe-mental-health-problems/

NHS England. (2024). *Health and Care Passport*. www.england.nhs.uk/long-read/health-and-care-passport-plain-english

NICE. (2018). *Post-traumatic Stress Disorder: NG116*. www.nice.org.uk/guidance/ng116/chapter/Recommendations#care-for-people-with-ptsd-and-complex-needs

NICE (2020). *Antenatal and Postnatal Mental Health: Clinical Management and Service Guidance: CG192*. www.nice.org.uk/guidance/cg192

Nijenhuis, E. R., Spinhoven, P., van Dyck, R., van der Hart, O., & Vanderlinden, J. (1998). Degree of somatoform and psychological dissociation in dissociative disorder is correlated with reported trauma. *Journal of the Trauma Stress*, *11*(4), 711–730. https://doi.org/10.1023/A:1024493332751

Nijenhuis, E. R. S. (1999). *Somatoform Dissociation: Phenomena, Measurement, and Theoretical Issues*. Van Gorcum: Assen, Drenthe.

Nijenhuis, E. R. S. (2015). *The Trinity of Trauma: Ignorance, Fragility, and Control*. Vandenhoeck & Ruprecht: Gottingen.

Nijenhuis, E. R. S., Spinhoven, P., Van Dyck, R., Van Der Hart, O., & Vanderlinden, J. (1996). The development and psychometric characteristics of the Somatoform Dissociation Questionnaire (SDQ-20). *Journal of Nervous and Mental Disease*, *184*(11), 688–694. https://doi.org/10.1097/00005053-199611000-00006

Nuñez, L., Fernández, S., Alamo, N., Midgley, N., Capella, C., & Krause, M. (2022). The therapeutic relationship and change processes in child psychotherapy: A qualitative, longitudinal study of the views of children, parents and therapists. *Research Psychotherapy*, *25*(1). https://doi.org/10.4081/ripppo.2022.556

Oakwater, H. (2008). *The Cost of Trauma*. www.fabparents.co.uk/blog/the-cost-of-trauma

O'Connor, R. C. (2011). The integrated motivational-volitional model of suicidal behavior. *Crisis*, *32*(6), 295–298. https://doi.org/10.1027/0227-5910/a000120

O'Connor, R. C., & Portzky, G. (2018). The relationship between entrapment and suicidal behavior through the lens of the integrated motivational-volitional model of suicidal behavior. *Current in Opinion Psychology*, *22*, 12–17. https://doi.org/10.1016/j.cop syc.2017.07.021

Ogawa, J. R., Sroufe, L. A., Weinfield, N. S., Carlson, E. A., & Egeland, B. (1997). Development and the fragmented self: longitudinal study of dissociative symptomatology in a nonclinical sample. *Developmental Psychopathology*, *9*(4), 855–879. https://doi.org/10.1017/s0954579497001478

Ogden, P., & Fisher, J. (2015). *Sensorimotor Psychotherapy: Interventions for Trauma and Attachment*. W W Norton: New York.

Orbach, I. (1994). Dissociation, physical pain, and suicide: A hypothesis. *Suicide Life Threat Behaviour*, *24*(1), 68–79. https://doi.org/10.1111/j.1943-278x.1994.tb00664.x

O'Neill, R. E., Horner, R. H., Albin, R. W., Sprague, R. R., Storey, K., & Newton, J. S. (1997). *Functional Assessment and Program Development for Problem Behaviour: A Practical Handbook*. Brooks/Cole: Pacific Grove, CA.

Palmisano, G. L., Innamorati, M., Susca, G., Traetta, D., Sarracino, D., & Vanderlinden, J. (2018). Childhood traumatic experiences and dissociative phenomena in eating disorders: Level and association with the severity of binge eating symptoms. *Journal of Trauma & Dissociation*, *19*(1), 88–107. https://doi.org/10.1080/15299732.2017.1304490

Panisch, L. S., Rogers, R. G., Breen, M. T., Nutt, S., Dahud, S., & Salazar, C. A. (2023). Dissociation among women with chronic pelvic pain: Relation to surgical treatment, pelvic pain severity, and health-related quality of life. *Journal of Trauma & Dissociation*, *24*(2), 296–311. https://doi.org/10.1080/15299732.2023.2168828

Paris, J. (2012). The rise and fall of dissociative identity disorder. *Journal of Nervous and Mental Disease*, *200*(12), 1076–1079. https://doi.org/10.1097/NMD.0b013e318275d285

Parry, S., Lloyd, M., & Wilson, H. (2022). Using digital mediums to provide trauma-informed support to people with complex presentations. In H. Wilson (Ed.), *Digital Delivery of Mental Health Therapies: A Guide to the Benefits, Challenges and Making it Work*. Jessica Kingsley: London.

Patel, A., Ness, J., & Waters, K. (2024). A much-needed focus on self-harm in older adults. *International Psychogeriatrics*, *36*(5), 332–335. https://doi.org/10.1017/s1041610223004520

Paulsen, S. L., & Golston, J. (2014). Stabilizing the relationship among self-states. In U. Lanius, S. L. Paulsen & F. M. Corrigan (Eds.), *Neurobiology and Treatment of Traumatic Dissociation: Toward an Embodied Self* (pp. 321–340). Springer Publishing Company: London. https://doi.org/10.1891/9780826106322

Pause. (2022). *Set Up to Fail: Women's Experiences of Psychiatric and Psychological Expert Witness Assessments During Care Proceedings*. www.pause.org.uk/wp-content/uploads/2022/07/Set-Up-to-Fail-July-2022.pdf

Payne, E., Watt, A., Rogers, P., & McMurran, M. (2008). Offence characteristics, trauma histories and post-traumatic stress disorder symptoms in life sentenced prisoners. *The British Journal of Forensic Practice*, *10*(1), 17–25. https://doi.org/10.1108/14636646200800004

Payton, J. (2014). "Honor", collectivity, and agnation: Emerging risk factors in "honor"-based violence. *Journal of Interpersonal Violence*, *29*(16), 2863–2883. https://doi.org/10.1177/0886260514527171

Perry, B. (2009). Examining child maltreatment through a neurodevelopmental lens: Clinical applications of the neurosequential model of therapeutics. *Journal of Loss and Trauma*, *14*, 240–255. https://doi.org/10.1080/15325020903004350

Perry, B. (2020). The Neurosequential Model: A developmentally-sensitive, neuroscience-informed approach to clinical problem solving. In J. Mitchell, J. Tucci, & E. Tronick

(Eds.), *The Handbook of Therapeutic Child Care for Children* (pp. 137–155). Jessica Kingsley: London.

Pierorazio, N. A., Dardis, C. M., & Brand, B. L. (2023). *Multicultural Considerations for the Past, Present and Future of Our Field*. American Psychological Association- Division 56- Trauma Psychology. https://apatraumadivision.org/summer-2023-vol-18-no-2/

Pierorazio, N. A., Robertson, J. L., Nester, M. S., & Brand, B. L. (2024). "They thought I was just making it up": Dissociative individuals' understandings of their dissociation, perceptions of their clinicians' conceptualizations of dissociation, and discrepancies between them. *Psychological Trauma: Theory, Research, Practice, and Policy*, No Pagination Specified-No Pagination Specified. https://doi.org/10.1037/tra0001800

Pietkiewicz, I. J., Bańbura-Nowak, A., Tomalski, R., & Boon, S. (2021). Revisiting false-positive and imitated dissociative identity disorder. *Frontiers in Psychology*, *12*, 637929. https://doi.org/10.3389/fpsyg.2021.637929

Pless Kaiser, A., Cook, J. M., Glick, D. M., & Moye, J. (2019). Posttraumatic stress disorder in older adults: A conceptual review. *Clinical Gerontology*, *42*(4), 359–376. https://doi.org/10.1080/07317115.2018.1539801

Poon, C. Y. M. (2014). Meeting the mental health needs of older adults using the attachment perspective. In A.N. Danquah., & K. Berry (Eds.), *Attachment Theory in Adult Mental Health: A Guide to Clinical Practice* (pp. 183–196). Routledge/Taylor & Francis Group: Abingdon, Ox.

Porges, S. W. (2022). Polyvagal theory: A science of safety. *Frontiers in Integrated Neuroscience*, *16*, 871227. https://doi.org/10.3389/fnint.2022.871227

Porges, S. W., & Furman, S. A. (2011). The early development of the autonomic nervous system provides a neural platform for social behavior: A polyvagal perspective. *Infant and Child Development*, *20*(1), 106–118. https://doi.org/10.1002/icd.688

Porter, J. L. B. (2022). EMDR therapy with people who have intellectual disabilities: Process, adaptations and outcomes. *Advances in Mental Health and Intellectual Disabilities*, *16*(1), 32–43. https://doi.org/10.1108/AMHID-07-2021-0033

Potgieter-Marks, R. (2012). When the sleeping tiger roars- perpetrator introjects in children. In R. Vogt (Ed.), *Perpetrator Introjects – Psychotherapeutic Diagnostics and Treatment Models* (pp. 87–110). AnsangerVerlag.

Potgieter-Marks, R. (2016). Pre-birth trauma- the missing link in full recovery? *ESTD Newsletter*, *5*(4), 16–23.

Potgieter-Marks, R. (2017). Systems and organisational dissociation in treating dissociative children. *ETSD Newsletter*, *6*(4), 10.

Prasko, J., Raszka, M., Adamcova, K., Grambal, A., Koprivova, J., Kudrnovská, H., ... & Vyskocilová, J. (2009). Predicting the therapeutic response to cognitive behavioural therapy in patients with pharmacoresistant obsessive-compulsive disorder. *Neuroendocrinology Letters*, *30*(5), 615–623. https://doi.org/10.2147/ndt.s101721

Prati, G., & Pietrantoni, L. (2009). Optimism, social support, and coping strategies as factors contributing to posttraumatic growth: A meta-analysis. *Journal of Loss and Trauma*, *14*(5), 364–388. https://doi.org/10.1080/15325020902724271

Proctor, B. (2010). Training for the supervision alliance. In J.R. Cutcliffe, K. Hyrkas, J. Fowler (Eds.), *Routledge Handbook of Clinical Supervision* (pp 51–62). Routledge: Abingdon, Ox.

Prosser, D., Johnson, S., Kuipers, E., Szmukler, G., Bebbington, P., & Thornicroft, G. (1996). Mental health, "burnout" and job satisfaction among hospital and community-based mental health staff. *The British Journal of Psychiatry*, *169*(3), 334–337. https://doi.org/10.1192/bjp.169.3.334

Psychological Professions Network. (2020). *Leadership and Management in the Psychological Professions: Discussion Paper*. https://ppn.nhs.uk/resources-url/publi cations/35-leadership-and-management-in-the-psychological-professions-discussion-paper/file

Pugh, M., & Waller, G. (2016). The anorexic voice and severity of eating pathology in anorexia nervosa. *International Journal of Eating Disorders*, *49*(6), 622–625. https://doi.org/10.1002/eat.22499

Pugh, M., Waller, G., & Esposito, M. (2018). Childhood trauma, dissociation, and the internal eating disorder 'voice'. *Child Abuse and Neglect*, *86*, 197–205. https://doi.org/10.1016/j.chiabu.2018.10.005

Punzi, E., & Singer, C. (2018). 'Any room won't do'. Clinical psychologists' understanding of the consulting room. An interview study. *Psychodynamic Practice*, *24*, 1–15.

Putnam, F. W. (1989). *Diagnosis and Treatment of Multiple Personality Disorder*. Guilford Press: New York.

Putnam, F. W., Helmers, K., & Trickett, P. K. (1993). Development, reliability, and validity of a child dissociation scale. *Child Abuse and Neglect*, *17*(6), 731–741. https://doi.org/10.1016/S0145-2134(08)80004-X

Putnam, F. W., & Trickett, P. K. (1997). Psychobiological effects of sexual abuse. A longitudinal study. *Annual of New York Academy Science*, *821*, 150–159. https://doi.org/10.1111/j.1749-6632.1997.tb48276.x

Quimby, L. G., & Putnam, F. W. (1991). Dissociative symptoms and aggression in a state mental hospital. *Dissociation: Progress in the Dissociative Disorders*, *4*(1), 21–24. https://psycnet.apa.org/record/1992-12764-001

Rabasco, A., & Andover, M. S. (2020). The interaction of dissociation, pain tolerance, and suicidal ideation in predicting suicide attempts. *Psychiatry Research*, *284*, 112661. https://doi.org/10.1016/j.psychres.2019.112661

Rabito-Alcón, M. F., Baile, J. I., & Vanderlinden, J. (2020). Child trauma experiences and dissociative symptoms in women with eating disorders: Case-control study. *Children (Basel)*, *7*(12), 274. https://doi.org/10.3390/children7120274

Raymaker, D. M., Teo, A. R., Steckler, N. A., Lentz, B., Scharer, M., Delos Santos, A., Kapp, S. K., Hunter, M., Joyce, A., & Nicolaidis, C. (2020). Having all of your internal resources exhausted beyond measure and being left with no clean-up crew: Defining autistic burnout. *Autism in Adulthood: Challenges and Management*, *2*(2), 132–143. https://doi.org/10.1089/aut.2019.0079

Rea, J. N. M., Broczek, K. M., Cevenini, E., Celani, L., Rea, S. A. J., Sikora, E., … & Rea, I. M. (2022). Insights into sibling relationships and longevity from genetics of healthy ageing nonagenarians: The importance of optimisation, resilience and social networks. *Frontiers in Psychology*, *13*, 722286. https://doi.org/10.3389/fpsyg.2022.722286

Reavis, J. A., Looman, J., Franco, K. A., & Rojas, B. (2013). Adverse childhood experiences and adult criminality: How long must we live before we possess our own lives? *Perm Journal*, *17*(2), 44–48. https://doi.org/10.7812/tpp/12-072

Reinders, A. A., Willemsen, A. T., Vissia, E. M., Vos, H. P., den Boer, J. A., & Nijenhuis, E. R. (2016). The psychobiology of authentic and simulated dissociative personality states: The full monty. *Journal of Nervous and Mental Disease*, *204*(6), 445–457. https://doi.org/10.1097/NMD.0000000000000522

Reinders, A. A. T. S., Marquand, A. F., Schlumpf, Y. R., Chalavi, S., Vissia, E. M., Nijenhuis, E. R. S., … & Veltman, D. J. (2019). Aiding the diagnosis of dissociative identity disorder: Pattern recognition study of brain biomarkers. *British J Psychiatry, 215*(3), 536–544. https://doi.org/10.1192/bjp.2018.255

Reinders, A. A. T. S., & Veltman, D. J. (2021). Dissociative identity disorder: out of the shadows at last? *British J Psychiatry, 219*(2), 413–414. https://doi.org/10.1192/bjp.2020.168

Reinders, A. A. T. S., Young, A. H., & Veltman, D. J. (2023). Biomarkers of dissociation. *BJPsych Open, 9*(4), e119. https://doi.org/10.1192/bjo.2023.511

Renard, S. B., Huntjens, R. J., Lysaker, P. H., Moskowitz, A., Aleman, A., & Pijnenborg, G. H. (2017). Unique and overlapping symptoms in schizophrenia spectrum and dissociative disorders in relation to models of psychopathology: A systematic review. *Schizophrenia Bulletin, 43*(1), 108–121. https://doi.org/10.1093/schbul/sbw063

Reuben, K. (2023). *Clinical Reflections. Co-occurring Autism and Trauma, Posttraumatic Stress and Dissociation.* International Society for the Study of Trauma and Dissociation. https://news.isst-d.org/co-occurring-autism-and-trauma-posttraumatic-stress-and-dissociation/

Reuben, K. E., & Parish, A. (2022). Dissociation in autism spectrum disorders: An underrecognized symptom. In E. Christensen (Ed.), *Perspectives of Dissociative Identity Response: Ethical, Historical and Cultural Issues* (pp. 151–183). HWC Press: Philadelphia.

Reuben, K. E., Stanzione, C. M., & Singleton, J. L. (2021). Interpersonal trauma and posttraumatic stress in autistic adults. *Autism in Adulthood, 3*(3), 247–256. https://doi.org/10.1089/aut.2020.0073

Rhue, J. W., & Lynn, S. J. (1987). Fantasy proneness: Developmental antecedents. *Journal of Personality, 55*(1), 121–137. https://doi.org/10.1111/j.1467-6494.1987.tb00431.x

Richardson, S. (2018). *The trauma and dissociation field in the UK: Reflections on the last 3 decades. ISSTD news international spotlight.* Retrieved May 9, 2025, from https://news.isst-d.org/the-trauma-and-dissociation-field-in-the-uk-reflections-on-the-last-3-decades

Roberts, A. L., Liu, J., Lawn, R. B., Jha, S. C., Sumner, J. A., Kang, J. H., … & Koenen, K. C. (2022). Association of posttraumatic stress disorder With accelerated cognitive decline in middle-aged women. *JAMA Netw Open, 5*(6), e2217698. https://doi.org/10.1001/jamanetworkopen.2022.17698

Romeo, A., Tesio, V., Ghiggia, A., Di Tella, M., Geminiani, G. C., Farina, B., & Castelli, L. (2022). Traumatic experiences and somatoform dissociation in women with fibromyalgia. *Psychologica Trauma, 14*(1), 116–123. https://doi.org/10.1037/tra0000907

Ross, C. A. (1991). Epidemiology of multiple personality disorder and dissociation. *Psychiatric Clinics of North America, 14*(3), 503–517. https://doi.org/10.1016/s0193-953x(18)30286-7

Ross, C. A., Heber, S., Norton, G. R., & Anderson, G. (1989). Differences between multiple personality disorder and other diagnostic groups on structured interview. *Journal of Nervous and Mental Disease, 177*(8), 487–491. https://doi.org/10.1097/00005053-198908000-00006

Ross, C. A., Miller, S. D., Reagor, P., Bjornson, L., Fraser, G. A., & Anderson, G. (1990). Structured interview data on 102 cases of multiple personality disorder from four centers. *Amercian Journal of Psychiatry, 147*(5), 596–601. https://doi.org/10.1176/ajp.147.5.596

Rothbaum, F., Weisz, J., Pott, M., Miyake, K., & Morelli, G. (2000). Attachment and culture: Security in the United States and Japan. *American Psychologist, 55*(10), 1093–1104. https://doi.org/10.1037/0003-066X.55.10.1093

Rothschild, B. (2004). Mirror mirror: Emotion in the consulting room is more contagious than we thought. *Psychotherapy Networker, 28*(5). www.psychotherapynetworker.org/article/mirror-mirror

Rothschild, B. (2017). *The Body Remembers: Revolutionizing Trauma Treatment* (Vol. 2). W. W. Norton: New York.

Rouf, K., & Waites, B. (2023). *Guidance on Responding to Disclosures of Non-recent (Historic) Child Sexual Abuse: Safeguarding and Support Implications. The British Psychological Society.*

Royal College of Obstetricians and Gynaecologists. (2022). *Top Tips for Health Professionals: Cervical Screening.* www.rcog.org.uk/news/top-tips-for-healthcare-profes sionals-cervical-screenings/

Rufer, M., Fricke, S., Moritz, S., Kloss, M., & Hand, I. (2006). Symptom dimensions in obsessive-compulsive disorder: Prediction of cognitive-behavior therapy outcome. *Acta Psychiatrica Scandinavica, 113*(5), 440–446. https://doi.org/10.1111/j.1600-0447.2005.00682.x

Ruismaki, M., Friberg, L., & Mankila, P. (2014). *Stabilization groups for dissociative parents.* European Society for Trauma and Dissociation Conference, Copenhagen, Denmark.

Rumball, F., Brook, L., Happé, F., & Karl, A. (2021). Heightened risk of posttraumatic stress disorder in adults with autism spectrum disorder: The role of cumulative trauma and memory deficits. *Research in Developmental Disabilities, 110*, 103848. https://doi.org/10.1016/j.ridd.2020.103848

Rüfenacht, E., Shaverin, L., Stubley, J., Smits, M. L., Bateman, A., Fonagy, P., & Luyten, P. (2023). Addressing dissociation symptoms with trauma-focused mentalization-based treatment. *Psychoanalytic Psychotherapy, 37*(4), 467–491. https://doi.org/10.1080/02668 734.2023.2272765

Sachs, A. (2015). Who done it actually? Dissociative identity disorder for the criminologist. *International Journal for Crime, Justice and Social Democracy, 4*(2), 65–76.

Sachs, A. (2025). The parts, the whole and the real person. In S. Richardson, M. Goodwin, E. Jack, & M. Jowett (Eds.), *Dissociative Identities: Attachment Based Approaches to Psychotherapy.* Taylor & Francis Group: Abingdon, Ox.

Salter, M. (2012). *Organised Sexual Abuse* (1st ed.). Taylor & Francis Group: Abingdon, Ox.

Salter, M. (2017). Organized abuse in adulthood: Survivor and professional perspectives. *Journal of Trauma & Dissociation, 18*(3), 441–453. https://doi.org/10.1080/15299 732.2017.1295426

Salter, M. (2023). Presidential Editorial: The facts and fantasies of dissociation. *Journal of Trauma and Dissociation, 24*(1), 1–7. https://doi.org/10.1080/15299732.2022.2157620

Salter, M., & Blizard, R. (2022). False memories and the science of credibility: Who gets to be heard? *Journal of Trauma & Dissociation, 23*(2), 141–147. https://doi.org/10.1080/15299732.2022.2028219

Salter, M., Brand, B. L., Robinson, M., Loewenstein, R., Silberg, J., & Korzekwa, M. (2025). Self-diagnosed cases of dissociative identity disorder on social media: Conceptualization, assessment, and treatment. *Harvard Review Psychiatry, 33*(1), 41–48. https://doi.org/10.1097/HRP.0000000000000416

Şar, V. (2011). Epidemiology of dissociative disorders: An overview. *Epidemiology Research International, 1*, 404538. https://doi.org/10.1155/2011/404538

Şar, V. (2014). The many faces of dissociation: Opportunities for innovative research in psychiatry. *Clinical Psychopharmacology and Neuroscience, 12*(3), 171–179. https://doi.org/10.9758/cpn.2014.12.3.171

Şar, V. (2022). Dissociation across cultures: A transdiagnostic guide for clinical assessment and management. *Alpha Psychiatry, 23*(3), 95–103. https://doi.org/10.5152/alphapsychia try.2022.21556

Şar, V., Akyüz, G., & Doğan, O. (2007). Prevalence of dissociative disorders among women in the general population. *Psychiatry Research, 149*(1–3), 169–176. https://doi.org/10.1016/j.psychres.2006.01.005

Şar, V., Koyuncu, A., Ozturk, E., Yargic, L. I., Kundakci, T., Yazici, A., ... & Aksüt, D. (2007). Dissociative disorders in the psychiatric emergency ward. *General Hospital Psychiatry, 29*(1), 45–50. https://doi.org/10.1016/j.genhosppsych.2006.10.009

Şar, V., Middleton, W., & Dorahy, M. J. (2012). The scientific status of childhood dissociative identity disorder: A review of published research. *Psychotherapy and Psychosomatics, 81*, 183–184. https://doi.org/10.1159/000333361

Sawrikar, P. (2017). *Working Effectively with Ethnic Minorities and Across Cultures in Western Child Protection Systems*. Routledge: Abingdon, Ox.

Sawrikar, P. (2020). A conceptual framework for the prevention and treatment of child sexual abuse (CSA) in ethnic minority communities. In *Child Sexual Abuse: Forensic Issues in Evidence, Impact, and Management* (pp. 625–641). Elsevier Academic Press. https://doi.org/10.1016/B978-0-12-819434-8.00028-3

Saxe, G. N., Chawla, N., & Van der Kolk, B. (2002). Self-destructive behavior in patients with dissociative disorders. *Suicide Life Threat Behav, 32*(3), 313–320. https://doi.org/10.1521/suli.32.3.313.22174

Saxe, G. N., van der Kolk, B. A., Berkowitz, R., Chinman, G., Hall, K., Lieberg, G., & Schwartz, J. (1993). Dissociative disorders in psychiatric inpatients. *Amercian Jornal of Psychiatry, 150*(7), 1037–1042. https://doi.org/10.1176/ajp.150.7.1037

Scaer, R. C. (2014). *The Body Bears the Burden: Trauma, Dissociation, and Disease* (3rd ed.). Routledge: Abingdon, Ox.

Schalinski, I., Schauer, M., & Elbert, T. (2015). The shutdown dissociation scale (Shut-D). *European Journal of Psychotraumatology, 6*, Article 25652.

Scharff, A., Ortiz, S. N., Forrest, L. N., & Smith, A. R. (2021). Comparing the clinical presentation of eating disorder patients with and without trauma history and/or comorbid PTSD. *Eating Disorders, 29*(1), 88–102. https://doi.org/10.1080/10640266.2019.1642035

Schielke, H., Brand, B., & Marsic, A. (2017). Assessing therapeutic change in patients with severe dissociative disorders: The Progress in Treatment Questionnaire, therapist and patient measures. *European Journal of Psychotraumatology, 8*(1), 12–12. https://doi.org/10.1080/20008198.2017.1380471

Schielke, H. J., Brand, B. L., & Lanius, R. A. (2022). *The Finding Solid Ground Program Workbook: Overcoming Obstacles in Trauma Recovery* (1st ed.). Oxford University Press: Oxford.

Schnurr, P. P. (2015). Understanding pathways from traumatic exposure to physical health. In U. Schnyder & M. Cloitre (Eds.), *Evidence-based Treatments for Trauma-related Psychological Disorders* (pp. 271–284). Springer: London.

Schnurr, P. P., & Green, B. L. (2004). Understanding relationships among trauma, posttramatic stress disorder, and health outcomes. *Advances in Mind-Body Medicine, 20*(1), 18–29. https://psycnet.apa.org/record/2004-12266-003

Schofield, L. (2021). *Understanding Dissociative Identity Disorder: A Guidebook for Survivors and Practitioners and Our House: Making Sense of Dissociative Identity Disorder*. Routledge: Abingdon, Ox.

Schore, A. N. (2003). *Affect Dysregulation & Disorders of the Self* (1st ed.). Norton: New York.

Schwartz, A. (2021). *Complex PTSD: Video Course.* www.nscience.uk/product/complex-ptsd-an-integrative-mind-body-approach-to-treating-clients-with-chronic-repeated-and-or-developmental-trauma-video/

Schwartz, R. C. (2021). *No Bad Parts: Healing Trauma & Restoring Wholeness with the Internal Family Systems Model.* Sounds True: Louisville, CO.

Scioli-Salter, E. R., Johnides, B. D., Mitchell, K. S., Smith, B. N., Resick, P. A., & Rasmusson, A. M. (2016). Depression and dissociation as predictors of physical health symptoms among female rape survivors with posttraumatic stress disorder. *Psychological Trauma: Theory, Research, Practice, and Policy, 8*(5), 585–591. https://doi.org/10.1037/tra0000135

Scior, K. (2016). Toward understanding intellectual disability stigma: Introduction. In K. Scior and S. Werner (Eds.), *Intellectual Disability and Stigma: Stepping Out from the Margins* (pp. 3–13). Palgrave Macmillan/Springer Nature: London. https://doi.org/10.1057/978-1-137-52499-7_1

Seagar, M. (2014). Using attachment theory to inform psychologically minded care services, systems and environments. In A. N. Danquah & K. Berry (Eds.), *Attachment Theory in Adult Mental Health: A Guide to Clinical Practice* (pp. 63–77). Routledge: Abingdon, Ox.

Seligman, R., & Kirmayer, L. J. (2008). Dissociative experience and cultural neuroscience: Narrative, metaphor and mechanism. *Culture, Medicine, and Psychiatry, 32*(1), 31–64. https://doi.org/10.1007/s11013-007-9077-8

Semiz, U. B., Inanc, L., & Bezgin, C. H. (2014). Are trauma and dissociation related to treatment resistance in patients with obsessive-compulsive disorder? *Society Psychiatry Psychiatric Epidemiology, 49*(8), 1287–1296. https://doi.org/10.1007/s00127-013-0787-7

Serra, R., Kiekens, G., Tarsitani, L., Vrieze, E., Bruffaerts, R., Loriedo, C., ... & Vanderlinden, J. (2020). The effect of trauma and dissociation on the outcome of cognitive behavioural therapy for binge eating disorder: A 6-month prospective study. *European Eating Disorders Review, 28*(3), 309–317. https://doi.org/10.1002/erv.2722

Severs, E., James, T., Letrondo, P., Løvland, L., Marchant, N. L., & Mukadam, N. (2023). Traumatic life events and risk for dementia: A systematic review and meta-analysis. *BMC Geriatrics, 23*(1), 587. https://doi.org/10.1186/s12877-023-04287-1

Sharma, E., Sharma, L. P., Balachander, S., Lin, B., Manohar, H., Khanna, P., ... & Stewart, S. E. (2021). Comorbidities in obsessive-compulsive disorder across the lifespan: A systematic review and meta-analysis. *Frontiers in Psychiatry, 12*, 703701. https://doi.org/10.3389/fpsyt.2021.703701

Shimmens, V., & Skelly, A. (2023). *Love, Attachment and Intellectual Disability: Meeting Emotional Needs and Developmental Trauma.* Pavillion: West Sussex.

Shonkoff, J. P., & Garner, A. S. (2012). The lifelong effects of early childhood adversity and toxic stress. *Pediatrics, 129*(1), e232–246. https://doi.org/10.1542/peds.2011-2663

Shorvon, H. J. (1946). The depersonalisation syndrome. *Proceedings of the Royal Society of Medicine, 39*(12), 779–792. https://doi.org/10.1177/003591574603901206

Silani, G., Bird, G., Brindley, R., Singer, T., Frith, C., & Frith, U. (2008). Levels of emotional awareness and autism: An fMRI study. *Social Neuroscience, 3*(2), 97–112. https://doi.org/10.1080/17470910701577020

Silberg, J. L. (2022). *The Child Survivor: Healing Developmental Trauma and Dissociation* (2nd ed.). Routledge/Taylor & Francis Group: Abingdon, Ox.

Silva, J. A., Derecho, D. V., Leong, G. B., Weinstock, R., & Ferrari, M. M. (2001). A classification of psychological factors leading to violent behavior in posttraumatic stress disorder. *Journal of Forensic Sciences, 46*(2), 309–316. https://doi.org/10.1520/jfs14963j

Simeon, D., & Putnam, F. (2022). Pathological dissociation in the national Comorbidity Survey Replication (NCS-R): Prevalence, morbidity, comorbidity, and childhood maltreatment. *Journal of Trauma & Dissociation, 23*(5), 490–503. https://doi.org/10.1080/15299732.2022.2064580

Simoneti, S., Scott, E. C., & Murphy, C. M. (2000). Dissociative experiences in partner-assaultive men. *Journal of Interpersonal Violence, 15*(12), 1262–1283. https://doi.org/10.1177/088626000015012002

Sinason, V. (2010). *Mental Handicap and the Human Condition* (2nd ed.). Tavistock: London.

Sinason, V., & Potgieter-Marks, R. (2022). *Treating Children with Dissociative Disorders: Attachment, Trauma, Theory and Practice.* Routledge: Abingdon, Ox.

Sinason, V., & Silver, A. S. (2008). Treating dissociative and psychotic disorders psychodynamically. In A. Moskowitz, I. Schafer, & M. J. Dorahy (Eds.), *Psychosis, Trauma, and Dissociation: Emerging Perspectives on Severe Pathology.* Wiley: New Jersey.

Skelly, A. (2020). Trauma exposure and the importance of attachment in people with intellectual disabilities. *Bulletin of the Faculty for People with Intellectual Disabilities, 18*(1), 15–19. https://doi.org/10.53841/bpsfpid.2020.18.1.15

Skelly, A. (2024). Factor structure of the quality of early relationships rating scale (QuERRS-2): Attachment representations predict case severity and length of psychological therapy in a community learning disabilities team. *Bulletin of the Faculty for People with Intellectual Disabilities, 22*(1), 43–54. https://doi.org/10.53841/bpsfpid.2024.22.1.43

Smith, E. K. (2023). Strategies to survive: Engaging transgender and gender diverse older adults experiencing suicidality and dissociative states. *Clinical Social Work Journal, 51*(3), 262–272. https://doi.org/10.1007/s10615-023-00867-1

Smith, M. L., Bergeron, C. D., Riggle, S. D., Meng, L., Towne, S. D., Jr., Ahn, S., & Ory, M. G. (2017). Self-care difficulties and reliance on support among vulnerable middle-aged and older adults with chronic conditions: A cross-sectional study. *Maturitas, 104*, 1–10. https://doi.org/10.1016/j.maturitas.2017.06.030

Snyder, B. L., Boyer, S. M., Caplan, J. E., Nester, M. S., & Brand, B. (2024). It's not just a movie: Perceived impact of misportrayals of dissociative identity disorder in the media on self and treatment. *European Journal of Trauma & Dissociation, 8*(3). https://doi.org/10.1016/j.ejtd.2024.100429

Soares, S., Rocha, V., Kelly-Irving, M., Stringhini, S., & Fraga, S. (2021). Adverse childhood events and health biomarkers: A systematic review. *Front Public Health, 9*, 649825. https://doi.org/10.3389/fpubh.2021.649825

Soffer-Dudek, N. (2023). Obsessive-compulsive symptoms and dissociative experiences: Suggested underlying mechanisms and implications for science and practice. *Frontiers in Psychology, 14*, 1132800. https://doi.org/10.3389/fpsyg.2023.1132800

Soh, K. C., Tay, Y. H., & Darjee, R. (2023). Those who commit violent crimes can be traumatised by their offences: A systematic review of offence-specific post-traumatic stress disorder. *Journal of Aggression, Maltreatment & Trauma, 32*(12), 1705–1725. https://doi.org/10.1080/10926771.2023.2186299

Spiegel, D. (2018). Integrating dissociation. *Amercian Journal of Psychiatry, 175*(1), 4–5. https://doi.org/10.1176/appi.ajp.2017.17101176

Spiegel, D., Loewenstein, R. J., Lewis-Fernández, R., Sar, V., Simeon, D., Vermetten, E., ... & Dell, P. F. (2011). Dissociative disorders in DSM-5. *Depress Anxiety, 28*(12), E17–45. https://doi.org/10.1002/da.20923

Steele, K. (2018). Dependency in the psychotherapy of chronically traumatized individuals: Using motivational systems to guide effective treatment. *Cognitivismo Clinico, 15*(2), 221–226. https://apc.it/wp-content/uploads/2013/03/18_Steele_CC18-2-2.pdf

Steele, K., Boon, S., & Van der Hart, O. (2017). *Treating Trauma-related Dissociation: A Practical, Integrative Approach*. W. W. Norton: New York.

Steele, K., Van der Hart, O., & Nijenhuis, E. R. S. (2001). Dependency in the treatment of complex posttraumatic stress disorder and dissociative disorders. *Journal of Trauma & Dissociation*, *2*(4), 79–116. https://doi.org/10.1300/J229v02n04_05

Steinberg, M. (1995). *Handbook for the Assessment of Dissociation: A Clinical Guide* (1st ed.). American Psychiatric Press: Washington DC.

Steinberg, M. (2023). *The SCID-D Interview: Dissociative Assessment in Therapy, Forensics, and Research*. American Psychiatric Association: Washington DC.

Steinberg, M., & Siegel, H. D. (2008). Advances in assessment: The differential diagnosis of dissociative identity disorder and schizophrenia. In A. Moskowitz, I. Schäfer, & M. J. Dorahy (Eds.), *Psychosis, Trauma and Dissociation: Emerging Perspectives on Severe Psychopathology* (pp. 177–189). Wiley Blackwell: Chichester, West Sussex. https://doi.org/10.1002/9780470699652.ch13

Stenfert-Kroese, B., Willott, S., Taylor, F., Smith, P., Graham, R., Rutter, T., ... & Willner, P. (2016). Trauma-focussed cognitive-behaviour therapy for people with mild intellectual disabilities: Outcomes of a pilot study. *Advances in Mental Health and Intellectual Disabilities*, *10*, 299–310. https://doi.org/10.1108/amhid-05-2016-0008

Stierum, A. (2016). Mastering traumatic memories. In F. S. Waters (Ed.), *Healing the Fractured Child: Diagnosis and Treatment of Youth with Dissociation* (p. 280). Springer: London.

Stolbach, B.C. (1997). *The Children's Dissociative Experiences Scale and Posttraumatic Symptom Inventory: Rationale, Development, and Validation of a Self-report Measure*. University of Colorado.

Stolbach, B. (2005). Psychotherapy of a dissociative 8 year old boy burned at age 3. *Psychiatric Annals*, *35*, 685–694. https://complextrauma.org/wp-content/uploads/2019/01/Case-Studies-5.pdf

Struik, A. (2019). *Treating Chronically Traumatized Children: The Sleeping Dogs Method* (2nd ed.). Routledge: Abingdon, Ox.

Substance Abuse and Mental Health Services Administration. (2014). *SAMHSA's Concept of Trauma and Guidance for a Trauma-informed Approach*. Rockville, MD

Sun, P., Alvarez-Jimenez, M., Lawrence, K., Simpson, K., Peach, N., & Bendall, S. (2019). Investigating the prevalence of dissociative disorders and severe dissociative symptoms in first episode psychosis. *Early Intervention in Psychiatry*, *13*(6), 1366–1372. https://doi.org/10.1111/eip.12773

Sunderland, M. (2006). *Science of Parenting: Practical Guidance on Sleep, Crying, Creative Play, Sibling Rivalry, and More - Based on Over 700 Studies*. Dorling Kindersley: London.

Sunderland, M., & Hancock, N. (2003). *Helping Children Locked in Rage or Hate: A Guidebook*. Routledge: Abingdon, Ox.

Sung, K., & Kim, H. S. (2003). Elder respect among young adults: Exploration of behavioral forms in Korea. *Ageing International*, *28*(3), 279–294. https://doi.org/10.1007/s12126-002-1008-y

Sutar, R. & Sahu, S. (2019) Pharmacotherapy for dissociative disorders: A systematic review. *Psychiatry Research*, *281*, 112529. https://doi.org/10.1016/j.psychres.2019.112529

Tanay, E. (1969). Psychiatric study of homicide. *Amercian Journal of Psychiatry*, *125*(9), 1252–1257. https://doi.org/10.1176/ajp.125.9.1252

Tatlı, M., Cetinkaya, O., & Maner, F. (2018). Evaluation of relationship between obsessive-compulsive disorder and dissociative experiences. *Clinical in Psychopharmacology Neuroscience*, *16*(2), 161–167. https://doi.org/10.9758/cpn.2018.16.2.161

Taylor, J. (2021). Compassion in custody: Developing a trauma sensitive intervention for men with developmental disabilities who have convictions for sexual offending. *Advances in Mental Health and Intellectual Disabilities, 15*(5), 185–200. https://doi.org/10.1108/AMHID-01-2021-0004

Teague, S. J., Gray, K. M., Tonge, B. J., & Newman, L. K. (2017). Attachment in children with autism spectrum disorder: A systematic review. *Research in Autism Spectrum Disorders, 35*, 35–50. https://doi.org/10.1016/j.rasd.2016.12.002

Temple, M. (2019). Understanding, identifying and managing severe dissociative disorders in general psychiatric settings. *BJPscyh Advances, 25*(1), 14–25. https://doi.org/10.1192/bja.2018.54

Ternes, M., Cooper, B. S., & Griesel, D. (2020). The perpetration of violence and the experience of trauma: Exploring predictors of PTSD symptoms in male violent offenders. *The International Journal of Forensic Mental Health, 19*(1), 68–83. https://doi.org/10.1080/14999013.2019.1643428

Thalmayer, A. G., Toscanelli, C., & Arnett, J. J. (2021). The neglected 95% revisited: Is American psychology becoming less American? *American Psychologist, 76*(1), 116–129. https://doi.org/10.1037/amp0000622

The British Psychological Society (BPS) (2011). *'Good Practice Guidelines on the Use of Psychological Information.' Division of Clinical Psychology*, December. Leicester, UK: The British Psychological Society. https://explore.bps.org.uk/content/report-guideline/bpsrep.2011.rep100

Thompson, E., & Zahavi, D. (2007). Philosophical issues: Phenomenology. In P.D. Zelazo, M. Moscovitch, & E. Thompson, (Eds.), *The Cambridge Handbook of Consciousness* (pp. 67–87). Cambridge University Press: Cambridge. https://doi.org/10.1017/CBO9780511816789.005

Tobin, D. L., Molteni, A. L., & Elin, M. R. (1995). Early trauma, dissociation, and late onset in the eating disorders. *International Journal of Eating Disorders, 17*(3), 305–308. https://doi.org/10.1002/1098-108x(199504)17:3<305::aid-eat2260170312>3.0.co;2-f

Trevillion, K., Oram, S., Feder, G., & Howard, L. M. (2012). Experiences of domestic violence and mental disorders: A systematic review and meta-analysis. *PLoS One, 7*(12), e51740. https://doi.org/10.1371/journal.pone.0051740

Tronick, E., Als, H., Adamson, L., Wise, S., & Brazelton, T. (1978). The infant's response to entrapment between contradictory messages in face-to-face interaction. *Journal of the American Academy of Child Psychiatry, 17*, 1–13. https://doi.org/10.1016/s0002-7138(09)62273-1

Tschoeke, S., Steinert, T., & Bichescu-Burian, D. (2019). Causal connection between dissociation and ongoing interpersonal violence: A systematic review. *Neuroscience & Biobehaviour Reviews, 107*, 424–437. https://doi.org/10.1016/j.neubiorev.2019.09.030

Turkus, J. A., & Kahler, J. A. (2006). Therapeutic interventions in the treatment of dissociative disorders. *Psychiatric Clinics of North America, 29*(1), 245–262. https://doi.org/10.1016/j.psc.2005.10.015

Twombly, J. H. (2000). Incorporating EMDR and EMDR adaptations into the treatment of clients with dissociative identity disorder. *Journal of Trauma & Dissociation, 1*(2), 61–81. https://doi.org/10.1300/J229v01n02_05

UK Government. (2022). *Working Definition of Trauma-informed Practice*. www.gov.uk/government/publications/working-definition-of-trauma-informed-practice

Upton, J. (2009). When words are not enough: Creative therapeutic approaches. In T. Cottis. (Ed.), *Intellectual Disability, Trauma and Psychotherapy*. Routledge: Abingdon, Ox.

Van der Hart, O., Nijenhuis, E. R. S., & Steele, K. (2006). *The Haunted Self-structural Dissociation and the Treatment of Chronic Traumatization* (1st ed.). W.W. Norton: New York.

Van der Hoech, J. (2022). *Beastie Boy and the Brand New Mummy*. JV Trauma Tools and Training.

van der Kolk, B. A. (2005). Developmental trauma disorder: Toward a rational diagnosis for children with complex trauma histories. *Psychiatric Annals, 35*(5), 401–408. https://doi.org/10.3928/00485713-20050501-06

Van der Kolk, B. A. (2014). The Body Keeps the Score: Mind, Brain and Body in the Transformation of Trauma. Penguin: London.

Van Derbur, M. (2003). *Miss America by Day: Lessons Learned from Ultimate Betrayals and Unconditional Love*. Oak Hill Ridge Press: Leicester.

Vanderlinden, J., & Palmisano, G. S. (2019). Trauma and eating disorders: The state of the art. In A. Seubert & P. Virdi (Eds.), *Trauma-informed Approaches to Eating Disorders* (pp. 13–30). Springer: London.

Vanderlinden, J., Vandereycken, W., van Dyck, R., & Vertommen, H. (1993). Dissociative experiences and trauma in eating disorders. *International Journal of Eating Disorders, 13*(2), 187–193. https://doi.org/10.1002/1098-108x(199303)13:2<187::aid-eat2260130206>3.0.co;2-9

Varese, F., Douglas, M., Dudley, R., Bowe, S., Christodoulides, T., Common, S., … & Turkington, D. (2021). Targeting dissociation using cognitive behavioural therapy in voice hearers with psychosis and a history of interpersonal trauma: A case series. *Psychology and Psychotherpy, 94*(2), 247–265. https://doi.org/10.1111/papt.12304

Varese, F., Smeets, F., Drukker, M., Lieverse, R., Lataster, T., Viechtbauer, W., … & Bentall, R. P. (2012). Childhood adversities increase the risk of psychosis: A meta-analysis of patient-control, prospective- and cross-sectional cohort studies. *Schizophrenia Bulletin, 38*(4), 661–671. https://doi.org/10.1093/schbul/sbs050

Vermetten, E., Schmahl, C., Lindner, S., Loewenstein, R. J., & Bremner, J. D. (2006). Hippocampal and amygdalar volumes in dissociative identity disorder. *Amercian Journal of Psychiatry, 163*(4), 630–636. https://doi.org/10.1176/ajp.2006.163.4.630

Vogt, R. (2012). *Perpetrator Introjects: Psychotherapeutic Diagnostics and Treatment Models*. Asanger Verlag.

Voswinkel, M. M., Rijkers, C., van Delden, J. J. M., & van Elburg, A. A. (2021). Externalizing your eating disorder: A qualitative interview study. *Journal of Eating Disorders, 9*(1), 128. https://doi.org/10.1186/s40337-021-00486-6

Wallin, D. J., & Ebscohost. (2007). *Attachment in Psychotherapy*. Guilford Press: New York.

Waters, F. S. (2016). *Healing the fractured child: Diagnosis and treatment of youth with dissociation*. Springer: London.

Watson, D., Wu, K. D., & Cutshall, C. (2004). Symptom subtypes of obsessive-compulsive disorder and their relation to dissociation. *Journal of Anxiety Disorders, 18*(4), 435–458. https://doi.org/10.1016/s0887-6185(03)00029-x

Webb, C., Dawson, D., & Langthorne, P. (2025). *An evaluation of trauma-informed care (TIC) and dissociation training to staff in adult community mental health services*. University of Nottingham.

Webermann, A. R., & Brand, B. L. (2017). Mental illness and violent behavior: The role of dissociation. *Borderline Personality Disorder Emotional Dysregulation, 4*, 2. https://doi.org/10.1186/s40479-017-0053-9

Webermann, A. R., Brand, B. L., & Chasson, G. S. (2014). Childhood maltreatment and intimate partner violence in dissociative disorder patients. *European Journal of Psychotraumatology, 5*, Article 24568. https://doi.org/10.3402/ejpt.v5.24568

Webermann, A. R., Brand, B. L., & Kumar, S. A. (2021). Intimate partner violence among patients with dissociative disorders. *Journal of Interpersonal Violence, 36*(3–4), NP1441–NP1462. https://doi.org/10.1177/0886260517746943

Welfare, H. R., & Hollin, C. R. (2015). Childhood and offense-related trauma in young people imprisoned in England and Wales for murder and other acts of serious violence: A descriptive study. *Journal of Aggression, Maltreatment & Trauma, 24*(8), 955–969. https://doi.org/10.1080/10926771.2015.1070230

West, M. J., Somer, E., & Eigsti, I. M. (2023). Immersive and maladaptive daydreaming and divergent thinking in autism spectrum disorders. *Imagin Cogn Pers, 42*(4), 372–398. https://doi.org/10.1177/02762366221129819

Wieland, E. (2015). *Dissociation in Traumatized Children and Adolescents: Theory and Clinical Interventions.* Routledge: Abingdon, Ox.

Wigham, S., Hatton, C., & Taylor, J. L. (2011). The Lancaster and Northgate Trauma Scales (LANTS): The development and psychometric properties of a measure of trauma for people with mild to moderate intellectual disabilities. *Research in Developmental Disabilities, 32*(6), 2651–2659. https://doi.org/10.1016/j.ridd.2011.06.008

Wigham, S., Taylor, J. L., & Hatton, C. (2014). A prospective study of the relationship between adverse life events and trauma in adults with mild to moderate intellectual disabilities. *Journal of Intellectual and Disability Research, 58*(12), 1131–1140. https://doi.org/10.1111/jir.12107

Wilkinson, S., & DeJongh, M. (2021). Dissociative identity disorder: A developmental perspective. *BJPsych Advances, 27*(2), 96–98. https://doi.org/10.1192/bja.2020.35

Williams, K., Moehler, E., Kaess, M., Resch, F., & Fuchs, A. (2022). Dissociation links maternal history of childhood abuse to impaired parenting. *Journal of Trauma and Dissociation, 23*, 37–51. https://doi.org/10.1080/15299732.2021.1934938

Willis, H. A., Sosoo, E. E., Bernard, D. L., Neal, A., & Neblett, E. W. (2021). The associations between internalized racism, racial identity, and psychological distress. *Emerging Adulthood, 9*(4), 384–400. https://doi.org/10.1177/21676968211005598

Willmot, P., & Jones, L. (2022). *Trauma-informed Forensic Practice.* Routledge: Abingdon, Ox. https://doi.org/10.4324/9781003120766

Wilson, J. E., Andrews, P., Ainsworth, A., Roy, K., Ely, E. W., & Oldham, M. A. (2021). Pseudodelirium: Psychiatric conditions to consider on the differential for delirium. *Journal of Neuropsychiatry and Clinical Neuroscience, 33*(4), 356–364. https://doi.org/10.1176/appi.neuropsych.20120316

Wojciechowski, T. W. (2020). PTSD as a risk factor for the development of violence among Juvenile offenders: A group-based trajectory modeling approach. *Journal of Interpersonal Violence, 35*(13–14), 2511–2535. https://doi.org/10.1177/0886260517704231

Xu, Y. E., Barron, D. A., Sudol, K., Zisook, S., & Oquendo, M. A. (2023). Suicidal behavior across a broad range of psychiatric disorders. *Molecular Psychiatry, 28*(7), 2764–2810. https://doi.org/10.1038/s41380-022-01935-7

Yehuda, R., & Lehrner, A. (2018). Intergenerational transmission of trauma effects: putative role of epigenetic mechanisms. *World Psychiatry, 17*(3), 243–257. https://doi.org/10.1002/wps.20568

Yu, J., Ross, C. A., Keyes, B. B., Li, Y., Dai, Y., Zhang, T., ... & Xiao, Z. (2010). Dissociative disorders among Chinese inpatients diagnosed with schizophrenia. *Journal of Trauma & Dissociation, 11*(3), 358–372. https://doi.org/10.1080/15299731003793468

Zamir, O., Szepsenwol, O., Englund, M. M., & Simpson, J. A. (2018). The role of dissociation in revictimization across the lifespan: A 32-year prospective study. *Child Abuse and Neglect, 79*, 144–153. https://doi.org/10.1016/j.chiabu.2018.02.001

Zheng, P., & Gray, M. J. (2015). Posttraumatic coping and distress: An evaluation of Western conceptualization of trauma and its applicability to Chinese culture. *Journal of Cross-Cultural Psychology, 46*(5), 723–736. https://doi.org/10.1177/0022022115580848

Index

Note: Page numbers in *italics* and **bold** denote figures and tables, respectively.

For Product Safety Concerns and Information please contact our EU
representative GPSR@taylorandfrancis.com
Taylor & Francis Verlag GmbH, Kaufingerstraße 24, 80331 München, Germany

www.ingramcontent.com/pod-product-compliance
Lightning Source LLC
Chambersburg PA
CBHW050330270326
41926CB00016B/3390